The Encyclopedia of
CARS

The Encyclopedia of
CARS

Peter Henshaw

Published in 2005 by

Regency House Publishing Ltd

24-26 Boulton Road

Stevenage

Hertfordshire

SG1 4QX

United Kingdom

ISBN 1 85361 519 6

Printed in China

The 20th century was an era of change. Electricity, the consumer society, mass-production and, in two world wars, mass-destruction were among the things that transformed the way ordinary people lived in many parts of the world. Increasingly, they lived and worked in cities rather than on the land; they enjoyed a higher standard of living than their parents and, sometimes, a good deal more leisure time.

Mobility was the key to many of these changes, and the private car became a symbol of this mobility or, as some called it, this faster pace of life. The car expanded horizons, both geographically and mentally. No longer tied to a railway timetable, the new generation of motorist could choose where to holiday, where to work and where to have friends. In practice, of course, most people still chose to holiday in the same place as everyone else, sitting in traffic jams to get there, but maybe that says something about human nature. A massive industry employing thousands of people grew up to make, sell and service cars. Thousands more were employed to build roads, filling stations, and those must-have trinkets such as a radio, a steering wheel glove or sunroof. In the 1950s and 1960s it seemed as if the car could do no wrong: it

was the sexy, prestigious freedom machine that more and more people could afford.

But that was the sting in the tail. It did not take a genius to work out that more and more cars demanded more and more roads, though it was not until the very end of the 20th century that the awful truth began to dawn that new and bigger roads did not solve the problem, they simply generated extra traffic. In fact, the open-road dream of the 1960s had come to appear decidedly tarnished by the 1990s. Despite advances in safety and emissions, cars still killed people and polluted the atmosphere. Moreover, the 20th-century lifestyle they represented (bigger, better, faster … and damn the consequences) was finally being called into question.

But this book is not a social history, nor a prediction of what might happen in the future. Instead, it is an encyclopedia of all the major marques and many of the smaller ones. Has any other industry attracted such a multiplicity of makes? Many of the people who founded these companies were enthusiasts as much as businessmen, for the dream of building cars has always been a seductive one. So there is much ground to cover. France and Germany were the pioneers, with Benz building what is

generally considered to be the first petrol-driven car in the world, in 1885. Soon after, De Dion Bouton of France introduced a much higher-speed engine. Henry Ford was a pioneer too, but it was not until 1914 that he applied mass-production techniques to the Model T, making the car cheaper and more accessible than ever before. With the newly formed General Motors and Chrysler as arch-rivals, Ford made the U.S. motor industry the biggest in the world. It held that position for decades, but meanwhile the Europeans were in the full flood of their vintage era, and the 1920s were a time of expensive, well-engineered sports cars from the likes of Lancia, Bentley and Mercedes-Benz. But the 1929 Wall Street Crash, and the worldwide economic slump that followed it, brought a reality check. Take the Bugatti Royale saloon, a glorious folly powered by a 300-bhp (224-kW) 15-litre engine: it was magnificent, but only six were made. Many smaller manufacturers collapsed, others were taken over by the bigger ones. Morris, Austin, Renault, Fiat had all learnt the lesson of piling high and selling cheap, just as Ford had done. Not everyone in Europe, or even the U.S.A., could afford a car, but it was moving that way.

World War II put a virtual halt to civilian car production, but in 1945 the major manufacturers lost no time in getting back to work, often with pre-war designs. In Britain industry was exhorted to 'Export or Die', while post-war Europe slowly rebuilt itself out of wartime devastation. Volkswagen's was the most extraordinary story. A devastated factory was brought into production by a British army officer, and within a decade VW was one of Europe's biggest manufacturers. Ford, GM and Chrysler were in a better position in 1945, and continued to supply their vast home market with ever more flamboyant constructions of steel, chrome and tailfins, reflecting a boundless post-war optimism. But car production was now well established in the U.S.S.R. and the Eastern Bloc as well. The utilitarian Lada, Skoda and Wartburg cars began to head west, their low prices attracting impecunious buyers.

Far more significant were the first trickles of exports from Japan. Although some Japanese makes had pre-war roots, the 1950s and 1960s saw them blossom into full-scale production, often with 22-cu in (360-cc) micro-cars. Never more obvious than in cars, Japan's

The Ford Model T. Testing chassis at Highland Park in 1914.

manufacturing and economic 'miracle' was making the West sit up and take notice.

In fact, it looked as though the motor industry could do no wrong, but then the bubble burst. Undercurrents of concern about safety and exhaust emissions finally came to the fore in the early 1970s. As if on cue, two oil crises came and went, leaving behind the knowledge that oil, on which the whole industry ran, would not last forever. Still, that did not deter new entrants. Ssangyong and Daewoo of Korea, for example, used Japanese technology to kick-start production and join the world club of car-producing nations.

But somehow the old days of optimism had gone. Further economic troubles through the 1980s and 1990s forced a series of mergers, as manufacturers sought to survive in an increasingly tough world. Even respected names like Rolls-Royce and Bentley failed to survive independently, while Chrysler merged with Daimler-Benz. In the 21st century, it seems, company survival depends on being either very big or, in the case of manufacturers such as Morgan, very small.

9

ABARTH (Italy 1941-1971)

Carlo Abarth started building racing cars in 1949, and in the following year launched his first production racer, the 204 Berlinetta. This used a tuned 67.1-cu in (1100-cc) Fiat engine (Abarth was to have a long association with the Italian giant) and Porsche-type torsion bar suspension (he was already acting as Porsche's representative in Italy).

The link with Fiat was formalized by an agreement of 1956. From that time on, many Abarths for road or race were tuned Fiats, though Carlo did build a Simca-based sports car in 1966. The Fiat-Abarth 600 was the first of many, with stunning coupés (designed by Zagato, among others) following in the 1960s. The company also did good business selling tuning parts.

Alas, it was not enough, and the whole caboodle was taken over by Fiat in 1971, when Abarth's financial problems became too pressing; but the man himself was kept on as a consultant. But it is an indication of the strength of his name that even the modern Fiat Cinquecento wore the Abarth scorpion logo.

ABC (Great Britain 1920s)
The air-cooled ABC was the brainchild of
engineer Granville Bradshaw. It was a
popular and stylish car, though Bradshaw
equipped it with a false radiator and filler
cap to assuage the fears of a conservative
buying public, which by the 1920s was
firmly wedded to the concept of water-
cooling. It was not just for show, however,
for the fake radiator filler cap acted as a
fuel filler. Improved from 1925, from
which time the chief ABC model was
known as the Super Sports, it was powered
by a 73.4-cu in (1203-cc) two-cylinder
engine, producing a respectable 35bhp
(26.1kW) at 3,400rpm. Production ended
in 1929.

RIGHT
1941 ABC Regent.

OPPOSITE
ABOVE: Fiat Abarth 750 Zagato.

*BELOW LEFT: Abarth 750s at Le Mans in
1960.*

*BELOW RIGHT: Fiat Abarth 750 Double-
Bubble.*

AC (Great Britain 1904 to date)

AC will always be associated with the fearsome Ford V8-powered Cobra, a rip-roaring sportster that surely deserved the epithet 'hairy-chested sports car'. But the company started out with a far more modest (not to mention useful) product, namely three-wheel load carriers for small firms that could not afford a van.

Partners John Weller and John Portwine, who had set up Autocars & Accessories in 1904, made quite a success of these basic commercial vehicles, changing the company name to Autocarriers after three years. A passenger version, the AC Sociable, was launched in 1908 and by the time World War I was declared in 1914, it had been joined by a small four-wheeled car, powered by a 10-hp (7.46-kW) Fivet engine.

The company had a difficult 1920s. Its founders left in 1922, the year after S.F. Edge, from Napier, had joined the board. There were more name changes, to AC Cars and then AC (Acedes), none of which prevented liquidation in 1929. Limited production restarted the following year under new owners, but it was not until the late 1940s that AC began to find its feet once more. One long-running sideline was the three-wheeled invalid car that became a common sight on British roads for the next 30 years.

But AC is remembered for something else. The attractive Ace sports car was launched in the early 1950s, followed by the Aceca coupé and four-seater Greyhound, all powered by Bristol or AC's own six-cylinder engines. It was so far, so English up to this time. Then American racing driver Caroll Shelby had the bright idea of levering a Ford V8 under the Ace's bonnet. This became the infamous Cobra, of which just over 1,000 were built between

ABOVE
1933 AC 16/60.

RIGHT
1938 AC 16/80-bhp drophead coupé.

1962 and 1969. The combination of this lightweight sports car with the muscular Ford engine could be downright scary at times, though it was certainly fast: 0-60mph (0-97km/h) in 4.2 seconds for the 427-cu in version.

More civilized versions followed, such

as the new 427 and 428, with a larger, more luxurious bodyshell. The hairy edge had gone, though. AC introduced the modern, mid-engined ME3000 in 1979, now with a milder Ford 465-cu in (3-litre) V6 engine as the oil crisis had put paid to those big, thirsty V8s. Less than 100 MEs were made, and a plan to build them in Scotland lasted only a year. But that was not the end of AC. The Cobra had become a legend in its own right, and Surrey-based engineer Brian Angliss was still building them under licence from Ford. Late in 1986 Angliss unveiled an all-new AC Ace, still powered by a Ford engine, of course. In the following year Ford took a controlling interest in AC, though Angliss was kept on as managing director. Angliss bought out Ford's share in 1991, when a new two-seater Ace was announced, but receivership followed in 1996. Almost immediately, the company was saved by businessman Alan Lubinsky, and six years on was offering

four variations on the basic Cobra theme: the carbonfibre-bodied 302 CRS and 212 S/C, and the hand-beaten aluminium-bodied 289 and 427, the latter with a 400-bhp (299.2-kW) Ford V8 of 427-cu in (7-litre) capacity.

ABOVE
AC Aceca.

RIGHT
AC 427-ci (7-litre) Cobra.

FAR RIGHT ABOVE
Autokraft AC Mk IV Cobra.

FAR RIGHT CENTRE
AC Cobra, with 427-ci V8 engine.

ADAMS (Great Britain)

Established in 1905, the Adams car was also known as the Adams-Hewitt, with miniature cycle cars being built as well as full-size models. The first single-cylinder Adams appeared in 1905, and sold well for five years, the 9/10 variant being powered by a 103.56 cu in (1697-cc) engine. There were a couple of twin-cylinder models as well, but most Adams were larger cars – there were five four-cylinder cars and two 30-hp (22.37-kW) six-cylinder types. Even a very early V8 was offered in 1908, as the 443.89-cu in (7.274-litre) 35/40.

ADLER (Germany 1900-1939)

Adler began building cars in 1900, but it was a famous maker of typewriters and bicycles long before that. It was making its own engines within a couple of years (the first cars had used De Dion units) and was offering singles, V-twins and fours by 1905. The new line was a great success, and by 1914 one car in five in Germany was an Adler.

Some of these pre-war models were reintroduced in 1919, with a six-cylinder car added in 1925, and a straight-eight three years later, though the best-seller remained the four-cylinder 91.5-cu in (1.5-litre) Favorit.

The more advanced front-wheel-drive Trumpf, another 1.5-litre model, was launched in 1932. It sold well, and was followed by the smaller 61.02-cu in (1-litre) Trumpf Junior, while the original gained 103.7cu in (1.7 litres) and later 115.9-cu in (1.9-litre) engines. It also handled well by the standards of the day, and did well in competition. Alongside the front-drive Trumpfs, a conventional rear-drive 91.5-cu in (1.5-litre) type was offered, and larger six-cylinder Adlers such as the streamlined 152.6-cu in (2.5-litre) car of 1937. Adler car production ceased on the outbreak of war in 1939, and never resumed, though the company continued building motorcycles until 1957.

BELOW LEFT
A very different Adams – a Jaguar-based kit car.

BELOW
The 1913 Morgan-Adler Carette seated driver and passenger in tandem.

BOTTOM
Alfa Romeo P1 racer, driven by Sivocci.

ALFA ROMEO (Italy 1909 to date)

Italy has produced more than its fair share of evocative motoring names, but Alfa Romeo must be somewhere near the top. It speaks volumes that the name has managed to retain some mystique while selling thousands of mainstream family cars. The secret has been to endow nearly all of them, from the little Alfasud upwards, with a distinctive sporting character.

Alfa's origins actually lay in France. Alexandre Darracq established a factory near Milan to build cars out of French-supplied parts. But it was not a success, and the venture was taken over in 1909 by Anonima Lombardo Fabbrica Automobil (ALFA). The Romeo side of the name arrived in 1915, when racing enthusiast and engineer Nicolà Romeo joined the company and began its transformation into a race-winner. Under Romeo's guidance, Alfa Romeo concentrated on sports and racing cars, dropping its early four-cylinder models in favour of more exotic sixes and

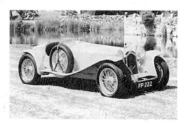

eights. It built no fours at all between 1925 and 1950.

Those early racing Alfas sported twin

LEFT (from top to bottom).
1924 supercharged P2 racer.
1923-28 six-cylinder RL.
1928 6C Sport Zagato 1500.
1932 finely-proportioned Monza.

FAR LEFT ABOVE
1910 Alfa Romeo with 24-hp engine.

FAR LEFT BELOW
1912 15/20 in racing trim.

overhead camshafts and superchargers: the Tipo B Bimotore featured two eight-cylinder engines, and there was also a 274.6-cu in (4.5-litre) V12. With cars like this, the race wins were soon rolling in, though there were also 12-hp (8.95-kW) and 24-hp (17.89-kW) four-seater road cars. There was a six-cylinder limousine, the RL, sold in the 1920s, but the most memorable road-going Alfas derived from the race cars, like the 1928 6C Sport Zagato, or the straight-eight Spyder in 1932, both open two-seaters.

This was all very well, but did not make financial sense, and Alfa was taken over by the Italian government. Like Adolf Hitler, Benito Mussolini wanted to promote national prestige through motor racing, and Alfa Romeo obliged, with no less than 11 Mille Miglia wins in the 1930s, and four at Le Mans. And in a piece of giant-killing, the great driver Nuvolari beat mighty Mercedes and Auto-Union on their home ground, in the 1935 German Grand Prix.

After World War II, Alfa Romeo faced a very different world. Its factory was mostly destroyed, and a devastated Italy wanted cheap, basic transport such as Fiat cars and Vespa scooters, not glorious sports

cars. Nevertheless, the company kicked off in 1947 with the 152.6-cu in (2.5-litre) Freccia d'Oro (Golden Arrow), though the 115.9-cu in (1.9-litre) saloon of 1950 was more down to earth. Being an Alfa, though, it had to be a sports saloon, and Super and Sprint versions soon followed, as well as the striking Disco Volante open two-seater show car. Four years later, Alfa Romeo clearly showed its new direction with the little 79.3-cu in (1.3-litre) Giulietta. Introduced as a svelte Bertone-designed coupé, more significant was the four-door four-seat saloon that followed in the following year but with the same four-cylinder twin-cam engine. This was the first in a long line of affordable, but sporting, Alfa saloons.

A bigger Giulia followed in 1962, with a 95.8-cu in (1.57-litre) engine and five-speed gearbox, while the 1900 Super got a capacity boost to 122.1cu in (2 litres) in the same year, and a new 158.7-cu in (2.6-litre) twin-cam six was introduced as the new flagship. That in turn was topped in 1967 by the Montreal sports car. Bertone designed this creature, which was powered by a 2.6-litre twin-cam V8, derived from the 2-litre V8 of the Tipo 33 racing car. With fuel injection and a five-speed gearbox, it could almost top 140mph (225km/h), and nearly 4,000 were built before production ceased in 1975.

Far more significant for Alfa's future was the all-new Alfasud, unveiled in 1971. The Italian government had persuaded the company to build a new factory near Naples, in an area of high unemployment. Everything about the front-wheel-drive Alfasud was new, from its 72.37-cu in (1.186-litre) flat-four engine to the Giugiaro styling. It immediately impressed with its lively performance and fine roadholding, and despite its doubtful build quality

thousands were sold, with 79.3-, 91.5- and 103.7-cu in (1.3-, 1.5- and 1.7-litre) versions following. At the other end of the range, the early 1970s also saw the Alfetta 2+2 coupé, now with a 119.73-cu in (1.962-litre) version of Alfa's classic twin-cam engine, allied to a rear-mounted clutch and gearbox for optimum weight distribution. It later came in saloon form as well. With the Montreal gone, Alfa's only pure sports car was now the open-top Spider, which would stay in production right into the 1990s.

Meanwhile, the Alfasud was replaced by the bigger 33, and the Alfetta by the oddly styled 75. The company returned to the big car market in 1987 with the 164, a joint design with PSA, and in this form powered by Alfa's smooth V6, which was updated into quad-cam 24-valve form in

LEFT
1929 Alfa Romeo Series III.

OPPOSITE, TOP ROW (left to right)
1939 6C 2500 Coloniale.
8C 35 and 12C 36 in 1937.
1958-61 2000 saloon.
1971 1750 GTV.

SECOND ROW (left to right)
1952 Disco Volante or Flying Saucer.
1971 1750 Berlina.

THIRD ROW (left to right)
1953-55 1900 saloon.
1952 1900-cc doc Berlina.

BOTTOM ROW (left to right)
1954 six-cylinder cabriolet.
1954 four-cylinder Giulietta Sprint by
  Bertone.
1973 front-wheel-drive Alfasud.

LEFT
1933 2.3-litre straight eight.

BELOW LEFT
Alfa Romeo touring coupé.

BELOW
1750-hp Alfa Romeo.

OPPOSITE
TOP LEFT: Alfa Romeo 164.

TOP RIGHT
1600 Giulia Sprint.

BELOW LEFT
Montreal V8.

BELOW RIGHT
1968 convertible Spider.

1992. The 164 was a clean-looking and uncontroversial car, but the same could not be said of the Zagato-styled SZ and convertible RZ of 1990 and 1992 respectively. Stubby, brutal and by no means beautiful, they were never big sellers.

But after that, Alfas began to acquire a little more grace. The awkward 75 was replaced by the smoother-nosed 155 (first with 2-litre Twin Spark and then 2.5-litre V6 engines) and though not everyone liked the three-door 145 (a 1994 replacement for the 33) the five-door 146 which followed a year later was less controversial. Both the 145 and 146 carried over the Alfasud flat-four engine until 1996, when they adopted the Fiat-based Twin Spark motor in 85.4-, 97.6-, 109.8- and 122.1-cu in (1.4-, 1.6-, 1.8- and 2-litre) forms. One new option for Alfa was a 115.9-cu in (1.9-litre) turbo diesel.

The Spider was finally replaced in 1996, along with a hardtop GTV version, both styled jointly by Alfa Romeo/Fiat and Pininfarina. Both were true to the new smooth and rounded Alfa look. Once again, the 2-litre engine was Fiat-based, with Alfa's own twin-cam, Twin Spark head, while a 3-litre quad-cam V6 was added later. It was still in production in 2002, with a replacement slated for 2004, but Alfa Romeo had never replaced the big 164, concentrating instead on its three-strong range of small and mid-size saloons: 147, 156 and 166.

RIGHT
Alfa Romeo Z33 racer.

BELOW RIGHT
The Spider, launched in 1997.

FAR RIGHT
Alfa Romeo 156.

FAR RIGHT BELOW
147 GTA.

BELOW
Nuvola.

OPPOSITE
1951 Super Sport.

ALLARD (Great Britain 1937-1960)

Sydney Allard of south London loved big American V8 engines, and made a living out of shoehorning them into his small open-top sports cars and large saloons. This was probably based on his pre-World War II experience with a modified Ford V8 built with a Bugatti tail. He made a dozen V8-powered cars before war broke out, and formed Allard Motors in 1945.

Allard worked fast, and the first new post-war cars left the factory in 1946, still with many Ford components, and bodies sourced from Whittingham & Mitchel and Paramount Sheet Metal. The definitive Allard was probably the J2 of 1949, powered by a 196-cu in (3.2-litre) 140-bhp (104.38-kW) Mercury engine, which gave a top speed of 110mph (177km/h). Two-seater Allards like this continued to be favourites in trials and other motor sports, but the company also built the P-type saloon (with a large 'woody' Safari variant).

Unfortunately, cheaper competition from Jaguar damaged Allard sales, and the company stopped producing cars in 1960. It went on to become the world manufacturer/distributor of Shorrock superchargers.

ABOVE RIGHT
1953 Allard J2R with 6921-cc V8.

RIGHT
1952 Allard J2X.

FAR RIGHT
1-litre Alpine Renault at Le Mans in 1963.

ALPINE (France 1955-1994)

Mainstream car manufacturers often have close links with specialists dedicated to producing more exotic machines based on their mass-production components: Fiat had Abarth, Ford had AC, and Renault had Alpine. The Renault/Alpine link was so strong that the little Dieppe-based concern used no other engines but Renaults, and this went right back to the beginning. Jean Redélé was the son of a Renault dealer, and rallied a Renault 4CV with sufficient success in the mid-1950s to persuade him not to join the family business, but set up on his own as Société Automobiles Alpine. To celebrate winning the 45.76-cu in (750-cc) class of the Mille Miglia, his first car was 4CV-based and called the Mille Miles. It was a glassfibre-bodied coupé, styled by Michelotti of Italy, with Redélé's own five-speed gearbox an option.

Tuned 51.57-cu in (845-cc) or bigger 55.17-cu in (904-cc) and 57.85-cu in (948-cc) engines (from the Renault Dauphine) were made available in 1957, as was an open-top version of the A106, as it was now known. Production was still limited to around 100 cars per year in the early 1960s, but in 1960 Alpine unveiled its most successful car ever, the rear-engined A110. The A110 was to distinguish itself in

many types of competition, winning the Monte Carlo Rally in 1971 and World Rally Championship two years later. The later A210 often won the Index of Performance prize at Le Mans.

A new A310 was launched in 1971, still rear-engined and Renault-powered, first with a tuned Renault 16 engine of 140hp (104.38kW), later with the 164.7-cu in (2.7-litre) V6. In the following year Renault took control of Alpine, securing its long-term future. Ten years later, the new GTA continued the Alpine tradition, still Renault V6-powered, in turbo or non-turbo form. The final 177-cu in (2.9-litre) A610 left production in 1994.

BELOW
Le Mans, 1964, co-driven by Delagenest.

BOTTOM
Alpine 1600 coupé with A110 body.

ALVIS (Great Britain 1920-1967)

Alvis is a name with which to conjure, for there were four- and six-cylinder vintage sports tourers with names like 'Speed 20' and 'Silver Eagle'. Always associated with high-quality sporting cars, Alvis was also an innovator, experimenting with front-wheel-drive in the 1920s.

The company was founded in Coventry in 1919 by T.G. John and started with the modest side-valve 10/30, a design bought from another manufacturer. More typical was the 91.5-cu in (1.5-litre) overhead-camshaft 12/50, built from 1923 to 1932. By the late 1930s, Alvis was a true rival to Bentley, offering a 100-mph (161-km/h) model with a 262.4-cu in (4.3-litre) engine. Things progressed slowly after

World War II, the new TA14 owing much to pre-war designs, though it was updated with independent front suspension and 465-cu in (3-litre) engine in 1950 as the TA21. Power increased for the 100-mph TC21 'Grey Lady' of 1955, but the final line of Alvis cars were the TD, TE and TF21 from 1959, all with Graber-styled two-door bodies. There were plans for a new Alvis to replace them, but after a merger with Rover in 1965, this never appeared. The last TF21 was built in 1967, and ever since the company has concentrated on military vehicles.

BELOW
Alvis 12/50 tourer.

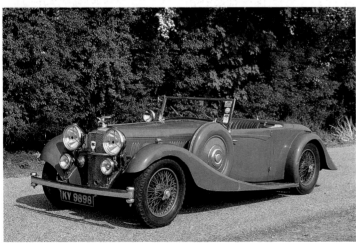

OPPOSITE
TOP LEFT: Alvis four-wheel-drive racer.

TOP RIGHT: 1928 Alvis tourer.

BELOW LEFT: 1935 Alvis Speed.

BELOW RIGHT: 1950 14-hp Alvis drophead.

BELOW
AMC Rambler Ambassador.

AMC (U.S.A. 1954-1988)

AMC (American Motors Corporation) resulted from a 1954 merger between Nash and Hudson. Backbone of the range was the Nash Rambler, which by 1957 covered a sprawling range of 20 models. That was topped in 1959 by the V8 Ambassador. AMC also did well with its sporty four-seat Javelin, but its best move was undoubtedly buying Kaiser-Jeep in 1970. For years, the good-selling Jeep range was the strongest part of the AMC line-up, but in the conventional car market, as opposed to four-wheel-drive market, the company was finding it increasingly difficult to compete with the big three of America, namely Ford, GM and Chrysler.

Still, in 1974 AMC did launch the unusual Pacer, a classy hatchback that looked like a typical European compact car blown up to U.S.A. dimensions. Short but wide, it aimed to provide a big car feel in a compact package. AMC acquired some genuine European technology the following

year, building and selling the Renault 18 in North America. Other Renaults followed, sold alongside AMC's own Eagle Series saloon and estate cars. In fact, Renault bought a 41.6 per cent stake in AMC in 1980. The end came seven years later, when Chrysler took over AMC. The new owner did not want the AMC name, nor the Eagle, nor the U.S.-built Renaults, just Jeep.

ABOVE
AMC's 1984 CJ-7 Laredo Jeep.

BELOW LEFT
1956 Rambler station wagon.

BELOW
The Javelin SST, introduced in 1968.

AMILCAR (France 1921-1939)

Amilcar built its reputation on lightweight, sporting cars in the finest vintage tradition. Founded in 1921 (with a name derived from that of its co-founders, Messrs. Lamy and Akar), its first cars were all open two-seaters powered by a 61-cu in (1-litre) four-cylinder side-valve engine. In 1924 they were topped by the overhead-valve CGS, with a top speed of nearly 80mph (128km/h); it was just as well that this was the first Amilcar with four-wheel braking. More sporting still was the CGSS Surbaissé model, lower-slung than the CGS and with a more powerful 67.1-cu in (1.1-litre) engine. Within a few years, Amilcar was producing much bigger, faster cars, such as the six-cylinder C6, with twin overhead camshafts and a 120-mph (193-km/h) capability. As if that were not quick enough, Amilcar also offered the straight-eight-cylinder C8. Successful in competition and sought-after for the road, Amilcar was making 12,000 cars a year by the late 1920s.

But World War II put an end to Amilcar production, and the company failed to resurface in 1945.

LEFT
A typical light sporting Amilcar.

BELOW
The Amilcar CGS from the 1920s.

ARMSTRONG-SIDDELEY
(Great Britain 1919-1960)

Armstrong built large, solid six-cylinder tourers, often with pre-selector gearboxes, an early type of semi-automatic transmission. The company appeared in 1919 when Armstrong-Whitworth merged with Siddeley-Deasy.

The first new car to emerge was a 30-hp (22.4-kW) six, which stayed in production for 13 years, though a smaller 18-hp (13.4-kW) version joined it in 1925. A four-cylinder 14-hp (10.4-kW) was added in 1925, but this only lasted a few years before Armstrong-Siddeley reverted to its quality six-cylinder line. From 1929 until

the outbreak of World War I, all of the company's cars had six cylinders, even the little 12, and from 1933 all were fitted with Wilson pre-selector gearboxes, with a new overhead-valve 121.5-cu in (1.991-litre) engine appearing in 1938. The first post-war cars drew on this 1930s technology, but the new Sapphire 346 of 1953 embodied some new thinking, albeit still with a separate chassis. But despite the addition of smaller 234 and 236 Sapphires, plus the more powerful fully-automatic Star Sapphire, sales were disappointing. Production ended in 1960, when Armstrong-Siddeley's parent company merged with aircraft maker Bristol.

LEFT
1929 Armstrong-Siddeley Whitley.

FAR LEFT (top to bottom)
1926 14-hp with a 1825-cc engine.
1928 30-hp six-cylinder London.
1934 12-hp tourer, a popular model.

BELOW
1959 3990-cc Star Sapphire.

ARROL-JOHNSTON/ARROL-ASTER (Great Britain 1895-1929)

Arrol-Johnston was one of the motoring pioneers: Scottish engineer George Johnston designed a four-piston opposed-twin engine and fitted it to a dogcart. Each pair of opposed pistons shared a cylinder, but were linked to a common crankshaft by rocking beams. It worked, and Johnston's car was in production for over a decade, from 1895 to 1906. A bigger 231.9-cu in (3.8-litre) version won the first ever Isle of Man Tourist Trophy race in 1905, beating the Rolls-Royce of Percy Northey.

Despite this success, Johnston then turned to more orthodox engines, such as the four-cylinder unit which powered the 24/30 of 1906, and a 537-cu in (8.8-litre) version followed in 1907. A new range of smaller cars with a 15.9-hp (11.86-kW) engine of 170.87-cu in (2.8-litre) capacity, was announced in the same year, with Renault-style dashboard radiator and, unusually for the time, four-wheel braking. One interesting diversion was the run of 50 electric cars built for Edison in 1913.

But the company's days were numbered. The 164.8-cu in (2.7-litre) Victory of 1919 was described as, 'unsellable and unreliable'. Arrol-Johnston merged with engine maker Aster in 1927 to form Arrol-Aster, whose cars then used Aster sleeve-valve units. But even this was

not enough to save the company, and production ceased two years later.

ASIA MOTORS (Korea)

The U.S. Willys Jeep has inspired countless other four-wheel-drives, such as the very Jeep-like Asia, an offshoot of Korean manufacturer Kia. For many years this was supplied to the Korean army, but in 1994 Kia decided to try exporting it to the booming 4x4 market in Europe.

So with smart new paintwork and alloy wheels, plus a flashy new name, the Asia Rocsta burst onto the scene. Unfortunately, the superficial additions could not detract from the fact that this was a simple, tough commercial vehicle, without any of the sophistication of 'lifestyle' four-wheel-drives. Power came from 109.8-cu in (1.8- litre) petrol or 134.25-cu in (2.2-litre) diesel four-cylinder engines, both majoring on lugging ability rather than refinement or sheer power. Slow and uncomfortable the Rocsta might have been, but it was also much cheaper than the European or Japanese opposition.

ABOVE LEFT
Circa 1901 Arrol-Johnston.

LEFT
1927 six-cylinder model.

FAR LEFT
Charlesworth-bodied 15.8-hp model.

TOP
Asia Motors tried hard to promote the
Rocsta as a lifestyle vehicle.

LEFT and ABOVE
The Rocsta's low price and rugged build
made it a good heavy-duty working vehicle
for farmers. The soft top was rather crude,
but it remained more popular than the
hardtop model.

ASTON MARTIN (Great Britain 1922 to date)

Aston Martin has had a chequered past, not only in its competition history but also in the frequent bankruptcies this sports car maker has suffered over the years. Not until 1987, when it was taken over by Ford, did a more certain future beckon. Aston's troubles started early. It built its first road cars in 1923, but went into receivership during the following year. The company had actually been in existence for over ten years by then, set up by engineer Robert Bamford and Lionel Martin to build one-off racing cars. Its name reflected both the man who financed its early years, and his success at the Aston Clinton hill climb in Buckinghamshire. After the 1924 collapse, the company was bought by consulting engineers Renwick and Bertilli, but it was

another three years before a new Aston Martin was announced, using a four-cylinder overhead-cam engine designed by Bertilli. But production was limited, and by 1931, the company was in trouble again, mainly due to the cost of its racing programme.

After another two ownership changes, Aston had a happier 1930s, with more competition success and 91.5-cu in (1.5-litre) then 122-cu in (2-litre) overhead-cam engines. In 1947 came yet another owner, the tractor manufacturer David Brown, but this heralded a new period of stability. Brown used the new Lagonda 152.6-cu in (2.5-litre) six-cylinder engine to create the Aston Martin DB2, introduced in 1950. The DB4 was all-new in 1959, and its DB5 successor was immortalized as a James Bond car in the film *Goldfinger*. The DB5

LEFT
1930 Aston Martin Lagonda 3-litre engine.

BELOW LEFT
1934 Aston Martin 1.5-litre tourer.

BELOW
DB2.

in turn gave way to the DB6 and 323.4-cu in (5.3-litre) V8 DBS.

Getting the V8 into production had cost Aston dear, however, and the company was sold to Company Developments in 1972. Two years later it was insolvent again, only to be saved by a consortium headed by Canadian Rolls-Royce importer George Minden and American Peter Sprague. Their

LEFT
DB1.

FAR LEFT
1954 Aston Martin DB3S 2.6-litre engine.

BELOW LEFT
DB3S.

BELOW RIGHT
DB4GT Zagato.

PAGE 32: Aston Martin Bulldog.

PAGE 33: DB7, as used by James Bond, 007.

LEFT
1959 DB2/4.

BELOW LEFT
Aston Martin DB7.

BELOW
Aston Martin Volante.

LEFT
Aston Martin V8 Vantage Le Mans.

BELOW LEFT
The DB7 coupé was the 'cheap' Aston.

set-up lasted five years, until Victor Gauntlett of Pace Petroleum and Tim Healey (CH Industrials) took over. Production settled down to the now familiar V8 Vantage and Volante convertible, as well as the striking Lagonda wedge-shaped saloon. By the mid-1980s, Aston had undergone yet another ownership change, with 75 per cent of the company owned by the Greek Livanos shipping family.

New Aston Martins started to reappear only in the late 1980s, after the Ford takeover. The new Virage replaced the existing V8s, though still powered by Aston's own hand-built engine, with an open-top Volante version appearing the year after. The in-house V8 was now getting old, but for 1992 engineers coaxed yet more power out of it by fitting twin Roots-type Eaton superchargers, which

gave the latest Vantage 550bhp (410.1kW) and a time of 4.5 seconds to 60mph (97km/h).

But cars of this type were increasingly out of tune with their times. The new DB7 of 1993 was the first of a new school, rather than the last of the old, with a TWR six-cylinder engine and coupé or open-top bodywork. A 420-bhp (313.2-kW) V12 followed from the Vantage version. As if that were not enough, in 2002 Aston unveiled a DB7 GT, with 435bhp (324.4kW) from the same V12.

OPPOSITE
Aston Martin Vantage Project.

ABOVE
Aston Martin Vantage Volante.

ABOVE TOP RIGHT
The Auburn Beauty Six was announced in 1919.

ABOVE RIGHT
The 1935 Auburn 851 was available with or without supercharger.

FAR RIGHT
The 80-8 with straight-eight engine.

AUBURN (U.S.A. 1900-1937)

Today Auburn is best remembered for its glamorous, supercharged Speedster of the mid-1930s. This made up but a small amount of total production, arriving only a few years before the company collapsed in 1937.

Auburn cars had come a long way since 1900, when Frank and Morris Eckhardt began making limited numbers of horseless carriages in their native Auburn, Indiana. It was three years before they started production proper, with a single-cylinder chain-driven car, the Runabout. Reflecting the rapid development of American car design at that time, a twin-cylinder model was added in 1905, a four in 1910 and a six in 1912. But Auburn did not produce its own engines, instead buying them in from Continental, Rutenber and Teetor. There was a new commitment to

style in the 1919 Beauty Six, which soon evolved into the 6-51 sports car. But the U.S. car industry was going through a difficult early 1920s, and Auburn was taken over by Erret Lobban Cord, who also build cars under his own name.

Cord ordered a completely new range of advanced Auburns for 1925, and the company bounced back, even weathering the depression well with its six- and eight-cylinder sedans, though the luxury V12 had to be dropped despite a price tag of less than $1,000. Sleek new styling had come in 1931 with the 8-98, but it was the 653 six-cylinder, 851 eight-cylinder and (most of

all) the supercharged Speedster, with its guaranteed 100mph (161km/h), that caught the public imagination. These were the cars of their affluent era, but Auburn lost money on every one of the Speedsters. Auburn went into liquidation in 1937.

AUDI (Germany 1910-1939, and 1965 to date)

Audi has a long history, but it divides neatly into two parts, before and after World War II, with a 26-year gap in between. The hiatus occurred because Audi was part of a larger group from 1931, Auto-Union, which itself was nationalized after the war and re-entered the private sector in 1949, but allowed the Audi name to lapse. Cars were still built at the Audi factory in Zwickau, but they were DKW designs, and badged as such.

August Horch was Audi's founder. This was his second motor industry start-up, for cars bearing his own name were already well established by 1909, when Horch had a disagreement with his partners and left. But he could not use his own name again on a car, and therefore took the name of his second venture from the Latin for the literal German translation of his own name.

Horch was a hands-on sort of man, and so entered the new Audi Type B for the 1911 Austrian Alpine trials, leading the team of drivers himself. He won without a single penalty point, and Audi Type Cs won the 1914 and 1915 events. But these cars were only made in limited quantities, and in World War I Audi turned to making two-ton trucks, based on the Type C, as well as military vehicles. After the war, the Types C, D and E were reintroduced, as well as a new Type G. But the challenge had gone for Horch, who left Audi in 1920.

The company carried on, its range culminating in a range of six- and eight-cylinder saloons such as the Type R Imperator of 1928. However, this was not a success, and Audi's fortunes took a turn that same year when J.S. Rasmussen of DKW bought a controlling share in the company. Under his leadership, Audi began to produce smaller cars using a whole range

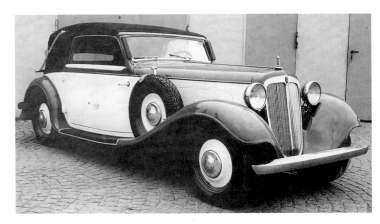

RIGHT
1934 Type 225 Front.

BELOW
Audi Wanderer.

of bought-in components. A new model in 1931, for example, consisted of a DKW chassis and a 67.1-cu in (1.1-litre) Peugeot engine, while U.S.-designed Rickenbacker engines were made under licence. In 1932, Audi became part of the Auto-Union concern, along with DKW, Wanderer and Horch, a fact that explains the four-ringed badge that Audis use to this day.

Nationalized after World War II and re-established under Mercedes control in 1949, Auto-Union made no use of the Audi name, until 1965, when VW gained a majority shareholding and introduced an all-new front-wheel-drive saloon. This 1700 was the start of Audi's new era of modern front-wheel-drive cars. The range expanded rapidly as Audi became the VW group's upmarket brand. It was a technologically-driven company, introducing a five-cylinder engine, turbocharging and four-wheel-drive in the late 1970s and early 1980s.

It was the Quattro, which combined all three of these features, that helped transform Audi's image. The Quattro, the first four-wheel-drive rally car, was a tremendous success, winning many major national and international rallies. It also heralded a new era of four-wheel-drive for performance road cars: with a few exceptions, until that time four-wheel-drive had been restricted to off-road vehicles. Audi was also at the forefront of aerodynamics, with the new 100 of 1983 boasting a drag coefficient of only 0.30. A

LEFT ABOVE
Auto-Union Monza coupé.

LEFT BELOW
Auto-Union 1700 saloon.

TOP
The 1977 100 saloon, the first Audi with a five-cylinder engine.

ABOVE
1990-specification Audi 80 2.0E.

RIGHT
The A3 gave Audi a new entry-level car to attract a new breed of younger potential Audi buyers.

BELOW
The Audi A6, launched in 1997, was good enough to frighten BMW. It competed directly with the BMW 5-series, which had also been updated in the same year.

BELOW RIGHT
The 1997 Audi cabriolet range. There was a 2.0-litre four and two V6s, one of 2.6 litres, the other of 2.8 litres.

few years later, the company was concentrating on high-technology diesel engines, with electronic diesel injection and a long-striding six-speed gearbox allowing the 100TDI of the early 1990s to use remarkably little fuel for so large a car. The smaller 80 and 90 continued (though the 90 badge, used to denote the five-cylinder petrol engine, was dropped in 1991) with their own TDI and high-powered petrol versions. Also in the 1990s, the original Coupé was replaced by a more

ABOVE
The Audi A6.

ABOVE LEFT
Audi's estate cars were always well-regarded. This is a 1997 A4.

LEFT
Top of the range was the A8. It used a 4.2-litre V8 in an all-aluminium bodyshell.

rounded version, and the 80 and 100 were replaced by the A4 and A6 respectively. The Audi range expanded in both directions through the 1990s. The A8 was an all-new executive car, offering up to 340bhp (253.5kW) by 1997, with standard four-wheel-drive, and for the first time it looked as though Audi had a credible BMW/Mercedes competitor. Meanwhile, the small/medium A3 was based on the VW Golf platform and the compact A2 took Audi back to the small car market. Cars like the V8-powered S4, with well over 300bhp (223.68kW), challenged BMW in the sports saloon market. After its long lapse, Audi was the born-again car marque.

OPPOSITE
The Audi TT.

ABOVE
The newly restyled Audi A8.

RIGHT
The Audi A2 1.6 FSI.

PAGE 44: The Audi Project 'Rosemeyer'
concept car.

PAGE 45:
The Audi Pikes Peak Quattro design study.

AUSTIN (Britain 1905-1989)
One of Great Britain's major manufacturers for decades, Austin made its mark with small cars like the ubiquitous Seven and revolutionary Mini. In fact, during the 1960s it was one of the most innovative mainstream car makers, wedded to front-wheel-drive and hydraulic suspension systems. Sadly, it went into a long, slow decline as part of the giant British Leyland, and while the famous Longbridge, Birmingham, factory lives on as part of the Rover group, the Austin name has died.

Herbert Austin's first car was actually built for Frederick Wolseley. Austin had met Wolseley while working in Australia for the latter's sheep-shearing company. That first car was a three-wheeler, but Austin soon went on to produce cars under his own name, beginning in 1905 at Longbridge, where Austins would always be built. Although Austin was later to be famous for small cars, this first chain-driven model was a four-cylinder, developing 25/30hp (18.6/22.4kW), and sixes up to a 591.9-cu in (9.7-litre) type delivering 60hp (44.74kW) would also come out of Longbridge.

But the most popular of these early Austins was the mid-range Twenty, joined by a Ten in 1910. In fact, the Twenty was Austin's sole model for a while, just after World War I, using a 219.7-cu in (3.6-litre) side-valve engine, and was on sale right up to 1929. There was a six-cylinder version from 1927, plus smaller four-cylinder Twelve and six-cylinder Sixteen. But the car that really made Austin was the diminutive Seven, often described as Great Britain's Model T. Austin was, so the story goes, so inspired by his dislike of motorcycle sidecars that he determined to build a car for the same price. The little Seven of 1922, usually powered by a

45.58-cu in (747-cc) side-valve engine of 13bhp (9.7kW), could transport two adults and two children at minimum cost, and was a great success. A long-wheelbased Big Seven with a 54.92-cu in (900-cc) motor was added later, and the original was made under licence all over the world. One step up was the 1932 Ten, known as the Cambridge from 1937, a reflection of Austin's fondness for giving his cars very English place names. As well as these small Austins, the range included bigger Eighteens and Twenty-Eights in the late 1930s.

Like many manufacturers, Austin reintroduced its pre-war range in the first years after World War II, but 1947 saw the unveiling of the new A125 Sheerline saloon as well as that of the little A40 Devon/Dorset. Continuing the county

theme, this was later joined by the A70 Hampshire. Quite different was the A90 Atlantic coupé, specifically designed to appeal to American buyers. Another interesting diversion aimed at the American market was the much smaller Metropolitan, built for Nash by Austin. Austin merged with arch-rival Morris in 1952 to form the British Motor Corporation, which would eventually gather up most of the British motor industry. Also that year, the little A30 (initially named 'New Seven') appeared, powered by an 48.82-cu in (800-cc) overhead-valve engine.

The cars were all updated through the 1950s as the A40, A50 and six-cylinder A90, but a new look came in 1958 with the Farina-styled A40, and a similar finned style for the A55 and A99 the following year. But of course, 1959 is most remembered for the Mini. By mounting the little 51.75-cu in (848-cc) engine transversely to drive the front wheels,

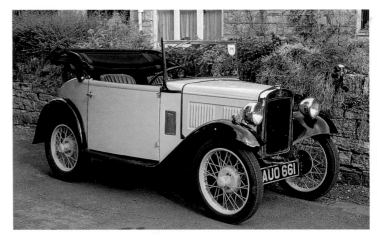

AUSTIN A30 SEVEN 2-DOOR SALOON

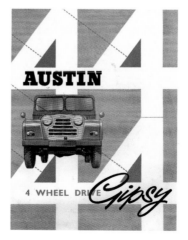

ABOVE
Sales brochure for the Austin A30.

ABOVE LEFT
Sales brochure for the Austin A30
Countryman.

LEFT
Sales brochure for the Austin Gipsy.

FAR LEFT
1951 Austin Atlantic convertible.

OPPOSITE
ABOVE: 1931 Austin Ulster.

BELOW: Austin 7 tourer.

designer Alec Issigonis produced a four-seater car in a tiny package. It was fun to drive as well, a world away from the stodgy saloons of the 1950s, and derivatives soon appeared, such as a van, the Countryman estate and what else but the Mini Cooper. The latter became a legend in its own right, winning international rallies outright against far bigger, more powerful cars. The ultimate road-going model was the Mini Cooper S whose 77.8-cu in (1.275-litre) engine provided 76bhp (56.67kW).

So successful was the Mini's front-wheel-drive concept that it was extended to the whole range. The 1100 was introduced in 1963 and was soon joined by a 1300 version, the big 1800 in 1965 and the five-speed Maxi (one of the first hatchbacks) in 1969. Less daring were the later Mini derivatives: the Clubman of 1969 added a larger hood and 60.9-cu in (998-cc) engine.

Austin had a less happy 1970s, though the Allegro, with its hydragas suspension, replaced the 1100/1300 and sold well for a time. The startling wedge-shaped Princess replaced the old 1800, still with front-wheel-drive and choice of 279-cu in (1.8-litre) four- and 134.25-cu in (2.2-litre) six-cylinder engines. These were soon replaced by the new O-series four in 103.7- and 122-cu in (1.7- and 2-litre) forms. The Metro of 1980 created a huge impact, and helped support the company through some very difficult times. It continued with the Mini's 998- and 1275-cc engines, albeit in updated forms, but was otherwise completely new, with a three-door hatchback body and hydragas suspension. A patriotic TV advert of the time showed Metros rampant on the White Cliffs of Dover, ready to repel the hordes of imported cars. For a few months, it seemed as if the whole country had gone Metro mad. The truth was, everyone was desperate for Austin-Rover, as it now was,

ABOVE
1959 Austin 7 Mini.

RIGHT
1952 Austin Atlantic coupé.

OPPOSITE
LEFT: Rover Mini Cooper.

RIGHT: A 998-cc Mini Cooper at Silverstone race track.

to produce a good modern, well-built car, a commodity it had lacked for some years.

Meanwhile, the Princess became the hatchback Ambassador in 1982, but never really fulfilled its promise as a roomy, practical family car. It was joined by the

Maestro in the following year as Austin's new mid-range hatchback, which the company hoped would echo the Metro's success. It came in 79.3- and 97.6-cu in (1.3- and 1.6-litre) forms, and later in 2-litre and 2-litre turbo forms. A saloon car version, the bigger Montego, was announced in the following year, with similar engine options. Like the Maestro, this was available with an ultra-economical Perkins turbo-diesel engine, but it too was plagued with indifferent build quality.

As part of British Leyland, Austin had been nationalized in the mid-1970s, and with its fate a political issue, it was often in the news for the wrong reasons. Several reorganizations followed, with new chief Michael Edwardes of the late 1970s determined to turn the company round. Part of his strategy was to make use of the many famous marques that came under the British Leyland umbrella, Austin among them. The company was renamed Austin-Rover, but by the late 1980s it was clear that the Rover name carried far more kudos, and the Austin name was gradually dropped: the Metro was rebadged as a Rover, and the Maestro, Montego and Ambassador were all replaced by Rover-badged cars. This was the end of Austin, but its Longbridge home lived on.

AUSTIN-HEALEY (Great Britain 1953-1971)

As a marque, Austin-Healey came about almost by accident, rather than as a carefully conceived plan. Donald Healey had been making sports cars since 1945, using engines from Riley, Nash and Alvis, though production was on a relatively small scale. The turning point came in late 1951, when Healey and his son Geoffrey decided to build an all-new open sports car based on Austin components. Austin agreed to supply the engine and running gear from its A90 Atlantic, the four-cylinder four-seat coupé aimed at the North American market. But the new Healey 100 was very different from that, a classic British two-seater, styled by Gerry Coker. Sleek and sporting, the latest Healey caused a sensation at the 1952 Earls Court Motor Show, and the company was swamped with orders: so many orders, in fact, that the little Healey concern had no hope of meeting them. At this point, Leonard Lord, head of BMC, of which Austin was now a part, stepped in and offered to make the car in large numbers. It thus became the Austin-Healey 100, and a new marque was born.

Variants and updates of the first 100 soon appeared. A four-speed gearbox was a useful change, but the car was also popular in competition, so the 100S had a lighter aluminium body and disc brakes. Alongside it, the 100M featured the A90 four-cylinder engine tuned to Le Mans specification. In 1956, the four was replaced with Austin's new six-cylinder C-series engine of 158.7 cu in (2.6 litres). The new 100 Six produced 102bhp (76.05kW), and three years later was upgraded as the Austin-Healey 3000 with the latest 176.97-cu in (2.9-litre) C-series engine.

This was the definitive 'Big Healey', with 124bhp (89.5kW) and a top speed of

ABOVE
Austin-Healey prototype 3000 MK III.

LEFT
Sales brochure for the Austin-Healey 3000.

OPPOSITE
ABOVE LEFT: Austin-Healey 100/4.

ABOVE RIGHT: Austin-Healey 100/6.

BELOW: Austin-Healey 3000 coupé special.

nearly 120mph (193km/h). Cheaper than an E-Type Jaguar, it continued to offer an uncompromising British sports car experience right through to 1967, by which time it came in triple-carburettor 132-bhp (98.4-kW) form. Prototypes were built with a 4-litre Rolls-Royce engine, but the big Healey was never replaced.

But it wasn't the only Austin-Healey. Back in 1958, Geoffrey Healey and Gerry Coker designed the little Sprite, this time based on the Austin A35 engine, gearbox and front suspension. With its cute, chubby looks, which led to its 'Frogeye' nickname,

the Sprite had great appeal and sold well. The 57.85-cu in (948-cc) engine was uprated with twin carburettors to give 43bhp (32.1kW), enough for some fun in the lightweight Sprite. In 1961, the Sprite was restyled along the same lines as the mechanically identical MG Midget, and was gradually updated with larger engines and disc brakes through the 1960s. But the MG name proved more alluring, and the Midget carried on after 1971, when the Sprite was dropped. The Austin-Healey name died with it.

AUSTRO-DAIMLER (Austria 1899-1936)

For a time Austro-Daimler was the biggest car manufacturer in Austria, though for the first few years of its life it was owned by the German Daimler concern. The story began in 1899, when the Vienna-based Bierenz-Fischer & Co. agreed to build 100 Daimler cars under licence. A new company was formed to do this but it soon ran into problems, and in 1902 Daimler's son Paul was sent to Vienna to sort things out.

But the Austrians had ambitions beyond building cars under licence, bolstered by the arrival of Ferdinand Porsche as director in 1903. A prolific and imaginative engineer, Porsche was keen to produce a new range of cars, and the Austrian company soon separated from its parent, though it did not achieve full financial independence until 1906 and only assumed the Austro-Daimler name five years later, when all links with Daimler were finally severed.

While Porsche's new ideas were being developed, the company built Maja cars for Emile Jellinek, consul-general for the Austro-Hungarian empire in Nice. Meanwhile, the first Porsche-designed cars came on stream, notably the Prince Henry Tour winner of 1910. The following year, a Porsche-designed Austro-Daimler won the Austrian Alpine Tour.

After building military vehicles (some of them both road- and rail-compatible) in World War I, Austro-Daimler resurrected some of its pre-war designs before unveiling some new fast touring cars; these too were successful in competition. But Porsche was dissatisfied, returning to Daimler in 1923. He was replaced by Karl Rabe, under whom the company linked up with Austro-Fiat and then merged with

Puch in 1928 to form Austro-Daimler-Puchwerke. Another merger in 1935, this time with Steyr-Werke to produce Steyr-Daimler-Puch, soon led to the Austro-Daimler name being dropped altogether.

TOP: 1909 Austro-Daimler charablanc.
CENTRE: 25/30-hp tourer.
ABOVE: Circa 1919 Sascha racing voiturette.

51

BALLOT (France 1919-1933)

Ernest Ballot's foray into road car manufacture was relatively short: only between 1921 and 1930 were Ballot-engined machines produced for the road. However, he had had a long and varied engineering career before that. He started out in the French merchant marine, setting up Ballot et Cie. in Paris in 1906 to build marine engines. The business had extended to other power units by 1914, and Ballot was producing commercial and racing engines for Delage, Mass and La Licorne.

With solid financial backing, Ballot was able to build his first racing car just after the end of the war. Designed by Ernest Henry, this 299-cu in (4.9-litre) eight-cylinder machine was intended specifically for the 1919 Indianapolis 500 in America. But a French company, of course, could not ignore the Grand Prix, and two years later Henry penned a smaller 3-litre car for Ballot to enter in the French GP. A 122-cu in (2-litre) four-cylinder racer was developed alongside it, and these racers formed the basis of the first Ballot road car, the 2LS. This is best described as a fast tourer, with four seats and four-wheel braking.

Other tourers based on the same theme followed, notably the 1924 overhead-camshaft 2LT, which came in open or closed saloon form, and the 158.66-cu in (2.6-litre) straight-eight RH saloon. The latter was introduced at the 1927 Paris Salon, and was an elegant machine, later enlarged to 3 litres for 1930. But with the Depression biting, this was not the time to sell big luxury cars.

TOP
1922 2-litre Grand Prix car.

ABOVE RIGHT
1924 overhead-camshaft 2LT tourer.

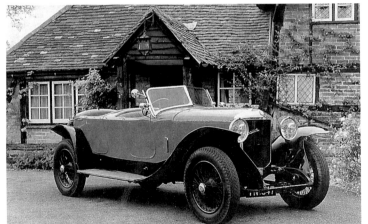

With sales slumping, Ballot was sacked from the company he had founded, and Hispano-Suiza staged a takeover. An-

Hispano-Suiza-engined Ballot was sold briefly before the factory was closed in 1933.

BENTLEY (Great Britain 1921 to date)

Bentley is a name forever associated with big, no-nonsense sports cars with massive four- and six-cylinder engines. Not for nothing did Ettore Bugatti refer to them as 'the fastest lorries in the world'. But the classic, brutish, Le Mans-winning Bentley was only in production for a few years, while for decades Bentleys were no more than badge-engineered Rolls-Royces, with no sporting aspirations whatsoever. Not until the mid-1980s did the marque start to re-emerge in its own right.

Walter Owen Bentley (the famous 'WO') started his working life by selling and modifying the French DFP car before realizing he could do better himself. Design work began in 1919, and the 183.1-cu in (3-litre) four-cylinder Bentley entered production two years later. For ten years, Bentleys came out of the same mould as big sporting cars of high quality and high price, five times winners of the Le Mans 24-hour race. But they sold in small numbers, and the racing programme was expensive. Bentley collapsed in 1925, was rescued, recovered and collapsed again in 1931, before being taken over by Rolls-Royce.

This was the start of a new era for Bentley, and whether it was for better or worse depends on one's point of view. They

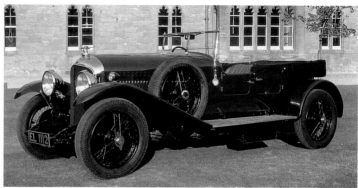

were now 'silent sports cars', modified and tuned Rolls-Royces which had little in common with the earlier muscular breed. The first was the 1933 213.6-cu in (3.5-litre) model based on the R-R 20/25, and which later became the 259.4-cu in (4.25-litre) model.

After World War II, Rolls-Royce/Bentley introduced its first standard steel bodies: before then, only the chassis had been offered, for which the customer could choose a coach-built body. The badge-engineering continued, with a Bentley Mark VI of 1946 following straight on from the pre-war cars. However, one or two Bentleys were unique to the marque. The graceful two-door R-type Continental of 1952 was one such, and was followed by

ABOVE
4.2-litre Bentley.

ABOVE LEFT
8.3-litre Bentley.

LEFT 1928 4.5-litre Bentley.

an S-type Continental in 1955. Both had more power than the equivalent Rolls-Royce, but most Bentleys were simply rebadged versions of the Silver Cloud and later Silver Shadow.

In 1982 the company finally began to capitalize on Bentley's performance heritage with the Mulsanne Turbo, combining Rolls-Royce ambience with sports car performance. A Turbo R followed, and a two-door Continental R in 1991, with a short-wheelbase Continental T five years later: these were unique Bentley models, with no Rolls-Royce equivalent. In fact, the Bentley name seemed to be withstanding the years better than its long-term partner. Late in 1991 the range included names like Red Label, Continental and Arnage, all powered by a 411.9-cu in (6.75-litre) V8 in 400-, 420- and 450-bhp (298.24-, 313.15- and 335.52-kW) forms. All of these were Bentleys, not that it was 100 per cent British any more. Rolls-Royce Bentley was taken over by Volkswagen in 1998, but within a few years was owned by BMW. The signs were that BMW was keen to differentiate the two marques.

RIGHT
Bentley Azure.

BELOW
Bentley Continental T.

BELOW RIGHT
Bentley Brooklands R.

OPPOSITE
ABOVE: Bentley 3-litre.

BELOW LEFT: Bentley Model R.

BELOW RIGHT: This modern Bentley has distinctive sporting lines.

TOP LEFT and RIGHT
The Bentley Azure final series.

RIGHT
The new Bentley Continental GT.

LEFT and ABOVE
The Bentley Arnage R.

BENZ (Germany 1885-1926)

Benz was there first as the world pioneer of car design. It is generally accepted that Karl Benz's first prototype of 1885 was the world's first petrol-powered car. It was a flimsy-looking affair, a lightweight three-wheeler whose single-cylinder four-stroke motor could propel it to a dizzying maximum of 10mph (16km/h): but it worked.

The young Benz had worked for both a carriage builder and stationary engine concern, so perhaps it was natural that this gifted engineer should try and combine the two. However, it was five years before his Tricycle finally reached limited production, when the arrival of two partners allowed him to concentrate on engineering. Things moved faster after that. The three-wheeler evolved into the four-wheeled Viktoria in 1891, which formed the basis of van and bus versions. There was also a cheaper model, the Velo, launched in 1894. All of these were considerable advances on the Tricycle, and Benz prospered: by the end of the decade his company had built an impressive 2,000 vehicles, with a capacity of 600 per year. It was, in effect, the world's leading car manufacturer.

But this was not to be for long. Rivals were springing up, producing advances which Benz was unwilling to meet. His cars began to look outdated, so soon after their pioneering early years, and sales began to fall. As a result, a new designer was engaged and Karl Benz left the firm that bore his name. Chief engineer Hans Nibel was now in charge, and from 1907 began a programme of motor racing aimed at restoring Benz fortunes. This culminated in the building of the remarkable 200-bhp (149.1-kW) Blitzen-Benz, powered by a 1,312-cu in (21.5-litre) airship engine. It was designed to take the world speed

record, and did so at a speed that remained unbeaten for over ten years.

Meanwhile, Nibel's new range of Benz road cars made gradual progress, and during World War I the company concentrated on trucks and aero engines. But it was facing hard times in Germany's shattered economy after 1918. Again, racing was used to publicize the breed, but most of the road cars were resurrected 1914 designs. The only way to survive was to merge, so in 1926 Benz joined with Daimler to form Daimler-Benz (later Mercedes-Benz).

TOP (from left to right)
Model 3 vis-à-vis car.
1892 Benz Viktoria.
1895 Benz omnibus.

CENTRE LEFT
The 1903 twin-cylinder Sport-Phaeton.

LEFT
The 1918 6/18 had a four-cylinder ohc engine.

BERLIET (France 1895-1939)

Berliet was one of the earliest car manufacturers, in limited production as early as 1895. Based in Lyon, the company built quite advanced cars for the time, featuring four-speed gearboxes and wheel-rather than tiller-controlled steering. Larger cars joined the range in 1901 when the Audibert-Lavirotte came under the Berliet umbrella.

In fact, Berliet began to concentrate on large cars from then on, with 384.5-cu in (6.3-litre) 40-hp (29.8-kW), 524.8-cu in (8.6-litre) 60-hp (44.7-kW) and 671.3-cu in (11-litre) 80-hp (59.6-kW) models available. Technical advances continued the Berliet tradition, with pressed steel chassis and overhead inlet valves featuring. Shaft drive arrived in 1907, replacing the ubiquitous chain. There were smaller twin-cylinder Berliets as well as the big sixes, and all were offered up to World War I.

After the war, Berliet cars continued to feature up-to-the-minute specifications, such as overhead valves, four-wheel braking and four-speed gearboxes, all offered in the mid-1920s. The range was still wide, from the 73.2-cu in (1.2-litre) 10/20 to the 244.1-cu in (4-litre) 23/70. A new line of restyled cars arrived in 1933, the new 97.6-cu in (1.6-litre) 9CV and 122-cu in (2-litre) 11CV Type 944, complete with an American look. There were de-luxe versions with independent suspension, and both overhead- and side-valve engines were available. Right up to the end, Berliets remained technically advanced, and the 1936 Dauphine had rack-and-pinion steering, independent front suspension and a synchromesh gearbox, though in the last few years before World War II Berliet bought its bodywork from Peugeot. The company did not restart car production after the war, but continues to build trucks.

TOP
Berliet 1911 four-cylinder 22-hp car.

ABOVE LEFT
1923 Model VI.

ABOVE
1936 2-litre Dauphine.

LEFT
The last Berliet car was a 1937 2-litre Dauphine.

FAR LEFT TOP
1901 Type B with chain-drive

FAR LEFT
1908 Double Phaeton.

BITTER (Germany 1973-1986)

Perhaps because of its strong mainstream motor industry, centred on companies such as VW, BMW, Mercedes and Porsche, Germany has produced fewer specialist manufacturers than some countries. Erich Bitter was the exception to this rule, though even his cars were really rebodied Opels. Bitter imported Abarth tuning parts from Italy in the late 1960s, as well as Intermeccanica cars. He was so disillusioned with the latter's poor build quality that he decided to build his own exotic car, based on proven mass-produced parts.

The Bitter CD 2+2 coupé was launched in 1973, based on a shortened Opel Diplomat chassis. The General Motors theme extended to the Chevrolet 323.4-cu in (5.3-litre) V8 engine, also used in the Diplomat saloon. In fact, nearly all of the components were of Opel concept, and even the shape was worked on by Dave Holls, Opel's head of styling. The bodies were built by Baur of Stuttgart. Sales were slow at first, as the first oil crisis hit shortly after the Bitter was launched, but eventually nearly 400 cars were sold.

A new Bitter, the SC coupé, convertible

BELOW
Bitter 6-cylinder SC.

and saloon was launched in 1981, and again Opel had a hand in the styling. But the SC, based on the latest Opel Senator, had a troubled early life. Erich Bitter was unable to find a German company to build bodies, so used OCRA of Turin. It soon became clear that OCRA quality was not up to scratch, with premature rust showing on finished cars. The contract was terminated after only 79 bodies had been delivered, and was awarded to another Turin firm. This time the arrangement worked, and SC bodies were delivered, fully trimmed, to the Bitter factory for Opel running gear to be added. Steyr did this assembly work from 1983, when Bitter ran out of space, which also boosted production to three or four cars per week. But production wound down in late 1985 and ceased altogether early the following year, after 488 SCs had been built.

Erich Bitter went on to produce several prototype cars in the late 1980s and early 1990s, including the Rallye coupé, Type 3 convertible and Berlina saloon, but none of these made it to production.

BMW (Germany 1928 to date)

The Bayerische Motoren Werke (BMW) now has one of the strongest images in Europe for building sporting cars that put the driver first. But this was not always the case: BMW's first car was a licence-built Austin Seven, and much of its income, which financed a new generation of sports saloons after World War II, came from the Isetta bubblecar, which the Bavarians built under licence.

But BMW has not always built cars. The company started out making aircraft engines in Munich, turning in 1923 to motorcycles in a process which continues very successfully to this day, and it was not until 1928 that it branched out into cars. BMW took over Dixi, which was already building an Austin Seven copy at Eisenach.

BELOW
1936 Dixi and BMW sports roadsters.

BMW's ambitions lay with more sporting cars, however, and the Dixi was rapidly joined by the sportier 3/15 and within five years by a long-wheelbased six-cylinder version. That six-cylinder engine was to form the basis of BMW's range of the late 1930s, growing to 122.05 cu in (2 litres) for the 1935 326, then powering the famous 328 two-seater of 1937. This was very successful in competition, winning the 1940 Mille Miglia, and by then was selling alongside the 152.6-cu in (2.5-litre) 335 saloon. During World War II the company concentrated on war work, such as motorcycle combinations, but in 1945 faced

a situation in which its Munich factories were destroyed by bombs, and the Eisenach plant was now isolated in East Germany. It was three years before motorcycle production could restart, but this helped finance a return to cars in 1952.

Oddly, given Germany's poor economic state, the first post-war BMW was the six-cylinder 501 limousine, with a V8 version following in 1955 and the svelte 507 V8 roadster the year after that. Not surprisingly, these expensive status symbols only sold in small numbers, but BMW found a more suitable product in 1955, building the Isetta bubblecar under licence from 1959, and the rear-engined 700 from the same year. The economy cars were selling well, but BMW was still facing near-bankruptcy in 1961, being saved only by the new 1500 saloon. This was the start of a new era, as the 1500 established the formula for nearly all subsequent BMWs, a high-quality, rear-wheel-drive sports saloon. The successful 80-bhp (59.6-kW) 1500 soon led to a whole range of two-door, four-door, cabriolet and later touring estate versions, culminating in the 170-bhp (126.8-kW) 2002 Turbo. So high was

demand that BMW needed extra production capacity, and bought the Glas company in 1967. As well as the mid-sized 1500-based saloons, BMW continued its range of large six-cylinder saloons and coupés, which were Bertone-styled from 1965 and powered by a 195.3-cu in (3.2-litre) engine by 1971.

In the 1970s BMW began to use its now familiar numbering system: the 3-series medium saloons (stemming from the original 1500), 5-series large saloons, 6-series coupés and 7-series luxury saloons. Engines ranged from 97.6-cu in (1.6-litre) fours to 213.6-cu in (3.5-litre) sixes. If

ABOVE
1939 328 sports roadster.

LEFT
1929 747-cc Dixi.

ABOVE
BMW 507 sports car.

BELOW LEFT
1971 M1.

FAR LEFT (from top to bottom)
327/28 cabriolet.
1975 1990-cc.
1987 320i.
5-series touring.

standard BMWs were not sporting enough, the Alpina range from 1978 offered a high-performance variant of all of these, echoed by the M-series cars of the early 1980s. The M3, M5, M535i and M635 Csi were all tuned versions of the standard cars, and all were built by BMW's Motorsport department. Meanwhile, BMW had built its first mid-engined sports car in 1978, the six-cylinder M1. By now, the company's sporting image was secure, bolstered by its successful Formula One racing engine. Less successful was the Z1 sports car, using the 170-bhp 2.5-litre six-cylinder engine from the 325i; but its high price restricted sales and production ended in the early 1990s.

But little else went wrong for BMW in the last decade of the 20th century. There were new 5- and 7-series cars, with an 8-series coupé replacing the '6'. BMW had

ABOVE
The Z3 was initially only available with four-cylinder engine.

BELOW
After the launch of the Z3, BMW announced that there was a coupé version on the drawing board.

TOP
The 3-series Compact provided a cheap entry-level car for younger buyers.

ABOVE
The V12-engined 850 was joined by the cheaper V8 840 in 1993.

LEFT
BMW 760i.

BELOW LEFT
BMW 3-series coupé.

BELOW
The X5 was BMW's first foray into the off-road market.

OPPOSITE
The new BMW Z4.

sports car, with a 3-litre six-cylinder engine producing 231bhp (172.2kW).

The late 1990s saw BMW take over Rover, with the successful Land Rover 4x4 an attractive prize. This did not work out, however, and Rover was sold back into British ownership after a few years. But BMW was left with the new 2001 Mini, which cleverly echoed the style of the original Mini. This was a great success, and in 2002 a 161-bhp (120.1-kW) Cooper S was announced, and another famous British name came under British control at the beginning of the 21st century. BMW had already sold its V8 engine to Rolls-Royce at Crewe, and also provided technical help, but by 2002 was fully in charge, building a new Rolls-Royce factory at Goodwood in Sussex. Meanwhile, on the drawing board was the 1-series, a small rear-wheel-drive car to come in hatchback or coupé form.

LEFT
The BMW Activity Concept Vehicle.

BELOW and OPPOSITE
The BMW Mini Cooper S.

progressed beyond six-cylinders now, with the top long-wheelbased 750iL powered by a 305.1-cu in (5-litre) V12, underlining BMW's determination to challenge Mercedes on its home ground. The 850i coupé used the same engine, and was limited to a top speed of 155mph (250km/h), a token gesture in response to environmental and safety concerns.

But the small 3-series remained the best-selling BMW, still offering a wide range of 1.6- to 2.5-litre (later 170.9-cu in/2.8-litre) engines through the 1990s, with the M3 now up to 321bhp (239.3kW) and one of the fastest production BMWs ever. A two-door coupé followed the saloon, and

there were cabriolet and touring estate versions. As the standard 3-series was slipping upmarket, a truncated hatchback version, the Compact, was introduced at a lower price. Meanwhile, the 5-series acquired V8 engines for the first time, of 183.1 or 244.1 cu in (3 or 4 litres), while 213.6- and 274.6-cu in (3.5- and 4.5-litre) V8s found a home in the 7-series. The Z3 was introduced as an entry-level 279-cu in (1.8-litre) sports car, but was soon followed by a 2.8-litre M3-engined version. Interestingly, the Z3 was built at BMW's new factory in Spartanburg, South Carolina. Its Z4 replacement, due early in 2003, looked like an altogether more serious

LEON BOLLEE (France 1895-1933)

Léon Bollée was one of the pioneers, building his first car in 1895, in a sense continuing the family tradition, as his father had produced steam carriages in the past. His little three-wheel Voiturette (little car) was quite successful, and fast for its time, capable of over 30mph (48km/h). With a 39.67-cu in (650-cc) single-cylinder 3-hp (2.2-kW) engine and three-speed gearbox, it was built by various companies over the following years.

Bollée, meanwhile, turned to larger cars, though these were less successful until he obtained backing from Vanderbilt. The 1907 726.2-cu in (11.9-litre) model, for example, was aimed at the U.S. market, and

there was a smaller 10/14-hp (7.5/10.4-kW) from 1909. Production (in one of Bollée Sr.'s factories, at Le Mans) was still limited to a maximum of 350 a year, and the venture was further affected by Léon's premature death in 1913. The company was struggling after World War I, with an increasingly outdated range, and the Le Mans factory was bought by Sir William Morris in 1924. Under his ownership, Morris chassis were fitted with elegant bodywork designed by Van Vestrant.

But the Morris regime ended with big losses, and the company sold out in 1931 to the Société Nouvelle Léon Bollée. This was a consortium which included Harry Smith, the Morris works manager at Le Mans. Sadly, this venture lasted for only two years, and the factory was closed in 1933.

BOND (Great Britain 1948-1974)

Lawrence 'Lawrie' Bond was a car designer who was fascinated by light weight and efficiency. He made his name building, racing and selling diminutive 30.51-cu in (500-cc) racing cars in early post-war Britain, specifically for hill climbing and the then-new National 500cc Formula. But even then he was considering his next

project: a basic three-wheeler that would cost a pittance to run, and would be perfect for a Britain in which petrol was still rationed and very few new full-sized cars were available.

This was the Bond Minicar, which went into full production in 1948, built for Bond by Sharps Commercials. Just as Bond envisaged, the Minicar was basic in the extreme: there was no rear suspension, and the 7.44-cu in (122-cc) Villiers two-stroke engine was started by pulling a cord! There was no roof, and there were cable brakes to the rear wheels only: in effect, the Minicar

ABOVE LEFT
The Bollée steam carriage, c.1880.

LEFT
The four-seater, four-door Type M of 1926.

ABOVE
1969 Bond Equipe convertible.

OPPOSITE LEFT
1956 Bond Minicar Mark C Villiers IIE.

was a late 1940s interpretation of the original cyclecar. The upside was that the Minicar weighed only 308lb (140kg), so it could cruise at 30mph (48km/h) while giving nearly 100mpg (37km/litre).

Through the 1950s the Minicar sold steadily, and gradually acquired more equipment, more room (four seats) and bigger engines (12.02- and 15.26-cu in/197- and 250-cc Villiers units). It was still slower and cruder than a four-cylinder three-wheel Reliant, but much cheaper, and like its Tamworth-built rival could be driven on a motorcycle licence. It was never designed as a long-distance car, but many enthusiastic owners made epic tours of Europe in their tiny Bonds.

The Minicar was dropped in 1962, but Bond replaced it with something very different. The Equipe GT Coupé was a distinctive looking 2+2, based on a Triumph Herald chassis and mechanical parts. It made quite an impact, offering GT looks at a modest price, and was later updated as the GT4S, with a 79.1-cu in (1.3-litre) Triumph engine. In 1967 it was joined by the Equipe 122- cu in (2- litre) GT, now with a cleaner fastback shape and power from Triumph's straight-six power unit, though it lasted only a few years and was joined by a convertible.

But three-wheelers remained at the heart of Bond, and in 1966 the company announced the new 875. This was designed to compete head-on with Reliant, using the all-alloy engine and transaxle from the Hillman Imp. The vehicle was so light that the Imp's lively overhead-cam engine was deemed too powerful, and in production the vehicle was fitted with a detuned unit, though it could still top 80mph (129km/h). Production was stopped when Reliant took over Bond in 1969.

But that was not the end for Bond, and in fact the company was to go out on a high and cheerful note. This was the bright orange, wedge-shaped Bond Bug. No one had seen anything like it on the road before, but the two-seater Bug was a serious attempt by Reliant to break into the youth market. To cut costs it used Reliant's 42.72-but later 45.77-cu in (700/750-cc) alloy engine and running gear, and there were no doors, just a large canopy that hinged up on a telescopic strut. The Bug was not fast (top speed was about 75mph/121km/h), but it certainly felt as if it was: the driver and passenger sat low, just inches from the ground. Reliant made the Bug between 1970 and 1974, with only 2,500 leaving the production lines. The end of the Bug also spelt the end of the Bond name, though the Bug was later revived as a kit car in three- and four-wheeled forms.

BRISTOL (Great Britain 1947 to date)
Bristol is an anachronism, surviving against all the odds in a modern world while so many others have fallen by the wayside. It has done so by building very exclusive, individual cars in tiny numbers, and buying-in major components from outside in a process that is much cheaper for a small company than any attempt to build its own. Some have contrasted Bristol's survival with Aston Martin's many crises, pointing out that Aston always insisted on building its own engines.

So too did Bristol, at first. It started out as a sideline for the Bristol Aeroplane Company, which was looking for new peacetime products after World War II. The cars it built were to aircraft quality and very expensive. It also had strong links with BMW's U.K. importer, so the first Bristol 400 of 1947 owed much to the pre-war BMW 328, especially in its 122-cu in (2-litre) six-cylinder engine.

The car gradually evolved into the aerodynamic 403, the beautiful 404 coupé and the four-door 405 (all other Bristols have always been two-doored). But there was no attempt to broaden the range or introduce a cheaper Bristol: the firm always remained wedded to the concept of big, high-quality two-door saloons. There was a big change with the 407 of 1961, which replaced the BMW-derived six with a Canadian Chrysler V8. From then on, Bristols were always effortless high-speed machines, even though their very

ABOVE
Bristol Zagato V8.

BELOW
Bristol 404 coupé.

conservative styling was dull in comparison with the early cars.

The brick-like Zagato-styled 412 of the 1970s was hardly an improvement, though it did gain more performance as the turbocharged Beaufighter in 1980, after Bristol had begun to name its cars after its aeronautical past, though the car business was now a separate venture. With their big thirsty V8s, separate chassis and sky-high prices, the individualistic Bristols – now with names like Brigand and Blenheim – carried on into the 21st century. But in 2002 there was a departure: the all-new Bristol Fighter is a gull-wing two-seater powered by a 525-bhp (391.4-kW) V10 engine and priced, in Britain, at a little over £200,000.

ABOVE
Bristol 405 drophead.

ABOVE RIGHT
1950s drophead.

RIGHT
Bristol 410.

FAR RIGHT
A 1925 Salmson Grand Sport taking part in a 1975 Light Car Rally.

BRITISH SALMSON
(Great Britain 1934-1947)
Salmson of France had its English equivalent. The French set up a factory at Raynes Park in London to make air-cooled radial aircraft engines, intended for a boom in small aircraft. When it came, the boom was smaller than expected, and to utilize its factory space, the company also began to make cars at Raynes Park.

Starting in 1934, the 91.5-cu in (1.5-litre) British Salmsons were available as two- or four-seater sports cars, a four-seat open tourer and two-door or four-door saloons. This was the S4C, and it was in production until 1938, powered by Salmson's own twin overhead-camshaft engine. It was joined by the larger 97.6-cu in (1.6-litre) S4D in 1936, which was quite advanced for its time with independent front suspension, rack-and-pinion steering, and Lockheed hydraulic brakes. A six-cylinder variant, the S6 or 20/90, was introduced the same year, with the same chassis and running gear but with a 152.6-cu in (2.5-litre) six-cylinder version of the Salmson engine. World War II put an end to Salmson production, when less than 400 cars had been made in all, though one more was assembled in 1947. It is said, though, that the inverted tappets used by Salmson influenced W.O. Bentley when he designed the V12 Lagonda engine.

BROOKE (Great Britain 1902-1913)

The Brooke was probably the first production car with a transverse-mounted three-cylinder engine, and went on sale in 1902. The 14-hp (10.4-kW) car was powered by a 146.34-cu in (2.398-litre) triple. However, most Brookes were conventional fours and sixes, such as the four-cylinder 14/20, of 195.3 cu in (3.2 litres) and 20hp (14.9kW), produced between 1905 and 1907. A variety of six-cylinder cars was offered, notably the 561.4-cu in (9.2-litre) 25/30, later developed as the 38 and finally 40. Brooke ceased car production in 1913, to concentrate on other products.

BROUGH SUPERIOR

(Great Britain 1935-1939)

George Brough made his name producing expensive, exclusive and much sought-after motorcycles. He turned to cars in 1935, following the then-popular practice of fitting American motors into relatively light British chassis: the Brough Superior was one of the more successful of these. Hudson straight-six and straight-eight engines were used at first, and the Brough cars soon became renowned for a similar high-quality, high-performance character as the motorcycles. But the cars were not stripped-down performance machines, for they had traditional coachwork for the convertibles, saloons and two-seater sports cars. World War II put a stop to production, but not before George Brough had produced his four-wheeled swansong, a 267.2-cu in (4.378-litre) V12 with a Charlesworth body.

ABOVE RIGHT
1935 Brough Superior.

RIGHT
1938 V12 Brough Superior.

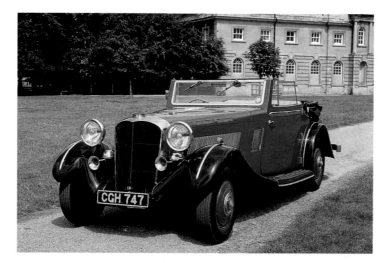

BSA (Great Britain 1907-1940)

Birmingham Small Arms (BSA) was a gun manufacturer based in Small Heath, Birmingham from 1861. It diversified into transport with the Otto Dicycle, and its first car was a 1908 copy of a 40-hp (29.8-kW) Itala. The first motorcycle followed two years later, and BSA became better known for these than for its cars. The company's real entrée to four wheels came about by buying the Daimler concern in 1910, and many early BSA cars were smaller versions of the Daimler, complete with sleeve-valve engines. The cheaper V-twin Ten three-wheeler was introduced after World War I, though it was actually outlived by the

TOP
1910 BSA 18/23-hp single laudaulette.

ABOVE
1914 13.9-hp BSA.

Daimler-derived car, which was built through to 1926. But the V-twin returned in 1929 and gained a fourth wheel three years later. In the following year a conventional four-cylinder engine was fitted, marking a departure from the motorcycle connection.

LEFT
1938 front-wheel-drive BSA Scout.

FAR LEFT
1924 BSA 'Ten'.

BELOW LEFT
BSA TW32-6.

BELOW
1937 BSA Scout series 4 de-luxe.

Production ceased for a year from 1934, but the car re-emerged as the front-wheel-drive Scout in 1935. There was also a neat Sports Coupé offered. These disappeared for good in 1940, when the company devoted itself to war work, notably with the Daimler armoured car and the armoured BSA Scout. The latter was very different to its peacetime namesake, powered by a 152.6-cu in (2.5-litre) Daimler engine and capable of 55mph (88.5km/h) in reverse! When peace returned in 1945, BSA decided to concentrate on motorcycles and never made another car.

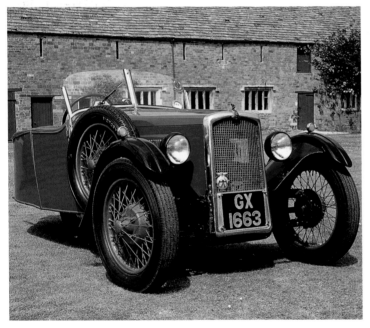

BUGATTI (Germany/France 1909-1956)
Bugatti remains one of the most evocative names in motoring. These lightweight, nimble cars made Ettore Bugatti the Colin Chapman of his day. Like Chapman, Bugatti was a gifted engineer, and had built a four-cylinder car by the time he was 20. Although born in Milan, Bugatti worked as a designer for several companies in Europe, including Benz, which was perhaps why he began making cars in France, rather than at home in Italy. While at Benz, Bugatti had built a small 73.72-cu in (1.208-litre) four-cylinder car with shaft drive. This formed the basis of the first Bugatti-badged cars, which he began to build in Molsheim, then part of Germany, in 1910. At first, Bugatti specialized in small cars, with the first 80.98-cu in (1.327-litre) machines followed by an 52.18-cu in (855-cc) model that Peugeot built as the Bébé (baby).

Meanwhile, the first Bugattis were winning races: Ernst Friederich won his class in the 1911 French Grand Prix. A bigger 305.1-cu in (5-litre) car followed in 1913, with the novel feature of three valves per cylinder (two inlet, one exhaust), and this led to the three-valve Type 30 and Type 37. During World War I Bugatti's factory turned over to war work for Germany, while the man himself worked in Paris!

Car production restarted soon after the war, in what was now eastern France, with the 16-valve Brescia, so named after it had won the Grand Prix de Voiturettes at Brescia, northern Italy. This was a great success, and Bugatti followed it with the 122-cu in (2-litre) straight-eight Type 30, which later developed into the famous Type 35. A departure came in 1926 with the monstrous Royale. With its 915.4-cu in (15-litre) engine and claimed 300bhp (223.7kW), this limousine was hardly the car to sell as the Depression loomed, and

indeed only three actually found buyers. To survive the Depression, Bugatti diversified, designing high-speed rail cars, aircraft and boats, while his son Jean looked after car production at Molsheim. Jean oversaw the last production Bugatti, the twin overhead-camshaft straight-eight Type 57. Nearly 700 of these were built between 1934 and '39, though Jean was sadly killed test driving a racing car near Molsheim in that final year.

During World War II, Bugatti Sr. moved to Bordeaux and continued to work on car projects with his younger son,

Roland. Together they produced the 91.54-cu in (1.5-litre) Type 73, though only a few had been made before Bugatti died in August 1947. Back at Molsheim, an updated Type 57 did go back into production in 1951, but only around 20 were built. A supercharged Type 101C was produced the following year, but this came to nothing, and other attempts to revive the marque failed. The Molsheim factory was bought by Hispano-Suiza in 1963, then the French aero engine company SNECMA. Much later, in 1987, a consortium of

TOP LEFT
A 1927 Bugatti 2.3-litre Type 43.

ABOVE LEFT
Kellner-bodied Type 41 Royale.

TOP
A British-owned 1925 Brescia model.

CENTRE
Type 35B, a very successful racer.

ABOVE
1925 1.5-litre Type 37.

European businesses bought the rights to the Bugatti name, later announcing it intended to build an all-new Bugatti.

For a short time, it did so. Bugatti Automobili S.p.A. was set up in Modena in 1987, and new owner Romano Artioli announced that the Bugatti for the 21st century would be a four-wheel-drive V12 supercar. When it was finally launched three years later, the EB110 GT did not disappoint the motoring press, and 98 cars were built in 1993. However, this was 30 per cent less than planned, and despite the appearance of the EB112 saloon at the Geneva Motor Show, it was clear that Bugatti was in trouble. Despite this, the company spent £30 million buying Lotus that same year. But in 1994 it drifted into bankruptcy and court hearings. Lotus was saved by the Malaysian company Proton, and the end seemed nigh for Bugatti.

This was not the end of the Bugatti story, however. In 2002 it was announced that another all-new Bugatti was on the

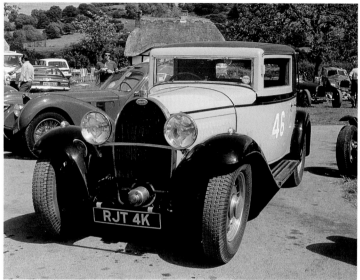

way, the Veynon 16.4. This promised to be a hyper sports car, with a reported 1,001hp (746.4kW) from the 16-cylinder engine. In August, it was claimed that the prototype had already run, and had turned in a 0-60mph (0-96.5km/h) time of less than three seconds. Production was promised for late 2003.

OPPOSITE
ABOVE: Bugatti Type 57 straight-eight supercharged.

BELOW LEFT: 1926 2.3-litre racer.

BELOW RIGHT: 1938 Bugatti 57SC 3.3-litre.

ABOVE
Bugatti 49.

LEFT
1938 Bugatti 400-bhp 59-50B.

RIGHT and BELOW RIGHT
The EB110S is the sports racing version of the EB110. It was stripped for lightness, and given an extra 40bhp and a fixed rear wing unlike the standard car, whose rear wing rose automatically at speed.

OPPOSITE
Bugatti boss, Romano Artioli's sense of tradition was tremendously strong and the standard EB100 was painted the unmistakable Bugatti blue. This was traditional but the construction was not. The EB100 used a carbonfibre monocoque designed by the French company, Aérospatiale.

BELOW
A classic Bugatti.

BUICK (U.S.A. 1903 to date)
Buick is one of the oldest names in the industry, celebrating its centenary in 2003. For all but five of those 100 years, Buick was part of the General Motors empire, and only enjoyed a single year of independence under its founder, David Dunbar Buick. William C. Durant bought the company in 1904, injected fresh capital, bought it a new factory and generally turned it around. The Model C, introduced the year after Durant's takeover, was such a success that by 1907 Buick was second only to Ford in the U.S. market.

From then on, Buick would always remain a top seller in its native land, though exports were small. The company was not afraid of introducing new features: Delco electric lighting and starting were made standard in 1914, the year a six-cylinder model, the B-55, was unveiled for the first time. In the U.S.A. this was a time when cars were getting bigger and more sophisticated by the year, and a straight-eight overhead-valve unit was introduced in 1931, available on all Buicks: the 1934 convertible, with 100bhp (74.6kW), was typical. In line with other General Motors divisions, the company followed this up with synchromesh gearboxes in 1932, with no-draught ventilation and a braced chassis the year after. In 1934 came independent front suspension and turret-top all-steel bodywork, with downdraught

ABOVE RIGHT
A 1937 Buick coupé.

RIGHT
A 1948 Buick sedan Roadmaster.

TOP LEFT
Founding member William Durant in 1906.

CENTRE LEFT
The first Flint Buick.

LEFT
1910 Buick Bug.

carburation and hydraulic brakes in 1936.
After World War II, the straight-eight Roadmasters and Centurys continued: the Century was for years the performance Buick, with the most powerful engine in a smaller bodyshell. But the days of straight-eights were numbered, and Buick's first V8 appeared in 1953, a 188-bhp (140.2-kW) overhead-valve unit that was fitted across

TOP
1980 Le Sabre sedan.

ABOVE
1980 turbocharged Regal Sport.

ABOVE LEFT
1990 Reatta convertible.

FAR LEFT TOP
1953 Buick Skylark.

FAR LEFT
1963 Buick Riviera.

the range from the following year. But sales slowed in the late 1950s, when Buicks lost some of their sparkle, and in the early 1960s the marque downsized its cars, again, following GM policy.

To suit the new smaller cars, there was an all-new aluminium V8 of 213.6 cu in (3.5 litres) that was later bought by Rover and used to good effect. But the big V8s survived in cars like the Riviera sports coupé of 1963, which offered 325bhp (242.3kW). Power and engine sizes continued to climb in the 1960s, but the mood (and legislation) changed in the 1970s, with a fresh wave of downsizing and catalytic converters fitted across the range. If one insisted, the big V8s were still available, but they were now sold alongside smaller V6s. From 1980 there was even a range of V8 diesels, with V6s from 1984. For the seriously economically-minded, Buick offered four-cylinder engines in its entry-level Skylark, which was really a rebadged Chevrolet in

RIGHT
1995 Century Special sedan.

CENTRE RIGHT
The 1998 Buick Park Avenue Ultra had a large amount of luxury features.

BELOW RIGHT
1998 Buick Le Sabre LTD.

BELOW
The stunning Riviera coupé was available with a supercharged V6 engine.

confirmation that the times had changed.

But sales fell through the 1980s, actually halving between 1984 and 1988 and not recovering until Buick began to creep back upmarket. It was, after all, one of GM's more prestigious brands, though the big V8s had gone for good. In the 1990s Buick instead concentrated on V6s of 189.2 to 231.9 cu in (3.1 to 3.8 litres), with supercharging giving up to 243bhp (181.2kW). The old names carried on:

Riviera, Regal and Le Sabre had all featured in Buick brochures before, underlining that the company was appealing to an essentially conservative audience. The Le Sabre, Buick's best-seller through much of the 1990s, was given only minor cosmetic changes, for Buick was never a company to spoil a winning formula. It was actually America's best-selling full-sized car for ten years running, and was still available in 2002. Meanwhile, the slightly cheaper Century was the entry-level Buick, while the Regal and Park Avenue covered the luxury end of the market. Buick had entered the 4x4 market as well, with the bulbous Rendezvous, and the bigger straight-six or V8-powered Rainier due to go on sale in 2004.

ABOVE
The Buick Rainier four-wheel-drive for 2004.

ABOVE LEFT
The 2002 Le Sabre model.

LEFT
The Buick Bengal roadster of 2002.

CADILLAC (U.S.A. 1902 to date)
For 95 years Cadillac has been General
Motors' top marque, the quintessential
American luxury car. Its development has
seesawed between periods of technical
innovation (it built the first mass-produced
V8) and times when style counted for more
than content. At other times, it was seen as
little more than a gilt-edged Oldsmobile,
and later faced the threat of technically
superior rivals from Japan and Europe. So
although Cadillac celebrated its centenary
in 2002, its path to success has not always
been smooth.

Cadillac's origins were in 1899 as the

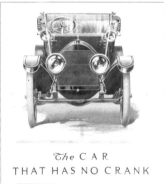

*The CAR
THAT HAS NO CRANK*

Detroit Automobile Company. This was
briefly known as the Henry Ford Company
in 1901 before being renamed Cadillac after
its original founder in 1902, the year it was
taken over by Henry Leland. Leland was
not a car maker, but already supplied
components, so he was familiar with the

industry. Early Cadillacs were very
different to their sybaritic descendants, for
they were modest single-cylinder runabouts
such as the 1902 Model A, which despite

LEFT
1909 model.

CENTRE LEFT
Advertising for a 1912 model.

FAR LEFT ABOVE
Model A.

FAR LEFT BELOW
1902 prototype.

BELOW
1912 model.

OPPOSITE
*ABOVE LEFT: 1918 Type 57 Victoria
coupé.*

BELOW LEFT
1930-31 V16 model.

its small engine was a full four-seater. But only three years later, Cadillac introduced its first four-cylinder engine, and in 1913 won the RAC Dewar Trophy for its pioneering use of electric lighting, starting and ignition. Another less obvious innovation was Leland's use of precision manufacturing, which allowed parts to be fitted to any car, and this was a vital stage in the transition from hand-built cars to mass-production.

In fact, Cadillac was doing so well that it was bought by William C. Durant in 1908 as the upmarket marque for his rapidly growing General Motors. As part of GM, Cadillac continued its innovations two years after those electric lights; its new Type 51 car was powered by the world's first viable production V8 engine, which was as powerful as a straight-six but more compact. Four-wheel brakes followed in

TOP
1927 La Salle convertible.

ABOVE
1949 model.

1923. Meanwhile, Durant gave Cadillac a sister marque, La Salle. The idea was to provide a slightly cheaper version to fill a niche between Buick and Cadillac. At first the La Salles were quite different from Cadillacs, with styling by Harley Earl, but later they became very similar and the

marque was dropped in 1940, the gap being filled by a new cheaper Cadillac, the Series 61.

Cadillac, for its part, seemed untroubled by the Depression, at least outwardly, though the reality was that sales of cheaper cars in the GM stable were keeping it afloat, and it is unlikely that Cadillac could have survived on its own. In any case, it forged on with a new 425-cu in (7-litre) V16 and 368-cu in (6-litre) V12 in 1930: the two engines shared many parts to

reduce costs, true products of General Motors. More modest Cadillacs retained the V8, and were now styled by Harley Earl, though the big multi-cylinder limousines, such as the Fleetwood, came with a wide choice of bodywork.

But sales continued to slide until a new raft of innovations arrived in the mid-1930s, courtesy of General Motors: all-steel turret-top bodies, hydraulic brakes and a new monobloc V8 with hydraulic valve-lifters. But really it was style that

ABOVE
1980 Elegant model.

ABOVE LEFT
1953 Eldorado.

LEFT
1959 Fleetwood Convertible.

FAR LEFT ABOVE
1951 advertisement.

FAR LEFT
President Eisenhower in an Eldorado.

OPPOSITE
ABOVE LEFT: 1976 Eldorado.

BELOW LEFT: 1983 Seville.

RIGHT: 1998 Touring coupé.

opposite direction, from the 1955 Eldorado to the 1959 Fleetwood Sixty Special. Of course, there were some useful technical advances as well: a new compact overhead-valve V8 in 1949 gave Cadillacs class-leading 100-mph (161-km/h) performance and was also successful in racing; there was standard automatic transmission from 1951; air suspension on the late-1950s Eldorado; and central locking and cruise control for 1960.

But within a few years the tailfins were gone, and early 1960s Cadillacs were noted for their toned-down, squared-off appearance, though the long, low, wide look continued, helped by a more compact V8 in 1963 and new perimeter chassis in 1965. There were gimmicks like automatic headlamps ('the Twilight Sentinel') and auto air conditioning, or the padded vinyl roof, a feature adopted right across the world in the years that followed. But from the late 1960s, real technical advances came back to the fore. The 1967 Eldorado had front-wheel-drive, a layout borrowed

from the Oldsmobile Tornado, and engineers began to spend more time on meeting new safety and emissions regulations.

Indeed, as the 1970s progressed, government regulation seemed to be the biggest influence on design. Thanks to restrictions on fuel consumption, cars had to get smaller, and by 1975 the Seville was a whole 2ft (0.6m) shorter than the De Ville, while even the big Eldorado had shrunk a little. The big V8s reduced in size too, and were joined by diesel variants in 1978 and a V6 in 1981. An example of lateral thinking was a V8 that could run on four, six or all eight cylinders, depending on the power required. There was a small, Euro-sized Cadillac as well, the 110-cu in (1.8-litre) four-cylinder Cimarron. In the climate of the times, this all made good sense. The trouble lay in the fact that the American buying public was still wedded to the idea of big, luxurious cars powered by large, thirsty V8 engines. Gasoline prices may have been rising in the U.S.A.,

underlined Cadillac's success for the next 20 years. The 1938 60 Special (once more designed by the Harley Earl studio) was followed by rear-wheel spats in 1941 and fastback styling in the following year. However, it was after World War II that Cadillac styling was at its most flamboyant, when the company became 'king of the

fins'. It started modestly enough, as two small kicked-up edges on the 1948 two-door Sedanet. The 'dream cars' that Cadillac unveiled at motor shows were only slightly more outlandish than the cars one could buy from a local dealer. But year on year, the cars became longer, lower and wider, and the tailfins sprouted in the

LEFT
The Cadillac De Ville D'Elegance featured more chrome than the standard car.

BELOW CENTRE
Cadillac De Ville Concours.

BELOW FAR LEFT
1997 Cadillac Catera.

BELOW CENTRE
1999 Cadillac Concours.

BELOW
1999 Eldorado.

but they were still among the cheapest in the Western world. And Cadillac, above all other American marques, was strongly associated with this type of traditional American car. It was recognized as quite conservative, but of high status: young professionals might go for an imported BMW or Mercedes, but the old money favoured 'Caddies', so the idea of an economy Cadillac just did not wash.

Nor did the Allanté convertible, an attempt by Cadillac to produce an Italianate convertible classed as a 'personal car' and powered by a 170-bhp (126.75-kW) V8. Aimed directly at the Mercedes SL, the Allanté was styled by renowned Italian design studio Pininfarina. In fact, to ensure some Euro-credibility, the Allanté's bodyshell was built by Pininfarina as well, then flown across the Atlantic for final assembly by Cadillac. It was a horrendously expensive way of building a car, and would surely have had William C. Durant turning in his grave.

Cadillac was now facing a new generation of imported luxury saloons, from Japan as well as Europe, all of which made traditional Cadillacs look sadly outdated. It was the early 1990s when the company finally began to respond, returning to its core business of luxury cars, and

introducing a whole raft of technically advanced new models. By the middle of the decade, the entire range had been renewed. Central to this was the Northstar engine, an all-alloy V8 with four valves per cylinder and up to 300bhp (223.68kW). It was designed to run 100,000 miles (160,930km) between services, which was astonishingly long even for a U.S. V8, and in the event of a coolant leak, was able to carry on by cycling air through deactivated cylinders to

ABOVE LEFT
2001 Catera.

ABOVE
2003 De Ville DTS.

LEFT 2004 CTS M.

ABOVE LEFT
2004 SRX.

ABOVE
EXT.

LEFT
Cien Concept Car.

OPPOSITE
ABOVE LEFT: 2004 Nieman Marcus XLR.

ABOVE RIGHT: 2004 Escalade ESV
Platinum.

BELOW: LMP Northstar racing car.

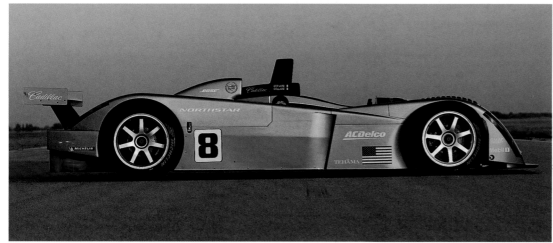

cool the engine. As well as the Northstar, there were other techno-goodies to compete with the Japanese: anti-lock braking, traction control and computer-controlled dampers, to name but three.

In 1996, Cadillac drew on General Motors' European expertise with the Catera, an Americanized version of the Opel Omega V6. The idea was to provide an entry-level Cadillac to compete with the BMW 3-series. Meanwhile, the big traditional Caddies carried on, now Northstar-powered: the Eldorado two-door, De Ville four-door and Seville. The last was new for 1998, and there were ambitious plans for exports, with a planned 20 per cent of production going abroad. In fact, Cadillac seemed determined to take on the Europeans at their own game; in 2002 the XLR coupé was being tested as a rival for the Mercedes SL, complete with large V12 engine.

CATERHAM (Great Britain 1973 to date)

Graham Nearn of Caterham Cars saved the Lotus Seven. In 1973, Colin Chapman was on the verge of dropping it, determined as he was to take Lotus upmarket from its spartan, kit-car origins. There was an outcry. The Seven had built up a tremendous following, not only in Britain but also all over the world, as a pure, teeth-rattling, almost vintage sports car driving experience. Nothing else at the time came even close.

Nearn bought all the spares, jigs and moulds from Lotus, and the renamed

Caterham Seven was back in business. There were a few minor changes here and there, such as the adoption of a stronger Ford RS2000 rear axle, but engine options remained Ford 1600GT or Lotus 98-cu in (1.6-litre) twin-cam in big-valve form. When supplies of the famous twin-cam dried up, tuned versions of the Ford overhead-valve engine were offered, then in the late 1980s a 165-bhp (123-kW) unit from the Vauxhall Astra GTE. This offered so much power in the lightweight Seven that every car came with a high-performance driving course: as well as reducing the likelihood of new owners

disappearing backward into hedges, it was a cunning piece of publicity. And if 165bhp was not enough, the 'Jonathan Palmer Evolution' of 1992 tuned the Vauxhall engine to 250bhp (186.5kW).

There were more changes as the years went by. Those with long legs had always felt cramped in the Seven, so the optional Long Cockpit version gave more room and an adjustable seat. And De Dion independent rear suspension replaced the old live axle. But outwardly, the Seven looked much the same as it always had. Under the bonnet, the 1990s saw the arrival of the 85.5-cu in (1.4-litre) Rover K-series

engine, first in 95-bhp (71-kW) form, later as a 97.5-cu in (1.6-litre) unit with far more power. By 2002, the ultimate Caterham Seven was the R300 Superlight. The name was inspired by its power/weight ratio of 300bhp/tonne (224kW/tonne). This is not the most powerful Seven ever, with 160bhp (119kW), but by shaving 143lb (65kg) off the weight to make it just 1,080 lb (490kg) seems like much, much more.

CENSUS (Great Britain 1998 to date)

Andrew Baker and Robin Hall set up FBS cars of Northamptonshire in 1998 to make their own composite-bodied design. Mounted on a steel monocoque shell, the body has a torsional stiffness of 17,000Nm per degree, claimed to be the stiffest in its class. A near-perfect 51/49 weight distribution is also claimed and an overall weight of just 2,138lb (970kg). So while the Census may not have Ferrari power, its 2.5-litre V6 is sufficiently powerful (170ps) to give a top speed of 140mph (225km/h), with acceleration to 100mph in a little over 15 seconds. If the standard Census seems too tame, 2003 saw the unveiling of the Census R, intended as a road-legal race or track day car, with Avon ACB soft compound tyres, wide wheels, lowered ride height, racing seat and harness and other options.

CHADWICK (U.S.A. 1904-1916)
Lee Sherman Chadwick was a perfectionist and great innovator. He was also very resourceful. Working as an engineer for a ball-bearing manufacturer, he built motor cars purely to demonstrate his employer's product. Then he went to work for the Searchmont Motor Co., where he designed a four-cylinder car. When the plans fell through, he simply rolled up his sleeves and built it himself during 1903.

This encouraged Chadwick to set up the Fairmont Engineering Works in the following year, with the express purpose of making Chadwick cars as well as repairing other makes. The business was a success, and over the next two years he produced 40 cars, including an 683.5-cu in (11.2-litre) giant. Another two years on and the company had become the Chadwick Engineering Works, expanded into a larger factory and employing 90 men.

Chadwick cars were not in the Model T class. They were luxurious high-performance machines, with hand-stitched leather seats and massive, powerful

OPPOSITE
FAR LEFT: Caterham Super Seven 1700-cc 135-bhp Ford Seven.

LEFT: 2002 Census.

RIGHT (top to bottom)
1914 Chevrolet Baby Grand.
1912 Chevrolet Classic Six.
1914 Chevrolet tourer.
1917 Chevrolet Type 490.

FAR RIGHT ABOVE
1922 Type 490 four-door sedan.

engines. One stripped-down model was timed at over 100mph (161km/h), and Chadwicks were successful in hill climbing and racing. This gave Chadwick a chance to experiment, and the cars he entered in the 1908 Vanderbilt Cup and Savannah Grand Prize were the first with supercharged petrol engines. But innovation costs, and by 1910 the company was in financial trouble. The last straw came when a major supplier pulled out. Chadwick himself left the industry, going to work for a stove manufacturer. The company he had founded lasted another four years before winding up in 1916.

CHEVROLET (U.S.A. 1911 to date)
Louis Chevrolet was Swiss and, like so many well known in U.S. commercial history as 'American', actually had foreign roots. Bill Harley of Harley-Davidson, for example, was the son of parents who had emigrated to the U.S.A. from England, and the Davidson brothers' parents came from Scotland. None of this, however, prevented Chevrolet from becoming one of the quintessential American marques. As General Motors' mass-market badge, it was the best-seller for decades, outselling Ford and becoming the biggest car manufacturer in the world in 1929.

Louis Chevrolet emigrated to the U.S.A. as a young man, along with brothers Arthur and Gaston. By then, he had already worked for Mors, and was soon busy in his new home, going on to work for several car manufacturers as well as becoming a well-known racing driver. Louis actually built his own racer, based on a Buick, which caught the attention of William Durant, founder (but no longer owner) of General Motors. Durant the entrepreneur and Chevrolet the car designer soon went into business together, launching the Classic Six in 1911

at Grand River Avenue, Detroit. Production was not considered on a Ford scale, but almost 3,000 Classic Sixes had been built by 1912, a respectable number for the time.

As Chevrolet the company expanded, so did its model range, with the Little Four (a 'Chevvy'-built version of Durant's own Little Runabout) and in 1913 the four-cylinder Baby Grand Tourer, the first car to carry the company's famous blue-and-white badge. Chevrolet also marketed a single-seat version known as the Royal Mail.

But in the same year, Louis Chevrolet decided to leave, and he and his brother Arthur were behind new companies such as the Chevrolet Aircraft Corporation. Apart from a brief spell in the 1930s, Louis had no more to do with the company that bore his name before his death in obscurity during 1941. Meanwhile, Chevrolet itself went from strength to strength. Expanding fast, it bought the Maxwell Motor Co. factory in New York during 1914 as a means of boosting production, and in the following year launched the Model 490. This four-door sedan came at the low price of $490, hence the name, and underlined Chevrolet's intention to out-Ford Henry Ford. By 1916 the company was well on the way to achieving this objective, producing over 70,000 cars in that year alone and further boosting production with new derivatives: closed sedans were offered from 1917, and the Ton Truck the year after. By 1919, the year Chevrolet was absorbed by General Motors, production reached almost 150,000.

91

LEFT (Top row)
LEFT: 1924 Superior Series F coach.

RIGHT: 1925 Superior Series K coach.

LEFT (second row)
LEFT: 1926 Superior Series V Landau sedan.

RIGHT: 1928 National Series AB cabriolet.

LEFT (third row)
1931 Independence coupé.

LEFT (fourth row)
LEFT:
1934 Master two-door Town sedan.

RIGHT: 1935 Master De-Luxe coach.

ABOVE RIGHT
1928 coupé.

RIGHT
1930 Universal sport roadster.

GM lost millions of dollars in the slump of the early 1920s, but company boss Pierre S. Dupont ignored a consultant's report advising him to close Chevrolet. Instead he introduced new models, and Chevrolet's low prices continued to attract customers, boosting production yet again: over 240,000 'Chevvies' rolled off the line in 1922, and over a million in 1927. Not all the new cars were a success (the air-cooled Superior had to be recalled), but a new six-cylinder engine kept the momentum going. Continuing to offer good-value motoring, Chevrolet sold its way through the

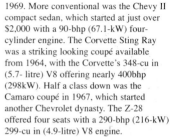

1969. More conventional was the Chevy II compact sedan, which started at just over $2,000 with a 90-bhp (67.1-kW) four-cylinder engine. The Corvette Sting Ray was a striking looking coupé available from 1964, with the Corvette's 348-cu in (5.7- litre) V8 offering nearly 400bhp (298kW). Half a class down was the Camaro coupé in 1967, which started another Chevrolet dynasty. The Z-28 offered four seats with a 290-bhp (216-kW) 299-cu in (4.9-litre) V8 engine.

Times were changing, though. The fuel crisis caused Chevrolet, along with every other car manufacturer, to think again about its product range. As a short cut to a more compact line-up, it bought shares in the Japanese Isuzu company, and began to rebadge Isuzus as sub-compact Chevrolets. The company was in a better position to do this than its GM partner Cadillac: in the U.S.A., Chevrolets had always been the mainstream, mass-produced option, so a small, cut-price Chevrolet made more sense to U.S. buyers than an economy Cadillac. However, the company did build its own sub-compact, the Vega, from 1971, followed by the Chevette five years later.

Depression of the early 1930s, and emerged in good financial shape. The company produced its ten-millionth car in 1935.

When production resumed after World War II, it was with pre-war cars, but 1949 saw an all-new look for the Styleline series and the Bel Air hardtop the following year. Bigger news was the Corvette sports car of 1954, a Ford Thunderbird rival that was the first of a long line of sporting Chevrolets. More avant-garde was the rear-engined Corvair of 1959, using a flat-six power unit. Famously damned by Ralph Nader as 'unsafe at any speed', the Corvair slumped in sales but remained in production until

ABOVE
1955 Bel Air.

RIGHT
1967 Camaro.

But Chevrolet had not abandoned the big cars, and the 1972 line-up included the Monte Carlo, Bel Air and luxury Caprice, as well as the Camaro coupé, Corvette sportster and Blazer four-wheel-drive.

There was a departure in 1980 with the compact front-wheel-drive Citation, and in common with other GM marques, Chevrolet offered a V8 diesel. In the mid-1980s the company's compact range was further boosted by the Cavalier, a great success, and more rebadged Isuzus and now Suzukis as well. The little four-wheel-drive Tracker, for example, was really a Suzuki Vitara, while the new Nova in 1984 was the result of a collaboration with Toyota.

Despite all this effort, Chevrolet was no longer the largest manufacturer in the world, having lost this accolade in 1980. Sales and market share were falling, reflecting the poor health of General Motors as a whole. In Chevrolet's case, it

LEFT
1954 Bel Air cabriolet.

BELOW LEFT
1956 Bel Air Nomad.

BELOW
1957 Bel Air convertible.

OPPOSITE
ABOVE LEFT
1957 convertible.

ABOVE RIGHT
Impala.

BELOW LEFT
1961 Corvette V8.

BELOW RIGHT
Malibu.

was not so much outdated cars (its Japanese-influenced compacts were far more competitive than the traditional Cadillacs, for example), but poor efficiency. Chevrolet took 30 per cent longer to build a car than Ford, Chrysler or AMC, let alone the Japanese. The range sprawled across 38 different car models and 80 trucks, and something had to be done.

Fortunately for Chevrolet, something was. The number of vehicle platforms was slashed from 21 to just seven, cutting costs by increasing the number of common components. The big rear-wheel-drive Caprice was dropped, and its production space given to pick-ups, which were enjoying a new popularity in the U.S.A. in the 1990s, for the simple reason that they were exempt from fuel economy regulations. At the same time, production methods were streamlined and management updated. Chevrolet continued to import

ABOVE LEFT
1963 Corvair.

ABOVE
1953 Corvette.

LEFT
1967 Camaro with 350-cu in V8.

RIGHT
Z28.

compacts to fill out its lower line (such as the Geo Metro) while carrying on such well-respected lines as the Corvette and four-wheel-drive Blazer. Out of all the GM's divisions, Chevrolet (still the biggest) looked to be entering the 21st century on a firm footing.

ABOVE
1969–70 Corvette.

ABOVE RIGHT
1998 Blazer four-door LT.

RIGHT
The 1997 Corvette coupé is shown with its ancestors, the previous four styles of Corvette sports car.

LEFT
2003 Cheyenne four-door pick-up truck.

CENTRE LEFT
S-series pick-up truck.

BELOW LEFT
Regular wheelbase Venture.

BELOW
Monte Carlo coupé.

LEFT
Camaro coupé.

BELOW LEFT
Corvette coupé.

BELOW
Corvette convertible.

OPPOSITE
*2003 SS concept car, a modern
interpretation of Chevrolet's sports car
heritage.*

CHRYSLER (U.S.A. 1923 to date)
Chrysler was a relative latecomer to the
line-up of North American car
manufacturers; Ford and Cadillac were
pioneers of the industry, Chevrolet was
formed in 1911, but the Chrysler
Corporation didn't come into being until
the mid-1920s.

The man who gave us the name was

Walter P. Chrysler, who bought his way into
the industry in November 1921, purchasing
the Maxwell Motor Corporation. In doing
so, he outbid Willys, White, William
Durant and Studebaker, so he was clearly
determined to get into the car-making
business. After a couple of years carrying
on the Maxwell name, Chrysler brought in
Owen Skelton, Fred Zeder and Carl Breer,
all three former Studebaker engineers, and
they designed the first car to bear
Chrysler's own name, the 70. There was
already a good dealer network in place to
sell the Maxwell, and Chrysler made use of
this to sell 30,000 70s in their first year of
production. That same year, the Chrysler
Corporation was formed, and the Maxwell
name was dropped: Chrysler had arrived.

It was a big company with big
resources, as it needed to be to compete

with the likes of Ford and Chevrolet. With
seven factories and capital of $400 million,
Chrysler was able to expand its model
range to four for 1926, including a new
Chrysler 60, and the Imperial. The latter
was a new marque, as Chrysler was to take
the GM route in maintaining several
marque names as well as its own, in an
attempt to reach the widest possible
audience. Another example was the De

Soto, intended to compete with mid-range
lines such as Pontiac, Oldsmobile and some
Nashes. As for Ford and Chevy, Chrysler
introduced Plymouth as its low-cost, good-
value name. Both Plymouth and De Soto

were launched in 1928. In the same year (it
must have been a busy one) Chrysler
bought Dodge for $175 million, which gave
a fourth marque, this one positioned just
above De Soto. More to the point, Dodge

LEFT
1930 Series 70 roadster.

BELOW LEFT
1957 Coronet police car.

BELOW
1957 Chrysler (U.K.) Hunter de-luxe.

OPPOSITE
TOP LEFT: 1926 Imperial E-80.

TOP RIGHT: 1934 Airflow.

CENTRE LEFT: 1927 Imperial Phaeton.

BELOW LEFT: 1928 72 cabriolet.

*BELOW RIGHT: 1930 Model 70
Sportsman's Coupé.*

the damage had already been done.

However, it would take more than this to upset the company which had successfully weathered the early 1930s Depression, making a profit in every year apart from 1932. It followed up the early 1930s innovations with independent front suspension in 1937 and a torque convertor and steering column gearchange in 1939. Walter Chrysler died in 1940, and his place as chief executive was taken by K.T. Keller, who had been in charge of manufacturing since 1927.

During the war years, Chrysler had been fully occupied building tanks and aircraft fuselages, among other things, but car production resumed in 1946. In the absence of genuine new models, 'Town & Country' wood trim was applied to existing cars. These 'woody' estates were popular for several years, and were a peculiarly Anglo-American preference that harked back to much earlier horse-drawn 'shooting brakes'.

Nineteen fifty-one saw more substantial change, with an all-new overhead-valve V8 replacing the old side-valve six, though that was still available on some Chryslers

was a going concern, and a large company which increased the group's factory space five-fold, and moved Chrysler up to third place in the U.S. sales charts.

To back up all this effort given to marketing and image, Chrysler had a strong streak of innovation. In 1932 alone, it introduced power brakes and an automatic clutch. The following year saw rubber mounting for engines, named 'Floating Power' in Chrysler's marketing-speak. This

was soon taken up by Citroën, a compliment indeed from that arch-innovator of European manufacturers. But these features seemed tame next to the 1934 Airflow, a striking, aerodynamic saloon with automatic overdrive. Unfortunately, it was a little too radical for the buying public (a decade or so later, and things could have been different), and the Airflow flopped. Chrysler responded rapidly with the less radical Airstream the following year, but

through to 1955. The new engine was a good one, partly designed by Owen Skelton (one of the original ex-Studebaker men taken on nearly 30 years earlier), which found favour with small manufacturers such as Allard and Jensen. To go with the V8, a new Power Flight automatic transmission followed in 1953. There was a

whole range of dream cars through the 1950s, and Chrysler also began to experiment with gas turbine engines, though these never reached production.

The De Soto name was dropped in 1960, but Plymouth was doing well, with the new compact Valiant range launched that same year. A few years later, it was further boosted by the V8 Barracuda fastback, based on the Valiant. This was a time when Chrysler was beginning to expand into Europe by acquisition. Simca of France was soon followed by the English Rootes Group (Rootes in particular faced a difficult 1970s), and Chrysler's European interests were sold off to Peugeot-Citroën in 1979. Behind the scenes, Chrysler had

TOP LEFT (clockwise)
1990 Eagle Talon sports coupé.
1990 New Yorker luxury sedan.
Le Baron Turbo GTC.

ABOVE
1990 Chrysler TC by Maserati.

BELOW
1990 Eagle Premier ES Limited.

been badly hit by the oil crisis. It often lost money in the 1970s, and at one point had a billion dollars' worth of debt. The company responded by rationalizing its overseas operations and dropping the Imperial line.

But a link with Mitsubishi was proving useful: Chrysler had taken a 15 per cent stake in the Japanese company in 1970 and Mitsubishi engines were increasingly being used in the smaller Chryslers; consequently the company was back in profit by 1982. A tie-up with Maserati in 1986 produced a Chrysler-engined (but Maserati-tuned) convertible. The marriage was not a happy one, and Chrysler severed the link when it bought Lamborghini late in the decade. A more successful project was the purchase of American Motors in 1987 – not for AMC itself, but for the highly successful and respected Jeep line-up it brought with it. Ever since, Jeeps have been part of Chrysler.

But like all the big U.S. manufacturers, Chrysler had to undergo some painful surgery in the late 1980s and early '90s, just to survive. The range was rationalized, and the company introduced its own compact, the modern 'L/H' line, with its forward-mounted cabins. This flew in the face of using imported compacts (which Chrysler itself had done with Mitsubishis), but it

TOP
1980 Cherokee Chief.

ABOVE
1989 Conquest TS1.

ABOVE RIGHT
The Jeep Cherokee was updated under the
skin in 1996 but was outwardly exactly the
same.

RIGHT
1997 Chrysler Neon.

worked. The L/H was such a success that Chrysler followed it with the compact Neon in 1997; using new production and design techniques meant that the entire Neon project cost $1.3 billion, something of a bargain for a brand new car. This all filtered through into impressive profit-per-car figures.

In 1998, Chrysler announced that it was to merge with Daimler-Benz to create a U.S.-German giant worth an alleged $24 billion. This looked promising, allowing the two companies to spread their costs, and giving Chrysler the chance to concentrate on pick-ups and 4x4s. This was reflected in the Voyager people-carrier and retro-styled PT Cruiser, which evoked a vaguely 1940s feel but was really only a modern family car in disguise. This was not enough to prevent Chrysler from losing a massive $1.3 billion in the first quarter of 2001.

RIGHT
2003 Sebring Xi coupé.

CENTRE RIGHT
Jeep Grand Cherokee Overland.

BELOW
2003 Jeep Wrangler X.

BELOW RIGHT
Voyager LX.

OPPOSITE
ABOVE LEFT: 2003 Crossfire.

ABOVE RIGHT: Chrysler PT.

BELOW LEFT Chrysler 300 M.

BELOW RIGHT: 2004 Stratus sedan.

LEFT
2003 Chrysler Sebring LXi coupé.

BELOW LEFT
2003 Town and Country.

BELOW
2003 Voyager LX.

RIGHT
2003 Chrysler Sebring convertible.

CISITALIA (Italy 1946-1965)

Cisitalia had a short but glamorous life as a maker of racing cars and svelte sports coupés. It was founded before World War II by Piero Dusio, a professional footballer who had retired through injury. He built up a business empire through which he was able to indulge his passion, running a racing team, Scuderia Torino.

After the war, Dusio was determined to have his own car built, and employed ex-Fiat man Dante Giacosa to design one. It was naturally based on Fiat components, a pure racer designed to be cheap to build. This, the D46, scored race wins almost immediately, and a second place in the 1947 Mille Miglia brought in a flood of orders that Cisitalia had trouble coping with. But Dusio's first love was racing, and he began a project to enter Grand Prix. It soon ran hopelessly over budget, and by 1949 Dusio himself was bankrupt.

He sold the remains of his empire and attempted to revive the Cisitalia name, but three attempts all ended in failure and the last Fiat-powered Cisitalia Coupé Tourism Special was built in 1965.

ABOVE
The bodywork on this 1947 Cisitalia 202 coupé was by Pininfarina. The engine was a 1090-cc Fiat four-cylinder, tuned to produce 60bhp. Few were made before financial troubles overtook the company.

CITROEN (France 1919 to date)

André-Gustave Citroën was the French Henry Ford. Not only did he become a national household name, but he possessed a genius for organizing mass-production. This was to be a factor as important in his success as it was in that of Ford. He also had a talent for publicity: in short, Citroën had all the right ingredients for a successful car tycoon. These natural talents were developed by study at the Ecole Polytechnique, France's top technical university, and a spell in the French army as an engineering officer. In 1908 Citroën became chief engineer at Mors, and was soon putting his production talents into practice. Five years later, Citroën was in business on his own, producing helix gear wheels, which explains the double-chevron badge that Citroëns wear to this day. Citroën's genius for streamlined production had not gone unnoticed, and during World War I the French government helped him to buy a large factory in Paris. In return, it got an efficient plant for mass-producing munitions, and at the end of the war Citroën was left with a modern factory full of American machine tools.

He lost no time launching his first car, and the Type A appeared in 1919, a mass-produced car that was cheap to buy and run. It was replaced two years later by the B2, similar but with a larger engine, and was joined in 1921 by the small 52.25-cu in (856-cc) type C. All were low-cost cars made in large numbers, and all established Citroën as a major French manufacturer. Citroën himself was an insatiable entrepreneur, expanding into buses and trucks (based on the B2), a taxi company, and nationwide bus and coach services: of course, all of these used Citroën vehicles. He also showed his flair for publicity, for example, by writing his name in lights on

TOP
1922 Citroën Type A 5CV two-seater.

ABOVE
1922 B2 'Caddy' roadster.

OPPOSITE
ABOVE LEFT: 1934 Ranelagh tourer.

ABOVE RIGHT: 1953 1991-cc Citroën Light 15.

BELOW LEFT: 1932 C6 coach.

BELOW RIGHT: 1948 375-cc 2CV.

the Eiffel Tower, and in the sky over Paris, using a smoke-trailing aircraft. The Citroën Kégresse half-tracks were proved by long endurance runs across inhospitable terrain.

But his cars at this time were relatively conventional, technically up-to-the-minute (with all-steel bodies from 1924 and the four-cylinder C4 and six-cylinder C6 later on), but not radical. This all changed in 1934, when the Citroën Rosalie was replaced by the stunning new Traction Avant. The name stemmed from the fact that it really was a front-wheel-drive car, decades before they became popular. With unitary monocoque construction, fully-independent suspension and overhead-valve engine, the Traction Avant was years ahead of the opposition. It was successful, too, though the sheer cost of getting it into production drove Citroën into bankruptcy, and thus into the welcoming arms of Michelin.

World War II intervened, and it was another 14 years before the next major new Citroën appeared. In its way, the 2CV was just as radical as the Traction Avant had been. Soft, long-travel suspension and a low-revving flat-twin engine made it comfortable rural transport. Like Germany's VW Beetle, Italy's Fiat 500 and Great Britain's Mini, it became a cult car of its time and beyond: production in Europe did not end until 1988. At the other end of the scale, the big DS broke new ground. For 1955, this big saloon was astonishingly advanced: a high-pressure hydraulic system powered the brakes, steering, and gear-change, as well as providing self-levelling suspension. It was the first production car with disc brakes as standard and had a unique inner steel 'skeleton' to which unstressed body panels were bolted. Again, it was long-lived, not replaced by the CX (still with hydraulic suspension) until 1974.

That in turn was dropped in favour of the 1989 XM, with styling by Bertone and 'hydractive' suspension which automatically adjusted the spring and damper settings to suit the road surface. Like the CX, it won the Car of the Year award.

In the mid-range, Citroën offered the GS from 1971, with hydraulic suspension (now almost a given on modern Citroëns) and a high-revving flat-four engine of just 61.9 cu in (1.015 litres). Its BX successor in 1983 had more conventional four-cylinder engines of 85.4 to 115.9 cu in (1.4 to 1.9 litres), but retained self-levelling hydropneumatic suspension. The power units came from Peugeot, which had bought Citroën eight years previously, but the distinctive styling by Bertone and the hydraulic suspension underlined the fact that this was no badge-engineered Peugeot.

Some Citroëns were more clearly Peugeot-influenced. The LN of the late 1970s was no more than a Peugeot powered by Citroën's flat-twin, while the Visa used a Peugeot floorpan and engine, though the flat-twin was still an option. The new AX of 1988 was a continuation of this process, offering only Peugeot engines. It was a true economy car, however, very light in weight and fuel-economical in its 85.4-cu in (1.4-litre) diesel form.

Peugeot and Citroën were becoming diesel market leaders in Europe at the time. The 1992 ZX was also more conventional than previous Citroëns, again owing much to Peugeot (it shared a floorpan with the 306) and with steel springs rather than hydropneumatics. For all that, it was very successful, both fast and economical in turbo-diesel form. Moreover, for Citroën traditionalists, the Xantia, which replaced the BX in 1992, offered hydraulic active suspension that was claimed to cancel out body roll during cornering. But the reality was that Citroëns were becoming ever closer to their Peugeot counterparts: the Synergie people-carrier was almost identical to the Peugeot 806, and the Saxo, which replaced the AX in 1995, to the 106. The same went for the van-derived Berlingo mini people-carrier and C8 full-sized people-carrier. The cars were perhaps no longer quirky, but at least Citroën had survived. There are signs of a change with the little C2, due late in 2003, still Peugeot-based but with more individual styling.

ABOVE
1954 big 1911-cc '15'.

LEFT
602-cc Mahari.

FAR LEFT
Citroën Maserati V6.

CENTRE
1973 Opéra Berline.

LEFT
DS21.

BELOW
DS19.

LEFT
Citroën Xsara world rally car.

BELOW LEFT
Berlingo Multispace.

BELOW
Citroën C3 1.4HDi 16V.

OPPOSITE
FAR LEFT: *The XM was a traditional Citroën with strange looks and even stranger mechanics: it wasn't a big seller.*

TOP RIGHT: *The ZX was the company's best-selling model.*

CENTRE RIGHT: *The innovative Xsara Picasso was launched in 2000.*

BELOW RIGHT *The Xsara coupé replaced the ZX and was a close relative of Peugeot's 306.*

CIZETA (Italy 1993-1995)

Every so often Italy announces another supercar to rival the products of Ferrari, Maserati and Lamborghini: many fall by the wayside, but the astonishing V16 Cizeta actually reached production, albeit briefly. It was the brainchild of ex-Lamborghini man Claudio Zampolli, who from 1985 began to plan a new V16 mid-engined sports car that would out-flank Ferrari in the wow-factor stakes. In the Modena region of Italy, building a brand new supercar is not as difficult as it might seem, since the area teems with skilled artisans, craftsmen and engineers, backed by generations of sports car production. Zampolli's dream was aided by financial backing from the composer Giorgio Moroder, a man with three Oscars under his belt for film scores, and who composed the music for both the Los Angeles and Seoul Olympics.

When it was unveiled in the early 1990s, the Cizeta amazed everyone. The only V16 available, its 366-cu in (6-litre) engine was said to have been developed from two Ferrari V8s spliced together: there were 64 valves, eight camshafts and two radiators. Accommodating so long an engine in the normal way would have given the Cizeta an unacceptably lengthy wheelbase, so it was mounted transversely, with the gearbox sticking out of the middle to form a truncated 'T' – hence the car's full name, V16T. This also made the Cizeta very wide, 3.15in (80mm) wider than a 512 Ferrari. But with its all-leather interior and exclusivity, the Cizeta was not intended as an ultimate driver's car to rival Ferrari, notwithstanding a power output of 520bhp (378kW) at 7,500rpm. Under the wedge-shaped body (designed by Marcello Gandini), the chassis was of tubular steel with aluminium and carbonfibre

reinforcement; suspension was by transverse links and there were Brembo ventilated disc brakes all round. The tyres were Pirelli or Michelin, with ultra-low profiles of 40 front and 35 rear. But the Cizeta lasted less than three years in production, with just 20 cars completed. Three of them were bought by the Sultan of Brunei.

CLYNO (Great Britain 1922-1929)

Clyno was a relatively small company, based in Wolverhampton in the English Midlands, that managed to sell cars for the same price as the giant Morris, but still only survived for seven years in the motor trade.

Led by Frank Smith, Clyno had started life as a manufacturer of motorcycles before turning to cars in 1922. The first 10.8-hp (8.05-kW) Clyno soon developed a reputation for reliability, with its sturdy 85.5-cu in (1.4-litre) Coventry Climax engine and three-speed gearbox. Despite the company's small size, it was able to sell the 10.8 for the same price as the rival Morris Cowley, but with four-wheel brakes where the Morris had only two. It was justifiably popular, and Clyno soon expanded to repeat the trick with a bigger 12/28 to rival the Morris Oxford. The cars were starting to look old-fashioned by the late 1920s, however, and Clyno simply did not have the resources to redesign them as selling at such low prices had meant small profits and little reinvestment. A straight-

eight 22-hp (16.4-kW) Clyno reached prototype form, but it was not to be, and Clyno closed in 1929.

CONTINENTAL (U.S.A. 1955-1960)

Continental was a short-lived attempt by Ford to create a superior marque to rival Cadillac. General Motors had Cadillac, Chrysler had De Soto and Dodge, while Ford set up Lincoln and Mercury as its own prestige badges. The original Lincoln Continental had been respected but never replaced since ceasing production in 1948.

Eight years later, a successor finally appeared after numerous outside consultants had put their designs forward. The chosen one came from Ford's own Special Products Division, designed by Harley F. Copp with a low chassis to allow a low roofline. Hand-built with a special Lincoln V8 and three-speed automatic transmission, the new Continental Mk II sold for a sky-high $10,000, reflecting the fact that Ford was after a flagship rather than volume sales. Unfortunately, sales were too slow even to guarantee exclusivity. Consequently, the Mark III of 1959 was much cheaper (though still not cheap, at $6,000) and was based on a standard Lincoln. Again, sales were poor, and in 1960 the Continental marque was reabsorbed by Lincoln.

CORD (U.S.A. 1929-1937)

Cars with the Cord badge were in production for a sum total of only five years, yet today they are one of the best-

ABOVE LEFT
The popular 1926 10.8-hp Clyno.

LEFT
1994 Cizeta V16.

BELOW
1930 Cord L-29 touring sedan.

BELOW CENTRE
1936 Cord 810.

BELOW RIGHT
1929 19.6-hp Crossley.

known examples of 1930s American motoring and, in some circles, are positively revered. Why did such a short-lived car make such a long-term impact? Erret Lobban Cord made his name as a salesman. As a teenager he traded Model T Fords around his native Los Angeles, later going on to sell Victory cars at a Moon

dealership in Chicago. And a salesman Cord might have remained, had he not been offered the chance to reorganize the moribund Auburn company, then in the hands of the receiver.

In less than a year, Cord had turned the company round. Five years on, and he had launched the Cord L-29 (still built by Auburn and sold through its dealers) as a big straight-eight, whose Lycoming engine produced 125bhp (93.2kW). Its unique feature was its front-wheel-drive, which caused great interest, though it was also a fatal flaw as it led to universal joint failure. Even so, over 4,400 were produced before production was halted by the Depression in 1932.

It was four years before Cord launched

another car. This was the legendary 810, still with front-wheel-drive but now with avant-garde styling complete with flip-up headlamps. It was actually cited as a work of art by the Museum of Modern Art. Alas, it was perhaps too radical for the buying public, despite the addition of a supercharged version of the Lycoming V8 offering 195hp (145.4kW). Only 2,320 had been sold by the time production was halted in 1937. But the U.S.A.'s fascination continued and even grew in later years, and several replicas were offered, the most interesting being Glenn Pray's car, built between 1964 and 1972, powered by a Chevrolet Corvair motor arranged for front-wheel-drive. As for Cord the man, he was reputed to have been made bankrupt, but he

somehow held on to the Lycoming engine factory he also owned. He went on to build aero engines during World War II.

CROSSLEY (Great Britain 1907-1937)
Crossley, based in Manchester, was part of Great Britain's embryonic motor industry, producing a chain-drive 22-hp (16.4-kW) four-cylinder car as early as 1904. The company and its engineers, J.S. Critchley and W.M. MacFarland, were evidently quite forward-looking, switching to shaft drive in 1906 and offering all-wheel braking as early as 1910: four-wheel brakes did not reach the mainstream for another ten years. Two new cars were introduced for 1910, the 12/14 and 244-cu in (4-litre) 20-hp (14.9-kW), and these were later developed

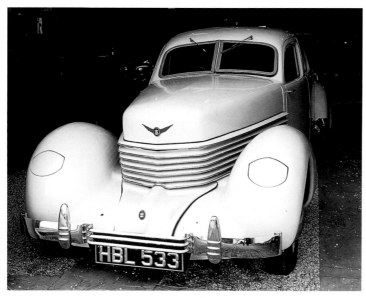

CUNNINGHAM (U.S.A. 1907-1937 and 1951-1955)

James Cunningham, Son & Co. of Rochester, New York was a carriage builder, and had been since 1842. It introduced an electric car in 1907, and soon followed that with four-cylinder petrol power, the engines made by Continental or produced by itself. By 1915 Cunningham was making its own V8, and its expensive cars were very well-regarded and highly prestigious. But even this small niche was squeezed during the Depression, and Cunningham ceased making cars in 1931, though it carried on producing bodies for other chassis until 1937.

Some 14 years later another Cunningham appeared, quite unrelated to the first. Briggs Swift Cunningham was a wealthy man who loved ocean sailing and motor racing, and was able to finance the production of several Cunningham sports cars, designed specifically for racing. The first C1 of 1951 was powered by a Cadillac V8, though the C-2R which followed, with both open and closed bodywork, used Chrysler's latest V8, tuned to produce 300bhp (224kW). Entered in the Le Mans that year, the three Cunninghams failed to finish, though in 1952 Briggs Cunningham himself drove a C-4R to fourth place in the classic French endurance race. The following year Cunninghams were placed third, seventh and tenth, but this was to be their best result at Le Mans. In 1955 Briggs Cunningham decided to cease production of his exclusive sports racers and concentrate on racing other people's cars. In a Chevrolet Corvette, he won the GT category of Le Mans in 1960.

LEFT
Ex-WWI 4.5-litre Crossley 25/30.

BELOW
1912 Model 'J' Cunningham limousine.

into 15-hp (11.2-kW) and 20/25-hp (14.9/18.6-kW) models. The bigger 20/25 was used as part of Britain's war effort in World War I and after the war became the larger 274.6-cu in (4.5-litre) 25/30. It was followed by the 19.6-hp (14.6-kW) in 1921, designed by T.D. Wishart, and the sports 20/70 version was guaranteed to top 75mph (120km/h).

In 1926 the company shifted from side-valve four-cylinder engines to overhead-valve sixes, of which the 158.7-cu in (2.6-litre) 18/50 was one. This was later uprated to 20.9hp (15.6kW) when the engine was enlarged to 195.3 cu in (3.2 litres). The smaller 15.7-hp (11.7-kW) was 122-cu in (2-litre)-powered, with a sports Shelsey (after the famous hill climb event) version available from 1929. The 15.7's six-cylinder engine was also used by Lagonda, as well as the more intriguing Crossley-Burney of 1934. This was a rear-engined car, looking a little like a monstrous VW Beetle from the rear. But it was not a success, and only two dozen were made. In any case, all Crossley car production; including that of the more conventional Regis, was discontinued in 1937.

DAEWOO (South Korea 1980 to date)
Few people had heard of Daewoo when it began to sell cars in Europe in the mid-1990s. But even then it was building more cars than the largest British company (it had started a decade-and-a-half earlier) and the parent company was the 33rd largest on the planet, which also made it bigger than Coca-Cola. Still, it was not a promising start in marketing terms, especially as few Westerners could work out how to pronounce the name. Not only that, but the Daewoo Nexia and Espero were based on the old-model Vauxhall Astra and Cavalier respectively. What really helped Daewoo establish itself were low prices, which came as an all-round package which covered all service consumables for three years. There was a generous three-year warranty and Daewoo cut out the middle man by selling cars direct to the public,

meaning that there were no dealers in the traditional sense.

A few years on, and this freshness of approach had somewhat pall. Daewoos still offered the same straightforward three-year deal, but in the meantime other manufacturers had cut their prices, extended their warranties, or both. Worse still for Daewoo, its own home-grown cars, which replaced the old Vauxhall-derived models, were looking sadly outdated, not long after they had been launched. Daewoo's car operation was eventually taken over by General Motors, which aimed to launch a new mid-sized car to rival the Ford Mondeo in early 2003.

ABOVE LEFT
Daewoo four-door Nubira CDX.

LEFT
2002 Daewoo Kalos.

FAR LEFT ABOVE
Daewoo 1.8 Espero CDi.

FAR LEFT BELOW
Four-door Nexia GLXi.

DAF (Netherlands 1958-1975)

For years, car transmissions had hardly changed. There were simple manual gearboxes and complex, inefficient automatics, the latter rarely available on anything but big luxury cars. So the Dutch Daf was unique in 1958 as a small economy car that used a fully automatic transmission. Instead of gears (whether automatic or manual), the Daf had two vee-belts running over two sets of expanding pulleys, which effectively changed size according to road conditions, the change being effected by a centrifugal clutch. This system gave an infinite variety of ratios within a fixed range, and was completely automatic; all the driver had to do was select forward or reverse.

In the Daf 33, announced in 1958, this was coupled with a little air-cooled flat-twin engine of 36 cu in (590cc), soon followed by a slightly larger 4.6-cu in (750-cc) unit which gave 30bhp (22.4kW) and a top speed of 65mph (105km/h). Then came

the bigger Michelotti-styled Daf 44 in which the flat-twin now pumped up to 51.5 cu in (844cc) and 40bhp (29.8kW) for a top speed of nearly 80mph (129km/h). The Daf 55 of 1968 moved up a class, using a four-cylinder Renault engine of 67.6 cu in (1108cc). That year, Dafs were entered in the London-Sydney Marathon rally, and finished. To celebrate, Daf launched the 55 Marathon, complete with sports stripes and the Renault engine uprated to 55bhp (41kW), allowing 80mph (129km/h) cruising speed.

The final update was the 66 in 1972, with a little more power, and a 79.3-cu in (1300-cc) option added in 1973. Daf stopped making cars in 1975, but was then taken over by Volvo, which completely restyled the 66 and launched it as the Volvo 343.

The Daf may have gone, but its transmission lives on. Its modern equivalent is the CVT (continuously variable transmission) used in some small cars and all two-wheel scooters.

DAIHATSU (Japan 1907 to date)

Based in Ikeda, Japan, the parent firm of Daihatsu was founded in 1907 to make internal combustion engines, with three-wheeled vans appearing in the 1930s. Its first passenger car wasn't launched until the early 1950s, though still owed much to those early vans, with its three-wheel layout and rear-mounted 540-cc air-cooled twin-cylinder engine. Four-wheelers followed in 1963, though these were still small cars, and the Campagno saloon, sports and station wagons all used 797-cc four-cylinder power units.

Three years later, the engine was up to 58.5 cu in (958cc) and this sophisticated little Daihatsu boasted such advanced features as front disc brakes and fuel

injection, producing 65bhp, an impressive output at the time. Daihatsu returned to the mini-car market with the 21.7-cu in (356-cc) two-stroke Fellow in 1967, which was built into the early 1970s. By this time, Daihatsu had been absorbed by Toyota, and subsequent models became increasingly based on Toyota equivalents – the Consorte, for example (which replaced the Compagno), was really a thinly disguised Toyota Corolla. The 1975 Charmant was also based on Toyota technology.

However, there were some independent Daihatsus, such as the four-wheel-drive Taft, a mini-Jeep powered by a 958-cc four-cylinder engine. This would lead to a long line of profitable Daihatsu 4x4s. By 1977 the Fellow had grown up with a 33.4-cu in (547-cc) four-stroke engine, with toothed-belt ohc drive. But the real pointer to the future was the front-wheel-drive Cuore announced a year later, with a transverse-mounted engine. This spawned the bigger Charade, again with front-wheel-drive, but with a unique 60.6-cu in (993-cc) three-cylinder engine and five-

speed gearbox. First in petrol, and later in ultra-economical turbo-diesel form, the Charade was for many years the only three-cylinder car available. Its engine was also used in the Italian-built Innocenti. By the early 1980s, the Daihatsu range covered Cuore, Charade, Charmant, Taft and the Delta, an eight-seater estate

ABOVE
2003 Daihatsu YRV.

LEFT ABOVE
1967 DAF 44 estate car.

BELOW LEFT
1974 DAF 55 Marathon coupé.

OPPOSITE
ABOVE LEFT: 1897 Daimler,

ABOVE RIGHT: 1909 four-cylinder tourer.

RIGHT: 1904 28-hp Landaulette.

with 1.8-litre four-cylinder engine.

One of Daihatsu's most successful models, the Land Rover-like Fourtrak, appeared soon afterwards. It was basic and rugged, unlike the new generation of luxury four-wheel-drives, and gained a good reputation as a working vehicle. Later Fourtraks, most of them powered by a 2.5-litre turbo-diesel, did acquire more creature comforts, especially with the Fourtrak Independent of the mid-1990s, with its independent suspension giving a more comfortable ride than the original bone-jarring 'cart' springs. Even in 2003 the faithful Fourtrak was still available, backed up by the smaller four-wheel-drive Terios, the latest version of the Cuore, tall YRV and Sirion supermini.

DAIMLER (Great Britain 1896 to date) Daimler of Great Britain was an entirely different company from the German pioneer. Although the British firm started as the Daimler Motor Syndicate in 1893, intended to build the German car under licence, the British soon began making their own twin-cylinder cars and then a whole range. Within five years, there was nothing to link the two Daimlers.

By the mid-1900s, the English arm was specializing in large four-cylinder cars, made fashionable when the then Prince of Wales (later Edward VII) acquired a Daimler in 1900. The company was taken over by BSA in 1910, and continued to specialize in big limousines, with upright, dignified lines and uncannily smooth and quiet sleeve-valve engines.

In 1927 Daimler announced its first V12, the 433.3-cu in (7.1-litre) Double Six, and it would make many more V12s up to 1938. The standard gearbox was not a conventional automatic, but a Wilson pre-selector with fluid flywheel, which remained the standard fitment until the 1950s. But Daimler was not just about stately limousines. There were mid-sized cars for the owner-driver, and an almost rakish two-door convertible, the 1931 Light straight-eight. Daimler also built buses (and

had done since 1908), while it marketed small cars under the BSA name. The smaller mid-range cars were badged Lanchesters, a company taken over by the parent firm in 1931.

After World War II, Daimler limousines continued with vehicles such as the straight-eight 335.6-cu in (5.5-litre) DE39 of 1949, but there were also the smaller Lanchester, the Conquest drophead coupé and Majestic, which came in 231.9-cu in (3.8-litre) Majestic Major form among others. But the real departure came in 1959 with the SP250 sports car. Powered by a free-revving 152.6-cu in (2.5-litre) V8, this came with brash, modern glassfibre bodywork, a world away from the royalty-favoured limousines. There was a 274.6-cu in (4.5-litre) version of the same engine, used by the more staid Daimlers.

But the SP250, or Dart, was the last 'independent' Daimler. The company was bought by Jaguar in 1960, and from then on Daimlers relied increasingly on Jaguar

ABOVE
1910 15-hp Daimler JD15.

ABOVE RIGHT
Daimler DB18 Hooper convertible.

RIGHT
1968 Daimler V8 250.

OPPOSITE
Daimler Corsica Jaguar concept car.

components. The Daimler V8 saloon used a Jaguar Mk II body shell, for example, and by the mid-1970s all Daimlers were no more than Jaguars with different badges and trim. The one exception was the Daimler DS420 limousine, Jaguar-engined,

and a favourite for weddings and funerals; many were converted into hearses. The last DS420 limousine was sold in 1988 (the year before Ford took over Jaguar/Daimler) and the last hearse in 1992, though a final batch of DS420s was built in 1996. Also

that year, to celebrate the British motor industry's centenary, Jaguar built a batch of 100 Daimler-badged saloons. Otherwise, the Daimler name had no part to play in Jaguar's future.

DARRACQ (France 1896-1920)

Alexandre Darracq did not like driving, yet loved cars and engineering of all sorts, and his name is prominent among the French pioneers of motoring. His first venture was to build bicycles with the Gladiator cycle company, later designing electric taxis, though the latter were not a success.

Then Darracq turned to the new petrol engine and sold tricycles inspired by the Léon Bollée. These did so well that he paid £10,000 for Bollée's new four-wheel design. Unfortunately, this was a flop. But the Darracq fortunes improved again in 1900 with his own little 6.5-hp (4.85-kW) voiturette, powered by a 47.9-cu in (785-cc) single-cylinder engine. Unusually, it was shaft-driven and within three years had been joined by two- and four-cylinder cars. There were racing successes too, with second, third and seventh places taken at the 1908 Isle of Man Tourist Trophy races.

But that was the high point. An ill-advised venture into steam buses brought only problems, and the company's factory in Milan was not a success. In 1912, when a new range of cars (many fitted with Henroid rotary-valve engines) also failed to turn the company round, Alexandre Darracq resigned. Darracq the company was saved by an Englishman, Owen Clegg, who introduced another new range based on his successful Rover Twelve design. For several years, the Suresnes factory enjoyed full production, and supplied big 4-litre cars to the French army.

After World War I an advanced new V8, with four-speed gearbox and four-wheel braking, was not a success, and the company was taken over by Sunbeam-Talbot in 1920. The name survived for another 20 years, with Talbots badged as Darracqs in France and Talbot-Darracqs in Great Britain.

RIGHT
1903 Darracq 20-hp racer.

BELOW
1906 10/12-hp.

BELOW RIGHT
1904 8-hp single-cylinder.

DE DIETRICH (France 1897-1934)

Many companies sprang up in France in the late 1890s to build cars, either of their own design or (more usually) one of the pioneer designs under licence. The De Dietrich company had a background in railway rolling stock, but in 1897 Adrien de Turckheim, son of one of the principle shareholders, acquired a licence to build Bollée cars, which he did in De Dietrich's factories at Luneville in France and Alsace (then part of Germany). Other licence-built cars followed, with designs from Léon Turcar and Simon Méry.

Turckheim left in 1904 to build Lorraine-Dietrichs, taking over Ariel of England and Isotta-Fraschini of Italy in 1907. Alas, his new company was shown to be losing money only two years later, and both of these had to be sold again. But a more modern range of cars, and an alarming 915.4-cu in (15-litre) Grand Prix

racer, enabled it to make a recovery.

After World War I, the 15CV Lorraine-Dietrich was a six-cylinder tourer capable of 60mph (97km/h), and enjoyed some success. There were some race wins, notably twice at Le Mans in the 1920s, but the company's focus was moving away from cars. It began to concentrate on aero engines in the 1930s, closing its car department in 1934.

BELOW
1907 24/30-hp Lorraine-Dietrich.

BELOW CENTRE
1894 De Dion Bouton petrol tricycle.

FAR RIGHT TOP
1899 De Dion single-cylinder model.

FAR RIGHT BELOW
1902 De Dion 402-cc model.

DE DION BOUTON (France 1883-1932)

Two well-known names from the pioneer days of motoring, Count Albert de Dion and engineer Georges Bouton, went into business together in 1883. Initially making steam tricycles, they soon began to experiment with petrol engines, and one of their prototypes set the fastest time in the Paris-Rouen Trials of 1894. The secret lay in Bouton's high-speed engines, which at 2,000rpm ran about twice as fast as their contemporaries, and the De Dion axle system (actually designed by Bouton's brother-in-law) which separated the load-bearing chassis and drive transmission. The company's first four-wheel voiturette appeared in 1899 (it had stuck with tricycles until then), with the first front-engined car four years later. There were also forays into electric cars, commercial vehicles and bicycles.

By 1910, after a couple of reorganizations, De Dion Bouton was producing a V8, and its simple single-cylinder engines were dropped a couple of years later, while commercial vehicles became more important than cars. The V8 was continued after World War I, alongside a four-cylinder engine, but the company really lacked the resources to enter large-scale production, and could not compete with the new giants of the industry. De Dion closed in 1927, though there was a short-lived revival, backed by the French government, which lasted until 1932.

DELAGE (France 1905-1954)

Delage made sporting tourers and racers throughout its heyday in the 1920s, but failed to survive the Depression as a true manufacturer. Demand for Louis Delage's early cars boomed as they won races, first with De Dion but later with Delage's own engines.

After making munitions during World War I, the company returned to its sports touring cars, such as the 1924 D1 Super Sports and the later D8 eight-cylinder. Bodies were often supplied by specialist coach builders, such as Albany and Kolsch. A super-sports version of the 244.1-cu in (4-litre) D8, available from 1932, was capable of 112mph (180km/h). But such magnificent machines could not survive the Depression. Belatedly, Delage rushed smaller-engined cars into production, which without sufficient testing proved more trouble than they were worth.

In 1935, Delage effectively ceased to exist as an independent car maker, when its Paris agent, Walter Watney, bought the whole outfit and promptly sold off most of its engineering capacity. Instead, he built Delahayes under licence but with Delage badges. This arrangement lasted until 1954, when the company merged with Hotchkiss.

RIGHT
1930 Delage D8, by Chapron.

OPPOSITE
ABOVE LEFT: 1913 Delage D1.

BELOW LEFT: 1927 Albany-bodied DM.

FAR RIGHT: 1929 Delage Tourer.

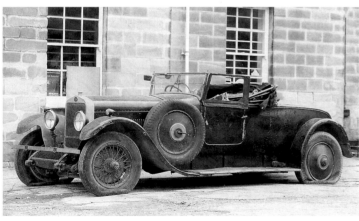

DELAHAYE (France 1894-1905)

Delahaye always bore the name of its founder, Emile, but he retired in 1901 and for the next half-century it was run by one man, Charles Weiffenback, who had joined the company in 1898. Under his leadership it suffered troughs of depression as well as enjoying the heights of success.

Delahaye's reputation was forged in racing and the long-distance public road events such as the Paris-Marseilles-Paris. Although Delahaye pulled out of this increasingly expensive sport, its experience showed in the advanced and sophisticated cars that it sold. The 10B of 1902, for example, had a steering wheel (not a tiller), three-speed gearbox and chain drive. Three years later, a 488.2-cu in (8-litre) Delahaye was chosen by King Alfonso of Spain, and by the outbreak of World War I the company had introduced such innovations as a V6 engine and pressure-lubricated suspension.

The years following World War I were less happy, with more conventional cars sold as Charles Weiffenbach attempted to build an automotive empire. By the early 1930s, sales had slumped, but the company staged a comeback by returning to its roots. Designer Jean François came up with a series of lightweight powerful cars. Once again, Delahayes were winning races, and the company went back to building sleek luxurious tourers.

Unlike some contemporaries, Delahaye recovered well after World War II and carried on building its prestigious cars; but this time the golden age was short-lived. French taxation laws made big engines very expensive, and despite a core business of building trucks, and an attempt to make a Jeep for the French army, Delahaye could not survive on its own and was taken over by Hotchkiss in 1954.

ABOVE
1936 3.5-litre Delahaye 135 with Carlton body.

LEFT
1952 Delahaye Figoni Type 235 coupé .

DELAUNAY-BELLEVILLE
(France 1904-1950)

Louis Delaunay joined the boiler maker Belleville of Paris in the 1860s, married the boss's daughter, changed his name to Delaunay-Belleville and went into the car business. His four- and six-cylinder machines were quiet and refined, attracting customers like Tsar Nicholas II of Russia. (After the Revolution, Trotsky and Lenin continued the tradition). In some ways, this was the French Rolls-Royce. The founder died in 1912, but was succeeded by his son, Robert, who continued to build cars with the characteristic rounded hood. However, the company was in a weaker position in the 1930s, forced to buy Continental engines from the U.S.A., while the 1936 R16 owed much to the contemporary Mercedes-Benz 230. Production resumed after World War II, but the company concentrated on a 27.46-cu in (450-cc) mini-car, the Rovin, and its cars and trucks were available up to 1950. The name survives as a maker of automotive radiators.

DELLOW
(Great Britain 1947-1959)

Dellows were trials cars, pure and simple, though they were also road-legal, and provided a simple, attractive open car for the impecunious. There were innumerable such 'specials', built in Great Britain after World War II, often based on Ford 10 components and intended for hill climbs as well as trials. Steep muddy lanes made up a typical trials section, so light weight, good ground clearance and decent traction were the priorities, rather than outright power.

Reflecting this, Dellows were powered by Ford's standard side-valve four-cylinder engine, in low-compression (6.16:1) or high-compression (7:1) versions giving 31 or 36bhp (23.1 or 26.8kW) respectively. Inevitably, there were variations over the years, and some Dellows were fitted with superchargers. They were one of the most successful of the Ford-based specials, and one car in particular won more than 400 awards.

ABOVE LEFT
A 15-hp Delaunay-Belleville for the British market.

LEFT
Delaunay-Belleville six-cylinder 26-hp model.

BELOW LEFT
Delaunay-Belleville 1906/07 four-cylinder 20-hp model.

BELOW
1910 Delaunay-Belleville 15-hp coach-built special.

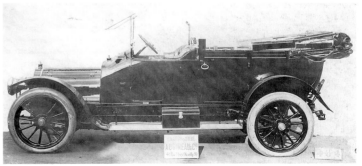

DE LOREAN

(Great Britain/U.S.A. 1981-1982)

It was like something out of a novel. John Zachary De Lorean worked his way up to the top ranks of General Motors. He left in 1973, and as the oil crisis bit and General Motors was left thousands of thirsty, unsaleable V8s, De Lorean was cast in the role of the thinking motor executive, the one who had warned his employers about consorting with dinosaurs. And now De Lorean had a dream. He would go it alone, produce an all-new lightweight and efficient sports car that would show the big boys how to do it. It seemed almost too good to be true, and it was.

De Lorean certainly stood out. He was tall and handsome, with a West Coast tan, though it was said that his famous jutting chin was really the result of cosmetic surgery. He was also a born salesman and managed to persuade the British government to help fund his project with a brand-new factory in Northern Ireland. The Irish government, as it happened, turned him down, but the British were desperate to provide jobs in the north, where Belfast was an unemployment black spot riven by political and religious strife.

It all looked very promising. The De Lorean car was a mid-engined machine, distinctive with its gull-wing doors and

ABOVE RIGHT and RIGHT
The De Lorean DMC-12 coupé of 1981.

stainless-steel finish. Power came from a proven 164.8-cu in (2.7-litre) V6 already in use by Peugeot, Renault and Volvo. De Lorean the man promised he could sell 20,000 of these cars in the U.S. alone, where buyers would welcome an economical, distinctive machine. Better still, 2,500 jobs would be created in Belfast, where some people of working age had never had a full-time job.

Lotus was brought in to help make the

car production-ready, and that is when the warning signs began to appear. The car was proving too heavy as it neared production, and had great trouble meeting the EPA emissions and fuel consumption regulations. Without those certificates, it could not be sold in the U.S.A., and without American buyers, the car was not worth building. There were also disturbing signs that De Lorean was treating government money as his own: he rented an expensive suite of offices in New York, and always crossed the Atlantic on Concorde. There were endless delays, and meanwhile the bills mounted. Even before the car was ready, De Lorean was forced to go cap-in-hand to the British government for more money. He also owed $20 million to the Bank of America.

Eventually, the De Lorean car staggered into production, but the talk of 20,000 sales a year proved groundless: it was just too expensive to sell in these numbers, and when in 1982 the company went into receivership, only 6,500 had been shipped to America, and a mere 1,655 had actually reached De Lorean dealers. After eight months of receivership, the De Lorean Motor Company was finally wound up. John De Lorean himself was arrested and jailed on drug trafficking charges. It turned out that over $17 million had been siphoned out of the company. As for the car, it became something of a collector's item.

DE SOTO (U.S.A. 1928-1960)

The 'Big Three' American car manufacturers, General Motors, Ford and Chrysler, may not have had the snob appeal of long-established European names, but they understood the value of marketing. Times had changed since Henry Ford was able to sell thousands of identical black Model Ts simply because they were cheap. As the market expanded, customers wanted something special, something different, maybe something even better than their neighbour's car.

So each one of the Big Three bought up or invented upmarket names for their cars. Ford had Mercury, General Motors

had a whole line-up of divisions from Chevrolet to Cadillac, and for Chrysler, Plymouth was its entry-level marque and Dodge the mid-range, while De Soto filled the gap in between. All of these were treated as different makes, but under the skin shared most of their components, reducing costs and cutting overheads. The differences ranged from simple badge and trim jobs, to completely different cars that might just share running gear.

So the first 1928 De Sotos were very similar to contemporary Chryslers, though later cars were models in their own right. The De Soto Airflow, though, was a straight rebadge of the Chrysler Airflow, and like the original its advanced streamlined styling frightened the customers away. Early De Sotos used straight-eights, though straight-sixes soon followed, and V8s were only available after 1955, notably the oversquare overhead-valve V8 which had been introduced three years earlier. The V8s came in Firedome or more powerful Fireflite forms, the latter powering the Adventurer hardtop of 1956. Styling advances echoed those of other Chryslers, such as Virgil Exner's 'Forward Look' of 1957. But De Soto sales were slumping in the late 1950s, squeezed by a general fall in mid-range demand. Chrysler merged it with Plymouth in 1958 and the final De Soto-badged car was produced in late 1960.

TOP
1961 De Soto Styline hardtop coupé.

ABOVE
1934 De Soto Airflow saloon.

LEFT
1928 De Soto Series K model.

DE TOMASO (Italy 1956 to date)

Alejandro de Tomaso was an Argentinian, the son of a former prime minister. Expected to take over the family estate, he fled the country in 1955 after political pressure. He went to Italy, the perfect place for a young man of his type who loved racing cars. After meeting the Maserati brothers, he raced their OSCA cars and founded his own company in 1959 to build racing cars using OSCA engines.

De Tomaso's long association with Ford began in 1963, when he launched his first road car, the Vallunga. Only 50 were made over the next two years, but the Vallunga established the concept of an exotic Italian sports car powered by a simple, reliable American V8. This same concept was to stay with De Tomaso for the next 30 years: it had particular attractions for exports to North America, where there was a big market for high-performance sports cars; but the complexity and expense of Ferrari or Lamborghini engines may well have deterred many buyers.

De Tomaso tried again with the mid-engined Mangusta in 1966; he already had an opening into the U.S. market as his well-connected American wife, Elizabeth, was related to the chairman of Rowan Industries of New Jersey. Rowan invested in De Tomaso's business, allowing him to take over the Ghia coach builder in 1967 and to export Mangustas to the U.S.A. Ghia had already styled a car for De Tomaso, the open-top Pampero of 1966. The Mangusta was a success, earning £1 million of sales in 1968 alone, though it had cost the company a great deal of money to launch.

In 1970 it was replaced by the Pantera, another mid-engined Ford V8-powered sports car, now with a 348-cu in (5.7-litre) engine capable of propelling it to 162mph (260km/h). Unusually for a sports car of the time, the Pantera was equipped like a luxury saloon, with air conditioning and leather seats, and there was an even more luxurious version, the Pantera L. But it was also a serious sports car; the GT4, for example, used a tuned version of the Ford engine to produce 500bhp (373kW). Other cars followed, as De Tomaso attempted to diversify away from mid-engined sports cars. The Deauville was a four-door luxury saloon and the Longchamps a Mercedes SL-like coupé.

All this time, De Tomaso was busy with other interests. He took control of the Moto Guzzi and Benelli motorcycle makers in the 1970s, as well as the British Leyland Innocenti, a three-door hatchback based on Mini running gear. An agreement was later reached with Daihatsu to supply modern three-cylinder engines for the car. And as if that were not enough, De Tomaso bought Maserati in 1975.

The last Pantera was delivered in 1992, and in the following year De Tomaso unveiled the Guara. Like its predecessors, this was mid-engined, but broke with tradition by using a BMW 244-cu in (4-litre) V8 instead of a Ford engine. Production began, though in order to finance it Alejandro de Tomaso was forced to sell his long-standing interests in Moto Guzzi and Maserati.

ABOVE
De Tomaso Pantera.

ABOVE LEFT
De Tomaso Mangusta.

LEFT
The Guara coupé, first shown in 1993, uses
a mid-mounted BMW 4.0-litre V8 engine
with six-speed gearbox.

OPPOSITE
The De Tomaso Deauville, with 5.7-litre V8
and 300 bhp.

133

DETROIT ELECTRIC (U.S.A. 1907-1938)

Electric cars are often envisaged as the vehicles of the future, but in fact they were being made, sold and used over 100 years ago. Moreover, it was said that, at that time, Detroit Electric was the largest producer of electric cars in the world.

The Anderson Carriage Co. was a well-established maker of horse-drawn carriages of all kinds, but sensibly began to look for an alternative as mechanical horsepower took over. In 1907 it began building an electric car designed for town transport: electric vehicles enjoyed a brief boom at this time, being quieter and far easier to operate than the comparatively dirty, noisy and temperamental petrol-engined devices.

Riding the back of this boom, Anderson did well, changing its name to the Anderson Electric Car Co. in 1911 and building up to 1,000 vehicles a year. It also introduced a range of electric commercial vehicles.

But after World War I the electric boom ended and sales began to drop off. It was a sign of the times that Detroit Electric (a name it assumed in 1919) had to restyle its cars with fake hoods and radiator grilles to make them acceptable to the public. The commercial vehicles were dropped in 1927, and the cars were now made to order, often with contemporary bodywork from Willys-Overland. Finally, in 1938, Detroit Electric closed its doors.

DKW (Germany 1928-1966)

DKW, as every motorcyclist knows, stands for *Das Kleine Wunder* (The Little Wonder), a name given to DKW motorcycles and reflecting the fact that up to 40,000 a year were built, making DKW the largest motorcycle manufacturer in the world. But the famous initials originally stood for something very different – *Dampf-Kraft Wagen*.

This was a steam car, built by two Danish engineers in Zschopau, Germany. The partners went on to make their first petrol-engined car in 1928, using a two-stroke twin-cylinder engine and wooden chassis-less construction. This was soon followed by the front-wheel-drive F1 in 1931, actually based on an Audi design, as was the F2 that came later. The link with Audi was a close one, as the two companies shared a factory at Zwickau, and Audi was later to use front-wheel-drive transmissions produced by DKW.

There were bigger cars, too, such as the rear-drive F8 and the V4 4-8, built in Berlin, plus commercial vehicles. By 1934 DKW was the second best-selling manufacturer in Germany. The cars were also made under

licence in Switzerland and Sweden. Between 1948 and 1956 DKWs were made in what was then East Germany, and badged as IFAs. All of these were two-strokes and were built up to 1966, after which time the company concentrated on motorcycles.

LEFT
A 1953 two-stroke Auto-Union DKW.

ABOVE
A 1937 DKW model proves its strength.

BELOW
The very American DKW 1000 of 1959.

THE ENCYCLOPEDIA OF CARS

DOBLE (U.S.A. 1914-1931)

In America the development of steam cars continued long after the type had faded away in Europe. Quieter and easier to drive than petrol-driven cars, they took longer to start from cold and needed a pressurized boiler. Doble cars were thought to be the finest steamers of their time, and indeed Abner Doble never made anything else, building his first in 1911 at the age of 16.

With financial backing from his parents, he went into production in 1914, selling four steam-powered Model As, and building a fifth to develop into the Models B and C. His success attracted more cash from C.L. Lewis, resulting in the unveiling of the GEC Doble (or Doble-Detroit) in 1916. It was an exciting time, with a reputed 11,000 orders waiting in the pipeline; but wartime restrictions meant that Doble could not get the steel he needed to build cars, and the project faded away.

Seven years later, Doble resurfaced in California, announced the new Model E and planned to restart production the following year. Available as a four-door Phaeton or two-door De Luxe Runabout, the Model E was styled to look like a conventional car, despite being steam-powered, and development had overcome the traditional steam drawbacks. Again it looked as if Doble's dream was about to come true, with plans for up to 1,000 cars a year from his new factory in Emeryville. But again, fortune was not on his side. Abner Doble was cheated out of a large sum of money on the stock market, and had to sell the factory and land just to pay off his debts. Only a few Model Es and the succeeding F were made, and in 1931 the company collapsed. Undaunted, Abner went on to work on steam commercials in Germany, and on the post-war Paxton Phoenix and Keen cars, though none of these was successful.

TOP
The luxurious Doble Phaeton of 1923.

ABOVE
The De Luxe Runabout version.

DODGE (U.S.A. 1914 to date)

Dodge, so familiar a name to American drivers today, was at one time the second largest manufacturer in the U.S.A. after Ford. It had enjoyed a rapid rise to near the top, only to collapse equally rapidly: within a few years of that high point, it had been taken over by Chrysler. But under Chrysler, the name has survived, with the Viper V10 sports car bringing it to international attention in the 1990s.

John and Horace Dodge made bicycles before branching out into engine manufacture. They supplied engines to Ford, so successfully that they became

shareholders in Henry Ford's growing business. But the Dodge brothers were not content just to be industry suppliers, and began to develop their own car in 1911. When it finally went into production three years later, the Dodge 4 proved to be a tough and reliable machine, enough to make Dodge the third largest U.S. manufacturer in only the second year of production. By 1920, it was second only to Ford himself. But John and Horace died in that same year, and Fred J. Haynes took over as president. The Dodge range was still tough, but ageing, and sales began to slip away. In 1925 the company was sold to a firm of bankers, and three years later to Chrysler. As a division of Chrysler, Dodge benefited from cheaper components and rapid technological progress, and sales began to recover, though Dodges were now little different from the equivalent De Sotos and Plymouths.

Through the 1950s and 1960s Dodge offered typical V8 American sedans, such as the Polara Lancer of 1960, heavily tail-finned, dripping with chrome, and powered by a 360-cu in (5.9-litre) V8 engine. Dodge had long built commercial vehicles as well, and these continued alongside. Sports saloons have been part of the Dodge line-up since the Red Ram V8 of 1953 (Dodge had taken on the famous Ram mascot back in 1931), through to the Charger coupé of 1966 and the classic Daytona Charger. As well as offering large cars, Dodge dealers have also sold imported compacts: the Colt GT was a Mitsubishi, and the Omni of the 1970s was the Chrysler Horizon, supplied by the company's French arm.

Dodge could not escape Chrysler's hard times of the 1980s, however. Renault took over the European commercial vehicle business, and in line with the demands of the market many Dodges were downsized. Not that this was a one-way street: for the

remarkable Viper sports car, which finally reached production in 1992, it was an abrupt change of direction. With its 400-bhp (298-kW) 488-cu in (8-litre) V10 engine, this was a virtual racer for the road, a statement that Dodge was back in the performance business. So successful was the Viper in revitalizing the Dodge image that its V10 power unit was also used in a huge pick-up, the Ram. Ten years later, both were still listed as new models, the Viper SRT-10, now with 500bhp (373kW), alongside the smaller

Dakota pick-up and Caravan people-carrier. But along with these American-sized automobiles there were the more modest Neon and Stratus saloons.

LEFT TOP
1914, the first Dodge automobile.

LEFT ABOVE
The Victory 6, with hydraulic brakes.

TOP
1957 Dodge Royal.

ABOVE
1965 Dodge Charger.

RIGHT
2003 Dodge Caravan.

ABOVE
2003 Viper SRT.

ABOVE LEFT
2003 Dodge Ram.

LEFT ABOVE
1999 Dodge Avenger.

LEFT BELOW
1998 Dodge Intrepid ESX.

FAR LEFT
Dodge Prowler.

DONKERVOORT (Netherlands)

Several sports cars have been inspired by the original Lotus Seven, and the Dutch Donkervoort is one of the better examples. Starting in the mid-1980s, Joop Donkervoort began building Seven replicas in a small factory behind his house near Utrecht. But 'replica' does not really do justice to the car, which was far more plush than the original and, it is claimed, could cruise the autobahn at 100mph (160km/h) without letting in the rain!

In fact, only the shape was the same as the original, hiding Donkervoort's own spaceframe chassis and independent rear suspension. The front suspension was a set-up similar to that of Caterham's but with Donkervoort titanium and aluminium-alloy uprights. The S8AT model was powered by a Ford 122-cu in (2-litre) four-cylinder engine with fuel injection and a turbo to produce 170bhp (126.8kW) and driving through a five-speed Ford gearbox. Despite the extra equipment, the Donkervoort was still a featherweight car, and the turbo engine gave a 0-60mph (0-97km/h) time of 4.8 seconds. The top speed was 130mph (210km/h), hampered by the Seven's poor aerodynamics.

Attention to detail was evident in the twin aluminium fuel tanks, a brake balancer control to allow a choice between rear or front bias, and a rear-mounted battery to keep all weight as low as possible. The Donkervoort may not have been as spartan as the original Seven, but it was faithful to its driving experience.

S8AT Donkervoort.

DUESENBERG (U.S.A. 1920-1937)

Rarely have so many companies been associated with one name. Fred and August Duesenberg set up to build marine and racing engines: Fred had already designed a horizontal overhead-valve engine, after starting out building bicycles. In 1916, the two brothers joined J.R. Harbeck to form the Duesenberg Motors Corporation, which built Bugatti aero engines during World War I.

They left after the war to build their first car in 1920 under the aegis of the Duesenberg Automobile & Motors Co. But poor management and production problems prevented the eight-cylinder Model A from making much of an impression, and the receivers were called in during 1924. The following year, Fred and August popped up again, with the new Duesenberg Motor Co. They carried on with the Model A (now Model X) but it was ageing by this time, and the new company looked as if it would suffer the same fate as the old one. The company was saved by Erret Lobban Cord, who owned Auburn and had sufficient capital to invest. He told the Duesenberg brothers to go away and design a new car. The result was the eight-cylinder 421-cu in (6.9-litre) Model J of 1928, which was powerful and advanced, with twice the power of any American rival. Four years later, a supercharged SJ version appeared, though only 36 of these were made. Sadly, Cord now had financial problems of his own, and when the Cord Corporation collapsed, Duesenberg went with it.

Yet this was by no means the end of the Duesenberg story: Fred died in a car crash in 1932, but August tried to resurrect the marque in 1947, whicht came to nothing; but 20 years later his son Fritz unveiled the prototype for a new Chrysler-powered Duesenberg, styled by Virgil Exner. In 1979, it was the turn of Fred's sons, Harlan and Kenneth, plus August's brother Wesley, with a Cadillac-based limousine. Again, only a single prototype was built, and nothing more was heard. However, one can only admire the Duesenberg family for its sheer persistence.

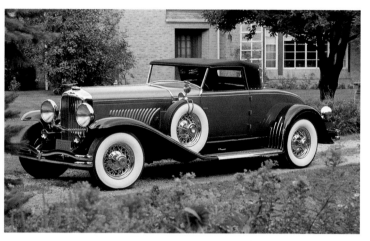

DU PONT (U.S.A. 1920-1932)

North America is supposed to have been the birthplace of mass-production techniques, especially when it came to cars. But not all U.S. manufacturers tried to emulate Henry Ford. Du Pont built only a few more than 500 cars, and this was in a period of some 12 years.

From the start, E. Paul du Pont wanted to make only high-quality cars in very low quantities. The first Du Pont, built in 1923, was powered by the company's own 250-cu in (4.1-litre) side-valve four-cylinder engine, though it was soon dropped in favour of six-cylinder units bought off the shelf from other manufacturers. It was a wise move, as four cylinders were just not enough in the American luxury car market.

The 1925 Model D came with a 305-cu in (5-litre) Wisconsin engine, driving up to 75bhp (55.9kW) through a four-speed transmission and with the advanced feature of Lockheed hydraulic brakes on all four wheels. The Model E that followed could be had with a supercharger, but the G of 1928 was the best known. Its straight-eight

317.3-cu in (5.2-litre) engine allowed a top speed of over 110mph (177km/h), and in Speedster guise it was a distinctive-looking car, with shrouded Woodlite headlamps and a curved grille to hide the radiator. If this was all too radical, there was a conventionally styled Roadster as well.

But the U.S.A. of 1929–30 was neither the place nor the time to be selling expensive, exclusive motor cars, and Du Pont sales began to decline, despite the introduction of the slightly bigger Model G. The company ceased production in 1932, leaving its owner to concentrate on Indian motorcycles, which he also owned.

LEFT
1930 Duesenberg Model J.

BELOW LEFT
1929 Duesenberg Model J with 420-ci engine.

BELOW Du Pont Model G Royal town car.

DURYEA (U.S.A. 1893-1916)

Duryea has a good claim to be the U.S.A.'s earliest car maker, and was certainly one of the pioneers. Charles Duryea began building his first car in 1891, but left his brother Frank to complete it. Four years later, the second prototype was Frank's work alone, and it won the 50-mile (80-km) *Chicago Times Herald* race in nine hours. Two years on, and the brothers got together to build cars for customers, even if they did not always see eye to eye about who was responsible for the first prototype!

But this arrangement did not last long. It was barely a year before Frank left in 1901 to join the Automobile Co. of America, then Stevens Arms, to design the Stevens-Duryea. He also designed a six-cylinder engine in 1906, said to be the first automotive six in the U.S.A. Meanwhile, Charles carried on making the original Duryea, in three- and four-wheeled forms. It was also made under licence in England,

Belgium and at Waterloo, Iowa. An interesting three-cylinder rotary-valve car was built in 1907, and a successful high-wheeled buggy introduced the following year. Charles built his last car, the Duryea-Gem, in 1916.

EXCELSIOR (Belgium 1903-1930)

Belgium did not produce many memorable car manufacturers, but along with Minerva Excelsior was one of them. The Compagnie Nationale Excelsior was established in 1903 by Arthur de Coninck, an engineer whose first cars used French Aster engines, Coninck being the Aster agent in Brussels.

Although the early Excelsiors were unexceptional cars, within four years their maker was offering three models, and in that same year moved into a larger factory in Liège. The company also began making its own engines and transmissions. The company was evidently doing well, as another factory was bought in 1909 and the first six-cylinder car, a D6, was launched the year after. There were forays into competition as well, with Excelsiors competing in the 1912 French Grand Prix, in Le Mans and in Belgian endurance events.

ABOVE
A 1928 Excelsior Imperia Monte Carlo Rally car.

LEFT
One offshoot of the Duryea company included Stevens-Duryea, of which this 1911 model is an example.

Excelsior suffered from the 1914-18 German occupation of Belgium, when all its plant machinery was taken. However, Coninck started again in 1919, and went on to produce the successful Adex C. Sadly, sales dropped away in the late 1920s, and despite exhibiting at the Brussels Salon in 1930, Excelsior did not survive into 1931.

FACEL VEGA (France 1954-1964)

Facel Vega experienced a single, troubled decade of production, attempting to produce a luxury car when French taxation laws made it very difficult. The company started in 1938, when it was formed to make machine tools for the aircraft industry. One of its many interests (it also built kitchen furniture and gas turbine parts among other things) was building car bodies for Simca and Panhard.

The first Facel car was launched at the Paris Salon in 1954. Named the Vega (soon incorporated into the company title) it was powered by a 274.6-cu in (4.5-litre) De Soto V8 of 180bhp (134kW). Expensive and exclusive, the Vega was built in small numbers: just 46 were delivered over 18 months. As the Facel Vega, in 1956, it received a 329.5-cu in (5.4-litre) V8, later upgraded to a 390.5-cu in (6.4-litre) engine delivering 350bhp (261kW) as the HK500 for 1958. All of these were the same two-door coupé style, and although a convertible was introduced, this was withdrawn after only a few had been made, due to insufficient rigidity, a problem that afflicted the 1957 pillarless Excellence coupé.

In 1960, came the little 97.6-cu in (1.6-litre) Facellia, a miniaturized version of the full-size coupé, in an attempt by Facel Vega to broaden its market. Unfortunately, its twin-cam four-cylinder was a disaster, being both noisy and unreliable. Despite an updated full-size Facel Vega, the company

was now in financial trouble, though it did carry on for a few years after the receiver had been called in. Attempts to use proven Volvo and Austin-Healey engines failed to provide the answer, and Facel Vega was declared bankrupt in 1965.

TOP
The Facel Vega HK500, a 1958 model.

ABOVE
The Facel II boasted even more power.

ABOVE RIGHT
The priceless 1948 Ferrari Type 166 Corsa Spider.

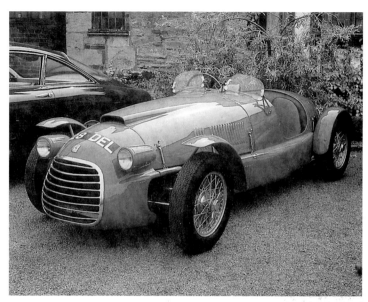

FERRARI (Italy 1940 to date)

Ferrari is surely the most evocative name in motoring. Whatever one thinks of the bright red cars from Maranello, there is no denying that they have presence, and their racing record is second to none. Racing, of course, has always been at the heart of Ferrari. It was Enzo Ferrari's passion, the reason why he began building cars in the first place. By the end of the 20th century, Ferrari had taken nearly 100 Formula One race wins, won the world championship nine times and Le Mans another nine. At the time of writing, in late 2002, Formula One racing stands accused of being boring, simply because the Ferraris are still so dominant!

From the age of 10, when he witnessed

his first race, Ferrari was hooked on motor racing, and was driving the family car by the time he was 13. But tragedy struck in 1916 when Enzo's father and brother Alfredo both died. In the following year, Enzo joined the Italian artillery as a farrier, later working on aero engines, the latter probably a better use of his talents. Invalided out of the army in 1918, he did what any motor-mad Italian youngster would have done, and tried to get a job with Fiat. He failed, but did find work with a Bolognese engineer, converting trucks to cars, then as a test driver for CMN. That, in turn, allowed him to start racing: his first event was the Parma Poggio di Berceto hill climb in 1919. A year later, he was working for Alfa Romeo as a test driver, and

finished second for Alfa in the Targa Florio. Other wins followed, and it was after one of these that he was congratulated by Count Enrico Baracca, father of the late Italian flying ace. The countess donated her son's prancing horse emblem to Ferrari, who was so touched that he kept it as his own, and to this day the emblem remains the universally recognized sign of Ferrari.

Ferrari stopped racing in 1932, when his son Dino was born, but forged on with team management, both with his own Scuderia Ferrari and as manager of Alfa Corse in 1938. He left the Alfa team after a year, but immediately set up his own company to make racing cars. The first 815 car was not called a Ferrari (there was a four-year ban on the use of his own name, part of his agreement with Alfa) but it showed promise with a straight-eight engine and bodywork by Touring.

The outbreak of World War II soon put an end to production, but Ferrari was able

to restart in late 1946, once his factory had been rebuilt after bomb damage. The new 91.5-cu in (1.5-litre) V12 racing sports car was designed by Gioacchino Colombo, and it was the first car called a Ferrari. Three of these were built, followed by the larger 159 and 166, the latter of which formed the basis of the first Ferrari road car, of which deliveries began in 1948. That same year saw Ferrari's Formula One debut (third place in the Italian GP) and first win.

Meanwhile, the road cars were acquiring their own following. The first U.S. export was made as early as 1949, and over 250 Inters, the early road cars, were built. The U.S.A. was to be a good market for Ferrari, with the 400 and 410 Superamericas of the 1950s designed specifically for the U.S., as well as the lightweight 410 Superfast and 400-bhp (298.2-kW) 500 Superfast of 1964-66. These were bigger, heavier, perhaps even cruder, than the more typical Ferraris for

LEFT
1984 Ferrari GTO.

BELOW LEFT
The 4.9-litre Berlinetta Boxer.

BELOW
An F40 at the factory.

OPPOSITE
ABOVE LEFT: 1965 V12 330GT.

ABOVE RIGHT: 275 Spider special.

BELOW RIGHT: 1971 365GT.

European consumption, such as the 250GT of 1956, which well and truly took Ferrari into the pure road car market. Several variations on the theme appeared over the years, including the 250 Lusso (Luxury), 2+2 (the first Ferrari with more than two seats) and short-wheelbased 250GTO, of which only 39 were built over two years.

Many people associate Ferrari with mid-engined cars, but the classic 183.1-cu in (3-litre) 250 was front-engined, as was the Daytona 365GTB4. With sensational styling by Pininfarina (it is hard to believe it went on sale as early as 1968), the Daytona was V12-powered and could reach 175mph (280km/h) making it, by some margin, the fastest car of its time. The same year saw the debut of a 'small' Ferrari, the Dino 206GT. Named after Ferrari's son (who had been tragically killed in 1956) it was aimed at the Porsche 911, and its

143

LEFT
Model 456.

BELOW
Daytona Spider with 4.4-litre V-12.

OPPOSITE
LEFT: 328GTS.

RIGHT ABOVE: 308GT4.

RIGHT BELOW: 1973 246 Dino.

Ferrari-designed V6 engine was built by Fiat. The Dino was later updated with a bigger engine as the 246GT and 246GTS Spider, part of a long line of smaller Ferraris.

Pininfarina made a good job of styling both the curvaceous Dino and Daytona, but Bertone designed the straighter-edged 308GT4 of 1973, Ferrari's first V8. Somehow, these straighter lines did not suit a Ferrari, and Pininfarina was called back for the 308GTB of 1976. A different target audience was aimed at in the 365GT4 2+2 in 1973, as was the 400 which replaced it. These were closer to full four-seaters than 2+2s, with coupé (not sports car) styling and later the option of automatic transmission.

A new generation of high-performance mid-engine Ferraris kicked off with the 365BB (Berlinetta Boxer). 'Berlinetta' translated as 'small saloon' (though there

was nothing saloon-like about this car) and 'Boxer' came courtesy of the 268.5-cu in (4.4-litre) flat-twelve engine, later upsized to 775cu in (5 litres). The Boxer was replaced in 1984 by the Testarossa (red head, after the colour of the cam covers). Also in the 1980s came the four-valve-per-cylinder Mondial in both open and closed forms, while other Ferraris were given larger engines: the 308 gave way to the 195.3-cu in (3.2-litre) 328 in 1985, then the 207.5-cu in (3.4-litre) 348GTB in 1989; the 400i near-four-seater became the more powerful 412 in 1985.

Ferrari needed a new flagship with which to celebrate 40 years in the business, and got it in 1987 with the F40, capable of over 200mph (320km/h) and 0-60mph (0-97km/h) in 4 seconds. The car was not elegant in the way of some Ferraris, but was thought by some to be the finest driving Ferrari ever made. Ferrari himself

lived to see the F40, though sadly he died the year after it was announced, aged 90.

In 1992 the 412 (the other car from Ferrari's straight-edge era) was replaced by the more voluptuous 465GT. Still with a massively powerful V12 under the bonnet, now offering 442bhp (329.6kW), it was a full four-seater. Two years later, the 348 mid-sized Ferrari was itself replaced by the 355, continuing the tradition of mid-engined Ferrari V8s which has now been running for 30 years. Now with 380bhp (283.3kW) from its engine, with five valves per cylinder, it used electronic control of the damping and came in hard-top GTB, targa-top GTS and later convertible Spider form. Just as the F40 was Ferrari's 40th birthday present, so the F50 filled a similar role ten years later. Like its predecessor, this was a stripped-out road car, now with a 286.8-cu in (4.7-litre) V12 and a speed of more than 200mph (320km/h).

But in the late 1990s Ferrari made a move back to the front-engined layout,

replacing the Testarossa with the 550 Maranello, using a rear transaxle for more even weight distribution. In 2002, as the 575M Maranello, this offered 515bhp (384kW) from its 347.8-cu in (5.7-litre) V12, with the latest in semi-automatic six-speed transmissions and electronic control of both steering and dampers. According to one road test, it was entertaining rather than intimidating, which would probably have pleased Enzo Ferrari.

ABOVE LEFT and RIGHT
The Enzo Ferrari.

LEFT
The 575M Maranello.

OPPOSITE
ABOVE LEFT: 1996 456GT.

ABOVE RIGHT: 1997 550 Maranello.

BELOW: 1996 F355 Spider.

FIAT (Italy 1899 to date)

Fiat is an Italian national institution. Having been the jewel in the Italian industrial crown for so long (it celebrated its 100th birthday in 1999), a European motor industry without Fiat seems almost unthinkable. A company with enviable racing success, all-time classics like the Topolino and 500, and a whole string of 'Car of the Year' awards, maybe that was why, late in 2002, after the company began to hit serious trouble, it was rumoured that the Italian government would step in to prevent the unthinkable from happening.

Like most car manufacturers, Fiat was set up to do just that, to build motor cars. Other new products (farm tractors for example) were built by well-established companies with a strong track record in a related field. Cars were different. The technology was so new that new start-ups were the best way to get to grips with it: very few horse-drawn carriage and buggy makers went on to build motor cars.

F.I.A.T. (Fabbrica Italiana Automobili Torino) was just such a start-up, established by Giovanni Agnelli di Bricherasio and Count Carlo Biscaretti di Ruffia. Agnelli was the leading light, which was appropriate, as the Agnelli family would be associated with Fiat for decades to come. The first car of 1899 was not designed by Fiat, but was based on a design by the Ceirano brothers, a 42.72-cu in (700-cc) 3.5-hp (2.61-kW) flat-twin with the engine mounted at the rear. It had 'vis-à-vis' bodywork, in which the driver and passengers faced each other, an arrangement more distracting than the conventional arrangement, but also more sociable. A larger 6/8-hp (4.47/5.96-kW) version appeared in the following year, and in 1901 Fiat's first front-engined car used a vertical-twin 66-cu in (1.08-litre) power unit.

So Fiat had started off with modest, small-engined cars, the sort of thing with which the company has long been associated. But in those early years, it went through a period of building monstrous racing machines with huge four- and six-cylinder engines. The first four-cylinder unit, a relatively modest 231.9 cu in (8 litres), appeared in 1902, and Fiat actually stopped making its small twins the following year. The first monster Fiat

arrived in 1905 in the form of the 622.4-cu in (10.2-litre) four-cylinder unit rated at 60hp (44.7kW), with a six-cylinder 671.3-cu in (11-litre) car following in 1907. These giants began a long Fiat association with motor racing, winning the Targa Florio, Kaiserpreis and French Grand Prix in 1907 alone. Smaller four-cylinder cars followed, such as the 122-cu in (2-litre) 10/14-hp (7.46/10.44-kW) of 1908, and Fiat's advanced technical stance was underlined by its early adoption of four-speed gearboxes and overhead camshafts. But it persisted with the big racers, such as the 1,110.6-cu in (18.2-litre) Mephistopheles, which raced at Brooklands, and the S76 of 1910, which sported a four-cylinder engine

ABOVE FAR LEFT
1927 ohc Fiat 509.

ABOVE CENTRE
1922 4.8-litre 519.

ABOVE
1921-22 6.8-litre V12 'Superfiat'.

BELOW LEFT
The first Fiat of 1899-1900.

BELOW
1911 28.3-litre Fiat S.76.

trucks during World War I, many of them for military use; the first genuine post-war car was the Tipo 501 of 1919. With a small 91.5-cu in (1.5-litre) side-valve engine and the option of four-wheel brakes from 1925, it earned a deserved reputation for reliability. Some 45,000 had been made by 1926, so Fiat was clearly in the mass-production league. There was also a little 509, with a 60.4-cu in (990-cc) overhead-camshaft engine, and 90,000 of these were sold in four years.

But Fiat was not forgetting its bigger cars. Alongside the 501, there were 140.4-cu in (2.3-litre) fours and 207.5-cu in (3.4-litre) sixes, designed along the same lines, while 1921 saw a new line of 'Superfiats'. The latter were exotic V12s of 415 cu in (6.8 litres), though only a few were made before being dropped in favour of the less ambitious six-cylinder Tipo 519. The Tipo

520 and 525 were sixes too, but in 1932 came another small Fiat, the Balilla. This was a very advanced little car for its time, with hydraulic brakes, short-stroke 60.72-cu in (995-cc) engine and four-speed synchromesh gearbox. Made under licence in both France and Poland, the Balilla was updated in 1937 as the new 508C Millecento. Again, there were more technical innovations for the latest Fiat: independent front suspension, and an overhead-valve 66.5-cu in (1089-cc) engine developing an impressive 32bhp (23.9kW). There were also bigger Fiats, of course, such as the six-cylinder 1500 of 1936, and the 122-cu in (2-litre) Ardita and six-cylinder 527, but Fiat's strategy was to make its small cars just as technically advanced as the larger ones.

Take the 1936 Topolino, the first in a long line of baby Fiats. It was tiny, seating

with a capacity of 1,604.9 cu in (26.3 litres). It could exceed 130mph (210km/h), a stratospheric speed for the time.

But alongside the high-speed racers, there were much smaller Fiats for road use. From 1910, the range included the 112.5-cu in (1844-litre) Type1B, mid-range Type 2 and 244.1-cu in (4-litre) Type 3, which later grew to 347.8 cu in (5.7 litres). Or there was the Fiat Zero, a bread-and-butter 15-hp (11.18-kW) four-seater, of which 2,000 were built between 1912 and 1915. More technical progress in 1914 led to electric lighting and starting for the larger cars, plus wire wheels. Fiat produced 35,000 cars and

ABOVE
1936 Balilla 508S TT.

RIGHT
1927 990-cc 509A tourer.

just two adults and powered by a side-valve 34.78-cu in (570-cc) engine mounted in the rear. So far, so price-cutting, but that little engine had four cylinders, and there were also independent front suspension, hydraulic brakes and a synchromesh gearbox. If a person wanted a small car, the reasoning went, why should they put up with less comfort and convenience than the driver of a large one? The Topolino was back in production in 1948, but the following year there were updated 67.1-cu in (1.1-litre) and 91.5-cu in (1.5-litre) Fiats, with steering column gearchange; they were joined by an overhead-valve 85.4-cu in (1.4-litre) in 1950, with unitary construction. The 1400 was a great success, selling 150,000 over nine years, and branching out into the cross-country Campagnola and (unusually) a diesel version. Meanwhile, the little Topolino was replaced in 1955 by the 600, still with rear-

engined four-cylinder unit, but otherwise all-new, with unitary construction; the practical Multipla derivative came later, a sort of mini-people-carrier.

But the definitive small Fiat came two years later. The 500 was arguably the true successor to the Topolino, providing the smallest possible motorized package short of a Lambretta. Its twin-cylinder air-cooled engine was tucked away at the back, allowing space for two smallish children as well as two adults; its 16.5bhp (12.3kW) was adequate. Like the 600, it was in production right into the 1970s, and acquired a huge following.

In the 1960s Fiat's mid-sized saloons were a departure from the cute, rounded 500 and 600, with ever more squared-off and boxy styling. The 1100 was joined by a 1200, 1300 and 1500, but while they may have looked a little boring, these family Fiats had plenty of pep and zest, especially

in the later 1966 124 and twin overhead-camshaft 125: the latter enjoyed 90bhp (67.1kW) and 100mph (160km/h), making it one of the first modern sports saloons. The little 850 was also surprisingly lively for a 40-bhp (29.8-kW) family car. There were other more exotic Fiats, such as the bigger 1800 and 2300, plus of course the Dino coupé, unveiled in 1970 complete with Ferrari-designed 2-litre V6.

Fiat entered the front-wheel-drive era in 1969 with the 128, with a choice of two overhead-cam engines, which was voted European Car of the Year in 1970. In 1971, the three-door 127 continued the 850 tradition with a lively 55.1-cu in (903-cc) overhead-valve engine and enough space for a small family. Later joined by an overhead-camshaft 64.1-cu in (1.05-litre) version, this too won the European Car of the Year award. But there was no front-wheel-drive for the smallest Fiat, the baby

126 replaced the 500 in 1973, still with rear-mounted twin-cylinder engine. Bigger Fiats stuck with rear-wheel-drive too, the 132 (with up to 109.8 cu in/1.8 litres) and 79.3/248-cu in (1.3/1.6-litre) 131. Nor should one forget the little X1-9, a miniature mid-engined sports car based on 128 mechanics, and built from 1977 to 1989.

But from the late 1970s, nearly all new Fiats had front-wheel-drive. The Ritmo (named the more mellifluous-sounding Strada in some markets) had quirky styling and a huge range of engines, from 67.1 cu in (1.1 litres) to 2 litres in the Abarth 130TC. The small Panda was an attempt to return to basic motoring, with boxy hatchback body and very simple interior. It used the 127's 903-cc engine and later Fiat's new FIRE engine range. There was an interesting four-wheel-drive variant as well, modified by Steyr-Puch. But the Uno was Fiat's biggest success of the 1980s. Yet another Car of the Year winner, it offered maximum space inside a three- or five-door hatchback bodyshell, with engines ranging from 903cc to 79.4 cu in (1301cc), plus a 103.6-cu in (1697-cc) diesel. Meanwhile the Regata took over as the mid-sized Fiat, with the big Croma aimed at executives from 1986.

In 1988, the Tipo made its debut as the replacement for the Ritmo. And before one asks, yes, it did indeed win Car of the Year! It continued that slightly quirky tradition of the smaller Fiats, but offered a large amount of interior space. Innovations included a 115.9-cu in (1.9-litre) turbocharged diesel and a galvanized body to combat corrosion, which was a common Fiat problem in damper northern climates. A saloon version, the Tempra, soon appeared alongside the Tipo, while 1991 saw the fourth-generation Fiat baby car, the

TOP
The striking 2000 Multipla.

ABOVE
Cinquecento Sporting.

LEFT ABOVE
The 2.0 20V Turbo Plus Coupé.

LEFT
2000 Barchetta.

OPPOSITE
ABOVE LEFT: The new Punto arrived in 1999.

ABOVE RIGHT: 1999 Bravo.

BELOW: 2000 Ulysse.

little Cinquecento. Like the 126, it was built in Poland to cut costs, and came with a 42.96-cu in (704-cc) twin or 54.86-cu in (899-cc) four, though the later Sporting with a 1.1-litre engine arguably had more impact. Fiat virtually took over Turin for the 1993 launch of the Punto, which replaced the Uno. This had more rounded, 1990s styling than previous Fiats, and again, maximum interior space was combined with peppy performance.

The success of the X1-9 encouraged Fiat to persevere with sports cars, and the 1990s saw the Pininfarina-styled Coupé (with up to 220bhp/164kW from a five-cylinder engine) and the retro-styled Barchetta, a traditional two-seater. But the focus was still on the small- and mid-sized hatchbacks that earned most of Fiat's profits. The three-door Bravo and five-door Brava replaced the Tipo in 1995, with more performance than ever before thanks to the new option of five cylinders. The latter was also used by the larger Marea, which replaced the Tempra. A collaboration with Peugeot/Citroën produced

the Ulysse people-carrier, actually not very different from the French-badged versions. A more imaginative design was the Multipla, offered from the late 1990s, with six seats and lots of luggage space, if one could live with the individual styling. The van-derived Doblo was yet another take on the people-carrier concept and by 2002 the Cinquecento had been updated as the Sciento, but now looked elderly, and the Bravo/Brava had been replaced by the Stilo, said to be a great improvement.

Despite all the new models, however, Fiat was facing an uncertain future. With home market sales falling drastically in 2002, it cut 8,000 jobs late that year. General Motors reduced its holding in the company, which worsened the situation, though the terms of the agreement meant that Fiat could force General Motors to buy the rest of its car business as well. The Italian government was rumoured to be considering stepping in to save Fiat – what other choice did it have? In the 21st century, after all, Fiat is still an Italian institution.

FORD (U.S.A. 1901 to date)

Asked to name the most significant car tycoon in history, most people will plump for Henry Ford. It is celebrity he deserves, but he was very far from perfect. The farmer's son from Michigan could be difficult and irascible: his world view was illogical, and he was not above using violence to prevent unions being formed in his factories. Moreover, contrary to popular belief, Ford did not invent mass-production, though he was the first to apply it to motor cars, and he did so with huge success. In so doing, he made cars cheap enough for untold millions of people to buy, and that was his real achievement.

Ford was not only a production man, he was also an engineer, building his first car, the Quadricycle in 1896. There was no question of plunging straight into production, and it was three years before a second quadricycle was running sufficiently well to convince a group of backers to form the Detroit Automobile Company to build it. But the car failed to sell, and with conflicting ideas on how to progress, Ford abandoned his financiers and started all over again.

He did not build another cheap runabout, but a 20-hp (14.9-kW) racer, which won a race at Grosse Point late in

RIGHT
The popular Model A of 1928.

BELOW
The 15-millionth Ford off the production line.

BELOW RIGHT
1912 Model T.

OPPOSITE
1931 Model A coupé.

upmarket Fords, such as the six-cylinder Model K, were less successful, and this was a lesson that Ford was to take to heart. The same year as the model N was introduced, Ford produced nearly 15,000 cars, but this was just a precursor of what was to come.

The Model T, announced in October 1908, was not a particularly advanced car, but it was built in the largest, most modern factory in the world. The use of precision components meant that any part would fit any car: workers did not have to undertake the laborious task of hand-finishing parts to persuade them to fit, but just bolted them on. That made the Model T quicker and easier to build than any competitor, and also cheaper. As Ford's mass-production techniques developed and volumes grew,

LEFT
1932 roadster.

BELOW
1935 V8 coupé.

OPPOSITE
ABOVE: 1934 V8 roadster.

BELOW: 1940 V8 convertible coupé.

1901. This attracted sufficient publicity for him to set up the Henry Ford Company, only a month after winning that race, but this arrangement was even more short-lived than the first. After three months, Ford upped and left and the company went on to become Cadillac.

But it was third time lucky. More success with the big 80-hp (59.6-kW) racers '999' and 'Arrow' saw more people willing to invest in another Ford venture, and the Ford Motor Company was born in June 1903. Having used racing to kick-start his venture, Ford now concentrated on making affordable cars. The Model A, as a first offering, was certainly that, a little 8-hp (5.96-kW) machine that sold well and made the new company over $30,000 of profit in its first three-and-a-half months. Bigger cars, the Models B, C and F followed in 1904, when sales reached nearly 9,000, while the Model N of 1906 was the prototypical Model T, inasmuch as it was simple and relatively cheap. Interestingly, attempts to produce more

the first low-priced V8-powered car was announced, another milestone, as it was the first to be mass-produced and therefore cheap. (The V8 had formerly been reserved for luxury cars.) Like the Models A and T, the new V8 was a great success, and was joined by a smaller version in 1937. Despite this, Ford's model range was still limited, and this was largely the reason for the fact that the company had been overtaken by Chevrolet in the 1930s. Ford's insistence on sticking with a live front axle and mechanical brakes, at a time when all General Motors' cars had gone over to independent front suspension and hydraulic brakes, was another factor.

Ford was entering an age of uncertainty, with boardroom battles over who should run the company when Henry Ford, who was now nearly 80 and becoming increasingly eccentric, retired. Sadly, it could not be his son Edsel, who had died in 1943. The level-headed Edsel had done much to curb his father's

the cars became cheaper and cheaper to make. Many businessmen would have stashed away the consequent fat profits, but not Henry Ford. He ploughed them back into the company, cutting the price of the Model T from $950 in 1911 to just $290 by 1925, and selling more and more cars in the process. Even at $230, he was averaging a respectable $50-dollar profit on each one. He spent money on his workforce, too, paying a guaranteed $5 per hour, which was nearly twice the going rate; this, of course, ensured loyalty, and good work and morale.

It was not until the mid-1920s, when the Model T was at its cheapest, that cracks began to appear. American buyers now wanted more comfort and sophistication; rugged value for money was no longer enough and the Model T, by now nearly 20

years old, was looking very dated. Reluctantly at first, Ford realized that he could not hang on to the Model T forever, but, typically, refused to do things by halves. Model T production ceased in May 1927, and there was a seven-month hiatus while his factories were completely stripped out and re-equipped for an all-new car.

When it appeared, the Model A did not seem very innovative, but under the skin it was right up to date, with three-speed transmission and four-wheel brakes. And it proved hugely popular, with almost 160,000 rolling off the lines in the first full month of production. But Ford had learned another lesson with the Model T: no longer could a manufacturer depend on a single model, however popular it was. So in 1932

excesses, and went far to ensure the success of the Model A, V8 and upmarket Lincoln division. In fact, this was said to have caused a fundamental split between father and son: Henry wanted to make the cheapest car in the world, while Edsel wanted to make the best. Meanwhile, a power struggle was going on between

production chief Charles Sorensen and Harry Bennett, the tough guy who was Henry Ford's right-hand man. Bennett managed to persuade Henry to get rid of Sorensen, who left to join Willys-Overland, but all this intrigue and instability worried the U.S. government as the Ford company was now essential to the war effort. So it stepped in and insisted that Edsel's son, Henry Ford II, become vice-president.

ABOVE
Pick-up truck.

FAR LEFT TOP
1949 station wagon.

FAR LEFT CENTRE
1950 Mercury.

FAR LEFT BOTTOM
1950 Mercury convertible.

LEFT ABOVE
1964 Mustang.

LEFT
1955 Thunderbird.

OPPOSITE
1958 Ford Edsel.

Aged just 26, Henry II rejoined the company, becoming president two years later after his grandfather had (with difficulty) been persuaded to hand over the reins. Henry Ford died in 1947.

The young Henry faced immense problems: Ford was losing up to $10 million per month, but he managed to turn the company round with fresh blood and new ideas. The first Ford under the new regime, the 1948 Custom Deluxe Tudor, was a success, and a price-cutting war in the early 1950s put Ford back into serious contention with Chevrolet, though it failed to close the sales gap. A particular success was the compact Falcon range of 1960, while inspired manager Lee Iacocca was the man behind the incredibly successful Mustang, a car that combined sports styling and image with affordability. Alongside traditional Fords like the Fairlane and Galaxy, these gave the company a more dynamic image.

Like other U.S. manufacturers, Ford faced a difficult 1970s, with two oil crises calling into question the whole ethos of

ABOVE
1978 Thunderbird.

ABOVE LEFT
1958 Thunderbird.

CENTRE LEFT
1969 Marauder.

BOTTOM LEFT
1978 Mustang.

BOTTOM RIGHT
1983 Mustang.

OPPOSITE
ABOVE LEFT: 1980 Fairmount.

ABOVE RIGHT: 1986 Mustang.

BELOW LEFT: 1986 Taurus LX.

BELOW RIGHT: 1996 Windstar.

building big cars that guzzled cheap fuel. The Pinto compact was one response, though a design fault which made its fuel tank vulnerable to fire in rear-end collisions led to a multi-million dollar lawsuit. With recession following in the early 1980s, Ford lost nearly $3.3 billion in 1982 and began a radical rationalization plan which saw the loss of many jobs. Light began to appear in the tunnel in the mid-1980s, when the all-new Taurus proved that U.S. manufacturers could beat the Japanese at their own game.

Ford's new factory at Atlanta was highly efficient, enabling it to sell the Taurus at a competitive price. Meanwhile, older names continued, with a new downsized 1980s Mustang offering a turbocharged four-cylinder engine as well as the traditional V8.

By the late 1980s, Ford U.S. was back in profit, and actually reported a $3.7-billion surplus for the first nine months of 1987. But it could not afford to stand still. An agreement with Mazda (Ford owned 25 per cent of the Japanese company) meant

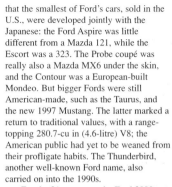

that the smallest of Ford's cars, sold in the U.S., were developed jointly with the Japanese: the Ford Aspire was little different from a Mazda 121, while the Escort was a 323. The Probe coupé was really also a Mazda MX6 under the skin, and the Contour was a European-built Mondeo. But bigger Fords were still American-made, such as the Taurus, and the new 1997 Mustang. The latter marked a return to traditional values, with a range-topping 280.7-cu in (4.6-litre) V8; the American public had yet to be weaned from their profligate habits. The Thunderbird, another well-known Ford name, also carried on into the 1990s.

For the 21st century, the Ford 2000 programme promised more world cars. No longer would the company produce a multiplicity of models all over the world intended for local conditions. Instead, all Fords would be designed for export worldwide, to maximize efficiency and minimize unit costs. Henry Ford's lessons had been well learned.

LEFT
2003 Taurus.

OPPOSITE
TOP LEFT: 1998 Contour.

TOP CENTRE: 1997 Mustang GT.

TOP RIGHT: 1999 Taurus SE.

BELOW LEFT: 2000 Taurus Wagon.

BELOW RIGHT: Explorer.

ABOVE
2000 STV Contour.

ABOVE LEFT
STV Mustang Cobra.

LEFT
2002 Thunderbird.

OPPOSITE
2003 Mustang Mach 1.

FORD (Europe 1911 to date)

Ford's European operations started as completely separate businesses, building different ranges of cars. But since the late 1960s the two main centres of production, Great Britain and Germany, have come closer and closer in terms of both operations and the types of cars they produce. The factories in Britain and mainland Europe are now effectively the same company, producing a single, integrated range of cars. Over the coming years, this process is likely to continue, integrating Ford production on a worldwide basis.

Although Britain and Germany have long been Ford's European focus, the company also began building cars in France before World War II, albeit under the Matford or Tracford names. The Matfords were 134.25-cu in (2.2-litre) V8s of American appearance, which achieved success in the Monte Carlo Rally. After the war, the V8 reappeared in the Ford Vedette,

RIGHT (fron top to bottom)
1935 Model C 10-hp saloon.
1948 Pilot 3.6-litre V8
1940 10-hp Prefect E93A
1937 'New Eight' (7Y).
1949 Anglia E494A.

FAR RIGHT TOP
1962 2.6-litre Zodiac.

FAR RIGHT CENTRE
The four-door Prefect 100E.

FAR RIGHT BOTTOM LEFT
1936-37 V-8 Type 48 Standard.

FAR RIGHT BOTTOM RIGHT
1933-34 Rhineland.

then from 1952 the Facel-bodied Comète coupé. Simca took over the operation in 1954, though the company continued to build the Vedette under its own name.

Germany's Ford history began in 1925, when Model Ts were assembled there. A new factory was built in Cologne, where the Models B and Y were also made as the Rheinland and Köln. V8s also came out of Cologne. After World War II, all German Fords assumed the Taunus name, with the 12M, 15M and 17M of the 1950s denoting their engine capacity. Cologne also built its own V4 and V6 engines, which were used in both German and British Fords. Instead of the Cortina, it built the front-drive Taunus 12M. But from the late 1960s Ford of Cologne began to share the same models as Dagenham in England.

In fact, Britain had been Ford's first foothold in Europe, and remains a significant part of its worldwide operation. Model Ts were being assembled in Manchester as early as 1911, and were very similar to the Detroit-built cars. This all changed when the giant Dagenham plant was opened in 1932: from that time onward, Ford of Britain designed its own cars. The little Model Y was the first thoroughly English Ford, with a 56.94-cu in (933-cc) side-valve engine, three-speed gearbox and transverse leaf front suspension. Simple and cheap (the two-

ABOVE LEFT
1956 Zephyr Zodiac.

ABOVE
1957 Ford Anglia de-luxe.

LEFT
1969 A right-hand-drive Escort.

167

door cost only £100), it was very popular, and was followed by the slightly bigger 10-hp (7.46-kW) Model C.

Dagenham also produced its own V8s, based on the American pattern, with a smaller 22-hp (16.4-kW) V8 from 1937. A name familiar to British Ford owners appeared in late 1939 as the Anglia, an 8-hp (5.96-kW) car very similar to the Model Y. Both the Anglia and 10-hp Prefect were reintroduced after World War II, with their

LEFT
1971 Capri.

BELOW LEFT
Cortina MkII.

BELOW
1968 Escort.

OPPOSITE
FAR LEFT: Consul.

TOP RIGHT
1972 Mk III Cortina 1600XL.

CENTRE RIGHT: 1972 Cortina MkIV 2000 Ghia.

BOTTOM RIGHT: A 1975 German Granada Ghia coupé.

side-valve engines continuing to be used. The Prefect was available right up to 1962, the last mainstream car in Britain with a side-valve engine. The V8 Pilot disappeared in the early 1950s, to be replaced by the four-cylinder 91.5-cu in (1.5-litre) Consul and six-cylinder 140.4-cu in (2.3-litre) Zephyr, with the luxury Zephyr Zodiac appearing in 1954.

These early post-war Fords were quite conservative in some ways, though their MacPherson strut front suspension was a step forward, but the early 1960s would see a new generation of flashier Fords, in keeping with the times. The 1959 Anglia, with its distinctive notchback styling and tailfins, used brand-new overhead-valve engines of 60.8 or 73.2 cu in (997cc or 1200cc). Both were oversquare, high-revving units that responded well to tuning,

quite different from the old side-valves. Two years later, the larger Classic followed the same lines as the Anglia, with 81.8-cu in (1.3-litre) and later 91.41-cu in (1.5-litre) versions of the new engines. But the Classic was outdated before its time, a heavy 1950s throwback that did not stay in production for long. The real pointer to Ford of Britain's future was the lightweight Cortina of 1962. With 1200- or 1498-cc units, and the choice of two or four doors, plus a capacious estate, it proved very successful: over a million were sold in just

four years, and the same was true of the 1.3/1.6-litre Cortina Mk II.

Up another class was the long, low Corsair announced the year after, with Ford of Germany V4 engines and again, a large estate version. By now, Ford was building a good reputation in motor sport, and capitalized on the fact with GT and Lotus-powered (warm and hot respectively) versions of the Cortina. That was especially true of the Escort, which replaced the Anglia in 1967: a wide range of engines culminated in the twin-cam Lotus 1.6-litre unit, and if this was not affordable then there was the milder 1300GT, plus a whole string of sporting Escorts over the years, such as the Mexico and RS2000.

But the closest thing Ford had to a

ABOVE
Cortina MkIII.

ABOVE LEFT
Escort MkII.

LEFT
1978 Capri.

Peugeot diesel engine for the first time.

The Escort went over to front-wheel-drive in 1980 with an all-new model in three- or five-door hatchback form. A four-door saloon version, the Orion, followed later. Hatchbacks had come to dominate European sales in the small- and mid-sized cars, but there was still demand for a traditional saloon. The long-awaited Cortina replacement of 1982 was a hatchback, but unexpectedly the new Sierra stuck with rear-wheel-drive. Underneath

sports car at this time was the Capri, a four-seater coupé based on the Cortina but looking very different. As ever with Ford, it offered a very wide range of engines (1.3-litre four to 3-litre V6) and different levels of trim, so that even the impecunious could afford to buy a basic Capri 1300. Meanwhile, the Cortina itself had grown into the Mk III, now with 1.6- or 2-litre overhead-cam 'Pinto' engines, while the Consul and Zephyr series had been replaced by the Granada in 1972. Perhaps more significant was the little Fiesta of 1976, Ford's belated entry to the small front-drive hatchback market. It was an instant hit, offering 957-, 1116- and 1298-cc engines. Meanwhile, the Cortina became the squared-off Mk IV and a new Granada (now built in Germany) offered a

ABOVE
1978 Fiesta van.

ABOVE CENTRE RIGHT
Escort XR3.

ABOVE FAR RIGHT
1992 Escort.

ABOVE RIGHT
1992 Orion.

RIGHT
1992 Fiesta Classic.

OPPOSITE
1987 Sierra Cosworth RS500.

LEFT
1990 RS200.

LEFT BELOW
1991 Escort Cosworth RS.

BELOW
Ford GT40.

LEFT
1994 Mondeo 24-valve V6.

BELOW LEFT
The Probe was not as popular with buyers as was originally envisaged.

BELOW
The Galaxy was the result of a joint project with Volkswagen.

OPPOSITE
ABOVE LEFT:The Puma, launched in 1997, used a 1.7-litre 16-valve engine.

ABOVE RIGHT: The Maverick is in fact a re-badged Nissan Terrano. This is a 2002 model.

BELOW LEFT: The Scorpio replaced the Granada in 1994. Its questionable styling did nothing to help sales figures.

the modernistic 'jelly mould' looks, the Sierra was very conventional, with 79.3-cu in (1.3-litre) to 170.9-cu in (2.8-litre) engines, including, once again, a 140.4-cu in (2.3-litre) diesel from Peugeot. The Sierra did well in saloon car racing, which helped to sell the 204-bhp (152.1-kW) Sierra RS Cosworth, with turbocharged 2-litre engine. The Granada went the hatchback route in 1985, though it too stuck with rear-wheel-drive, while the last Capri rolled off the line in 1987.

For 1990 the Escort received a much needed update, with the new 16-valve Zetec engine and an RS2000 for the boy racers. It was already using Ford's own

109.8-cu in (1.8-litre) diesel, which from 1993 was available in turbo form. A new Fiesta replaced the old one in 1989, bigger inside and out, with another big update in 1995. In 1993, Ford's mid-sized contender finally adopted front-wheel-drive, when the new Mondeo replaced the Sierra in both hatchback and saloon forms: it was also sold in the U.S.A. as the Contour. Initially it came only with four-cylinder engines, but a 152.5-cu in (2.5-litre) V6 followed in 1994. In the same year, the Granada bowed out in favour of the Scorpio: not everyone liked the styling, and it was increasingly hampered by the perceived lack of snob appeal attached to the Ford name. Next to

LEFT
2002-03 Focus RS.

BELOW
2002-03 Fusion.

OPPOSITE
ABOVE LEFT: Street Ka.

ABOVE RIGHT: 2002-03 Fiesta.

BELOW: 2002-03 Mondeo Zetec S.

a BMW, Audi or Mercedes, few company car drivers would willingly choose a Ford.

In the late 1990s, people-carriers were seen as the latest growth market, so Ford joined forces with Volkswagen to produce the Galaxy, a big five–seven-seater with Ford's 2-litre petrol engine or VW's VR6 petrol or 115.9-cu in (1.9-litre) turbo diesel. The little Ka was all Ford's own, though, based largely on Fiesta components but with radical rounded styling to attract younger urban buyers. It was followed by the Puma, a small coupé aimed directly at the Vauxhall Tigra, and powered by a 103.7-cu in (1.7-litre) engine. The Maverick 4x4 was a rebadged Nissan, underlining Ford's determination to cover all eventualities,

with a car for every niche in the market.

There was a new Fiesta in 2001, while the Focus had already replaced the Escort; but there were new question marks concerning Ford's overall model strategy in Europe. The Fusion of 2002 was a high-roofed rebodied Fiesta that offered nothing really new, while the C-Max people-carrier was criticized for offering only five rather than seven seats. However, there were plans for an all-new car to replace the Fiesta, with rumours of small cars from Volvo and Land Rover, both built on the same B3XX platform. Ford would still be here for a while yet.

FORD (Australia 1925 to date)
The Model T was assembled in Australia
from 1925, though the car had been
exported there from 1908. Model A bodies
were later made 'down under' as well, then
fitted to imported American chassis.
Starting out in Geelong, Victoria, Ford
assembly plants were later built in
Granville, Brisbane, Adelaide and
Fremantle. Ford V8s were introduced in
1932, but although well suited to Australian
conditions were simply too expensive,
while the Model T had become too old-
fashioned and, as a consequence, General
Motors was going unchallenged as the local
market leader.

But from 1934 Ford Australia began to
develop its own cars, the most significant
being the pick-up or utility vehicle – the
ubiquitous 'Ute'. This has become a virtual
Australian institution, long before pick-ups

were fashionable with urban dwellers in the
U.S.A. In the 1950s the Australian content
of these Fords was rapidly increased to over
90 per cent, and in 1960 a new plant at
Broadmeadows was built to produce the
new six-cylinder Falcon, which was aimed
directly at the market-leading Holden. A V8
Falcon was added in 1966, soon joined by
the bigger V8 Fairlane. These two, plus the
LTD V8, were different from American
Fords of the same name.

Australian Ford used the Mazda link,
just as its parent company had before, and
as a result the Laser, Telstar and Capri
convertible in the 1980s were all Mazda-

ABOVE
*The Ford Falcon 'Ute' was designed
especially for Australia.*

LEFT
The ever popular Fairlane, a 2000 model.

based. With that help, Ford Australia was
finally able to overtake Holden in the sales
charts in 1982. In 2002, the range was
wide, bolstered by imports from Europe of
vehicles such as the Ka and Focus, plus
four-wheel-drive off-roaders such as the 3-
litre Escape and big Explorer. But many
familiar names are still there: the Laser (in
1.6-, 1.8- and 2-litre form), Fairlane, LTD
and Falcon. And there is a new version of
the Falcon 'Ute', especially for Australia.

FRANKLIN (U.S.A. 1902-1934)
Franklins were unusual cars, with their air-
cooled engines and wooden chassis, and
yet for a time they were very successful,
selling up to 10,000 units a year
throughout the 1920s. Herbert H. Franklin
was not a car designer, but he ran a
successful die-casting firm in Syracuse,
New York. In 1901, however, he was
shown a prototype of the air-cooled car
designed by John Wilkinson. Franklin was
impressed, ordered a car, and in the
following year the type went into full
production bearing his name.

Four-cylinder Franklins were quickly
followed by a six (though a competition
straight-eight was unsuccessful), which
became the only engine from 1913. This
too was air-cooled. It was advanced, with
full-pressure lubrication and light weight,
which made it a popular engine for aircraft
use. Distinctive because of their lack of a
front radiator (though a false one was
added in 1929, a travesty which forced
John Wilkinson to resign!), Franklins sold
well, with bodywork available from
Derham, Willoughby, Holbrook, Dietrich
and J.F. de Causse. The 1928 Franklin was
christened the Airman, capitalizing on the
aero engine associations of air cooling, not
to mention the fact that Charles Lindbergh
and Amelia Earhart were both celebrity

Franklin owners. But a familiar story was about to unwind: Franklin sales slumped during the Depression and despite efforts by a new management team to make the cars cheaper, there was no saving it. The last Franklin was produced in 1934, when a mere 406 cars were built, though a water-cooled version of the famous engine was later used in the Tucker car.

ABOVE 1926 Franklin.

ABOVE RIGHT:
Circa 1924 Frazer-Nash tourer.

BELOW RIGHT
Frazer-Nash Sebring and AFN staff (left to right) Nelson Ledger, W.H. Aldington, George Sneath, H.J. Aldington and Harry Olrog.

FRAZER-NASH
(Great Britain 1924-1957)
Frazer-Nash cars were made in small numbers in Kingston, Surrey. Instead of a drive shaft and differential, they used a system of chains and dog-clutches that were lighter but cruder than the mainstream alternatives. Archie Frazer-Nash had previously been a partner in GN, only starting his new venture when that failed.

The Frazer-Nash changed little in its 15 years of production, using a 91.5-cu in (1.5-litre) overhead-valve Plus Power engine, later an Anzani. The company had had a chequered career: a merger with William G. Thomas lasted only two years before a new backer stepped in. Archie Frazer-Nash died in 1928 but long-term employee H.J. Aldington took the reins in his place, and remained at the head of the company until it closed. The company never made more than 50 Frazer-Nashes a year, but a link-up with the growing BMW was to provide a lifeline for the company, now known as AFN Ltd. The BMW 315 was imported as the Frazer-Nash-BMW Type 34, as well as the Type 40 (BMW 315 or 319) and Type 55 (315 Sports). By the late 1930s, sales of Frazer-Nash home-grown cars had dropped off completely, and only one was delivered in 1939.

But that was not the end of the story. After World War II, AFN built sports cars powered by Bristol engines (H.J. Aldington had worked for Bristol during the war), of which the most successful was the Le Mans replica. There was also an attempt to go upmarket with the BMW V8-powered Continental, but this proved too expensive and the company closed after just two had been made.

LEFT
The highly successful 1951 Frazer-Nash Le Mans replica.

FAR LEFT
1930 Frazer-Nash with 1.5-litre Meadows.

BELOW
Frazer-Nash Sebring.

OPPOSITE
1929 1.5-litre Frazer-Nash.

FSO (Poland 1946 to date)

FSO was one of the many East European makers of the Cold War era that built cars based on outdated Western technology, but which was still able to export to the West as a result of the low prices of its products. Fabryka Samochodow Osbowych (FSO) started life as a state-owned concern in 1946, building the two-stroke Russina Gaz and selling it as the Warszawa.

But in 1968 it reached an agreement with Fiat to make the FSO 125P, based on a combination of the old 124 body and 1300/1500 running gear. Already mildly out of date when introduced, the Polski-Fiat, as it was known, struggled on until 1991. By that time, however, FSO designers had already introduced the Polonez. Despite being restricted by the ancient Fiat base, FSO managed to produce a relatively

modern-looking five-door hatchback: it was unfortunate that it did not have a folding rear seat, however, which made the hatchback facility rather pointless. And under the skin were the same old Fiat pushrod engines.

In the harsh economic climate that followed the collapse of the Eastern Bloc, it seemed as if it was only a matter of time

ABOVE
FSO Caro pick-up truck.

LEFT
FSO Caro.

before FSO went the way of many ex-state-owned companies. But in 1993 a new management team freshened up the Polonez by softening its lines and introducing the 115.9-cu in (1.9-litre) Peugeot diesel and 85.4-cu in (1.4-litre) Rover K-series petrol engines. These modern power units gave the car a new lease of life, especially in one-ton diesel pick-up form, though it was still otherwise very outdated.

Korean maker Daewoo later took a stake in FSO, and the factory was increasingly used to assemble Daewoo Tico and Espero vehicles as well as Citroën C15

vans. Unfortunately, when General Motors bought the bankrupt Daewoo in 2002, the old FSO plant was not included. Late in 2002 it was rumoured that Rover would invest in the factory to build its 45 saloon for the east European market.

GAZ (U.S.S.R./Russia)

Not every Eastern Bloc car manufacturer wilted in the face of capitalism. The massive GAZ factory at Gorkiy claimed to have built over 190,000 vehicles in 2001, and was aiming for 200,000 in 2002. When built in 1932, this was claimed to be the

largest vehicle-manufacturing plant in the world, and was set up with a great deal of help from Ford. Henry Ford was actually of great assistance to the U.S.S.R., hoping that the formation of a more prosperous regime would help to prevent another world war.

So the first GAZ cars and trucks were very similar to contemporary Fords. The GAZ-A, for example, the first car to roll out of the massive plant, was based on the

ABOVE
1932 Ford Model T-based GAZ-A.

ABOVE LEFT
1940 GAZ-II-73.

LEFT
1969 Volga M.24, a 90-mph (145-km/h) saloon.

Model T. Its M-1 successor in 1940 also betrayed Ford influence, though with different 195.3-cu in (3.2-litre) four- and 207.5-cu in (3.4-litre) six-cylinder engines.

After World War II the new M-20 Probieda (victory) bore a resemblance to the Standard Vanguard, and was powered by a 128.2-cu in (2.1-litre) four-cylinder engine. Nearly a quarter of a million M-20s were made, some of them convertibles, some with four-wheel-drive. The larger M-12 was introduced in 1951, with a 213.6-cu in (3.5-litre) six-cylinder unit, and being more exclusive, only 21,000 were built over nine years, though some were exported to Finland and Sweden. Higher officials were allowed the 335.6-cu in (5.5-litre) V8 Chaika (Seagull), which GAZ built from 1959 to 1965, and this was reintroduced in 1977 with updated styling. Top Soviets, of course, enjoyed the luxury of a ZIS or ZIL limousine.

The M-20 was replaced by the 2.5-litre Volga in 1955, a long-running car that was updated in 1968 and 1982. It was also exported and was available with a Peugeot-designed 128.2- or 134.3-cu in (2.1- or 2.2-litre) diesel as well as GAZ's own petrol unit. During the 1980s, GAZ developed the 1102, a 67.1-cu in (1.1-litre) three-door car with front-wheel-drive, which was launched in 1988. But in 2002, GAZ appeared to have abandoned the market for small cars. Instead, one could still buy an updated Volga in saloon or estate form, powered by the GAZ 2.5-litre engine in 81-bhp (60.4-kW) low-compression or 131-bhp (97.7-kW) high-compression forms, plus a 2.1-litre Steyr turbo diesel of 95bhp (70.8kW) made under licence. That was the only passenger car listed, but GAZ also offered the Sobol minibus, Gazelle van and Sadko truck, with plans for a 1950s-style off-roader named the Combat.

GINETTA (Great Britain 1958 to date)
The Walklett brothers, Douglas, Trevor, Ivor and Bob, constitute Ginetta. Encouraged by their first sports car based on a Wolseley Hornet, and by friends asking for replicas, they went into production with the Ford-engined G2 in 1958. Typical of low-production British sports cars of the time, it consisted of an open fibreglass body mounted on a steel spaceframe chassis. About 100 were made.

Ginetta's big break was the little G4, unveiled in 1962. This was designed around the new Ford family of oversquare engines, in 73.2-, 81.8- and 91.5-cu in (1.2-, 1.3- and 1.5-litre) forms. It was designed as much for racing as the road, and was particularly successful on track, the modest power compensated by fine road-holding and low weight. But the Walkletts had

ambitions to conquer the U.S. market, and launched the more luxurious 286.8-cu in (4.7-litre) Ford V8-engined G10 in 1965. This was indeed luxurious compared to the G4: it even had wind-up windows. The G10 also made a promising competition debut, but component supply problems meant only six cars were finished before the type was dropped. It was followed by the similar-looking G11, this time with MGB 109.8-cu in (1.8-litre) powertrain: again parts supply held it up, and only 12 G11s were made. The G12 of 1966 was very different, claimed to be the first British mid-engined car and designed exclusively for racing, though some were used on the road.

Meanwhile, the Walklett brothers were looking around for a successor to the G4. When it arrived in 1967, however, the G15 was quite different. It was a pure road car, a

closed two-seater powered by the smooth, tuneable 53.4-cu in (875-cc) Hillman Imp engine. This turned out to be Ginetta's most successful car so far: it was cheap to insure, could top 100mph (160 km/h) and achieved 50mpg (17.7km/litre). The G15's success prompted Ginetta to abandon the attractive mid-engined G20 and delayed the more conventional G21, a pretty 2+2 coupé powered by a 77.8-cu in (1.7-litre) Hillman engine until 1973.

Ten years later, the G25 was unveiled as the spiritual successor to the G15, this time mid-engined, with Ford Fiesta components.

But it was abandoned when Toyota's MR2 appeared, underlining the fact that a Ginetta would need to offer at least the same level of performance. Instead, the G32 was developed, mid-engined again, but with the 105-bhp (78.3-kW) 97.6-cu in (1.6-litre) engine from the Ford XR3.

By 2002 Ginetta was offering a range of three cars, though it had gone back to its front-engined origins. The G20 was described as a modern G4, with a choice of Ford Pinto or Zetec engines and a glassfibre body and steel spaceframe, while the G27 was an updated G4 with the same engine options. Finally, the G33 was launched in 1990 as an upmarket car, slightly longer and wider than the G20/27 with Ford Zetec 2-litre or Rover V8 engines available. Mark Walklett (son of Trevor) was involved in the design.

LEFT
Ginetta G33.

OPPOSITE
TOP RIGHT
Ginetta 875-cc G15.

BELOW RIGHT
Ginetta 1600i G32 Ford.

BELOW LEFT
Ginetta G26, with a G31 in the background.

GN (Great Britain 1910-1925)

The name derives from the initials of its two founders, H.R. Godfrey and Captain Archibald Frazer-Nash, and the company built cyclecars. These were popular from around 1910 to the early 1920s, very lightweight and simple cars owing much to motorcycle technology. The idea was to offer car stability and protection at the same price as a motorcycle and sidecar.

The GN was typical, launched in 1910 with a choice of JAP or Peugeot air-cooled engines, though the company later made its own engine, using some Peugeot parts. Cyclecars usually used belt or chain transmission, and the GN was no exception.

After World War I, fresh owners moved GN to a new factory in Wandsworth, London, took on more staff and increased production, while GNs were also made under licence by Salmson in France.

The future had been looking bright but

was beginning to dim. Cheap, light cars like the Austin Seven were undermining the cyclecar market, offering better weather protection, more substantial mechanics and often four seats, for little more money. Sales slumped, and GN went into receivership. H.R. Godfrey set up a GN servicing company, while Frazer-Nash went on to make the cars that bore his name. GN Motors Ltd. was officially closed in 1923.

GRAHAM-PAIGE (U.S.A. 1927-1940)

The Graham brothers, Robert, Joseph and Ray, were entrepreneurs in the truest sense of the word. In varied careers, they dabbled in real estate, farm tractors, bottle making, trucks … and cars. In 1927 the Grahams found themselves cash-rich after selling their truck body business to Dodge, and an opportunity to spend it arose when the Paige car company came up for sale.

Paige had been around since 1908, and

had broken speed records at Daytona. But now it needed help, and the Graham brothers immediately set about reorganizing the company and putting their considerable skills as salesmen to work. They were astonishingly successful, and in 1928, the first full year of the new Graham-Paige regime, the company set a sales record. In the following year, over 80,000 cars were built, and the brothers were obliged to buy up several more factories to keep up with demand.

It could not last, for the Depression was far from kind to upmarket six-cylinder cars like the Graham-Paige, though the company did manage to survive the early 1930s, while many small manufacturers disappeared from view. Despite weathering this economic onslaught, however, the renamed Graham company seemed unable to take advantage of its new prosperity. The low sleek Blue Streak of 1932 was much admired, but sales did not reflect the fact, even after a supercharged model was added two years later. Selling a consignment of tooling for an obsolete model to Nissan of Japan was the only thing that saved Graham from collapse.

Other Grahams of the late 1930s and early 1940s, such as the 1938 Sharknose and 1940 Hollywood failed to save the company, and it stopped making cars during World War II. After the war, its car-making arm was taken over by Kaiser-Frazer, the Graham brothers went into real estate, and their successors now own Madison Square Gardens.

TOP LEFT
A distinctive GN 1914 tourer.

CENTRE LEFT
A 1921 French-built GN.

BELOW LEFT
Reproductions of early 1920s racers.

BELOW
1939 Graham-Paige chassis with Amherst Villers body.

GREGOIRE (France 1942-1970)
Designer Jean Albert Grégoire made sporadic but determined efforts to get his cars into production, starting with the aluminium AFG, designed during World War II. He was a very experienced engineer, having worked on front-wheel-drive cars for Tracta and Amilcar. But his latest was turned down by Peugeot, Simca, Citroën and Renault after the war. Panhard took it up, however, and built it as the Dyna, and some of these were even built under licence in England.

In the early 1950s Grégoire designed a four-cylinder car, which reached production as a joint venture with Hotchkiss, but only survived for a little while after that company collapsed. Undeterred, Grégoire produced a supercharged car actually designed by Henri Chapron, and made it in limited numbers until 1962. Grégoire's final design was an electric car, which reached prototype form in 1970 but never made it to production.

HAMPTON (Great Britain 1912-1931)
Produced in Birmingham and subsequently Stroud, Hampton cars used proprietary engines but the company's own gearboxes, reflecting its interest in transmission development. Among other things, it did development work on the Cowburn gearbox, which used coned rollers and springs instead of gears.

Before World War I, various cars were made, including an 8-hp (5.97-kW) cyclecar, a twin-cylinder two-stroke light car and conventional four-cylinder 12/16. Dorman engines were used for the post-war 91.5-cu in (1.5-litre) 10/16 and 109.8-cu in (1.8-litre) versions, with Meadows units of 73.2 and 109.8 cu in (1.2 and 1.8 litres) following in 1923. At around this time, Hampton became successful in hill climbs and motor racing, one lapping Brooklands at 90mph (145km/h). Financial problems meant reorganization in the mid-1920s, but the company emerged with the 103.7-cu in (1.7-litre) six-cylinder 15/45 in 1927, an 8-hp (5.96-kW) car was added the following year and the 183.1-cu in (3-litre) 20-hp (14.91-kW) car, Hampton's biggest yet, in 1929. But the problem of shaky finances arose yet again, and the company closed in 1931, when its cars included a 1.2-litre 12-hp (8.95-kW) and 134.25-cu in (2.2-litre) Rohr-powered straight-eight.

TOP LEFT
Grégoire's first design, sold by Panhard as the Panhard Dyna, c.1946.

CENTRE LEFT
The Socéma-Grégoire turbine car of 1954.

LEFT
The Grégoire 2.2-litre convertible of 1959, one of only ten ever made.

HEALEY (Great Britain 1946-1954)

A well-known British name, Healey actually only survived eight years as an independent manufacturer, after which the success of its Austin-powered Healey 100 led to the whole operation being taken over by Austin and renamed Austin-Healey.

Donald Healey worked for both Triumph and Riley before launching his own car in 1946. It was Riley-powered, using a 146.5-cu in (2.4-litre) four-cylinder engine, available as a chassis or with two-door saloon bodywork by Elliot or as a Westland convertible. It was also claimed to be the fastest production car in the world, and was timed at almost 112mph (180 km/h). The first Healey proved successful in competition as well, underlining its designer's motor sport background.

It was joined by the open-top Sportsmobile in 1948, and in 1950 new

Tickford saloon and Abbott drophead bodywork replaced the Elliot and Westland. The Silverstone, a lightweight two-seater that was more like a road-legal racer, joined the range that same year, and this too was Riley-powered. Bigger engines, the 183.1-cu in (3-litre) Alvis and 231.9-cu in (3.8-litre) Nash, soon became available, and the rebodied Nash-Healey was built up to 1954, the last pure Healey. By then, Austin had appeared on the scene. Healey's new Austin-powered 100 two-seater attracted a flood of orders that the little company could not hope to meet. So Austin took over, Austin-Healey was born, and Healey's days as an independent manufacturer were over.

TOP
1949 Healey Sportsmobile.

ABOVE
Nash Healey of 1952.

TOP LEFT
A distinctive Healey Tickford.

LEFT
1950 Healey Silverstone.

RIGHT
1931 prototype Hillman Minx.

HILLMAN (Great Britain 1907-1978)

Hillman Cars began in 1907, though the company is better known as a post-war member of the Rootes Group, which was a sort of mini-General Motors in which Hillman was the mainstream Chevrolet equivalent.

William Hillman's first car was a 25-hp (18.6-kW) four-cylinder machine, built specifically for the Tourist Trophy race. But it was in smaller family cars that Hillman specialized, introducing a 82.8-cu in (1.4-litre) 9-hp (6.71-kW) model in 1912 and a 10-hp (7.46-kW) car just after World War I. There were bigger Hillmans (up to a 591.9-cu in/9.7-litre six) but these were only made in small numbers. In fact, between 1926 and 1928 the company only made one model, the modest side-valve Fourteen. Safety was hardly a major issue then, but Hillman offered a 'Safety' derivative of the Fourteen, complete with toughened glass and servo-assisted brakes.

Hillman lost its independence to the Rootes Group in 1932: the Rootes brothers were successful car dealers who were building up a manufacturing empire. As well as Hillman, the Humber, Singer and Sunbeam companies all came under its umbrella, and each marque had its own purpose. Hillman was the mass-market brand, Singer was allowed a little more

(to celebrate its victory in the London-Sydney Marathon) and much hotter Hunter GLS of the 1970s.

There was, of course, a yawning gap between Imp and Hunter, filled in 1969 by the all-new Avenger. Chrysler had taken a controlling influence in the Rootes Group in 1967, and its cost-cutting measures manifested themselves in the Avenger, a simple, cheap-to-produce car aimed directly at Ford. It was an attractive car but with lacklustre 76.1-cu in (1.25-litre) or 91.4-cu in (1.5-litre) overhead-valve engines, and an estate and a 97.5-cu in (1.6-litre) unit were added later on. The Avenger was a success, but not enough to stem Chrysler U.K.'s financial problems. The American parent had money problems too, and only support from the British government in 1975 kept its U.K. operation alive. Meanwhile, the Hillman name gradually faded out in the mid-1970s to be replaced by Chrysler, and the remnants were bought by Peugeot-Citroën in 1979.

prestige, Sunbeam was for sporting types and Humber was the luxury brand.

Hillman's first new car under the new regime was the highly successful Minx, a 10-hp 72.3-cu in (1.2-litre) affair which sprouted a sports Aero version in 1933 and gained a synchromesh gearbox in 1935. After World War II the Minx continued, now with unitary construction, and was gradually updated through the 1950s with new bodywork (including the attractive Californian, a pillarless two-door coupé

with bodywork by Thrupp and Maberley) and an overhead-valve 84.8-cu in (1.4-litre) engine giving 43bhp (32.1kW). Another new Minx arrived in 1956, now with 51bhp (38kW) and offered semi-automatic 'Manumatic' transmission from the following year, with the fully-automatic 'Easidrive' from 1960. By 1962 it was up to 97.15 cu in (1.6 litres), alongside the bigger bodied Super Minx.

But what Hillman lacked was a small car to compete with the Mini, and it finally arrived in 1963 as the rear-engined Imp. Although clever and innovative in many ways (its all-alloy 53.4-cu in/875-cc engine

was derived from a racing Coventry Climax unit, the Imp was dogged by teething troubles, and later in life by poor quality. Nevertheless, it was advanced, with all-independent suspension, and was more comfortable than the rather basic Mini. It hung on in production until 1976.

In 1965, the new Hunter replaced the Super Minx, with a five-bearing 105.3-cu in (1.72-litre) engine, which was still developed from the original 1390-cc unit. This did well for Hillman, later replacing the Minx, and developing a capacious Estate version, the warmed-up Hunter GT

FAR LEFT (top to bottom)
1927 14-hp Hillman.
Hillmans bound for Australia in 1951.
1955 Hillman Minx Mk VIII.

TOP
M. Louis Coatelen and a 1907 Hillman.

ABOVE LEFT
1963 Hillman Imp.

ABOVE RIGHT
1973 Hillman Avenger GLS.

HISPANO-SUIZA (Spain 1904-1944)

Hispano-Suiza, despite being the most
famous Spanish car of all time, was really
an international effort, a combination of
Spanish finance, Swiss engineering and
Spanish/French manufacturing. Geneva-
born engineer Marc Birkigt had already
built a small 4.5-hp (3.36-kW) car in
Barcelona when he met Spanish financier
Damien Mateu, and the two joined forces to
form Hispano-Suiza.

One of the company's most famous
cars was the Alfonso, developed from a
1910 racer that won the Coupe de l'Auto
that year. Named in honour of King
Alfonso XIII of Spain, who was to be a
faithful aficionado of the marque, this was
a remarkably light car at 1,680lb (762kg).

It made the most of its 64-bhp (47.7-kW)
219.7-cu in (3.6-litre) engine, and the
Alfonso turned out to be one of Hispano-
Suiza's landmark cars. It was built in
Barcelona, but the Spanish factory was
beginning to concentrate on trucks and less
exotic cars, while a new French plant took
over the more prestigious projects. One of
these was the H6 and 6B of 1919, powered
by an overhead-camshaft alloy six-cylinder
engine, boasting 396.7 cu in (6.5 litres) and
130bhp (96.7kW). Torquey and flexible, it
could accelerate smoothly from 10 to
86mph (16 to 138km/h), all in top gear. The
H6 also won the Boulogne road race twice,
and was sixth in the 1924 Targa Florio.
Another of Hispano's landmark cars, it was
produced right up to 1934.

Meanwhile, the French factory had
unveiled the Type 68 in 1931, though a less
appropriate car for the depths of the
Depression would be hard to imagine. A
huge luxury saloon, it sported a 573.6- or
689.6-cu in (9.4- or 11.3-litre) V12 and,
unlike the Bugatti Royale, actually found
many customers. It was built up to 1938,
when Marc Birkigt decided to stop making
cars to concentrate on armaments and aero
engines. Hispano's factory in Paris did not
open again after World War II.

HOLDEN (Australia 1948 to date)

Holden, maker of the quintessential
Australian car, started out as a coach
builder and did not build a complete car
until 1948. But for decades it was the best-
selling manufacturer 'down under', losing
its top spot to Ford Australia only in the
early 1980s. However, it remains a close
and profitable second.

Holden & Frost of Adelaide originally
made bodywork for horse-drawn carriages,
producing the body for its first car in 1914
and doing the same for a series of imported
Morris chassis from 1920, when its name
was changed to Holden Motor Body
Builders Ltd. Taken over by General
Motors in 1931, the following decade saw
Holden rebody British and American GM
cars for the Australian market, though it
also worked on chassis from other U.S.
manufacturers such as Willys, Essex and
Chrysler. A fastback coupé was introduced
in 1938, years before the style became
popular in North America. Also known as
the Sloper, it was built on a variety of
different chassis.

A turning point for Holden came just
after World War II, when its managing
director, Sir Lawrence Hartnett, obtained
backing from the Australian government to

ABOVE FAR LEFT
King Alfonso and his 1908 model.

ABOVE CENTRE
*The 1913 'Alfonso', named after the king
of Spain.*

ABOVE RIGHT
1931 Type 68 with a V12 engine.

LEFT
Fernandes et Darvin-bodied K6.

build a complete car designed for Australian conditions. Hartnett realized that British cars were really too small for Australia and American cars too big. As it happened, General Motors rejected his advanced design and Sir Lawrence resigned in disgust. But his concept lived on in the FX, a four-door sedan launched in 1948. It

was a hit, and was joined by a utility three years later. The latter, the 'Ute', was a favourite of Australian farmers, and these closed-cab pick-ups became part of the Australian landscape.

So popular were the FX and the FJ215 that succeeded it, that by the mid-1950s Holden was building nearly half the private cars sold in Australia. Its large conventional saloons continued to be best-sellers for many years, with larger V8s such as the HK Belmont and Kingswood following on from

the smaller sixes. The Chevrolet-engined Monaro coupé gave Holden a sporting car, while the Gemini range of the 1970s was based on the Opel Kadett. Being part of GM also gave Holden access to Isuzu technology.

In 1979 the Commodore was launched, again owing something to the European GM divisions. In fact, Holden was becoming part of the GM global production web, exporting Opel engines to Sweden, whose emissions regulations were similar to those of Australia, and complete cars to countries, such as New Zealand, where

TOP LEFT
A 1934 Holden coupé, just before the fastback style was introduced.

TOP
1960 EH Holden.

LEFT
1970s Holden Torana GTR-X.

FAR LEFT (top to bottom)
1953 FJ utility.
1970s Statesman.
1970s Kingswood.

other GM divisions were not strong. The company was not restricted to GM products, however, the Holden Astra being an Australian-assembled Nissan Cherry.

Just as the Commodore had been Holden's best-seller in the 1980s, so the VS range was for the 1990s, based on the old Opel Senator. It seemed that the upper-

range European cars, rather than full-sized U.S. vehicles, were best suited to the Australian market. However, the engines were all-American: 231.9-cu in (3.8-litre) V6, 305.1-cu in (5-litre) V8 and 347.8-cu in (5.7-litre) V8. Though named as different models, the Calais, Berlina, Caprice and Acclaim differed in engine and trim levels only. Thus equipped, Holden was able to hold its close second place behind Ford Australia, and was said to be GM's favourite division in 2002, simply because it was making a profit. That same year, the four-wheel-drive SSX concept car was unveiled, V8-powered like the VS range but with a two-piece hatchback and four-wheel-drive. A range of high-performance 4x4 Holdens are predicted for 2004.

OPPOSITE
FAR LEFT TOP: 1980s VC Commodore.

FAR LEFT CENTRE: 1980s VL Calais.

FAR LEFT BOTTOM: 1990s Caprice.

ABOVE RIGHT: 1990s Aclaim.

BELOW RIGHT: 1990s Berlina.

THIS PAGE, TOP LEFT:
1990s Calais.

CENTRE LEFT:
2000 Barina SX3i.

CENTRE RIGHT: HRT 427.

BELOW FAR LEFT:
2000s Cruze.

BELOW CENTRE RIGHT:
2003 Rodeo with crew cab.

TOP:
Holden based on Vauxhall/Opel Vectra.

ABOVE:
2002 Statesman.

HONDA (Japan 1962 to date)

Honda, the world's largest motorcycle manufacturer, did not make its first car until 1963, and even that owed much to two-wheel technology. But by the 1990s, the company was well established as one of the most innovative car manufacturers in the world.

Soichiro Honda's story has parallels with that of Henry Ford. He came from a poor family (one of nine children, of whom only four survived), but as a gifted engineer with a level-headed business sense was able to build up a successful company. After helping his blacksmith father, Honda was apprenticed to a car repair shop, though he did not get the chance to drive cars until an earthquake hit Tokyo in 1923, and the young apprentice was kept busy ferrying people and supplies around the devastated city. He started his own repair shop, where he dallied with car racing for a while,

LEFT
1978 example of a Honda Civic.

BELOW
1965 L700 Estate.

BOTTOM LEFT
1979 Accord sedan.

though a serious accident put paid to that in 1935. Honda wisely gave up racing and concentrated on making piston rings, demonstrating his genius for production engineering.

After World War II Japan was desperately short of private transport, but very few people could afford a car. Honda hit on the idea of fitting ex-military two-

stroke engines to bicycles as cheap, basic transport. The first motorcycle, the Dream, followed in 1949 and the first four-stroke engine (Honda was always a four-stroke devotee) came soon after that. The motorcycle business boomed, and Honda the company prospered with it. But Honda the man had not forgotten cars, and launched a 21.97-cu in (360-cc) mini-van and 30.51-cu in (500-cc) chain-driven sports car in 1963. The sports car was quite unlike anything else, powered by a high-revving four-cylinder engine with four carburettors. This S500 was replaced by the shaft-driven S600 in 1964, and later by the

S800. But these were enthusiasts' cars, and more profits came from the little N360, a twin-cylinder micro-car whose name indicated its engine capacity. The range grew rapidly, with 36.61- and 42.72-cu in (600- and 700-cc) family cars soon following. Honda had already made a success of Formula One racing by this time, the V12 winning the Mexican Grand Prix in 1965.

Meanwhile, Honda road cars were becoming bigger and more conventional, with the 73.2-cu in (1.2-litre) Civic a particular success. The Civic was the first Honda to use CVCC (compound vortex

controlled combustion), a new Honda-designed method of reducing emissions, which in 1973 met the new U.S. standards two years ahead of schedule. Soichiro Honda retired soon afterwards (he was now 67), but continued to guide the company under the title of 'supreme advisor' for many years.

Honda moved out of the small car market in the mid-1970s with the Accord, a 97.6-cu in (1.6-litre) four-door saloon: in various forms this has been part of Honda's line-up ever since. A two-door coupé version, the Prelude, followed in 1978 and the 1980s saw the striking 122-cu in (2-litre) Accord Aerodeck and CRX sports coupé, the latter with 91.5- and 97.6-cu in (1.5- and 1.6-litre) engines. The 1980s also saw an agreement with Austin-Rover, the British manufacturer that had survived out of several incarnations of the same company. At the time, Great Britain had a 'gentleman's agreement' with Japan,

limiting imports of Japanese cars to 10 per cent of the market. The contract with Austin-Rover allowed Honda to sell more cars in Britain by having them assembled there, while the British got a modern small saloon to build. It was the Ballade, assembled and sold in Britain as the Triumph Acclaim and later in much updated form as the Rover 213/216. Other Honda/Rover projects followed, with the Concerto (Rover 214/216), the bigger

Accord/Rover 600-series and executive-class Honda Legend/Rover 800.

In North America, Honda sought to increase sales by launching the upmarket Acura brand, which sold the Integra hatchback and Legend V6. The latter came in both four-door saloon and two-door coupé form. For home consumption, the Civic Shuttle was a high-roofed small people-carrier based on the 1980s Civic, while the Accord had grown into a 134.25-

P
ised Accord of 1982.

P RIGHT
injection Accord.

iHT
8 Accord.

BALLADE

FAR LEFT
1985 Ballade.

LEFT
1986 Integra.

BELOW LEFT
1986 Honda CRX.

BOTTOM LEFT
1986 Prelude 2.0.

cu in (2.2-litre) fuel-injected saloon. But the NSX of 1989 was a real departure. This was a true supercar to challenge Porsche and Ferrari, with Honda pulling out all the stops to produce a high-tech sports car that bristled with advanced features: the first production car with an aluminium chassis; a 274-bhp (204.3-kW) V6 engine featuring Honda's V-TEC variable valve timing; near-perfect weight distribution; and being a Honda, it was well made and very easy to drive. For the first time, here was a supercar one could truly take shopping!

The NSX was such a success that it was still in production in 2002, now with a 195.3-cu in (3.2-litre) V6 and 280bhp (208.8kW). By then, the Rover link had gone, since the British manufacturer had been bought by BMW, but Honda now had a factory in Swindon, plus a huge range of cars, from the little Jazz, the latest Civic and Accord, and the clever petrol/electric Insight and CR-V people-carrier.

ABOVE
1990 Legend saloon.

LEFT
Four-wheel-drive Civic 1.6 Shuttle.

CENTRE FAR LEFT
Legend V6 saloon.

CENTRE LEFT
1990 Legend coupé.

BELOW LEFT
NSX sports car.

BELOW
1995 Accord EX sedan.

TOP
1997 CRX.

ABOVE
1997 Civic coupé.

LEFT
1997 Shuttle.

ABOVE RIGHT
1997 Civic five-door VTi.

RIGHT
2003 CR-V.

TOP LEFT
2000 Acura NSX.

CENTRE LEFT
2003 Accord coupé.

LEFT
2003 Civic Si.

TOP
2003 Civic Hybrid.

ABOVE
2002 Passport.

199

HORCH (Germany 1898-1940)

Horch of Germany made its name with large, luxurious cars, though it started in 1900 with a small 4/5-hp (2.98/3.73-kW) voiturette with seating for two. August Horch had worked for Benz as an engineering manager at Mannheim, but left to set up his own company in 1899. Ten of those little voiturettes were made, but Horch himself had ambitions to build bigger cars, moving to a bigger factory in 1904. Production and the workforce increased, and Horch cars were successful in competition, one winning the Herkomer Trophy in 1906. However, the straight-eight engine introduced that year was unsuccessful and disagreements over this and other issues led to Horch leaving the company in 1909. He went on to found Audi.

Horch the company prospered, the range expanding to include engines from 96.91 to 390.25 cu in (1588 to 6395cc), the six-cylinder 31/60 PS of 1910 being typical. In 1920, the firm was taken over by

Argus Motoren of Berlin. Arnold Zoller, then Paul Daimler, took charge, which led to some design improvements. Despite its

luxurious range, Horch managed to survive the Depression, in part because its prices were relatively low, but in 1931 it was sold again, this time to Auto-Union, which already owned DKW, Wanderer and Audi. Auto-Union is best remembered for its fearsome Porsche-designed Grand Prix cars, and these now came out of the Horch works, though the factory still made large luxury cars, such as the 853 straight-eight, a

V8 range (which lasted up to 1939) and even a few V12s.

During World War II, Horch car production was limited to a few four-wheel-drive command cars, powered by Ford engines. The name was resurrected in 1956 for a six-cylinder car built at Zwickau, but Auto-Union objected, so it was swiftly renamed.

ABOVE LEFT
1900 4/5-hp Horch voiturette.

BELOW LEFT
1910 31/60 PS six.

BELOW
1931 Type 670 six-litre cabriolet.

OPPOSITE
Honda VTi Sports.

HOTCHKISS (France 1903-1954)

Hotchkiss, a famous French manufacturer, was founded by an American, and for a while was owned by the British. Benjamin Hotchkiss was a U.S. munitions manufacturer who had done well out of the Civil War in the 1860s, and in the 1870s moved to Paris and set up a new company in the same business. During a fall in demand for munitions, the Hotchkiss company began to make parts for car manufacturers. The next step was to build its own, which it did in 1903.

It was designed by ex-Mors man, George Terrasse, and in fact was similar to the equivalent Mors but with a rounded radiator and hood that gave a distinctive look to the 17CV Hotchkiss. The company was soon specializing in large, luxury cars, incorporating the famous Hotchkiss Drive system, which combined shaft-drive with a live rear axle.

But a change of direction came in 1911 when the firm bought out its British board of directors (who had bought the concern 20 years before) and decided to build smaller middle-class cars.

During World War I the company had naturally been given over to munitions

OPPOSITE
ABOVE: *Hotchkiss sedan.*

BELOW LEFT: *A 1910 model with
distinctive hood.*

BELOW CENTRE: *1926 boat-tailed AM2.*

BELOW RIGHT: *An AM80S of 1932.*

BELOW
Hotchkiss Grégoire.

work, but as peace resumed it went straight back to cars, rejecting a prototype luxury car named the AK, and instead focusing on the mid-size AM. This was a success, on sale until 1928 when it was replaced by the 183.1-cu in (3-litre) AM80 and 213.6-cu in (3.5-litre) AM80S sports car. The latter won several races and rallies (including the Monte Carlo) and was to be part of the Hotchkiss line-up right into the 1950s. But this underlined Hotchkiss's greatest failing. It was a rather conservative company, preferring to stick with old, proven designs like the 3.5-litre rather than risk something new. It also remained wedded to right-hand-drive, long after every other French manufacturer had switched to the more sensible (for France) left-hand-drive. In any case, the company had already been weakened when its munitions business was nationalized by the French government in 1936. By 1954, sales had slowed to a trickle, and after merging with Peugeot and Delahaye, Hotchkiss car production was shut down altogether.

HRG (Great Britain 1936-1956)

A classic British sports car in the Morgan mould, HRG was set up by three enthusiasts named Halford, Robins and Godfrey. The first two were racing drivers, and H.R. 'Dan' Godfrey had been one half of the original GN partnership. Could this be a more English set-up?

Not surprisingly, the car that rolled out of their Surrey workshop in 1935 was an enthusiast's machine, with little consideration for comfort, weather protection or convenience. On the other hand, its 91.5-cu in (1.5-litre) Meadows engine was a well-proven and tuneable unit, and the car itself was very light, with responsive handling and keen acceleration. The brakes may have been cable-operated and a little crude, but they were effective enough for such a light car, and they could even be adjusted on the move!

For keen drivers, an HRG was 'just the ticket' (in the phraseology of the time), road-legal, but competitive in motor sport into the bargain. In the late 1930s, the Meadows engine was replaced by a Singer of 61 cu in (1 litre) or 1.5 litres, again of modest standard power but with great tuning potential, which HRG executed itself. So powered, HRGs won their class at Le Mans and in the Alpine and RAC Rallies, as well as in countless local events all over Britain.

Production resumed after the war, much as it had left off, with Singer still keen to supply engines. But HRG was not inclined to follow the Morgan example and ignore modern styling. The Aerodynamic model of 1947 (the prototype had been built in 1940) was the first British sports car with full-width styling, but in the event proved little faster than the standard car. HRG drivers were more concerned with sheer speed than new-fangled styling and the Aerodynamic was soon dropped. Undeterred, the company unveiled a more advanced car in 1955 with tubular spaceframe, independent suspension and disc brakes. But it was the swansong. Singer had been taken over by the Rootes Group, which discontinued its engine and prevented any more collaboration with HRG. There was even talk of Singer building the new car. HRG survived, but only by tuning and general light engineering. A spaceframe prototype sports car was shown in 1965, but it came to nothing, and HRG made no more cars.

BELOW
1939 HRG.

BOTTOM
1940 HRG Aerodynamic prototype.

BELOW RIGHT
1925 Hudson Phaeton

BOTTOM RIGHT
1929 Hudson Superb sedan.

HUDSON (U.S.A. 1909-1957)

Hudson lost its independence in 1954, merging with Nash to form American Motors, and its name disappeared altogether within a few years. Yet in the 1920s and '30s it was one of the U.S.A.'s major manufacturers, placed third in sales behind Chevrolet and Ford. The Hudson Motor Car Company was not one of the pioneers of motoring, having being formed in 1909 by Joseph L. Hudson – who owned a large Detroit department store – and a group of

sole model, though it came in a wide variety of body styles, including limousines and cabriolets.

But successful as it was, the Super Six was still too expensive to challenge Ford or Chevrolet, so in 1919 Hudson launched the Essex marque. This was aimed at the cheaper end of the market, and came first with a 177-cu in (2.9-litre) four-cylinder, later a 158.7-cu in (2.6-litre) six-cylinder engine. This too sold well, and it was in the late 1920s peak that Essex/Hudson

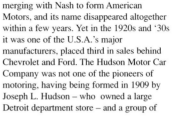

associates. Their first car was an instant hit, despite its decidedly ordinary specification, with a 152.6-cu in (2.5-litre) four-cylinder engine and orthodox layout. Joseph Hudson died in 1912, but the company that bore his name went from strength to strength, introducing its first six-cylinder car that same year, the Model 6-54.

In fact, sixes would become something of a Hudson trademark. The 6-54 came in both open and closed body styles and was such a success that by 1914 Hudson was claiming to be the world's largest manufacturer of six-cylinder cars. It dropped the fours in 1916, and concentrated on developing the 286.8-cu in (4.7-litre) Super Six, which for a while was the company's

combined captured third place in the sales charts. Hudson had clearly learned that it could not live by six cylinders alone. The year 1930 saw the introduction of the

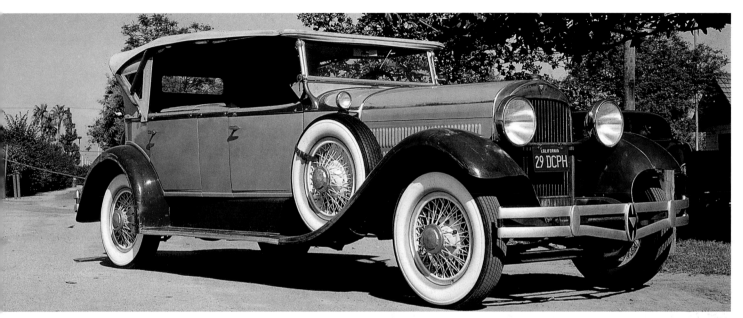

straight-eight, producing 95bhp (70.8kW), and by the time production ended in 1953 the Hudson eight was producing 128bhp (95.4kW). But the 1930s saw Hudson past its peak. The Essex line was killed off in 1932 and despite some innovations, like the 'Electric Hand' electric gear change and the 'safety engineered chassis' (Bendix hydraulic brakes with mechanical back-up) sales began to slide, and Hudson lost money in 1939 and '40.

The new post-war line did not make its debut until 1948, with the 'Step-Down Design' in which passengers stepped over the body sills and down onto a low floor. The line-up ranged from the 231.9-cu in (3.8-litre) six-cylinder Pacemaker to the

Here they measure real motor-car value right before your eyes

The results shown on these tough public proving grounds can help you choose your family car!

Stock-car events are held coast to coast. Two years ago, Hudson scored 47 wins in 55 events; became U.S. Champion for 1952

Each event equals 50,000 miles of ordinary driving. Last year, Hudson had 46 wins in 66 starts; became U.S. Champion for 1953

With a total of 119 wins in 3½ years, Hudson continues its victory stride! Hornets took the first five places at Langhorne in May, and they've already captured 13 firsts in 20 starts in 1954

New Hornet Special...New Low Price!

The instant power that gets Hudson Hornets out of tight spots and ahead on the track can whisk you out of danger on a crowded road; lets you drive relaxed and confident.

The low center of gravity that makes the Hornets steadier on tight track turns can save you on an unexpected highway curve. And that road-hugging feature also takes all effort out of driving, even on day-long trips.

The durability and stamina that bring Hudsons in first show this is a car that needs little mechanical attention—that saves you inconvenience and money.

Best yet, you can enjoy this great and lasting performance at a new low price—in the new Hornet Special—full Hornet power, full Hornet size! Power steering, power brakes optional. See your Hudson dealer.

HUDSON
HORNETS · WASPS · JETS
Products of
AMERICAN MOTORS

256.3-cu in (4.2-litre) Commodore eight, with the compact 201.4-cu in (3.3-litre) Jet joining the range in 1953. Despite all this effort, sales never recovered and Hudson completed that Nash merger the following year.

ABOVE
1937 Hudson Terraplane coupé.

LEFT
1950 Hudson Hornet.

BELOW LEFT
1949 Hudson Superb.

FAR LEFT
Advertisement for Hudson Hornet.

RIGHT
Hudson Hornet.

HUMBER (Great Britain 1899-1976)
One of the first companies in Britain to
build a car, Humber began by making
bicycles in 1867. It was involved in
producing the Pennington three-wheeler,
but unveiled its own 3.5-hp (2.61-kW)
single-cylinder car in 1899. The company
was unafraid of innovation, experimented
with front-wheel-drive, and was selling a
shaft-driven car, the De Dion-engined 4.5-
hp (3.36-kW), as early as 1901.

Humber also built motorized tricycles
up to 1905, as well as a voiturette, but by
that time was well established as a maker of
full-sized cars: 12- and 20-hp (8.95- and
14.91-kW) four-cylinder models were on
offer by 1903, along with a very unusual
three-cylinder device with mechanically
operated inlet valves (most pioneer engines
opened the inlet valve by intake suction).
Finally, there was the Humberette, a little
36.61-cu in (600-cc) car with shaft-drive
and two-speed gearbox. The name was
reintroduced in 1912 in the Humberette
cyclecar, now with an air-cooled 60.9-cu in
(998-cc) engine, but after World War I the
company concentrated on conventional
family cars.

Humber was doing well by the mid-
1920s, well enough to take over truck
maker Commer in 1926 and Hillman two
years later. These dovetailed nicely with
the bigger six-cylinder Humbers,
introduced in 1930 as the 128.15-cu in (2.1-
litre) 16/50 and 183.1-cu in (3-litre) Snipe.
But the company had overreached itself,
and was taken over in turn by the Rootes
Group in 1932. Although a smaller Humber
12 was introduced soon after, Humber's
forte was the conservative side-valve
saloons and limousines, though by the late
1930s these were being kept up to date
with independent front suspension and
hydraulic brakes.

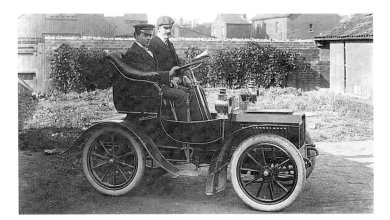

When peace returned at the end of
World War II, there was a new four-
cylinder Humber, the Hawk with a 115.9-cu
in (1.9-litre) engine, still with side valves,

but overhead valves were finally fitted across the range by 1953. A substantially new unitary-construction Hawk was launched in 1957 with all-new styling: the Hawk remained with the 140.4-cu in (2.3-litre) four-cylinder engine, while the Super Snipe, with the same bodyshell, used a 158.7-cu in (2.6-litre) but later a 3-litre six. Both came as saloon, estate or limousine.

During the 1960s Humbers were little more than badge-engineered versions of the equivalent Hillman, with the name used as the luxury brand of the Rootes Group. So the Sceptre of 1963 was a Hillman Super Minx with superior trim and an 85-bhp (63.4-kW) 1.6-litre engine. Its final incarnation was the Hunter-based 103.7-cu in (1.7-litre) Sceptre, which hung on up to 1976. By then, Chrysler was in charge, and its badge replaced all the old Rootes marques.

ABOVE RIGHT
1981 Hyundai Pony 1400 GLS.

CENTRE RIGHT
1982 Hyundai Pony 1200T.

RIGHT
1992 five-door Hyundai Sonnet.

HYUNDAI (South Korea 1973 to date)
One of South Korea's leading car manufacturers, Hyundai actually had strong links with Britain in its early days. Although it was the country's largest industrial enterprise, well established in shipping and civil engineering, Hyundai began by assembling British Ford cars and trucks in 1968. Five years on, when the Koreans decided to design and build their own car, it was with British financial backing. The man brought in to oversee this new regime was George Turnbull, fresh out of British Leyland. And Turnbull's ex-employer also supplied most of the bodyshell dies for the new Pony, which was finally unveiled in November 1974 (in London, where else).

In fact, the Pony was an international effort. Its modern five-door body was styled by Giugiaro and engineered by Ital Design, both of Italy, with power supplied by a Japanese Mitsubishi engine of 75.5 cu in (1238cc). Hardly a revolutionary design, as it stuck to rear-wheel-drive and proven mechanicals, the Pony was nonetheless well-built and reliable. It was generally well received, and over 50,000 were built in the first year, with nearly 400,000 after a decade. The Pony remained part of Hyundai's range for a long time, though with revised styling and the option of a 92-bhp (68.6-kW) 87.75-cu in (1438-cc) Mitsubishi unit from 1982.

In the following year the larger Stellar saloon was announced, still Mitsubishi-powered, and an all-new Pony in 1985 with a transverse engine and front-wheel-drive. The new Pony (known as the Excel in the U.S.) came in hatchback or saloon form. Hyundais were now being exported to North America in significant numbers by the mid-1980s, and for a while it was the fastest-growing export marque in the U.S.

By the mid-1990s, the company was building over a million cars per year. Meanwhile, the range continued to expand, with the large Sonata added in 1989, in 146.5-cu in (2.4-litre) four-cylinder or V6 forms, while other Hyundais received some much needed updating. The S Coupé was another new model, with sporting aspirations but such bland looks that it was never a success. Radically revamped in 1996 with Hyundai's own new 16-valve engines and Toyota Celica-like bodywork, it found its mark.

By the end of the century, Hyundai could boast a very wide range: the Amica mini-car, Accent hatchback (spiritual successor to the original Pony); mid-sized Elantra and upper-mid Sonata; compact and large people-carriers (Matrix and Trajet respectively); the still-respected Coupé; Santa Fe off-roader; and XG30 executive saloon. All offered lower prices than their European or Japanese competitors, but most were dynamically dull and suffered serious depreciation. However, determined to head upmarket, Hyundai launched the Equus executive in 2002, with a 274.6-cu in (4.5-litre) V8 and five-speed automatic transmission.

FAR LEFT (from top to bottom)
1997 Hyundai Accent 1.5 GLSi.
1997 Sonata V6.
1997 Lantra saloon.

ABOVE LEFT
The 1997 Coupé.

LEFT
In 1999 the Hyundai Coupé was given a facelift.

ABOVE LEFT
The 2000 Hyundai Atoz was designed with the city-dweller in mind.

ABOVE
2000 Lantra 2.0 CDX saloon.

LEFT
2003 Sonata model.

LEFT
2003 Tiburon.

BELOW LEFT
2003 Accent.

BELOW
2003 Elantra GLS.

OPPOSITE
2003 Santa Fe.

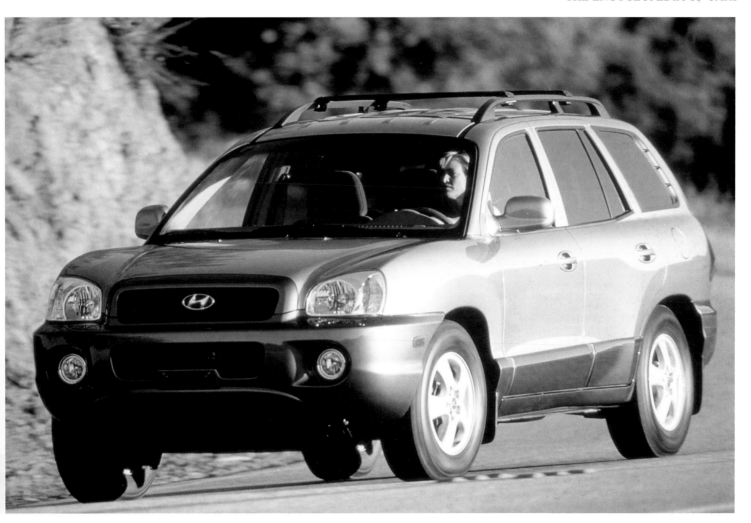

IMPERIAL (U.S.A. 1954-1975)
Imperial started out as an upmarket badge for the more expensive Chryslers in 1926, and would compete with General Motors' Cadillac and Ford's Lincoln. But after World War II Chrysler decided to give the marque stand-alone status: it would still use the Chrysler V8 engine and other mechanical parts, but the bodywork and interiors would be its own.

Although well-built and with quality interiors, styling was conservative until the Flite Sweep bodywork appeared. Disc brakes were added, as was the Le Baron name for a further upmarket touch (Le Baron had built coachwork for Imperials in the 1920s and 1930s.) As the 1950s wore on, Imperial features became ever more esoteric, and included intriguing extras such as automatically swivelling seats. But there were also genuine engineering advances: unitary construction was admittedly late in 1967, but Imperial was the first car in America to offer standard anti-lock brakes. Power still came from a Chrysler V8, of course, with up to 335bhp (249.8kW) available at one point.

But Imperial did not survive its parent company's huge problems of the 1970s. Chrysler made a loss of over $52 million in 1974, and a cost-cutting measure was to ditch the Imperial name. In any case, it was not a success by this time: for every Imperial that left the showroom, Ford was selling five Lincolns. However, Chrysler did revive the Le Baron name in the early 1980s on its compact front-wheel-drive cars.

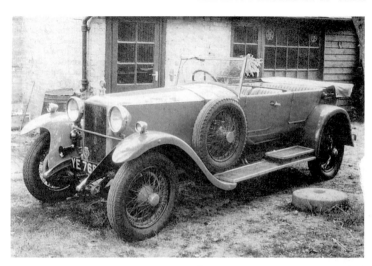

ABOVE
1927 3-litre Invicta.

LEFT
1972 Chrysler Imperial Le Baron.

BELOW FAR LEFT
Imperial Palace

BELOW LEFT
1931 CG Imperial Roadster. Luxury Chryslers from 1926 were designated 'Imperial'.

OPPOSITE
Hyundai LZ450.

INVICTA (Great Britain 1925-1936 and 1946-1950)
The first Invicta was a smooth, torquey machine that could be driven almost anywhere in top gear, thanks to its strong six-cylinder Meadows engine. The story goes that designer Noel Campbell Macklin was so impressed with the torque of an American Doble steam car that he determined to build a petrol car with similar characteristics.

Thus the 1925 Invicta was powered by a 158.7-cu in (2.6-litre) Meadows six, increased the following year to 183.1 cu in (3 litres) and then to 274.6 cu in (4.5 litres), all in search of the ultimate effortless machine. There were in fact two altogether different types of Invicta: the stately high-chassis saloon or tourer (sometimes with Mulliner coachwork), and the more sporting underslung chassis job, which could top 100mph (161km/h). As a sports car, the Invicta S Type was a formidable machine, despite its laid-back origins. Donald Healey won the 1931 Monte Carlo Rally in one, and the Cordery sisters made long-distance timed runs also in an Invicta.

Sadly, none of this was enough to save Invicta from the Depression, and sales steadily took a downward turn through the early 1930s. The cheaper 91.5-cu in (1.5-litre) Blackburne-engined 12/45 failed to save the company and in 1933 Noel Macklin sold out. There were plans for new Invictas, based on French Darracqs, but these came to nothing. But the name was revived again after World War II; the 1946 Black Prince was an advanced car with twin overhead-camshaft 3-litre Meadows engine, Brockhouse automatic transmission and all-round independent suspension. But it was too expensive and only a few were sold before the company closed in 1950. That

BELOW
1927 3-litre 'Doctor's coupé'.

RIGHT
Invicta 4¹/2-litre.

BELOW RIGHT
A modern Invicta.

was not the end of the Invicta name, however, for in 2002 came news of yet another revival. This time Chris Marsh (ex-Marcos designer) came up with an all-new carbonfibre-bodied sports car, powered by a 280.7-cu in (4.6-litre) Ford V8 of 320bhp (238.6kW). The new S1 had a claimed top speed of 170mph (274km/h) and the incredibly low weight of 2,425lb (1100kg). Production is planned to start in 2003.

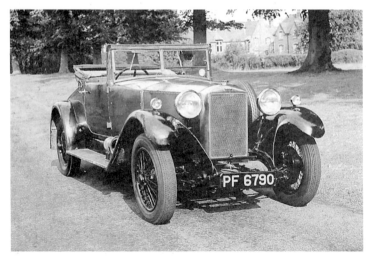

ISO (Italy 1962-1975)

Isothermos, Renzo Rivolta's company, built refrigerators before World War II. After the war, Rivolta turned his hand to scooters and then to the Isetta bubblecar, which was built between 1953 and '55. His next car could not have been more different. Launched in 1962, the Rivolta was an exotic two-door four-seat coupé, powered by a 327.03-cu in (5.3-litre) Chevrolet V8 engine. There was a choice of ZF four-speed manual gearbox or a Chevrolet automatic, with several stages of tune on offer, from 300 to 400bhp (223.7 to 298.2kW), the latter in ultimate four-carburettor form. The combination of Bertone styling and American V8 power proved attractive, and the Rivolta was equipped as a luxury car, with leather interior, electric sunroof and air conditioning all on the options list.

Perhaps the best-known, and probably best-looking, Iso was the Grifo, which appeared a year after the Rivolta. It was based on the earlier car, with the same engines, suspension, brakes and transmissions, but on a shorter wheelbase and with an all-new coupé body, again styled by Bertone. Unlike the 2+2 Rivolta, the low-slung Grifo was clearly designed as a sports car. Pop-up headlights were added in 1971, and a few targa-top cars were built, though the convertible Spider shown at the 1964 Geneva Motor Show came to nothing.

The Grifo was successful by Iso standards, remaining in production right up to 1975 when the company closed. Several different Chevrolet engines were fitted, each bigger than the last, up to the 451.6-cu in (7.4-litre) 'Can Am' V8 with 395bhp (294.5kW). This did not include the last 37 Grifos, which were fitted with a 353.9-cu in (5.8-litre) Ford V8. At the same time, Iso was offering the Fidia, a big four-door saloon styled by Ghia, available from 1967

and based on a stretched version of the Rivolta chassis. Less than 200 of these were built, most of them Chevrolet-powered. The last new Iso was the Lele, launched in 1969, with all-new bodywork by Bertone, this time in the form of a two-door 2+2 coupé. Launched with the Chevrolet V8, it changed to Ford power after 125 cars had been built.

Iso closed in 1975, following the oil crisis, and an ill-advised move into Formula One racing. Renzo Rivolta had died in 1966, leaving his son Piero to take over. Piero attempted to revive the marque in 1991 with the Grifo 90, once again Chevrolet V8-powered, but apart from a single prototype, this came to nothing.

LEFT
1968 ISO Grifo GL365.

BELOW
ISO Rivolta with 5.3-litre V8.

ISOTTA-FRASCHINI (Italy 1900-1949)

Isotta-Fraschini possessed all the right ingredients in a three-man partnership. Vincenzo Fraschini provided the passion, being a great car enthusiast, while Cesare Isotta provided the money and, better still, was a lawyer. They were soon joined by Giustino Cattaneo, a prolific and gifted engineer.

Isotta and Fraschini started modestly enough in 1898, importing Renaults and De Dions into Italy. After two years, they began to build their own cars, albeit with imported parts. The company really took off when Cattaneo joined the company, and came up with a string of designs, some of which were winning races before World War I. That did not prevent Isotta-Fraschini from facing a cash crisis in 1907, but joining forces with Lorraine-Dietrich for two years enabled it to survive.

After World War I Isotta-Fraschini entered its golden era. The new Type 8 of 1919 placed the company straight into

contention with Mercedes and Rolls-Royce. Cattaneo's advanced chassis was combined with a powerful 360-cu in (5.9-litre) engine, topped with coachwork from a choice of builders. In the early 1920s, an Isotta-Fraschini became the car to have, even among Hollywood movie stars, and it looked as though Italy had another prestigious car marque alongside Lancia.

But the company lost its way after only a few more years. Fraschini and Isotta both left in 1922, while new owner, Count Lodovico Mazzotti, sought to diversify still further into aero engines, leaving the Type 8 to take care of itself. As a result, the car

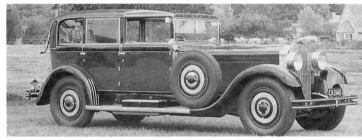

side of the business stagnated, and when it finally collapsed in 1933, the remains were bought up by aircraft maker Caproni, which was only interested in the company's expertise in aero engines. It went on to make engines for aircraft, trucks and boats during World War II.

After the war, there was a short-lived attempt to revive Isotta-Fraschini as a car maker, but the 8C Monterosa was too advanced for its own good. Only six were sold before the project was wound up, and the company has since concentrated on engines and industrial drivetrains.

TOP
The Type 8, introduced in 1919.

ABOVE
By 1929, the year of this model, the founders had left the company.

ABOVE LEFT
The post-war Type 8C.

LEFT
The 1906 18/22 was competent but hardly unique.

ISUZU (Japan 1953 to date)

Isuzu's roots stretch right back to 1918, when a heavy engineering company merged with the Tokyo Gas & Electric Company. They signed an agreement to build and sell Wolseleys in the Far East, though it was another four years before the first Japanese-built Wolseley appeared. From 1929, the company began to build its own cars, using various trade names including Isuzu (after a Japanese river). The company formally became Isuzu Motors only in 1949.

Four years later, another licensing deal was signed, this time with the British Rootes Group, and Isuzu built Hillman Minxes throughout the 1950s, first assembled from imported parts, later as a 100 per cent Japanese car. It was not until 1961 that Isuzu felt ready to launch its own in-house design, the Bellel, a conventional four-door saloon which came with either a 91.5-cu in (1.5-litre) petrol engine or, unusually, a 122-cu in (2-litre) diesel. The range soon flourished, with the smaller Bellet following in 1963 (as saloon or two-door coupé), then the 117 coupé and twin overhead-cam Florian saloon. But Isuzu, smaller than big Japanese players like Nissan, was struggling. Production halved between 1968 and 1970, and partnerships were sought with Mitsubishi, Nissan and Fuji.

In the end, it was General Motors which took a 34 per cent stake in Isuzu and set the Japanese company on a new, more prosperous course. Building its own versions of the smaller GM cars for both home and export markets gave Isuzu a ready-made range of up-to-date, cheap-to-produce cars. The 1974 Gemini was the first, an Isuzu-built version of the Opel Kadett/Vauxhall Chevette, with 96.66- or 110.88-cu in (1584- or 1817-cc) power

units. By the mid-1980s, the Gemini was front-wheel-driven, based on General Motors' R range. The long-running Piazza coupé was launched in 1981, its straight, clean lines designed by Giugiaro, and available with or without a turbo for its 2-litre engine. Isuzu also built light commercials for GM, but is best known for its wide range of four-wheel-drive off-road vehicles, notably the short- and long-

wheelbased Trooper, which is sold in Japan as the Bighorn. The 2002 range also included the Rodeo and Rodeo Sport (long- and short-wheelbase respectively, both with a 195.3-cu in/3.2-litre V6), the six-seat Ascender and the range-topping Axiom, with a 230-bhp (171.5-kW) 213.6-cu in (3.5-litre) V6 and electronically-controlled suspension.

BELOW
Isuzu 4x4.

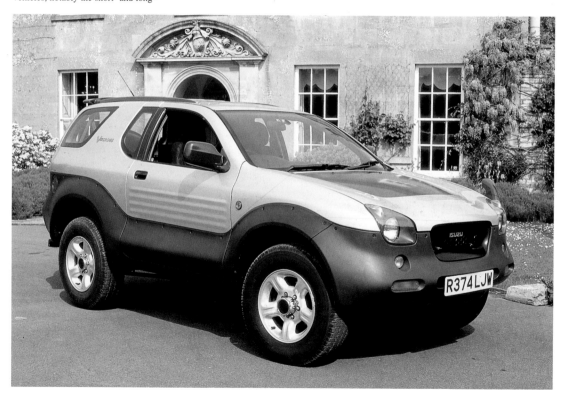

ITALA (Italy 1904-1934)

Itala's life was relatively short but nevertheless glorious, and a more apt cliché for the early Italian motor industry would be hard to find. The Ceirano brothers were central to the story. Between them, they had a hand in the development of seven different makes, including Fiat, but it was Matteo Ceirano, who left his elder brother's engineering works in 1903, who was to found Itala. With five partners, he set up shop in Turin, and the company's first car actually won a hill climb, the Susa-Mont Cenisio, in the following year, driven by Matteo himself. The year after, an Itala won the Coppa Florio and the year after that another took the Targa Florio. In the following year, 1907, Itala won an even higher profile event, when Prince Borghese won the Peking-Paris marathon, three weeks ahead of his nearest rival.

These sporting successes boosted sales no end, and Itala expanded fast, offering a wide range of cars by the outbreak of World War I. By this time, Ceirano had long since gone, leaving Itala in 1905 to set up SPA. But as was so often the case with exotic car makers, glittering success before the war turned to penury soon after. Itala suffered a loss on wartime contracts to make aero engines under licence, though it did manage to put the 51S into production, which won the Targa Florio in both 1922 and 1923. Within a couple of years, the company was being run by receivers, and despite a new Tipo 61 and a V12 racer, all attempts to revive the company ended in failure and Itala finally closed in 1934.

ABOVE RIGHT
Grandeur and grace – the 1907 Itala.

RIGHT
1908 Itala 12-litre racing model.

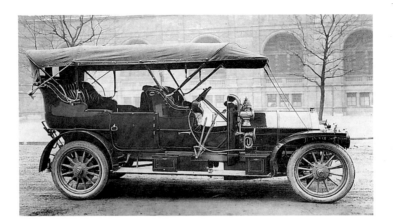

JAGUAR (Great Britain 1945 to date)

Although a 1945 start-up date is listed above, and Jaguar Cars did indeed start business in that year, its origins were in the early 1920s, with the Jaguar name first being used in 1935. Headed for decades by Sir William Lyons, its co-founder, Jaguar made its name with stylish, sporting cars that were surprisingly good value. Two milestone sports cars, the 1948 XK120 and 1961 E-Type, placed Jaguar in the international spotlight, followed by a whole string of highly successful saloons. There were bad times, too, but a takeover by Ford in 1989 finally gave Jaguar the financial stability it needed to develop a range of new cars.

Bill Lyons tried his hand at several jobs before setting up the company that would be his for life. Apprenticed to Crossley, he also helped out in his father's piano restoration business and for a while worked as a car salesman. But Lyons was also a keen motorcyclist, so he was attracted to the sleek aluminium sidecars built in small numbers by his neighbour, William Walmsley. He persuaded Walmsley that together they could make a real success of the business, so in 1922 Swallow Sidecars was born. Business boomed, and Swallow soon branched out into making car bodies, with the first Austin Swallow based on Lyons's own Austin Seven. That was followed by other Swallow-bodied cars based on Morris, Alvis and Clyno chassis. The idea was to offer exotic looks with tried and tested mechanicals at a low price. The formula worked, and worked so well that Swallow had to move to a larger factory. In 1931, the rakish Swallow SS1 was Standard-powered but based on the company's own chassis. Little by little, Swallow was becoming its own manufacturer.

Renamed SS Cars in 1933, it followed up with the magnificent SS90 and SS100

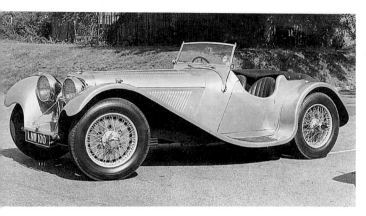

sports cars. Under their shapely bodies, these used decidedly ordinary 162.51-cu in (2.66-litre) engines which, as ever, kept the price down, something William Lyons rarely forgot. By the outbreak of World War II the company had built 5,000 cars and was turning a profit, albeit a small one. Another renaming in March 1945 finally set up Jaguar Cars, which at first carried on building the pre-war cars with 109.8-cu in (1.8-litre) four-cylinder or 164.8- and 213.6-cu in (2.7- and 3.5-litre) six-cylinder engines. The Swallow sidecar business was sold off, incidentally, ending up with Watsonian, which was still happily making sidecars in 2002.

Jaguar was still using adapted Standard engines at this point, but in 1948 it unveiled its first completely in-house engine. The twin overhead-camshaft 207.5-cu in (3.4-litre) straight-six was hidden under the shapely bonnet of the new XK120 two-seater. It caused a worldwide sensation, not only because of its exotic specification and 120-mph (193-km/h) top speed, but also because it cost just £1,273: once again, Lyons's determination to give value for money had triumphed. The XK120 was a huge success, most of the cars being exported, and was followed by the updated XK140 and XK150. The Mk VII of 1951 was powered by the same twin-cam engine, and sired a long line of big four-seat Jaguars.

*TOP
1936 Jaguar SS100.*

*ABOVE
A Swallow sidecar of the 1920s.*

*RIGHT
XK140 dhc.*

Sales of the road cars were bolstered by competition successes, Le Mans in particular: a Jaguar C-Type won the French endurance race in 1951, with the D-Type taking victory in 1953, 1955, 1956 and 1957. Booming sales allowed Jaguar to move to a bigger factory, the Browns Lane plant in Coventry it still occupies today, and to introduce the unitary-constructed 146.5-cu in (2.4-litre) vehicle. This more compact saloon (later dubbed the 'Mk I') was powered by a downsized version of the now famous twin-cam engine, and there followed 3.4-litre and 231.9-cu in (3.8-litre) versions. The succeeding Mk II became something of an early 1960s icon. It acquired the dubious honour of being favoured not only by the police but also by the villains they were chasing!

Despite a disastrous factory fire in 1957, it seemed as if nothing could stop the Jaguar bandwagon. Production was back on stream after just two months, the company bought Daimler in 1960 and the following year announced the most famous car it ever made, the E-Type. Just like the XK120 13 years earlier, the new sports car created a huge stir, thanks to three main features: its striking looks, its performance (Jaguar claimed 150mph/241km/h) and its price: at £2,100, the E-Type had the speed and charisma of cars costing two or three times as much. Like the XK120, it was a huge success (over 70,000 were built), with many cars exported, and most of these to the U.S.A.

Meanwhile, the saloon range was extending upward with the wide, imposing Mk X in 1962, first with the E-Type's 3.8-litre straight-six, later with an enlarged 256.3-cu in (4.2-litre) version which the E-Type also adopted in 1965. This was a Jaguar to compete with the biggest limousines, though it retained the low,

ABOVE
A 1964 Jaguar 4.2-litre E-Type in the original colour.

OPPOSITE
1950 3.4-litre XK120.

sporting roofline so beloved by Sir William (he was knighted in 1956) and, it seemed, his customers. The gap between the gargantuan Mk X and compact Mk II was filled in 1964 with the S-Type. This made clever use of existing parts, and was really a restyled Mk II with a longer trunk and the Mk X's independent rear suspension. Engine choices were the now ubiquitous twin-cam in 3.4- and 3.8-litre forms.

But Jaguar was soon to lose its independence. It merged with the British Motor Corporation in 1966 to form British

Motor Holdings, which in turn merged with bus and truck manufacturer Leyland two years later. Jaguar was now part of British Leyland, though Sir William remained in charge.

But for car watchers, 1968 was memorable for something else, namely the XJ6. This svelte new saloon effectively replaced the old Mk II, S-Type and Mk X in one fell swoop. It somehow managed to look up to date, but was instantly recognizable as a Jaguar. It set new standards of ride, refinement and handling

223

for a big saloon, and would be the backbone of Jaguar's range for nearly 20 years. Power came from the familiar 4.2-litre six-cylinder engine, or a new 170.9-cu in (2.8-litre) version designed to circumvent tax laws in certain markets. The smaller engine was less successful, however, and was later replaced by a 3.4-litre unit.

In fact, in these pre-oil crisis days, bigger was always deemed to better, especially when it came in the form of Jaguar's new 323.4-cu in (5.3-litre) V12 engine announced in 1971. This was

designed by (among others) William Heynes, who had been with Jaguar since the 1930s and underlined one of the secrets of its success, namely a strong engineering team. The creamy-smooth V12 was fitted to the E-Type (heavier and fatter by now) in 1971 and the XJ saloon the year after. Few cars won as much praise in the motoring press as the XJ12.

But the mid-1970s onwards were less happy times for Jaguar. Under the British Leyland regime, quality had slipped, and the cars were getting a reputation for

ABOVE
Jaguar 3.8-litre E-Type roadster.

TOP RIGHT
1961 E-Type roadster.

CENTRE RIGHT
1950 D-Type.

BOTTOM RIGHT
Engine of the E-Type 3.8 series.

shoddy workmanship and unreliability. And while everyone agreed that the new E-Type replacement, the XJS, was fast and silent, it lacked the grace of its predecessor. However, there was an elegant two-door version of the XJ, and from 1980 Jaguar gradually turned around under the leadership of John Egan, who worked hard

to improve quality. Sir William Lyons lived to see this, but died in 1985, while still honorary president.

The year after, the long-awaited successor to the XJ6, the Sovereign, was announced, with brand-new twin-cam six-cylinder engines of 177 and 219.7 cu in (2.9 and 3.6 litres), later supplemented by a 244.1-cu in (4-litre) unit. Again, there were mutterings concerning quality, and the fact that the latest car seemed to have lost some of its traditional Jaguar elegance. More seriously, the company was now heavily dependent on U.S. sales, and currency fluctuations in the 1980s were playing havoc with both sales and profits. Despite winning Le Mans once again in 1988, Jaguar was seriously looking for a partner, and began talks with General Motors.

Then Ford stepped in. The Jaguar marque was such a prize that Ford could hardly stand by and see its chief rival just walk in and take it. The company staged a

hostile takeover bid, which succeeded, and in November 1989 Jaguar became a wholly owned subsidiary of Ford. It was a brave, some even say foolhardy, move. Ford had paid $2.5 billion for the latest member of its family, which at that point was losing a million dollars a day. And despite the new backing, Jaguar continued to face hard times, forced to cut both jobs and production in 1992.

But Jaguar did enjoy a product-led revival in the 1990s, thanks to a combination of Ford investment and a return of that Jaguar elegance. Retro, classic styling that evoked the past was now heavily in vogue, and Jaguar made the most of it, drawing heavily on its own heritage. So the new XJ6 of 1994 was clearly inspired by its 1968 original, while the XK8 sports car of 1996 replaced the XJS but was clearly styled to bring back memories of the E-Type. There were new engines too, specifically an all-new 4-litre

ABOVE LEFT
1968 XJ6.

LEFT
1973 XJ6.

225

V8, and a supercharged version of the 4-litre six for a sporting XJR saloon.

The smaller S-Type was next to arrive, with that new V8 (later enlarged to 256.3 cu in/4.2 litres) and later a 152.6-cu in (2.5-litre) V6 as well. Once again, the styling was modern-retro, this time the 1960s S-Type supplying the inspiration. The big XJ became the XJ8, once again powered by that V8, which in supercharged form in the S-Type R, produced 400bhp. For years, there had been talk of a smaller Jaguar to rival the BMW 3-series, and it finally arrived with the four-wheel-drive X-Type, powered by a 3-litre V6 engine. A cheaper 2-litre two-wheel-drive version was unveiled in 2002. It looked as though Jaguar could do no wrong, apart from the fact that once again it was losing money, despite record-breaking sales. Ford's answer was another round of new models, including a new F-Type sports car.

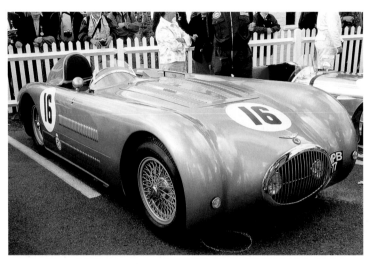

LEFT
1948 3.4-litre Alta-Jaguar Streamliner.

BELOW LEFT
1997 Jaguar Sovereign.

BELOW
1994 XJR.

LEFT
1994 6.0-litre XJS.

BELOW LEFT
2003 Jaguar S-Type.

BELOW
2004 Jaguar X-Type.

LEFT
2003 XK coupé.

OPPOSITE
2004 Jaguar XJR aluminium show car.

JEEP (U.S.A. 1963 to date)
The Willys-Overland Jeep originated, as just
about everyone knows, because of World
War II, but it did not become a marque in its
own right until 1963, when Kaiser-Jeep was
formed as an entity separate from Willys-
Overland. This also marked a splitting of
the Jeep line into two. The long-running CJ
series, descended directly from the G.I.'s
favourite workhorse of World War II,
continued, but alongside it came the
Wagoneer estate, obviously very much a
'civilian' vehicle, but still with the cachet of
the Jeep name, plus the option of four-
wheel-drive. In fact, the Wagoneer virtually
invented a new class of car: the four-wheel-
drive which is capable of off-road work, but
which rarely gets used for the purpose – in
short, the ubiquitous SUV.

But while the Wagoneer acquired a
329.5-cu in (5.4-litre) V8 option in 1965,

LEFT
1942 amphibious Jeep.

BELOW LEFT
The Jeep as a favourite workhorse.

BELOW
The 4x4 J20.

CJ reflected its more workaday role with 34.25-cu in (2.2-litre) four-cylinder ...rol engine or 195.3-cu in (3.2-litre) ...kins diesel, though one could have a ...5.8-cu in (3.7-litre) V6 bought from ...ick if one insisted. But far from being ...dated by its more flamboyant new stable ...tes, the CJ actually went from strength to ...ength. It was being built under licence all ...er the world by this time: in Japan by ...tsubishi, in Spain, Portugal, Israel and in ...uth Africa. But perhaps the most enduring ...ence-built Jeep was the Indian Mahindra. ...sembly began in 1947, and production ...tinues to this day, now with a 2.2-litre ...geot diesel engine. It was even exported ...urope in the 1980s, at a knockdown ...ce.

As for the original U.S.-built version, ...maker Kaiser-Jeep was simply too small ...survive on its own, even with such a ...cessful product, and Jeep merged with ...erican Motors in 1970. The range was ...eloped, with the company's own V6 ...ilable from 1971 and the new two-door

Cherokee three years later. The latter was along the same lines as the Wagoneer, though smaller, while the Wagoneer itself became available with automatic transmission, a first with four-wheel-drive.

In fact, these top-of-the-range Jeeps were beginning to bear a closer resemblance to luxury saloons than genuine off-roaders. The engine options reflected this, as the basic four was dropped in favour of a 256.3-cu in (4.2-litre) six, with V8s of 305.1, 360 and 402.75 cu in (5, 5.9 and 6.6 litres). There was an almost-grudging Perkins diesel option from 1978, but for export only; even after the oil crisis, the U.S.A. was still the land of cheap and plentiful gas. This divergence of Europe and America was underlined in the early 1980s, when the latest Cherokee could be had with a modern 152.6-cu in (2.5-litre) turbo diesel, from VM of Italy, while the CJ had a V8 petrol option for the first time.

Even by the early 21st century, it was business as usual: the CJ plodded on, by now looking increasingly outdated in a leisure-dominated market; the Cherokee acquired retro styling and a more on-road bias, while the range-topping Grand Cherokee offered 255-bhp (190.1-kW) petrol or a more realistic diesel option.

ABOVE
Willys and Wrangler Jeeps.

LEFT
CJ6.

ABOVE LEFT
Jeep pick-up.

ABOVE
1981 CJ7 Renegade.

LEFT
1984-85 Cherokee Chief.

OPPOSITE
ABOVE LEFT: *2001 Cherokee Classic.*

ABOVE RIGHT: *2003 Wrangler.*

BELOW LEFT: *2003 Liberty Sport.*

BELOW RIGHT: *2004 Grand Cherokee.*

JENSEN (Great Britain 1935-1976)
The Jensen brothers, Allan and Richard, made their name building special bodies for ordinary cars, and went on to make their own complete cars (usually powered by American V8s). In the 1960s they were the first to offer a car with both four-wheel-drive and anti-lock brakes.

Their first commission was to build a sporting two-seater body for the Standard Nine. It was so well-received that both brothers went to work for W.J. Smith, a small body-building concern. The brothers made such a difference to Smith's fortunes that they took the company over in 1934, renaming it Jensen Motors. Their first car was not long coming: the Jensen convertible came complete with four seats and a 219.7-cu in (3.6-litre) Ford V8. A four-door saloon version followed in 1935, plus the long-wheelbase Type H soon after.

The Jensens stuck with U.S. engines after the war, with the exception of the Austin-powered 541, and launched the PW, which used a Nash unit. Meanwhile, the body-building side of the business was growing too: Jensen supplied bodies for the Austin A40 Sports, and later the Austin-Healey, Sunbeam Tiger and Volvo P1800 sports cars. After the 244.1-cu in (4-litre) 541, Jensen returned to American muscle with the Chrysler V8-powered CV8 in 1963. The CV8 made history by being offered with four-wheel-drive and anti-lock brakes from 1965, but only a few were built before it was superseded by the Touring-designed Interceptor of the following year. The Interceptor was in a class of its own. Luxurious, fast and expensive, it was a four-seat GT that remained the only car on the market with anti-lock brakes and four-wheel-drive, though Jensen sold far more of the cheaper two-wheel-drive variant.

But by now Jensen was in trouble. Its body contracts were dropping away one by one, and the big, thirsty Interceptor was simply the wrong car to be making in the oil crisis era. The company was taken over in 1968, and produced the Lotus-powered Jensen-Healey, in open two-seater form and as a smart GT. Neither saved the company, however, and it closed down in 1976. But that was not quite the end, as ten years later a new Jensen company reintroduced the Interceptor, made to order at the rate of one a month.

1948 Jensen saloon with 4-litre Austin engine.

ABOVE LEFT
1959 Jensen 541R with 4-litre Austin
engine.

ABOVE
1975 Jensen-Healey MKII with Lotus
engine.

LEFT
1974 Jensen Interceptor.

JOWETT (Great Britain 1906-1953)
Jowett was unusual among British
manufacturers for persisting with a twin-
cylinder engine well into the 1930s, and a
flat-twin at that. But it gained a good
reputation, due to its economy, reliability
and surprisingly good pulling power: it was
known as 'the little engine with the big
pull'.

William and Benjamin Jowett, of
Bradford, Yorkshire, built V-twin engines
for other manufacturers before making their
first car in 1906. Four years later, they
introduced that famous flat-twin, which
would stay in production until the
company's demise in 1953. By 1913,
production had settled down to a little two-
seater car powered by a 49.86-cu in (817-
cc) side-valve version of the twin, later
enlarged to 55.35-cu in (907-cc).

The car was gradually updated, with an
electric starter added in 1923 and four-
wheel brakes plus detachable cylinder-
heads in 1929. By this time there was a
four-seat version as well, the Long Four,
and the fabric-bodied Black Prince. Until
now, Jowetts had been anything but sports
cars, but the sporting Kestrel and twin-
carburettor Weasel appeared in the 1930s,
along with a four-speed gearbox.

But the big news was Jowett's first
four-cylinder engine, a flat-four, of course,
producing a respectable 30bhp (22.4kW)
from 71.15 cu in (1.2 litres). Car production
ceased during World War II, but the
Bradford van carried on, powered by the
latest 25-bhp (18.64-kW) 61.02-cu in (1-
litre) flat-twin.

In 1947 Jowett unveiled the advanced
Javelin saloon, with streamlined styling,
independent suspension and a 50-bhp
(37.28-kW) 90.68-cu in (1.48-litre) flat-four
allowing over 80mph (129km/h). This was
followed by the two-seat Jupiter sports car,

powered by the same engine, and later the
glassfibre R4, capable of 100mph
(161km/h). The faithful Bradford van
continued alongside, and with 135 of these
produced weekly (plus 125 Javelins) the
future looked bright. Alas, sales did not
match up to production, and the final straw
came when Jowett's body supplier refused
to carry on. The company closed in 1953.

ABOVE
1923 Jowett 7-hp 'Short Two'.

RIGHT
1952 1.48-litre Jowett Javelin.

KAISER (U.S.A. 1946-1955)
Kaiser-Frazer was a short-lived attempt by
a relatively small American company to
challenge the industry's domination by
Ford, General Motors and Chrysler. It was a
classic swords to ploughshares operation:
Henry J. Kaiser built ships during World
War II, joined up with Joseph W. Frazer
(ex-Willys-Overland) and set up production
in a factory that until recently had built
Consolidated B-24 Liberator bombers!

The first prototype of 1946 was
ambitious and advanced, but Kaiser-Frazer
fortunately recognized that to manufacture
it was beyond the company's resources.
The first production car, the Custom Sedan,
was therefore a more conventional car. At
first, the company did well: its cars were up

to date and two line-ups were offered in the form of the standard Kaisers and luxury Frazers.

Unfortunately, from 1949 the industry's big guns began to introduce their own all-new post-war models with sleek styling and big V8s. But Kaiser still did not offer a V8 in 1952. Instead, it concentrated on a new economy car, the Henry J, introduced just when an affluent market wanted bigger and better. Even the muscle of Sears Roebuck, selling its own Allstate version, failed to boost Kaiser-Frazer sales. The money ran out, and in 1954 the company merged with Willys-Overland to form Kaiser-Willys. There was a new glassfibre-bodied sports car, the 161, but that did not work either (though it was built in Argentina for another seven years) and the company closed in 1955, though the name lived on as Kaiser-Jeep.

LEFT: Jowett Jupiter.

ABOVE: 1948 Kaiser Special four-door saloon.

KIA (Korea)

Kia began by supplying its home market, but by 2003 was exporting to the world, including Europe and the U.S.A. Like other south-east Asian manufacturers, the company made its name with straightforward, value-for-money cars. Even now, with the new executive-class Amanti, with several advanced features, challenging Audi and BMW, the value aspect is emphasized. But to most buyers, Kias such as the modest Rio, a thoroughly conventional three- or five-door hatchback with 1.3- or 1.5-litre engines are more familiar. The small 4x4 Sportage has also proved popular, and is a natural rival to the Suzuki Vitara. Kia offers another luxury 4x4, the Sorento, with self-levelling suspension and a choice of turbo-diesel or petrol engines. Then there are two people-carriers, the Carens and larger Sedona, the Magentus executive saloon and Shuma budget hatchback.

KISSEL (U.S.A. 1906-1930)

Kissels were unusual for their innovative body styles. The 'All-Year', for example, was an open touring four-seater with a detachable hardtop, complete with glass windows that could be bolted on or off as the weather dictated.

William and George Kissel determined that they would produce a car out of the family agricultural business, and were in

production by 1908 with the Kisselkar. In the same year they introduced commercial vehicles with Waukesha or Wisconsin engines; they also built their own power units, though the bigger models were tried with a Lycoming straight-eight and even (briefly) a Weidely V12.

After World War I the company concentrated on saloons such as the 6-45 Tourster and that All-Year, which was built

up to 1920. There were sports cars too, starting with the Silver Special Speedster and followed by the famous Gold Bug (the name stems from its colour), powered by a 262.4-cu in (4.3-litre) side-valve six. But these attractive Speedsters would be some of the last true Kissels. Falling sales forced the company to build cars under contract for other firms, but when the last of these fell through in 1930 car production ceased. The company was reorganized the following year to make engine parts, and was finally sold off in 1943.

ABOVE
1920 Kissel 6-45 Speedster.

LEFT
Kia Sorento.

LADA (U.S.S.R./Russia 1970 to date)

In the West cars are often bought because of their perceived glamour, performance and sophistication. The U.S.S.R., and indeed post-communist Russia, had different priorities: toughness and reliability came first, qualities that have long been reflected in the VAZ line-up, known in export markets as Lada.

This organization was set up in 1970 with help from Fiat which was, of course, also instrumental in establishing FSO in Poland. A new factory was built at Togliattigrad, west of Moscow, and production commenced of a Soviet version of the ageing Fiat 124. However, it was adapted for Russian conditions, made of thicker steel to suit the harsher climate, and given a Lada-designed 73.22-cu in (1.2-litre) engine. Crude and basic, this Fiat-based car is ubiquitous in the U.S.S.R., and some were sold abroad, where its toughness and low price are appreciated. Over 30 years on, this original Lada is still in production

There was a departure in 1979 with the all-Russian Niva, a small four-wheel-drive with good off-road capabilities and a low price. Again, this is still in production, now in three- and five-door forms as well as pick-up. The Samara hatchback followed in 1984 with a more modern layout with

ABOVE LEFT
1997 Lada Niva 4x4.

ABOVE
1996 Lada Riva estate.

LEFT
Lada Samara five-door hatchback.

OPPOSITE
RIGHT: 1970 Lada 1200 saloon.

239

front-wheel-drive, though it was let down by poor build quality. In 1996, the new 110 looked very different, with roly-poly 1990s styling and the option of 8- or 16-valve fuel injection 91.5-cu in (1.5-litre) engines with up to 94bhp (70.1kW). This comes as a four-door saloon, five-door hatchback or estate. Also offered in 2002 was the little 1111 three-door hatchback. Despite the economic upheavals in Russia, VAZ was able to report a profit for 2001, when it claimed to have built well over 700,000 cars.

LAGONDA (Great Britain 1906-1988)

Lagonda, that most English of cars, was actually brought into being by an American, Wilbur Gunn. It was also named after Lagonda Creek, near his home town of Springfield, Ohio. But in 1906 Wilbur was living in Staines, England, and was beginning to make tricars in a small workshop at the back of his house. The venture lasted only a year, but Gunn went on to build a few four-wheeled cars, notably a 14/16-hp (10.4-/11.9-kW) Coventry Simplex-engined machine.

So when he found new backing, and formed Lagonda Ltd. in 1913, Gunn was ready to produce a small advanced car with unitary construction and a 67.07-cu in (1.10-litre) engine. After World War I production resumed, with a larger 86.65-cu in (1.42-litre) engine added from 1921. But five years later Lagonda changed direction, aiming at the luxury sporting market which it has been associated with ever since.

The first 14/60 was powered by a 122-cu in (2-litre) twin overhead-camshaft

power unit, with advanced Rubery brakes. It was also expensive at £430, but Lagonda persevered with the larger 183.1-cu in (3-litre) six in 1928 and a supercharged 2-litre in 1930, some of which were raced at Le Mans. But despite cars like the magnificent 274.6-cu in (2.5-litre) Rapide, the company was not profitable and went into receivership in 1935.

It was saved by solicitor Alan Good who, with W.O. Bentley as designer, managed to revive the company. It was taken over again in 1947 by tractor manufacturer David Brown, which already owned Aston Martin. Brown put the new 152.6-cu in (2.5-litre) Lagonda into production two years later, and this survived until 1958 with a 3-litre engine.

1932 Lagonda tourer.

Thereafter, Lagonda saloons were sporadic variations of the equivalent Aston Martins: the DB4-based 244.1-cu in (4-litre) Rapide, a four-door version of the DBS, and the striking William Towns-designed Aston Martin Lagonda of the 1970s and 1980s. Now under Ford ownership, it would be surprising if this famous badge is never used again.

RIGHT
1980 5.3-litre Aston Martin Lagonda.

BELOW
1934 4.5-litre Lagonda.

BELOW RIGHT
1935 Lagonda Rapide.

LAMBORGHINI (Italy 1963 to date)
Ferruccio Lamborghini originally made his
fortune building tractors. He started out by
converting surplus war machinery, building
his own purpose-built tractors from 1949.
But Ferruccio was also a car enthusiast, and
raced a Fiat Topolino in the 1948 Mille

Miglia. Like any other wealthy Italian car
fanatic, he also owned a Ferrari. The story
goes that he took the car back to Enzo
Ferrari himself, complaining that it had a
noisy gearbox. In that case, retorted the
great man, you should stick to tractors! So
incensed was Lamborghini that he decided

to build a car to beat Ferrari, and another
exotic Italian sports car was born.
    Profits from the tractors, not to mention
those of the heating and air-conditioning
systems Lamborghini also produced,
allowed him to set up Automobili Ferruccio
Lamborghini S.p.A. in 1963. Unveiled at

1968 Lamborghini 400GT.

the Turin Show that year, the 350GTV was clearly aimed directly at Ferrari, with a 213.6-cu in (3.5-litre) V12 mounted up front, and striking looks. Unusually, almost every part was made at Lamborghini's new Sant'Agata factory, including a gearbox featuring synchromesh on reverse from 1964. The GTO proved a success, and was later superseded by the 400GT 2+2, now with 320bhp (290.8kW) from its bigger 238-cu in (3.9-litre) V12. It was joined by the mid-engined Miura P400 in 1965, a new form of supercar which gradually took over from the old front-engined GT, and was the first in a long line of mid-engined Lamborghinis. But the front-engine layout was retained for the V12 Espada of 1967: for years, the company offered both mid-

engined two-seat supercars and front-engined four-seaters or 2+2s, such as the Islero and Jaramo.

All of these were, of course, very expensive and Lamborghini attempted to build a cheaper car in 1971 with the 152.6-cu in (2.5-litre) V8 Urraco. But Sant'Agata is not remembered for the Urraco. The most memorable Lamborghini, and perhaps the most famous supercar of all time, was the Countach. Launched in 1973, this mid-engined V12 supercar had a sensational wedge-like shape and stunning performance. The engine was boosted from 244.1 to 305.1 cu in (4 to 5 litres) in 1982, with four-valve heads added in '85. It was finally replaced in 1990 by the Diablo.

Meanwhile, Lamborghini had been

ABOVE
1976 3-litre V8 Lamborghini Urraco.

LEFT
Lamborghini Espada.

RIGHT
Lamborghini Countach 5000.

BELOW
Lamborghini Islero 'S'.

BELOW LEFT and OPPOSITE
3.5-litre Lamborghini Jalpa.

through several changes of ownership since
Ferruccio himself retired in 1972. When
Chrysler took over in 1987, this apparently
ushered in a new era of stability, but the
American parent had its own problems,
forcing it to sell up after only five years and
Lamborghini is now owned by the VW
group. With nearly 500bhp (372.8kW), the
Diablo was Lamborghini's flagship
throughout the 1990s. There was also a
four-wheel- drive version, the VT, the
lightweight SV, and open-top Roadster.
Perhaps more intriguing was the LM002
V12-engined off-roader. By 2002, the
Diablo itself had been replaced by the
Murcielago, a mid-engined V12 in the
Lamborghini tradition, albeit with standard
four-wheel-drive, 580bhp (432.4kW) and a
claimed top speed of 205mph (330km/h).

RIGHT
Lamborghini Diablo.

OPPOSITE
Lamborghini Miura.

LANCHESTER (Great Britain 1895-1956)

In its early years, Lanchester was one of the most innovative English manufacturers. At a time when most motoring pioneers were producing copies of the French De Dion or German Benz, Frederick Lanchester was building his own prototype, with no outside influence from anywhere else. From that first 1895 machine, more followed, such as the 8-hp (5.96-kW) car of 1897, with its twin-cylinder engine mounted under the floor. Lanchester finally went into production in 1899, along with his brothers George and Frank and, though produced in very small numbers (six cars were made in 1900), Lanchesters soon became known for their innovative design. The company had a four-cylinder engine ready as early as 1904, for example, though it was declared bankrupt shortly after this, despite having a full order book.

George Lanchester set up a reorganized Lanchester Motor Co. and production resumed of the distinctive cars, with their very short hoods, due to the engine being mounted between driver and passenger. They also persisted with tiller steering until

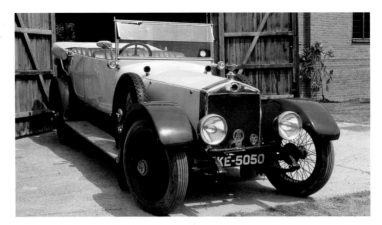

1911. From then on, Lanchesters became gradually more conventional, and perhaps it was no coincidence that Frederick Lanchester resigned in 1913.

As large, comfortable cars, Lanchesters such as the 378.3-cu in (6.2-litre) Sporting Forty acquired their own following (the writer Rudyard Kipling owned one), but by 1931 the company had again run out of money. It was taken over by Daimler, and from that time onward, and especially after World War II, Lanchesters were cheaper, badge-engineered Daimlers, until the name was dropped in 1956. Frederick Lanchester, a professional inventor, had died ten years previously, but both his brothers outlived the cars that bore their name.

TOP RIGHT
1921 Lanchester 40-hp tourer.

RIGHT
1913 38-hp Torpedo tourer.

OPPOSITE
1925 Lanchester 21 drophead.

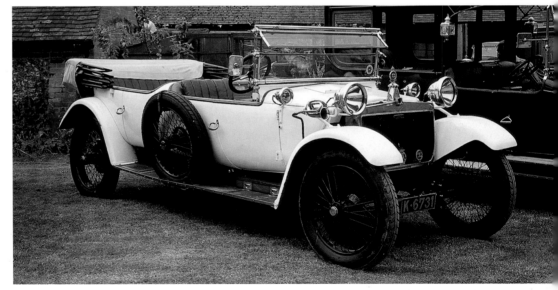

LANCIA (Italy 1906 to date)

Lancia is sometimes seen as an upmarket brand of Fiat, adding a vague sporting/luxury cachet to cheap and common mechanicals. But this long-lived Italian marque, one of Italy's oldest, can boast a whole string of innovations. It pioneered the use of unitary-constructed bodies, was an early proponent of V4, V6 and V12 engines, and claimed to offer the world's first five-speed gearbox in a production car. Along the way, it won more world rally championships than any other manufacturer.

The man behind it was Vincenzo Lancia, born in 1881, who was a man who had demonstrated mechanical aptitude at an early age. The young Lancia started work with a bicycle manufacturer, then joined the newly established FIAT as chief inspector. A gifted driver, he won his class first time out, with an 8-hp (5.96-kW) Fiat in 1900. More race wins followed, and by 1907, when Lancia decided to go into car making on his own account, he was already famous in motoring circles.

The first Lancias, which were the four-cylinder Tipo 51 and six-cylinder Dialpha, were made only in small numbers, but the company soon expanded into a larger factory in Turin, introducing the 244.1-cu in (4-litre) Delta and 305.1-cu in (5-litre) Eta. It was clear that Lancia was aiming high, well beyond the Fiat class. That was confirmed by a V8 and V12 in 1918, though Lancia sold more of its 5-litre Theta.

But the most innovative Lancia of all was just over the horizon. Vincenzo had already patented a design for a car with no chassis (unit construction), which was inspired by a ship's hull. In 1922, it went into production as the Lambda V4. Lighter and stronger than a conventional car, the

Lambda boasted independent front suspension and could top almost 70mph (113km/h); over 12,000 were made in nine years. It was another 30 years before unit construction became commonplace. Meanwhile, Lancia responded to the Depression with the little Augusta. Again V4-powered, a Lancia trademark, and with unit construction, it was the right car at the right time, and over 15,000 were sold. The Aprilia of 1937 was another significant advance, housing all-round independent suspension beneath its streamlined bodyshell. Admired for its 80-mph (129-km/h) performance and good roadholding, the Aprilia used a 82.44-cu in (1.35-litre) V4. In the same year, Vincenzo Lancia died, but his wife Adele took over control of the company, followed by their son Gianni in 1948. After World War II the Aprilia and Ardea went back into production, the latter offering a five-speed gearbox from 1948.

After two decades of building small

ABOVE
1908 Lancia with Alfa 2.5-litre side-valve.

RIGHT
1909 3-litre Beta four-cylinder.

OPPOSITE
ABOVE LEFT: 1923 2.1-litre V4 Lambda.

ABOVE RIGHT: 1957 2.5-litre Aurelia GT.

BELOW LEFT: 1931 3-litre V8 Astura.

BELOW RIGHT: 1929 Lambda Torpedo.

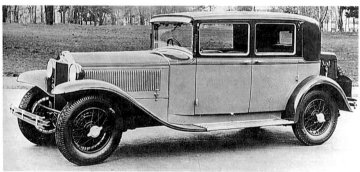

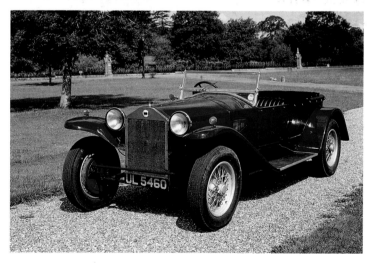

cars, however, Lancia was ready to go up-market again, with the 1950 Aurelia. Claimed to be the first production car with a V6 engine (not to mention semi-trailing independent rear suspension), the Aurelia was soon followed by the beautiful Pininfarina B20 Coupé, with 109.8 cu in (1.8 litres) and later 152.6-cu in (2.5-litre) V6s. The smaller V4 Appia was launched in 1953 and the big Flaminia V6 saloon in 1956, though the latter was unsuccessful.

Lancia entered the front-wheel-drive era early, with the Flavia, its first such vehicle, of 1961. It was powered by a 91.5-cu in (1.5-litre) flat-four, which was a departure for Lancia, and was followed by the highly successful front-drive Fulvia, of which over 300,000 were sold over a long lifespan. The Fulvia achieved great success in world-class rallies, which became something of a Lancia tradition. That was certainly upheld by the mid-engined Stratos, launched in 1972, and in no uncertain terms. Powered by a 146.5-cu in (2.4-litre) Ferrari Dino V6, this won the World Rally Championship in 1974, 1975 and 1976, and also scored five Monte Carlo wins. By this time, Lancia had been taken over by Fiat; despite the success of most of its cars, all this innovation had not come cheap, and Lancia was unable to survive on its own. In the 1950s, realization of the financial situation had forced an agreement with Fiat and Ferrari, which led to Lancia abandoning Formula One: it passed its D50 design on to Ferrari, which made a success of it. In the meantime, Lancia was taken over by cement maker Carlo Pesenti in 1955, and in 1969 by Fiat, which finally gave Lancia the financial stability it needed.

The downside of this process, so far as Lancia enthusiasts were concerned, was that Lancias were increasingly using Fiat components. The 1972 Beta hatchback and Monte Carlo sports car used Fiat four-cylinder engines. In fact, the Beta looked decidedly ordinary compared to previous Lancias, and to add insult to injury had a serious problem with rusting. Build quality was often poor and Lancia residuals slid downwards. The big Gamma saloon and Delta coupé of 1976 were a little more adventurous, powered by a 2.5-litre flat-four unique to Lancia, but neither was a success. Ironically, the Delta hatchback of 1980, which was a good seller, was actually made by Fiat, though it also ushered in

OPPOSITE
Lancia B24S Aurelia Spyder.

RIGHT
1938 Aprilia.

BELOW
Flaminia 3C convertible.

PAGE 254
Lancia Stratos.

PAGE 255
Lancia 1.6-litre Sport Zagato.

another generation of rally winners, culminating in the four-wheel-drive HF Integrale turbo. This was to win the world championship every year from 1987 to 1992.

But while they may have been based on Fiats, and even made by Fiat, Lancias continued to use their own bodyshells, which helped to keep the identity of the marque intact, even if the days of unique engines had gone. The Gamma was replaced by the Thema in 1985 as a joint project between Lancia, Fiat, Alfa Romeo and Saab, and offered a Ferrari-powered 8.32 flagship. At the other end of the range, the little Y10 was Lancia's equivalent of the Fiat Panda.

The Delta was updated with smoother bodywork in 1993, plus a three-door HPE version two years later. Meanwhile, the Y10 (nicknamed 'White Hen' by the mischievous) was replaced by the clean-looking Y. The Kappa of 1994 used Fiat's new five-cylinder engines, and was soon joined by an estate and coupé, all unique to Lancia. However, the Z people-carrier was a straight rebadge job on the PSA/Fiat people-carrier. But Lancia sales were still patchy. The Kappa was not a success and in 1994 Lancia stopped exporting to Britain altogether. In 2002, hopes were being pinned on the Thesis, a new high-tech executive car to replace the Kappa, with engines ranging from a 185-bhp (137.9-kW) 2-litre five to an Alfa Romeo 3-litre V6 offering 215bhp (160.3kW).

ABOVE
Lancia Dedra station wagon.

LEFT
Lancia Z.

OPPOSITE

LEFT TOP: Lancia Kappa coupé.

LEFT CENTRE: Lancia Kappa saloon.

LEFT BOTTOM: Lancia Dedra saloon.

RIGHT ABOVE: Lancia Delta 1.6-litre.

RIGHT BELOW: 1997 Lancia Y.

LEA-FRANCIS (Great Britain 1904-1953)

R.H. Lea and G.J. Francis did not actually intend to make cars. They set up shop in 1895 in Coventry to make bicycles, the Midlands city being the centre of Britain's cycle industry. They soon added motorcycles, which were offered right up to the 1920s, and a car was launched in 1904. However, this failed to attract buyers to Coventry, cheque books in hand, and only two were sold.

It was nearly 20 years before Lea and Francis made another attempt at cars. Once again there were a few false starts, but this time they persevered, aided by a link with the Vulcan car company. The breakthrough came when they acquired the rights to use the respected Meadows engine in their otherwise unremarkable cars. The 91.5-cu in (1.5-litre) Meadows was powerful and responded well to tuning, and it performed particularly well in Lea-Francis's lightweight 'Ten' chassis. It easily won the 1924 RAC Six Days Small Car Trials, rewarding its makers with a new sporting image.

From then on, there was always a sports car in the Lea-Francis line-up. The Hyper of the late 1920s, in TT or S-Type forms among others, was particularly effective, especially when four-wheel brakes and supercharging were added. After several years of trying, Lea-Francis produced its own six-cylinder power unit, the 'Ace of Spades'. This was all well and good, but the company was also spending a great deal of money developing a luxury saloon in the early 1930s. By 1935, it was bankrupt.

It returned from the grave two years later, but had little hope of surviving in wartime, so this revival was short-lived. When peace returned, the company was again frustrated by high taxation, shortages of materials, and the need to export. By 1953 car production was over, though the company carried on with other projects,

RIGHT ABOVE
1929 Lea-Francis TT Hyper.

RIGHT BELOW
The Jaguar-based 1980 version.

LEFT
The Vulcan-built LFS 14/40.

BELOW LEFT
1939 Avon-bodied coupé.

BELOW
One of the last, a 1952 saloon.

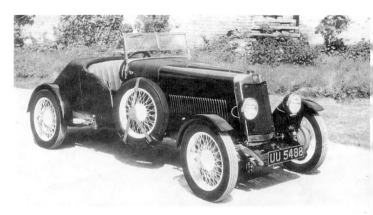

1929 Lea-Francis TT Hyper.

The Jaguar-based 1980 version.

such as agricultural equipment. There were a few attempts to revive the name on a car, such as the Ford-powered Lynx in 1960 and Jaguar-based retro sportster 20 years later, but neither succeeded.

OPPOSITE
ABOVE LEFT: 1996 Lexus LS450.

ABOVE RIGHT: 1996 GS300 Sport.

BELOW LEFT: 1996 Lexus LS400.

BELOW RIGHT: 1995 SC400.

LEXUS (Japan 1988 to date)
By the late 1980s Toyota, like all the major
Japanese makes, was a highly respected
marque, denoting solid, straightforward
engineering quality and reliability. But it
lacked prestige, so in an attempt to crack
the luxury car market Toyota created Lexus
as a completely new brand. This was not a
new idea, Ford, General Motors and
Chrysler having done the same half a
century earlier, but it was a great success.

The first Lexus was the LS400, a big
five-seat saloon with bland styling that

carried vague overtones of Mercedes-Benz.
Powered by a 244.1-cu in (4-litre) V8, it
offered a generous helping of standard
equipment allied to Toyota build quality.
Some said it lacked character, but then
many luxury car buyers did not want
'character', but rather Mercedes-style
dependability at a lower price, and that was
what the Lexus delivered. The LS400 was

followed by the SC300 and 400 coupés (the latter with a 183.1-cu in/3-litre six-cylinder engine) and the smaller (or maybe that should be 'less large') GS300 and 430, which were styled by Giugiaro.

In fact, the surest pointer to the success of the whole Lexus experiment was the steady rate at which the brand range grew through the 1990s. Luxury off-roaders were the trend of the time, and Lexus obliged with a re-badged version of the Toyota Land Cruiser, and later with its own RX300. The latter was thought better to drive than the equivalent Mercedes ML but not quite up to the BMW X5, though it was, of course, cheaper than both. The two German makes were clearly in Lexus's sights: the SC430 was a new convertible to rival the Mercedes SLK, sporting the brand's big 262.4-cu in (4.3- litre) V8 that was later adopted in the big LS. And Lexus made its smallest car yet in the IS200 and 300, a four-door mid-sized saloon aimed squarely at the BMW 3-series.

Bland maybe, Toyota had managed to create a brand-new badge that was capable of competing with the best that Europe and the U.S.A. could offer.

ABOVE
Lexus 2003 GX470.

ABOVE LEFT
2003 GS300.

CENTRE LEFT
2003 GS430.

CENTRE RIGHT
2003 IS300.

LEFT
2003 SC300.

LEYLAND (Great Britain 1920-1983)
Leyland was a maker of trucks and buses, but will always be associated on its home ground with the troubled British Leyland conglomerate. It started out as a family engineering concern in Leyland, Lancashire, turning to commercial vehicles in 1907. As a truck maker, Leyland flourished, though its first car was not a success. The Leyland Eight of 1920 was the brainchild of Henry Spurrier, one of the firm's financial backers. Spurrier directed that the company make the finest car in the world, regardless of cost. It was almost the company's downfall. Only 18 were sold, and Leyland almost slid into bankruptcy, recovering under new management only in the mid-1920s. Undeterred, it stayed in the car market, building more modest vehicles than the ostentatious Eight, such as the 10-hp (7.46-kW) Trojan.

By the early 1960s, Leyland was prosperous again, exporting its trucks, buses and coaches all over the world. It decided to diversify back into cars by taking over Standard Triumph in 1962 and Rover in 1967. In fact, this was the decade of mergers: Leyland joined up with British Motor Holdings in early 1968, bringing Austin, Morris, Jaguar, Daimler, MG, Riley, Wolseley and Leyland commercials

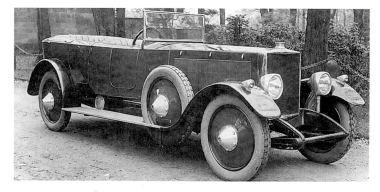

LEFT
1920 Leyland Eight show model.

BELOW LEFT
1959 948-cc Triumph Herald.

BELOW FAR LEFT
1925 Leyland Trojan 10-hp utility.

all together under one umbrella. In other words British Leyland now constituted most of the British-owned motor industry. But it didn't work. The new giant proved unwieldy and was eventually split up into smaller groups. Officially the cars were known for a while as 'Leyland Cars' but this ignored the strong brand loyalty to firms like Jaguar and Rover. In 1983, the group was split up for good: Leyland trucks and buses were eventually absorbed into Daf of the Netherlands, and its car-making days were over.

LINCOLN (U.S.A. 1920 to date)

Ford's luxury badge, Lincoln was no made-up brand to suit the marketing men. It started out as an independent manufacturer, though it had had links with Ford long before it became part of the company. Bob Leland and his son Wilfred ran a successful

machine-shop business, did some work for the original Henry Ford Company and for Cadillac, and in World War I built Liberty V12 aero engines.

It was not until 1920 that they built their first car. The first Lincoln was a very well-engineered luxury saloon, powered by

in taking over the company, but his son Edsel was more positive, so the deal was struck early in 1922. Sadly, the Lelands left within a few months: as so often happens with takeovers, there were very different ideas about who was now in charge.

Under the new regime, Lincoln sales picked up. Edsel had a nose for upmarket cars that would sell, just as his father had for cheap ones, and the original Lincoln V8 L series was soon making a profit. It was followed by the K series V12, which came with the bewildering choice of 23 body types. The gap between the two was filled in 1936 by the Lincoln Zephyr, while the arrival of the lower-priced Mercury division in 1939 confirmed Lincoln's position as Ford's luxury brand.

In the early 1950s, now under the new Henry Ford II regime, Lincoln made great

a 360-cu in (5.9-litre) V8. But it was a less than roaring success as a result of the recession of 1921 and the car's uninspired styling: the Lelands evidently put engineering first and style second. In little more than a year, the whole venture had collapsed into receivership. When first approached, Henry Ford was not interested

RIGHT
1997 Lincoln Continental.

FAR RIGHT
1997 Lincoln Mk VIII.

BELOW
1997 Lincoln Town Car.

OPPOSITE
LEFT:
TOP: 1922 Lincoln.

CENTRE LEFT: King George VI and
Queen Elizabeth stepping out of a Lincoln
on 22 June 1939 at Regina, Saskatchewan,
Canada.

CENTRE RIGHT: 1940 Lincoln
Continental coupé.

BOTTOM: Lincoln Zephyr.

RIGHT (from top to bottom)
1949 Continental.
1956 Continental MKII outside the factory.
1961 Continental.
BOTTOM LEFT: 1969 Continental Mk III.
BOTTOM RIGHT: 1970 Lincoln
Continental.

strides, taking 22 per cent of the U.S. luxury car market in 1953 but still way behind arch-rival Cadillac, though respectable enough. But Lincoln lost its way later in the decade, being without Cadillac's focused image, and only recovered with the 1961 Continental, a hugely successful car that turned the company round. By 1980, the Continental had grown into a 458-cu in (7.5-litre) V8

LEFT:
2002 Lincoln Blackwood with crewcab.

OPPOSITE
LEFT TOP: 2003 Lincoln Town Car.

LEFT BELOW: 2003 Navigator.

FAR RIGHT: 2003 Lincoln Aviator.

sedan, typical of the final generation of big American V8s, though Lincoln's attempt to sell the Versailles, a smaller car to compete with the Cadillac Seville, was less successful.

Lincoln was here to stay, however. It survived the recession of the early 1980s and followed in 1992 with the Mk VIII, still a big V8-powered saloon, but with modern styling and plenty of gadgets. The Continental had been updated in 1987, but for real traditionalists, there was always the Town Car of the late 1990s, a real throwback to 1970s values. As for Lincoln the name, its place as the upmarket Ford for American buyers looks secure.

LOCOMOBILE (U.S.A. 1899-1929)

Locomobile started not with petrol power, but with steam. A.L. Barber and J.B. Walker bought the rights to the Stanley steam car, and began producing steam buggies in 1899, though Walker left soon afterwards. He went on to build Mobiles, which were mechanically very similar to the Locomobiles.

A new era dawned for Locomobile when A.L. Riker joined the company as vice-president and chief engineer. Riker had been building electric cars before going on to produce petrol-engined vehicles, and after he arrived, Barber sold the steam patents back to Stanley, and rapidly introduced the first petrol-powered Locomobiles. The two men had upmarket aspirations, and by 1905 were offering powerful luxury cars in the Mercedes mould. Three years later, George Robertson won the Vanderbilt Cup in one of these vehicles. In 1911 Locomobile introduced its most famous car, the '48', which was to

cheaper Locomobile, the Junior 8, in an attempt to widen its appeal. With a 183.1-cu in (3-litre) engine, this outsold the bigger Locomobiles by eight to one, but it was still too expensive by General Motors' standards. The company closed in 1929.

last until the company's demise in 1929. During World War I the firm built tank engines, as well as staff cars and trucks, but following financial problems, merged with the Emlen Hare Motor Group in 1920.

Two years later the firm was acquired by Willam C. Durant, who used to produce Flint cars, though he also introduced a

ABOVE
1901 Steam buggy.

ABOVE LEFT
1901 6-hp twin-cylinder Steamer.

FAR LEFT
1916 six-cylinder Speedster.

LEFT
1900 Steam buggy.

LOTUS (Great Britain 1952 to date)
Lotus is the British Bugatti: it built, and
still does build, lightweight, nimble cars
that belied their small engines and
relatively modest power outputs with
superb handling and giant-killing
performance. If they failed to have mass-
production build quality, that was because
Colin Chapman, the power behind Lotus,
was an engineer through and through: it
was design and ideas that were his forte,
not production.

   Born in Richmond, Surrey, the young
Chapman was given his first car by his
parents in 1945. He sought to make a little
extra cash by buying and selling cars, but
the harsh economic conditions of post-war
Britain put paid to that idea. Instead, he
built a special, a trials car, based on an old

Austin Seven, which proved successful. His
day job was as a development engineer
with British Aluminium, but during the
evenings and weekends, Chapman built
cars. One went to Michael Allen, who was
so impressed that he suggested going into
partnership with Chapman, and Lotus
Engineering was born in January 1952,
working out of an old stable in north
London.

LEFT
Colin Chapman and Lotus 7.

BELOW LEFT
Lotus 6.

BELOW
1959 Series I Lotus 7.

Their first car was the Lotus Mk 4, which was also the first with a spaceframe chassis. This became a Chapman trademark, the ideal combination of strength with extreme lightness; the Mk 4 was intended for road use as well as competition. Allen left after a year, but Chapman's wife-to-be, Hazel Williams, stepped in with a cash injection of £25, enough to keep Lotus going. Slowly, for Colin Chapman was still working for British Aluminium at the time, the company built itself up. As well as producing competition/road cars, Chapman designed suspensions and chassis (always his speciality, rather than engines) for Grand Prix teams like BRM and Vanwall. But his next car was his most road-biased yet, the Lotus 7, unveiled at the 1957 Motor Show. Offered in kit form to take advantage of a tax loophole, the Seven could be fitted with 71.52-cu in (1.17-litre) Ford or 57.85-cu in

ABOVE LEFT
Lotus Esprit Turbo.

ABOVE RIGHT
Lotus Elan Sprint.

LEFT
Esprit GT3.

OPPOSITE
1961 Coventry Climax-powered Lotus Elite.

LEFT
Lotus 2.2-litre 180-bhp Excel SE.

BELOW LEFT
Lotus Elise.

BELOW
The GT1 used the Esprit's V8 engine in an Elise-style carbonfibre body.

OPPOSITE
The newly updated Elise.

948-cc) BMC engines. It was a landmark car, which developed a huge following, acquiring bigger engines over the years but staying true to the concept of a no-nonsense basic two-seater (comfort always came second in the Seven). So well-loved was the Lotus 7, that when the company stopped making it, Caterham Cars took it over. Forty-five years on, it was still possible to buy a new one.

With demand for the Seven running high, Lotus moved to a bigger factory and carried on developing racing cars: a Le Mans debut came in 1957 and Lotus won its first Grand Prix in 1960. Meanwhile, the first Lotus with a roof was announced as the glassfibre Elite. With a small Coventry Climax engine, the svelte little Elite caused a sensation, setting new standards for road-car handling. But it was too expensive to sell in large numbers, so for 1962 Chapman introduced the Elan, with a simple steel chassis replacing the complex spaceframe, and a Ford-based twin-cam engine of 95.1 cu in (1.6 litres). The successful Elan necessitated yet another move, this time to Hethel in Norfolk, and was followed in 1966 by the mid-engined Europa, which was powered by a Renault engine.

Despite some hard times in the late 1960s and early 1970s, Lotus survived to make its long-planned move upmarket with the four-seat Elite in 1974. This was totally new, with Lotus's own 122-cu in (2-litre) twin overhead-cam 16-valve power unit, a five-speed gearbox and striking wedge-shaped styling. A cheaper coupé, the Eclat, soon followed, with the arresting mid-engined Esprit in 1976, both using the same Lotus engine. In fact, that engine, originally developed for the Jensen-Healey sports car, was to prove very enduring; later enlarged to 134.25 cu in (2.2 litres) and fitted with a turbocharger, it took Lotus into the 1990s.

But the company struggled through a troubled 1980s. Partly tarnished by its association with the De Lorean project, it suffered a further blow when Colin Chapman died of a heart attack in 1982. The company was taken over by British Car Auctions, then in 1985 by General Motors. Meanwhile, the Esprit was gradually updated and a new two-seat Elan was unveiled in 1990. A management buyout in the early 1990s collapsed, but Lotus was taken over by Bugatti Automobili in 1993. When Bugatti itself collapsed, Lotus was rescued by Proton, the Malaysian car maker, in 1996. The late 1990s were to be happier times for Lotus. That same year, it unveiled the Elise, a mid-engined two-seater that seemed to be a reminder of what Lotus's bare essentials of handling, light weight and driving experience had once been. Powered by a Rover K-series engine of 109.8 cu in (1.8 litres), the Elise also used an unusual bonded alloy chassis. In the following year, an all-new 213.6-cu in (3.5- litre) V8 engine was fitted to the latest Esprit, with twin turbochargers to produce over 350bhp (261kW). Still produced in tiny numbers each year in the early 21st century, the Esprit has become something of an institution. The Elise has crept upmarket a little, but has remained a benchmark for its handling. Colin Chapman would have been pleased.

MARCOS (Great Britain 1959 to date)
Jem Marsh and Frank Costin met in a pub in
1959 and, so the story goes, decided to build
a wooden sports car to rival the Lotus 7.
Marsh already ran Speedex Castings, which
supplied parts for Austin 7 specials, while
Costin was an aerodynamicist who knew a
great deal about working with wood. So the
first Marcos really was made of stressed
marine ply, with only the nosecone of
glassfibre. It looked odd, with its bug-eyed
headlamps and gull-wing doors, but the car
was so light that the little Ford 100E engine
ensured it gave excellent performance.

Though intended primarily as a
competition car, the Marcos could also be
used on the road and by 1962 was being sold
in kit form. But the car that made Marcos
arrived two years later in the form of the
beautiful GT. Powered, incongruously
enough, by a 109.8-cu in (1.8-litre) Volvo
engine, the new Marcos resembled nothing
else on the road, apart, perhaps, from a
Ferrari or Maserati. It was styled by Dennis
Adams, the sleek glassfibre bodyshell
bonded to Marcos's trademark plywood
chassis; it became the classic Marcos.

Ford engines soon followed the Lotus:
a 91.41-cu in (1.5-litre) four-cylinder unit at
first, then 152.6-cu in (2.5-litre) and 183.1-
cu in (3-litre) V6 units, while in 1969 the
plywood chassis was discarded in favour of
a steel spaceframe, which made the cars
quicker and cheaper to build. The other
long-running model was the little Mini
Marcos, a kit car based around
Mini components. What this lacked in grace
it made up for in sheer affordability. This
would be taken over by D & H Fibreglass
Techniques in 1975, and developed into the
more sophisticated Midas in 1978. By that
time, Marcos itself was no more. The four-
seat Mantis of 1970 was not a success, and
the company was taken over the year after,

LEFT
Marcos 3-litre.

BELOW
Marcos Mantara.

OPPOSITE
Marcos with 3-litre Volvo engine.

with production ceasing in 1972.

That was not the end of the Marcos
story, however. In 1981 Jem Marsh put the
Marcos GT back into production at the old
factory in Westbury, Wiltshire. By 1986,
when two cars a week were rolling out of
the works, the Mantula was unveiled, with
the familiar Dennis Adams bodyshell now
powered by a 213.6-cu in (3.5-litre) Rover
V8 engine. And 20 years on from that
revival, one could still buy a new Marcos,
with all variations bearing a family
resemblance to the original GT. The two-
seater Mantis now offered a range of quad-
cam V8s: 280.7-cu in (4.6-litre) with 350bhp
(261kW), 305.1-cu in (5-litre) with 460bhp
(343kW) or 280.7-cu in (4.6-litre)
supercharged with just over 500bhp
(372.8kW). For racing, there was the
Chevrolet V8-powered LM600. Marcos has
come a long way since those original
'wooden wonders.'

MARENDAZ (Great Britain)

The name Marendaz sounds Spanish, or maybe Latin American, but the cars were thoroughly English, built in London and Maidenhead in the 1930s. Captain D.M.K. Marendaz, who had been a pilot in the Royal Flying Corps, began to build Maraseal cars after World War I at Brooklands. He later moved to Brixton Road in London, where Marendaz Specials were based for a few years, before moving to Maidenhead in 1932. The cars were only ever built in small numbers, and just 60 Marendaz cars were produced at Maidenhead over four years.

Famed for their style and sinuous chrome exhaust pipes (à la Mercedes), the Marendaz vehicles were sports cars intended for road or competition use. Many were used for trials, and the parents of racing driver Stirling Moss made good use of a 13/70 Marendaz in this way. They achieved many race victories and broke records: one particular 1926 car broke two records at Brooklands (the 3-hour and 311-mile/500-km) and four at Montlehéry (24-hour, 1,491-mile/2000-km, 621-mile/1000-km and 12-hour).

That car was powered by a 91.29-cu in (1.5-litre) Anzani engine, but later models used other units, such as the 1933 13/70 with a six-cylinder Continental engine topped with a Marendaz cylinder head. Three years later, Marendaz was producing the block as well.

LEFT
1926 1.5-litre Marendaz Special Brooklands Pacer.

OPPOSITE
1936 Marendaz Special.

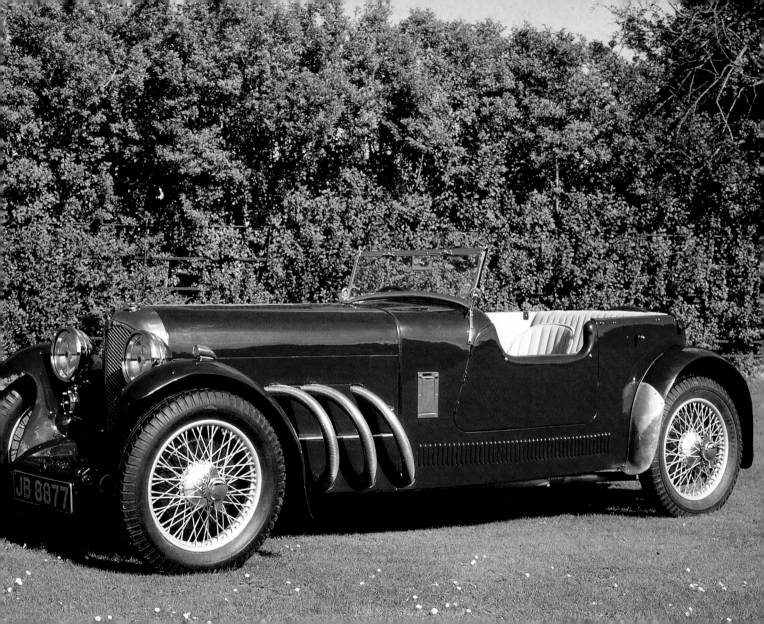

MARMON (U.S.A. 1902-1933)

Unusually for an American design, Howard Marmon's first car was an air-cooled V-twin, which he had begun to develop as early as 1898. It did not enter production, however, Marmon choosing instead to work on a four-cylinder version which appeared two years later. He remained with V4s until 1908 when he dropped them in favour of the more easily and therefore cheaper to produce in-line fours. But his fascination with vee power units continued: he experimented with a V6, built an unsuccessful V8 and finally produced the exotic V16 Sixteen as the company's swansong.

Meanwhile, Marmons were selling reasonably well, thanks to Ray Harroun's victory in the first-ever Indianapolis 500 of 1911, driving a Marmon 32. The 34 which succeeded it in 1916 was designed by Frederick Moskovics and Alanson Brush, and was unusual for being constructed mostly out of aluminium. When reintroduced after the end of World War I, the Model 34 used a cast-iron engine. But by now the company was facing hard times, and George M. Williams was brought in to turn it round. He succeeded by concentrating on cheaper cars, none of which prevented the company's rapid decline in the face of the Depression. In the circumstances, Howard Marmon's Sixteen, with its aluminium V16 motor of 488.2 cu in (8 litres), could hardly have been more inappropriate. The company was taken over by the American Automotive Corporation in 1933.

ABOVE RIGHT
The Marmon Wasp, the 1911 Indianapolis winner.
RIGHT
1929 Roosevelt 3.3.
FAR RIGHT
1930 Marmon straight-eight.

MASERATI (Italy 1926 to date)

There were five Maserati brothers (Alfieri, Bindo, Ettore, Ernesto and Mario), all involved with racing cars and motorcycles. A sixth, Carlo, died in 1910 and a seventh at birth. In 1926, the five brothers built their first car, a 91.5-cu in (1.5-litre) racer. In that same year Alfieri, a fine driver, had a class win in the Targa Florio. In fact, that racer was not their first, for the Maseratis had built a 122-cu in (2-litre) Grand Prix car for the Turin manufacturer Diatto in 1925, which was later sleeved down to produce the first 1.5-litre Maserati.

The brothers went into business for themselves, concentrating almost entirely on racing cars (the road cars would come later), which included a V16. By 1932, Alfieri was dead, the result of a racing accident, while Mario had left the business to become an artist. The remaining brothers carried on building cars, but in 1937 a controlling interest in their business was bought by industrialist Adolfo Orsi. The brothers signed a ten-year consultancy agreement with Orsi, but as soon as this expired they left to form OSCA sports cars.

In that same year Maserati unveiled its first true road car, the A6-1500. Fortunately, Orsi and his son Omer had found another design talent to fill the brothers' shoes. This was Gioacchino Colombo, who had already worked for Ferrari and Alfa Romeo. He was instrumental in producing the 250F in 1953,

one of the landmark Grand Prix racers: Juan Fangio won the drivers' championship in a 250F in 1957.

Meanwhile, Maserati was getting more serious about road cars, launching the 3500GT coupé in the same year that Fangio clinched his fifth world championship. By 1966 the range included the Quattro Porte saloon, Mexico V8-coupé and Ghibli, the latter first in coupé and later in open Spyder form. All of these were front-engined cars, but to rival Ferrari, Maserati needed a mid-engined design and produced the Bora V8 of 1971, which neatly fitted the bill.

The Orsi family had sold its interest in Maserati to Citroën in 1969: the French manufacturer wanted access to a producer

TOP RIGHT
1953-54 250F straight-six Grand Prix car.

TOP LEFT
Nuvolari in a 1934 8CM3000.

ABOVE
1959 2-litre 'Birdcage' Tipo 60.

ABOVE LEFT
Mistral coupé.

Far LEFT (top to bottom)
1956 twin-cam 250F F1 racer.
1960s 3500GT, first seen in 1957.
1964 Quattro Porte.

of high-performance engines for its forthcoming SM coupé. The SM was an odd mixture: unmistakably a Citroën, but with a Maserati V6 under the hood. Unfortunately, buyers were not attracted by this intriguing mix of European culture, and the SM did not last long. Having no further use for Maserati, Citroën started to look around for a buyer, and in May 1975 announced that the Modena factory was to go into voluntary liquidation. The prospect of this famous Italian name going under had the desired effect, and Alejandro de Tomaso came forward to take over, with backing from the Italian government.

Through the late 1970s and 1980s there was still no attempt to make a Maserati supercar, but the company persevered with its V8s, notably the Kyalami Coupé and Khamsin 2+2. A new smaller Maserati was the mid-engined V6 Merak, first in 2-litre but later in 3-litre forms. In 1982, the Biturbo was another departure, a compact luxury saloon powered by a twin-turbo 2-litre V6 producing 180bhp (134.2kW). Convertible and four-door saloons, with 152.6- and 170.9-cu in (2.5- and 2.8-litre) versions of the V6, followed.

But Maserati was in serious trouble by the early 1990s. It had made a profit back in 1982, but some said that was its first ever! In 1993, it was taken over by Fiat, and the dated Biturbo was given a much needed update, while a 256.3-cu in (4.2-litre) V8 Quattro Porte followed in 1995. Two years later, Maserati was taken over by none other than Ferrari. This led to a fresh injection of cash, with the Modena factory re-equipped

the following year and a new 3200GT. By 2002, the company was offering the Coupé and Spyder, both powered by a 256.3-cu in (4.2-litre) V8, with optional semi-automatic gearchange.

ABOVE
Maserati Indy.

LEFT
Maserati Mexico.

OPPOSITE
Maserati Mistral.

ABOVE
Maserati Merek.

ABOVE LEFT
Maserati Shamal.

LEFT
Maserati Bora.

OPPOSITE
2004 model.

MATHIS (Germany/France 1910-1950)
Emile Mathis was a dealer for Fiat, De Dietrich, Minerva and Panhard, but was to work with Bugatti and Henry Ford as well as building his own cars. The dual nationality of his company, incidentally, came from its Strasbourg location: the Alsace region was German before World War I, and was returned to France in 1918.

The first Mathis cars were actually built by Stoewer and sold in Germany as Stoewer-Mathis vehicles, but in 1912 came the little Babylette, a true Mathis, and within two years a range of five cars was on offer. Although the early Mathis cars were noted for their light weight, by the early 1930s the company had gone upmarket with big straight-eight engines. Mathis was not afraid of innovation, offering features like synchromesh gearboxes and independent front suspension years before such things reached the mainstream.

Despite their advanced features, Mathis cars were not selling well, but a new lucrative line was found by producing Fords at Strasbourg. A new Matford company was formed, and these cars were

soon outselling the Mathis cars. Emile Mathis sold the concern to Ford, though kept his factory. He lived in the U.S.A. during World War II, but returned to Strasbourg after 1945 in an effort to restart production. Two prototypes, the three-wheel VL333 and four-wheel 666, never made it. Mathis himself died in an accident during 1956.

MATRA (France 1965-1993)
Matra of France was an aeronautical engineering contractor, which in 1964 took over René Bonnet sports cars. At first, the René Bonnet Djet was sold as a Matra, but three years later the company transferred production to its own new factory at Romorantin, and launched the M530. This was a beautiful coupé powered by a Ford V4 engine, though a poor dealer network prevented it from becoming a success.

This underlined the fact that Matra was a very small manufacturer, and its best hope for success was to amalgamate with one of the big boys. So that is what the company did, forming an agreement with Simca to set up Matra-Simca in 1969. All this time, Matra had been heavily involved in racing, building Formula 1 cars in the mid-1960s and later on receiving substantial backing from the oil giant Elf and also from the French government to produce a new Formula 1 car. Matra was to carry on supplying Formula 1 engines to the Ligier team into the 1980s.

ABOVE
1920 Mathis Type P.

LEFT
1928 six-cylinder Mathis.

FAR LEFT
Circa 1913 four-cylinder sports.

RIGHT
Matra Murena.

BELOW
Matra Djet with 1-litre Renault engine.

BELOW RIGHT
Matra 530 with 1.7-litre Ford V4 engine.

Back with Simca, the first fruit of the Matra-Simca union appeared in 1973 as the mid-engined Bagheera sports car. A 79.3- or 85.4-cu in (1.3- or 1.4-litre) unit was mounted transversely in the glassfibre bodyshell; the Bagheera was unusual in that it accommodated three people, the driver and two passengers seated abreast. Another project was the Matro Rancho, in the style of a four-wheel-drive estate (without four-wheel-drive), again based on Simca components. The Bagheera was replaced in 1980 by the steel-bodied Murena, now with a 134.25-cu in (2.2-litre) Chrysler engine. Three years later, Matra left what had become the giant Peugeot-Citroën empire to join Renault. Here, its major contribution was the Espace, which virtually invented a new class of vehicle, the people-carrier.

MAYBACH (Germany 1921-1941)
Carl Maybach was responsible for
Maybach cars, but this may never have
happened but for the influence of his
engineer father, Wilhelm. The latter was a
brilliant designer, a partner of Gottlieb
Daimler, who is credited with developing
the spray carburettor and vertical-twin
engine layout. After Daimler died in 1900,
Maybach carried on working for Emil
Jellinek, perfecting his Mercedes cars, until
he left the company in 1907.

Disenchanted by cars, Wilhelm
involved himself in Germany's golden age
of airship development, producing the huge
piston engines needed for these
aeronautical behemoths. One type measured
1,288 cu in (21 litres) and, incredibly, an
example was used to power a racing car,
the Metallique-Maybach.

Germany was forbidden an aviation
industry after World War I, so while
Wilhelm Maybach retired (he died of
pneumonia in 1929) his son Carl returned
to cars. Like his father, Carl was something
of a perfectionist, so Maybach cars were
constructed on a grand scale. In memory of
their airship days, the 488.2-cu in (8-litre)
V12 limousine was named the Zeppelin.
The Maybach cars were natural rivals to the
Mercedes vehicles of the day, being heavy,
well-engineered saloons with every
conceivable luxury. The 1927 W5, for
example, was by no means Maybach's
biggest, but nonetheless it weighed some
7,826lb (3550kg). It also boasted a six-
cylinder engine of 427.2 cu in (7 litres) and
generated so much torque that only a two-
speed gearbox was needed.

Germany in the early 1930s was not an
ideal market for such extravagances,
however, and Maybach also built trucks,
which soon became the company's main
source of income. Car production ended in
World War II, never to resume, and the firm
survives as a maker of heavy-duty diesel
engines.

MAZDA (Japan 1960 to date)
The first Mazda car appeared in 1960, but
by then this well-known Japanese firm had
already been in existence for 40 years. Set
up as Toyo Cork Kogyo at Hiroshima in
1920, it built motorcycles for a short time,
as well as machine tools and drilling
equipment. By 1931, it had been renamed
Mazda (after both founder Jujior Matsuda,
and Mazda, god of light) and was
producing a light truck. A prototype car was
actually built in 1940, but World War II
prevented any further development.

Mazda was lucky not to suffer any
serious damage from the atomic bombing
of Hiroshima, though truck production did
not resume until the 1950s, and Mazda's
first true production-car finally appeared in
1960. It was a typical Japanese micro-car of
the time, a two-seater coupé powered by an
air-cooled V-twin of 21.72 cu in (356cc). Its
16bhp (11.93kW) was enough to push the
little car along at 56mph (90km/h), and
enough for Mazda to sell well over 20,000
in its first year. It was followed up by the
P-360 two years later, now with water-
cooling and two- or four-door saloon
bodywork. Enlarged to 35.76 cu in (586cc)
in 1964, the micro Mazda now boasted
28bhp (20.88kW).

In that year Mazda moved up a class to
full-sized cars with the Familia, a
'conventional' four-door saloon with a
47.72-cu in (782-cc) four-cylinder engine.
The vehicle was in fact not that
conventional, except in appearance, for the
overhead-valve engine was of light alloy
and Mazda offered a two-speed automatic
alongside the standard four-speed manual
gearbox. A 90-mph (145-km/h) coupé later
joined the range, with an overhead-
camshaft 60.11-cu in (985-cc) engine
giving 68bhp (50.7kW). The Familia sold
so well that Mazda became Japan's third
biggest car manufacturer by the mid-1960s,
selling over 80,000 cars in 1965. It was
encouraged to introduce the larger 929 (also
known as the Cosmo or Luce) in 1966,
which was styled by Bertone and came with
a 90.9-cu in (1.5-litre) four-cylinder engine.

So far, so conventional. But both the
Familia coupé and the 929 were to have
another engine option that only one other
company in the world was offering: a

BELOW
The 1967 Mazda 1000.

BOTTOM
The Italian styling of its 1500 cousin.

FAR LEFT
1973-74 RX-4, with a rotary engine.

FAR LEFT BELOW
The 1300 saloon, a big seller in the 1970s.

LEFT (top to bottom)
1985 RX-7 2+2.
1990 RX-7 turbo cabriolet.
1990 323F 1.8 GT injection.
1990 121 1.3 LX sun top.
1990 626 2.0-litre GLX Executive.

Its 59.93-cu in (982-cc) twin-rotor engine produced 110bhp (82kW), later boosted to 128bhp (95.4kW) for a top speed of 125mph (200km/h). So successful was the 110S that the rotary option was extended to other Mazdas. The 929 was developed into the twin-rotor RX-4, a 120-mph (193-km/h) saloon that became a great success. By 1978, Mazda had sold over a million rotary-engined cars, making it by far the most prolific producer in the world.

Meanwhile, exports were growing fast, and in 1970 the mid-sized Capella 616 was brought in to plug the gap between the small Familia and big 929. As well as 90.9- or 96.8-cu in (1.5- or 1.6-litre) piston engines, there was of course a Wankel option, in this case a 34.97-cu in (573-cc) twin-rotor unit. In the following year the Grand Familia 808 slotted in beneath the 616, with 77.6- or 90.9-cu in (1.3- or 1.5-litre) reciprocating or 29.96-cu in (491-cc) Wankel engine options, in saloon, coupé or estate car bodies.

Wankel rotary. Mazda had long shown an interest in the Wankel, and bought a licence from NSU to build its own version. It had built running units before the first sample engines were shipped over from Germany, and it is interesting that of all the automotive companies that became involved with the Wankel, whether experimentally or in production, only Mazda persevered and made a long-lasting

success of the concept. The company overcame the perennial problem of rapid rotor-seal wear, and many customers were prepared to pay extra for the smooth-running rotary, despite a higher fuel consumption, than a reciprocating piston engine.

Mazda's first rotary-engined car was the Cosmo 110S coupé, also the first mass-produced rotary-engined car in the world.

Brave though it was, the twin-engined strategy almost led to Mazda's collapse. Only extra financial backing from the Sumitomo Bank saved it, and Mazda responded by introducing the Familia 323 in 1975. This was as simple and conventional as the rotary-engined cars had been adventurous. It was reliable, cheap to make and sold in huge numbers, and it saved Mazda. From then on, rotary engines became increasingly restricted to the upmarket and sporting Mazdas. This was underlined by a new 626 with conventional four-cylinder engines and the rotary-powered RX-7 of 1978. The latter was a landmark car for Mazda, keeping the rotary idea alive and establishing it as a maker of serious sports cars. It was a good seller, in production for over 20 years, by which time it had transformed into a twin-turbo design to rival the Porsche 944.

Ford bought 24 per cent of Mazda's parent company in 1979, which further bolstered the recovery, and from then on the two firms co-operated on car development. Front-wheel-drive 323s and 626s followed, and Mazda gained access to the lucrative Australasian market, where the 323 in particular sold well. A little 121 in 1988 brought Mazda back to the small car class and for 1990 it unveiled the retro-styled MX-5, a conventional rear-wheel-

drive sports car influenced by the original Lotus Elan. A huge success, it was still in production over a decade later. Although Mazda cars could be regarded as conventional under the skin, they often had sleek styling, such as the fastback 323 of the mid-90s and Xedos saloon of 1991. Keen drivers liked the four-cylinder Mazda 6, though by 2002 most of Mazda's range had slipped back into boxy anonymity.

ABOVE
2002 Mazda pick-up truck.

FAR LEFT TOP
2001 Mazda MP3.

FAR LEFT CENTRE
626 LX.

FAR LEFT BOTTOM
2002 Sport Wagon.

BELOW LEFT
2002 Millenia.

OPPOSITE
ABOVE LEFT: Mazda MX-3 1.6.

ABOVE RIGHT: European Mazda 121.

BELOW LEFT: 1997 Mazda 626 five-door.

BELOW RIGHT: Mazda MX-5.

LEFT
Mazda MX-5 1.8i Sport.

BELOW LEFT
Mazda Demio.

BELOW
Mazda Premacy.

RIGHT
Mazda RX-8.

MERCEDES-BENZ (Germany 1901 to date)

Mercedes-Benz is often cited as one of the most widely recognized brands in the world, not only among car manufacturers but also as a worldwide brand to rival Coca-Cola and Nike. How did this maker of solid, unexciting but very well-engineered saloons achieve such pre-eminence? The answer is two-fold: alongside this apparent conservatism Mercedes is a pioneer of passive safety, with features like anti-lock brakes and fuel injection. Moreover, most car buyers the world over are not enthusiasts: what they want is utter dependability with a dash of snob appeal, and that is what Mercedes has always delivered.

It was an amalgam of two companies, Mercedes being the name given to later

Daimler cars. Daimler was a pioneer motor manufacturer, encouraged by financial banker Emil Jellinek to build the high-performance four-cylinder cars from 1901 that made its reputation. Mercedes was the name of Jellinek's daughter, first used as a pseudonym at an 1899 speed trial, and adopted for all Daimler cars in 1902. The company became well known for its luxurious quality cars, which used sleeve-valve Knight engines from 1911 and superchargers from 1921. But even with Ferdinand Porsche as chief designer, the company was not immune to recession, and was forced into a co-operative agreement with Benz, another German pioneer, in 1924. Two years later, the companies merged, and Mercedes-Benz was born.

Daimler had a history of supercharging, and Dr. Porsche made good use of it in a new generation of Mercedes-Benz sports-racers, beginning with the 1926 K. This was followed by the 1927 S and 1928 SSKL, the last of which was a 427.2-cu in (7-litre) monster that could muster 200bhp (149.1kW) with the supercharger engaged. When Porsche left in 1928 to be replaced by Hans Nibel, there was a greater

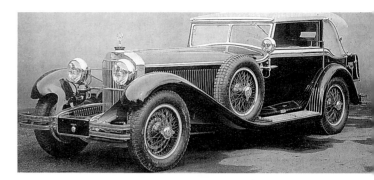

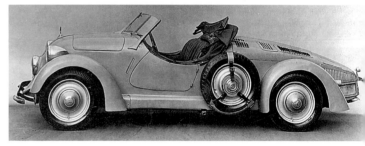

ABOVE LEFT
1922 6/25 PS limousine.

LEFT
Gottlieb Daimler and his 1886 car.

BELOW LEFT
1913 sleeve-valve Mercedes-Knight.

TOP
1928 Type SS cabriolet.

ABOVE
1934 Type 150 rear-engined sports.

OPPOSITE
Mercedes SSK.

emphasis on refinement, though big supercharged sportsters continued, such as the 1933 380 and 540K of 1936. The latter used a straight-eight 329.5-cu in (5.4-litre) engine giving 180bhp (134.2kW) with the supercharger doing its job.

But the big sellers were conventional saloons like the 170V, the most popular M-B, and the 2600, the world's first diesel-engined production car. There was also a range of small rear-engined cars, though these were not big sellers. Supercharging was also applied to the big limousines, such as the 770. But of course, the best known Mercedes of the 1930s were those monstrously fast Grand Prix cars,

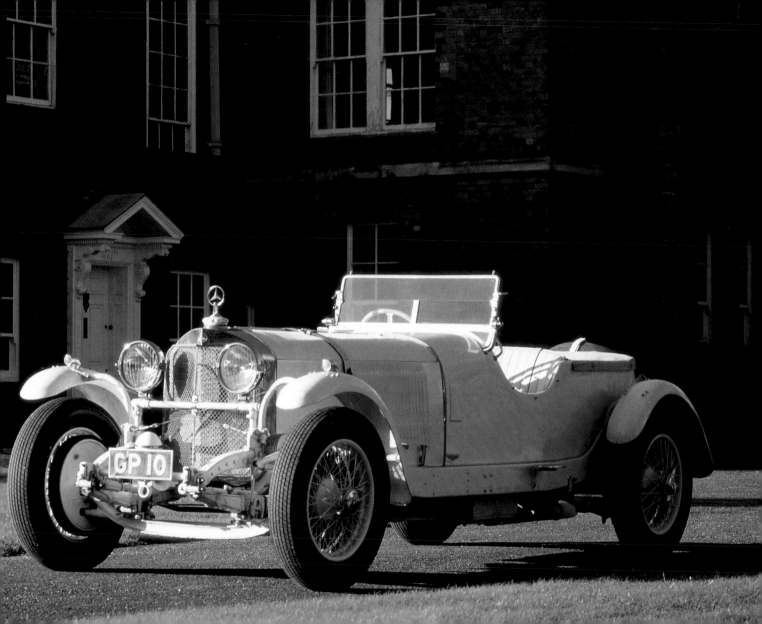

themselves were back into production, joined by a six-cylinder 220 in 1951. Both the 170 and 220 were available as saloon, coupé or cabriolet, with bare chassis sold to coachbuilders. A bigger 300 soon followed, making it clear that Mercedes was determined to return to its pre-war role of building prestige cars.

The company restarted a race programme at this time as well, with the 300SL 'Gullwing' combining the 220's power unit with a tubular steel spaceframe. This was developed into a road-going 300SL for 1954, complete with gull-wing doors and fuel injection, which became one of the classic sports cars of all time, remaining in production up to 1961.

A new generation of unitary-

construction cars began to appear in the mid-1950s, the saloons replacing the 170 and 220, and a new 190SL sports car. The 220SE adopted the 300SL's fuel injection in 1958, another pioneering move. Another new range of saloons in 1959 also pioneered passive safety, with deformable front and rear sections to protect the passenger cell. The range was large, from a diesel 1800 (Mercedes would always have a dependable diesel in its range) to the six-cylinder fuel-injected 300SL.

None of these were ultimate luxury cars, but in 1963 Mercedes-Benz sought to plug that gap with the big 600, a massive long-wheelbased limousine powered by a 384.5-cu in (6.3-litre) V8 engine. This powerful engine gave the heavy 600 a

developed with Hitler's personal encouragement. In the final years before World War II, these supercharged straight-eights and V12s dominated Grand Prix.

After the war, Mercedes was devastated, its factories bombed out and under the control of various Allied commands. But light trucks were soon rolling off the rebuilt production lines, based on the pre-war 170V saloon, and two years into peacetime, the pre-war cars

ABOVE
Mercedes 320 saloon.

RIGHT
Mercedes 190/170 sedan.

OPPOSITE
1934 Mercedes 500K.

surprising turn of speed, though it was even more sparkling in the mid-sized 300SEL 6.3 of 1968, whose conservative appearance concealed sports car performance. The 300 was part of the new S-class for 1965, the rest of which had six-cylinder engines.

For the 1970s Mercedes-Benz announced a new range of SL sports cars (though more coupés than out-and-out sports models) with removable steel hardtops. In 1974 a new S-class appeared, with the 300SEL flagship now even quicker, due to a 421.1-cu in (6.9-litre) version of the V8. But times were changing, and Mercedes-Benz was having to pay more attention to emissions and economy regulations, especially in the U.S.A. Its long diesel experience was paying dividends here, with a range of five-cylinder engines, some of which were turbocharged: Mercedes in fact pioneered the turbo-diesel saloon. An estate car joined the mid-sized saloons.

A departure came in 1979 with the G-Wagen four-wheel-drive off-roader, designed to rival the successful Range Rover and Toyota Land Cruiser. Although well-built and capable, the G-Wagen was simply too utilitarian to compete with these luxury 4x4s, though it remained part of the Mercedes-Benz line-up for many years. Another new market was sought with the 190 saloon of 1982, an attempt by Mercedes to compete with the smaller BMWs. It sold well, becoming the company's best-selling car, though it never had the sporting cachet of BMW, despite image-boosting derivatives such as the Cosworth-developed 190-2.3. Meanwhile, the mid-sized saloons, estates and coupés were replaced in 1985, followed by a new SL sports car in 1989. Beneath their staunchly conservative styling, these 1980s

Mercedes-Benzes were high-technology machines: anti-lock braking, four-wheel-drive and traction control all featured in certain models. The open-topped SL, for example, featured a fold-down roll-bar that sprang into place in a fraction of a second in the event of an accident.

But Mercedes-Benz was not weathering the recession well. Despite the 190, itself not a cheap car, it was depending heavily on expensive luxury cars that drank a lot of fuel. The C-class which replaced the 190 in 1993, was not such a big seller and the new curvier E-class of 1995, and the extravagant S-class (complete with double-glazed windows) were simply more of the same. But from the mid-1990s the company showed a new determination to crack different markets. The SL range had become hugely expensive, several classes

ABOVE and OPPOSITE
Mercedes 300SL Gullwing.

RIGHT
1965 230SL.

LEFT
1987 500SL.

BELOW
250TD estate.

BELOW LEFT
Mercedes 300.

up from the original 190SL, but the smaller, cheaper SLK of 1996 proved an instant hit. An steel electric folding roof was standard, and there were four-cylinder supercharged or V6 engines. Perhaps even more significant was the creatively conceived A-class launched in the following year. This mini-MPV put a Mercedes within the reach of Ford and VW buyers, and once initial scares concerning its handling had been resolved, proved very popular. Moving

ABOVE
1997 Mercedes SLK.

ABOVE LEFT
C-class Sport.

FAR LEFT
The V230 people carrier.

CENTRE and LEFT
E-class estate. and saloon.

LEFT
The luxury S-class.

FAR LEFT
500SL sports car.

even further down the price range, Mercedes collaborated on the Smart microcar, a joint project with Nicholas Hayek, inventor of the Swatch watch. With two seats and a 36.61-cu in (600-cc) engine tucked under the floor, it brought new chic to city cars.

In 1998, Daimler-Benz, the parent company of Mercedes, merged with Chrysler. This promised both companies the prospect of lower costs through sharing components, while each partner could concentrate on its strengths: Chrysler on pick-ups and SUVs, and Mercedes-Benz on saloons. Not that there was any chance of Mercedes-Benz abandoning its traditional plutocratic customers: the 2002 CL coupé and S-Class limousine were both available with a twin-turbo V12.

297

ABOVE
1997 A-class.

LEFT ABOVE
4-wheel-drive.

LEFT
1997 SLK.

ABOVE RIGHT
SLK 32 Sport .

RIGHT
C-class coupé.

RIGHT
2003 E500 sedan.

BELOW CLK500 cabriolet.

BOTTOM 2003 C32 AMG.

BELOW CENTRE
2003 S500 sedan.

FAR LEFT CENTRE
ML 500.

FAR LEFT BOTTOM
G500.

RIGHT
Mercedes 'Smart' car.

OPPOSITE
2004 Mercedes E-class wagon.

OVERLEAF
PAGE 302: The SLA small sports car
concept was based on that of the A-class.

PAGE 303: The Maybach concept car saw
Mercedes reviving a long-forgotten name.

MERCER (U.S.A. 1910-1925)

Mercer cars were fast, lightweight and almost totally devoid of creature comforts. The company which built them grew out of the Walter Automobile Co., setting up as Mercer in 1910.

Starting as it meant to go on, Mercer offered as its first products cars designed primarily for racing and powered by Beaver engines. In the following year, the Type 35 Raceabout was introduced as a spartan road car which put driving thrills above all else. Its 305.1-cu in (5-litre) four-cylinder Continental unit gave a modest 55bhp (41kW), but the Raceabout was so light that this was enough for a startling performance. A Raceabout won the American Grand Prize event at Indianapolis in 1914, driven by Eddie Pullen.

It was replaced in 1915 by the Type 22, which was more powerful but with more enclosed bodywork, so much of the Raceabout's raw appeal was lost. By 1920, Mercer was facing serious financial problems, and was taken over by Hare's Motor Group. The result was to move the company further away from it sporting roots, though the Rochester-engined six-cylinder car of 1923 was not exactly slow. But even this ceased production in 1925 and despite an attempt to revive the marque in 1931, no more was heard of Mercer.

MERCURY (U.S.A. 1938 to date)

Henry Ford made his Model T cheaper than any other car on the market by building nothing else. It was cheap because every Model T was exactly the same as all the others: there was no choice of engine, trim level or, perhaps most famously, colour. But by the late 1930s, even Henry Ford had to

LEFT
1914 Mercer Type 35 Raceabout.

ABOVE
1939 Mercury Eight.

RIGHT
1950 Mercury four-door sedan.

LEFT TOP
1957 Turnpike cruiser.

LEFT CENTRE
1966 Cyclone G.

LEFT
1968 Park Lane brougham.

TOP
1967 Cougar.

ABOVE
1969 Marauder.

accept that times had changed. The mass-market was more affluent now, and people could afford to spend a little extra to have a more prestigious car than their neighbours. Hence the introduction of the Lincoln marque, so that Ford could sell cars to richer people who would not be seen dead in anything as ordinary as a Ford.

Mercury did the same for the middle-class market. There was still a big gap between the basic Ford V8 and the Lincoln Zephyr, but Henry's son Edsel and Ford sales chief Jack Davis filled it with the new

305

Mercury Eight. The Eight was a huge success, selling over 70,000 in 1939, and making it a household name.

It was followed in 1941 by a larger Mercury (though this used a Ford

ABOVE
1995 Mystique LS.

LEFT
1997 Grand Marquis. This was the largest of the range.

FAR LEFT (from top to bottom)
1976 Grand Monarch Ghia.
1976 Bobcat.
1988 Tracer estate.
1988 Merkur Scorpio.
1900 high-performance Cougar.

bodyshell) but thereafter the brand moved closer to Lincoln, and the first new car after World War II, the Type 72 Coupé, used a Lincoln body. Smaller Mercury cars followed, with the compact Comet, which was derived from the Ford Falcon, in 1960, and the mid-sized Meteor a couple of years later. In fact, Mercury was developing a wide range, albeit with Ford components. The Cougar two-door coupé of 1967 was a Mustang competitor, while the Bobcat of 1973 was a sub-compact; its replacement, the Lynx of 1981, was based on the European Ford Escort. In the late 1980s, the Mercury Sable was part of Ford's DN5 programme, and an upmarket version of the Taurus. Meanwhile, the Cougar carried on, really the Ford Thunderbird with some different sheet metal and badges, and now called the XR7. The Tracer did the same with the U.S. Ford Escort while the

ABOVE
1997 Mercury Tracer.

TOP LEFT
1997 Cougar XR7.

CENTRE LEFT
The Mercury Villager is based on the Nissan Quest minivan.

LEFT
The Mountaineer was launched in 1996.

ABOVE
2002 Sable Wagoneer.

LEFT
2002 Mountaineer.

TOP RIGHT
2000 Mystique sport.

CENTRE RIGHT
2001 Cougar ZN.

RIGHT 2002 Cougar RX.

OPPOSITE
ABOVE LEFT: 2003 Marauder.

ABOVE RIGHT: 2002 Villager sport.

BELOW LEFT: 2003 Sable sedan.

BELOW RIGHT: Messenger concept car.

Mystique was a Ford Contour/Mondeo by another name. For its 1990s people-carrier, Mercury turned to Nissan: the Mercury Villager was a Nissan Quest in disguise, while that other niche market of the 1990s, the 4x4, was catered for by the Mountaineer, a Ford Explorer given the Mercury treatment.

MG (Great Britain 1924-1980 and 1985 to date)

Generations of British drivers grew up lusting after an MG, for the use of mass-production Morris components made it an affordable, fun sports car. Never at the forefront of technology, MG nevertheless inspired a loyal following, especially in Britain and the U.S.A., where in the 1950s it introduced Americans to the concept of a small, cheap and nimble sports car.

Although always associated with giants Austin and Morris, and despite the fact that its initials stood for Morris Garages, MG started out as an independent. Morris dealer, Cecil Kimber, based in the Morris home city of Oxford, fitted a few special four-seat bodies to Morris Cowleys in 1922, and sold them with the name Chummy. Other rebodied Morris cars followed: one of them was advertised as the MG V-Front Saloon, and the MG was born. The relationship with Morris remained close, and in 1927 Kimber accepted a £10,000 loan from William Morris himself, allowing him to move to a new factory. Two years later, increasing demand forced him to move again, this time to Abingdon, a few miles south of Oxford. It would remain the home of MG for the next 50 years.

Not that MGs were simply rebadged Morrises. From the late 1920s Kimber stopped buying complete chassis from Morris, taking his major components from

ABOVE
MG 'M' saloon.

LEFT
1939 MG TA Tickford.

OPPOSITE
ABOVE LEFT: 2.6-litre MG WA.

ABOVE RIGHT: 1930 MG 18/80 Tigress.

BELOW LEFT: SA saloon.

BELOW RIGHT: MG K2.

a variety of sources, though engines were invariably Morrises; this marked the birth of MG as a genuine car maker. A key model was the new Midget of 1928, with its little 51.69-cu in (847-cc) overhead-cam engine from the Morris Minor. There were bigger MGs as well, such as the 152.6-cu in (2.5-litre) six-cylinder 18/80 and later the 122-cu in (2-litre) SA saloon which was aimed at the SS Jaguar.

By the late 1930s MG was owned by Leonard Lord, a Yorkshire businessman who was later to head Austin. The hard-headed Lord soon closed down MG's competition department, which was successful but expensive, and insisted that cheaper pushrod (rather than overhead-cam) Morris motors be used. There was also a return to the use of more Morris components. None of this dented MG's popularity, however,

RIGHT
MG 'N' type Allingham.

BELOW
MG 14/40 2-seater tourer.

BELOW RIGHT
MG YB saloon.

OPPOSITE
1930 18/80 Mk II tourer.

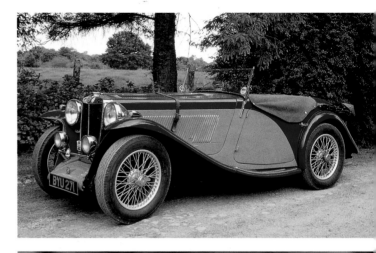

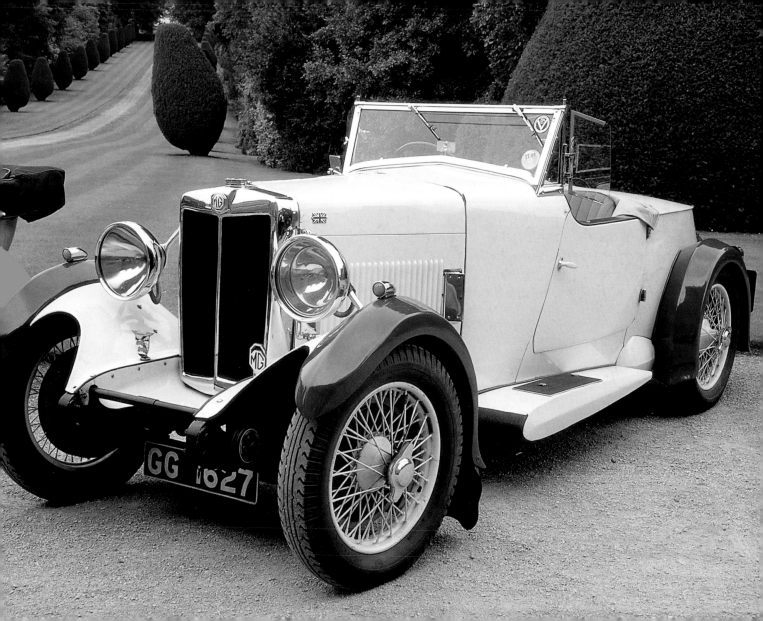

particularly not that of the TA/TB Midget.

After World War II MG simply re-introduced its pre-war cars: the new TC was a mildly updated TB, but its popularity was even greater than it had been before the war. Exports to the U.S.A. began in 1947, where the little MG was a big hit: 10,000 were built in five years. The succeeding TD was even more successful, and most of these were exported. Plans for a new Midget were dropped in 1953, as a result of the success of the Austin-Healey 100 and the fact that MG was now part of the giant British Motor Corporation; the downside of access to all those cheap mass-production components was that control of the company rested with top management in Cowley and Longbridge, rather than Abingdon.

BMC was keen to cut costs by sharing components between the large number of marques under its umbrella. So the new MG Magnette ZA saloon of 1954 used the same bodyshell as the Wolseley 4/44, while the

LEFT
1953 MG TF 1500.

BELOW
1950s MG TD tourer.

OPPOSITE
1960 MGB roadster.

later Magnette ZB had the same Farina body as every mid-sized BMC car, albeit with an MG radiator grille and badges. Through the 1950s and '60s a whole range of badge-engineered MG saloons appeared, a fact that horrified generations of enthusiasts, though if truth be told, there had long been MG saloons, and MGs had always relied on mass-production components, and always would.

However, there can be no denying the fact that MG sports cars were far more distinctive than the saloons. The new MGA of 1955 enclosed the corporate BMC mechanics in modern, aerodynamic bodywork: with sales of over 100,000, it was the most successful MG until its successor, the MGB, came along in 1962. With unitary construction and far more comfort than the MGA, this had sold over 460,000 by the time it was dropped in

ABOVE LEFT
1969 MG Midget Mk III.

ABOVE
MG RV8.

LEFT
MG 1.8i.

1980. The MGB GT was an attractive fastback version, and bigger-engined derivatives, the six-cylinder MGC and Rover-engined MGB GT V8, were fast but sold in much smaller numbers. Alongside these mid-sized success stories, the little Midget was revived in 1960, at first with a 57.85-cu in (948-cc) engine but later increased to 67, 77.8 and finally 91.1 cu in (1.10, 1.27 and 1.5 litres). It was really a rebadged version of the Austin-Healey Sprite, which had been made at Abingdon since 1958. And it was another success, revisiting the old Midget concept of a cheap, fun sports car. Like the MGB, the Midget had had a long life, though some would argue too long.

The beleaguered BMC, by then British Leyland, lacked either the funds or the foresight (or indeed both) to replace the two MGs, so they hung on into old age though they were still selling steadily.

In fact the parent group was in deep trouble by the late 1970s, and when the MGB ceased production in 1980, the Abingdon plant was shut down for good. But this was not the end of the MG story. The latest incarnation of BMC, Austin-Rover, recognized the value of the MG name, and in the late 1980s applied it to the small Metro, hatchback Maestro and Montego saloon. It was just like the old days!

But the name would soon be devalued by bolting it on to family cars alone, with no sports car to back it up. In 1992, the MG RV8 was a mildly updated Rover V8-powered MGB, more a statement of intent than a long-term proposition. A few years later, a thoroughly modern sports car arrived in the form of the MGF, complete with mid-engine (the latest Rover-built 97.6- or 109.8-cu in/1.6- or 1.8-litre units) and Hydragas suspension. It was an instant

hit, and in 2002 was substantially updated as the MG TF, with conventional steel springs.

Alongside it, the Rover saloons and hatches got the MG treatment as well. The changes were more extensive than in the old days, when they were confined to a new coat of paint and different trim. The MG ZR (Rover 25), ZS (Rover 45), ZT (75) and ZT-T (75 Estate) all had significant performance boosts as well as the badges, wide wheels and body kits. And the latest company name? MG Rover. MG had definitely returned.

MG Xpower SV.

MINERVA (Belgium 1899-1939)

Belgium is not renowned for its motor industry, but there was one, and Minerva was its most famous make. At one time it was the car of choice for the kings of Norway, Belgium and Sweden, and even Henry Ford once drove one!

Sylvain de Jong began making bicycles in his Antwerp workshop in 1897 and within a couple of years was showing prototype voiturettes, though he did not go into production until 1902. The first Minervas, such as the Minervette cyclecar, were small one- and two-cylinder machines, though a four soon followed and by 1907 a 378.3-cu in (6.2-litre) six-cylinder car was part of the range. Knight sleeve-valve engines were also used in the bigger Minervas, underlining their role as quiet, quality cars.

After World War I the company began exporting to the U.S.A., one typical model being the 323.4-cu in (5.3-litre) six-cylinder tourer. The biggest Minervas could be had with coach-built bodywork, such as the Saoutchik cabriolet arrangement on the AK 32/34 chassis. But the company went into a decline from the late 1920s, especially after the severe blow of Sylvain de Jong's death in 1928. There were numerous attempts at a revival: a return to smaller cars, intervention by the Belgian government, a takeover in 1935 – even Ettore Bugatti expressed interest. But Minerva's car-making days were essentially over, though it carried on building commercial vehicles during World War II, and a Land Rover-type 4x4 in 1955.

BELOW
1906 Minerva tourer.

RIGHT
1917 Mitsubishi Fiat-based Model A.

BELOW RIGHT
The bulbous Mitsubishi 500 of 1959.

BELOW FAR RIGHT
Colt was the name used on later models, like this 1100.

MITSUBISHI Japan 1917-1921 and 1953 to date)

Mitsubishi cars make up just one small part of the output of this giant Japanese corporation, one of the largest companies in the world, which makes everything from supertankers to recording equipment. It was established way back in 1870 as a shipping concern, and was a very early entrant to the Japanese motor industry, producing its first car in 1917. The Model A, influenced by a Fiat design, was actually one of the first Japanese-built cars, though only about 20 were made before it disappeared in 1921.

Mitsubishi then seemed to forget about cars for over 30 years, concentrating on trucks, buses and all the other things it produced, which included aircraft such as the famous A6M 'Zero' fighter of World War II.

It was not until 1953 that Mitsubishi began to produce Jeeps under licence, and another six years before its first car appeared. It was the basic little 500, a typical Japanese micro-car. Basic it may have been, but Mitsubishi quickly learned throughout the 1960s what increasingly affluent car buyers required. Its cars were renamed Colts, and grew in size from the

80' engine, with a balancer shaft to smooth out the vibration of its four-cylinder unit. Other Mitsubishi/Colts later adopted the system.

The company's export growth to the U.S.A. was given a substantial boost by a tie-up with Chrysler, which led to Mitsubishis being sold in America through Chrysler showrooms. The Colt Starion sports car, for example, was sold in the U.S.A. by Chrysler dealers as the Dodge

FAR LEFT (top to bottom)
The big six-cylinder Debonair saloon.
The Mitsubishi Galant, launched in 1974.
The early Colt 800.
The Colt 1500 GLX.

BELOW LEFT
The Galant GTO.

BOTTOM LEFT
1992 Shogun.

Conquest. The same deal held true for its successor, the Mitsubishi 3000GT, more familiar to U.S. buyers as the Dodge Stealth.

While many of its family saloons and hatchbacks were bland to the point of invisibility, Mitsubishi was still doing good business in niche markets. It was an early builder of people-carriers, with the Space Wagon of the 1980s, and the Shogun has been a strong competitor in the luxury 4x4 market. Known as Pajero in some markets, the Shogun was launched in 1984 as a diesel-only model, though a petrol option soon followed. It became one of Mitsubishi's best-sellers, with a substantial update in the 1990s and the choice of three-door short- and five-door long-wheelbased models. Meanwhile, the success of the Lancer saloon in world-class rallies (Tommi Makkinen won the world championship in one in 1996) led to a succession of road-going offshoots. In 2002, the latest of this four-wheel-drive Evo series offered over 300bhp (223.7kW) from its turbocharged 122-cu in (2-litre) four, though only at a considerable price. A direct-injection petrol engine was the main innovation at this time, for which Mitsubishi claimed diesel economy, but niche markets remained its strongest suit, with cars like the Pajero Mini 40.21-cu in (659-cc) off-roader and FTO coupé.

astback 800 to the 1100 saloon and big ix-cylinder Debonair. In the 1970s it ranched out into coupés as well, notably he Galant of 1974 and Sapporo of four ears later. The latter also used the 'Astron

TOP ROW, FAR LEFT
1997 Colt.

CENTRE
Colt 1.6 GLX.

LEFT
The Mitsubishi Lancer Evo III won the
World Rally Championship in 1996.

THIS ROW, FAR LEFT
Mitsubishi Carisma.

CENTRE and LEFT
1997 Galant.

BELOW LEFT
Carisma Evolution concept car by TWR.

BELOW
1997 The Shogun, also known as Pajero.

ABOVE
Mitsubishi 3000GT.

ABOVE RIGHT
A Mitsubishi pick-up with crewcab.

RIGHT
The 1999 Mitsubishi Shogun Pinin.

RIGHT
...000 Shogun sport 4x4.

BELOW
Colt 1.6 GLS.

BELOW RIGHT
Galant VR-4 estate.

OPPOSITE
Mitsubishi EVO VI.

MORGAN (Great Britain 1910 to date)
From the late 1990s and into the early 21st
century, retro styling was all the rage, and
in cars more than any other sphere. Even
the latest high-tech cars often included a
nod to the past, either to the manufacturer's
own or someone else's. It follows that
Morgan has to be the trendiest car
imaginable – not even a cunningly styled
retro, but the real thing.

With a clergyman father and
grandfather, H.F.S. Morgan might have

RIGHT
The Morgan three-wheeler Matchless.

BELOW
1939 Morgan 'F' sports with Ford engine.

BELOW RIGHT
Morgan brochure.

OPPOSITE
1954 Morgan four-seater.

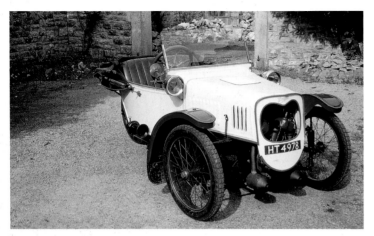

been expected to follow the family tradition and enter the church. It says much for his father's broad-mindedness that when it was clear that young H.F.S. had a talent for engineering, he was encouraged to study it at college, and to take up an apprenticeship with the Great Western Railway. Training over, the young Morgan set up as a car dealer in Malvern Link, Worcestershire, but in his spare time built cars of his own. One of these was a Peugeot-engined device with what would become two Morgan trademarks: three wheels and independent front suspension.

His father came up trumps again, financing the new Morgan Motor Company in 1910 so that H.F.S. could build and sell his three-wheelers, now with JAP engines. They were a success, with sales of up to 1,000 cars per year by 1914. After World War I sales continued to boom, especially after a four-seat Family Morgan was introduced in 1919. Although many were used by young families which could not

afford a car, Morgans were also popular with enthusiasts, especially with a big rorty air-cooled V-twin providing the power. Thus equipped, Morgans went into racing and trials, building up a loyal following.

The first four-wheel Morgan, the 4/4, was announced in 1935, just as three-wheeler sales were starting to drop off, and the final three-wheeled Morgan was built early in 1952. The 4/4 was replaced by the 128.2-cu in (2.1-litre) Plus Four in 1950, though the 4/4 was reintroduced a couple of years later, with a Ford Ten engine. A 'cheap' Morgan was to remain in the range for many years, with Ford 1600GT and later XR3 engines, as was a four-seater.

H.F.S. Morgan died in 1959, but left the firm in trust to his four daughters and son Peter, who carried on. Far from losing its way, Morgan flourished, unveiling the Rover V8-powered Plus 8 in 1968: this offered serious performance in the traditional Morgan two-seater, with that

same sliding pillar front suspension that H.F.S. had designed back in 1910. In fact, engines came and went but nothing else changed, while waiting lists remained as long as ever.

In a memorable TV documentary of the 1990s, troubleshooting businessman John Harvey-Jones could not understand how Morgan persisted in hand-building just two or three cars a week by antiquated means, when they could easily sell four times as many by introducing new machinery. But he missed the point of Morgan. The company had no wish to be a big player making big profits, it preferred to produce cars in very small numbers, with that three-year waiting list a comfortable buffer zone against economic ups and downs. Moreover, there was more going on at Morgan than one might have supposed. In 2001, the company announced the Aero 8, with up-to-date dynamics, aluminium chassis and BMW V8-power, but it still looked like a Morgan.

ABOVE LEFT
Morgan Family three-wheeler.

ABOVE
1966 Morgan four-seater.

OPPOSITE
2004 Morgan Aero.

MORRIS (Great Britain 1912-1984)
William Morris was the British Henry Ford, a self-made man who built and sold thousands of cars with the same 'pile 'em high, sell 'em cheap' philosophy. Yet in Britain Morris does not have the same image as Ford. Instead, there has always been a comfortable middle-class dependability about the name: the foreman of a local factory might drive a Model T, but bank clerks bought Morrises.

The man who made them was not a pioneer manufacturer, and actually produced motorcycles for several years before turning to cars. But this was not a hobby, and from the start William Morris (or Lord Nuffield as he became) intended that his cars should be a business proposition. The first, the Oxford, went on sale in 1912, nicknamed the 'Bullnose', because of its rounded radiator grille. Its official name came from the city where it was made, and Morris cars would be made at Cowley, on the outskirts of Oxford, right

TOP
1929 Morris Minor saloon.

ABOVE CENTRE
1935 Morris Ten-Four saloon.

ABOVE
1933 Ten-Six saloon.

RIGHT and OPPOSITE
1930 Morris Cowley two-seater.

up to the end. That first car was powered by a small White and Poppe four-cylinder engine of 10hp (7.46kW), and 1,000 were sold before the outbreak of World War I. It was soon joined by the bigger Cowley, which used a 91.2-cu in (1.5-litre) U.S.-built Continental engine.

Both received a bigger power unit after the war, the 96.7-cu in (1.58-litre) Hotchkiss from France, with the Cowley now the cheaper of the two, due to a lower level of trim. As production increased, Morris followed the Ford tradition and passed on savings to the customer, cutting the price of his cars by £100. That in turn led to increased demand, with 65,000 cars per year built in the early 1920s. As the profits rolled in, Morris used them intelligently, buying up his major suppliers: Hotchkiss engines, Wrigley transmissions, SU carburettors and Hillock & Pratt bodies. This guaranteed supplies and reduced the price still further.

The famous bull-nose radiator disappeared in 1927, replaced by a less distinctive flat design, but that year also saw the biggest Morris yet. The Empire Oxford was designed specifically for export to what was then the British Empire. To cope with primitive colonial roads, it had a big 152.6-cu in (2.5-litre) six-cylinder engine, a four-speed gearbox and worm final drive, which gave greater ground clearance. For British buyers, the little Minor of 1929 used an overhead-camshaft 51.69-cu in (847-cc) engine, and was a lively little car, but if one specified a cheaper side-valve unit, it cost just £100, making it the cheapest car in Britain. Sales soared.

The bigger Cowley and Oxford, the latter now with a six-cylinder engine, continued in production, and all Morris cars had hydraulic brakes from 1934. A new Ten-Four and long-wheelbased Ten-Six filled the gap between them and the Minor, while the new top model was the 213.6-cu in (3.5-litre) Twenty-Five. The Minor was replaced in 1935 by the 56.02-cu in (918-cc) side-valve Eight, available as saloon or open tourer; now the whole range was named after its horsepower rating. For 1939, a new Ten offered unitary-construction bodywork for the first time, with an overhead-valve 69.57-cu in (1.14-litre) engine, while the Eight was replaced by the Series E just before World War II broke out in 1939.

Both these pre-war cars went straight back into production in 1945, but only lasted three years before being replaced by the radically new Morris Minor. Designed by Alec Issigonis and A.V. Oak, this had been envisaged as an all-new car with front-wheel-drive and flat-four engine: cost and time dictated that it had to make do with the old 918-cc side-valve and rear-wheel-drive, but the new Minor was still radical enough. Rack-and-pinion steering, independent front suspension and unitary construction combined with a roomy interior, excellent handling and fuel economy. This latest Minor was a big hit, and stayed in production right up to 1971.

The whole Morris range received a boost after 1952 as a result of the merger of Morris with Austin, the other giant of the British motor industry, to form the British Motor Corporation (BMC). All the old side-valve engines were ditched in favour of the newer overhead-valve Austin units: the Minor now had the 49-cu in (803-cc) unit from the Austin A30; the 1954 Cowley received the 73.23-cu in (1.2-litre) B series and the Oxford used a 90.86-cu in (1.5-litre) version of the same engine. The biggest Morrises and Austins, however, used a new Morris-designed motor, the 158.7-cu in (2.6-litre) six-cylinder C series, which powered a new Morris Isis from 1955. In fact, from then onwards, Austin and Morris cars were increasingly badge-engineered versions of the same thing.

The revolutionary new Mini of 1959,

for example (another Issigonis design), came as the Austin Seven or Morris Mini-Minor, depending on which badge you preferred. Whatever badge it wore, the Mini made a huge impact, and virtually became a marque in its own right, ditching both Austin and Morris badges in the late 1960s. It was followed up by the even more advanced 1100 in 1962, again with front-wheel-drive, a larger 67-cu in (1.10-litre) engine and 'hydrolastic' hydraulic suspension. The biggest front-wheel-drive BMC car was the 1800, a large, roomy machine with the same transverse engine,

and front-drive layout as its smaller siblings. It later came as the 110-bhp (82-kW) 2200, with six cylinders squeezed together to fit transversely under the bonnet. All these, of course, came in both Morris and Austin forms.

Alongside these high-tech front-drivers, the old rear-wheel-drive Morris Oxford soldiered on. In 1959 it had received new finned styling by Pininfarina, which was fashionable at the time but dated quickly. It was slow, even with the later 99-cu in (1.62-litre) engine, and was showing its age by now, though the Estate was tough and

useful. The only other 'pure' Morris, the Minor, was ageing more gracefully, was gradually updated with bigger engines and was still selling steadily, in wood-trimmed Traveller guise as well as in the two- or four-door saloon.

But in 1971 there was a new Morris, with no Austin-badged equivalent – the Marina. With a choice of 77.8- or 109.72-cu in (1.3- or 1.8-litre) engines and in saloon, coupé or estate styles, this was designed to meet Ford head-on: cheap to build, with a wide range from which to choose. It did well too, a popular car that

was probably more profitable than any of the clever front-wheel-drive Austin/Morrises. But the Marina turned out to be the last Morris of all. It was updated with a new 103.4-cu in (1.7-litre) O series engine in 1979, but the new regime of

Austin-Rover clearly had little room for the Morris name. There was a final major update in 1980, when the Marina became the Morris Ital, with a modernized 1.3-litre engine and the option of a 2-litre O series plus automatic transmission. When it was dropped in 1984, the Morris name died with it.

TOP
1967-68 Mini Moke utility vehicle.

ABOVE LEFT
1972 Morris Marina 1.3 de-luxe coupé.

ABOVE FAR LEFT
1962 Morris 1100.

LEFT
1964 Morris Oxford Series VI.

OPPOSITE
LEFT:1934 Ten-Six tourer.

RIGHT (from top to bottom)
1951 Morris Minor convertible.
1954-55 Morris Six MS saloon.
1961 Morris Mini Minor.

MORS (France 1895-1925)

Mors is an excellent example of how racing success can boost sales. Riding high while it dominated the long-distance races of pioneer motoring, Mors soon went into decline when it was no longer winning races, though other factors contributed.

Emile and Louis Mors took over their father's electrical engineering business in 1880, but soon turned their attention to vehicles, building their first car in 1895, via steam vehicles and petrol-powered railway rolling stock. Unusually, though not so surprisingly, given the Mors's electrical background, it featured the brothers' own ignition system. The designer of that first car was Henri Brasier, who went on to design a whole string of competition cars for Mors.

These dominated the long-distance races held for a few years on public roads in France, before the high casualty rate (of both drivers and spectators) put an end to it. In 1899 a Mors won the Paris-St. Malo and Paris-Bordeaux races; in the following year it triumphed in the Paris-Toulouse-Paris and Bordeaux-Perigueux-Bordeaux; in 1901 it took the Paris-Bordeaux again, plus the Paris-Berlin. In 1903, now powered by a 70-bhp (52.2-kW) 683.5-cu in (11.2-litre) engine, a Mors won the Paris-Madrid race.

This was the high point. Two key designers, Henri Brasier and Charles Schmidt, left the company, and the race wins soon petered out. There were financial scandals too, and Mors had to withdraw from racing in 1908. That same year, Andre-Gustave Citroën was brought in to reorganize production: his talent was clear, but was not enough to help Mors. The production of commercial vehicles brought a short-lived revival, and Mors only really began to thrive again during World War I, busy making munitions and aero engines.

Citroën left to start the firm that was to bear his name, and which was gradually to absorb Mors. By 1925, Mors itself no longer existed.

NAPIER (Great Britain 1900-1924)

Napier, a famous British name, could just have easily been Edge. Montague Napier, who ran an engineering firm, was a keen racing cyclist, and fellow cyclist Selwyn Francis Edge asked him to design a new engine for his 1896 Panhard car. In the following year, Napier came up with a complete car, still based on the Panhard. But it was Edge who put Napier's

TOP
1913 Napier Type 44 Torpedo tourer.

ABOVE
1907 60-hp Napier.

RIGHT
1915 20-hp Napier Colonial.

cars into production in 1900. He also raced them successfully in 1901 and 1902, and was associated with the name until 1907, when a disagreement caused him to leave. Edge won the Gordon Bennett Trophy in 1902, the first major victory for a British car in an international race.

Demand for Napiers grew, and the fledgling company soon outgrew its little factory in Lambeth, south London, moving to larger premises in Acton. Other cars joined the range, such as the 18/30-hp (13.4/22.4-kW) six-cylinder, and it is for big cars like this that Napier is remembered. Although the name is often associated with big, rorty racing Edwardians, Napier sold many large limousines, and the 1910 catalogue listed over 160 prominent owners, all members of the aristocracy, army and

church. It was, without doubt, the 'establishment' car. Napier also built small cars, down to a 10-hp (7.46-kW) 79.3-cu in (1.3-litre), but its core production remained concentrated on large imposing machines like the 1922 40/50-hp (29.8/37.3-kW).

During World War I Napier first built aero engines under licence, and this led the company to produce its own, the Lion, which later powered land-speed record cars such as Malcolm Campbell's Bluebird. After the war, Montague Napier introduced the 378.3-cu in (6.2-litre) T75, though not many of these were made. Production ended in 1924, after less than 5,000 Napiers had been made in nearly a quarter of a century. As for the company, it concentrated on aero engines, and was taken over by English Electric in 1945.

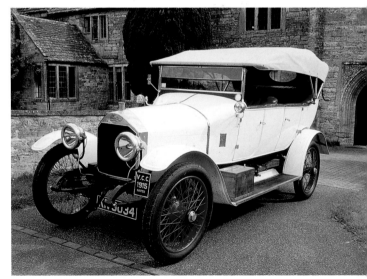

NASH (U.S.A. 1917-1957)

Charles W. Nash was a self-made man. Starting out as a farm labourer, by 1912 he was president of General Motors, but still he was not satisfied. He really wanted to be his own boss, though for most people being boss of GM would surely have qualified, so he left in 1916 and bought the Jeffery Motor Company and Nash cars were born.

In the following year the first Nash-badged car appeared, a 244.1-cu in (4-litre) six-cylinder machine, with roadsters and sports cars soon following. A smaller 152.6-cu in (2.5-litre) four, designed along the same lines, was introduced in 1920: together with the existing six, the Nash Four offered a total of nine different body styles. These were not upmarket cars, but sold well in the mid-range (upmarket from Ford, down from Cadillac). Nash desired a slice of the luxury market, however, and bought La Fayette Motors as a short cut. This company built a 341.7-cu in (5.6-litre) V8, but it did not sell well and the plan was abandoned.

Instead, Nash concentrated on the middle ground. The new 328 of 1928 was claimed to be the cheapest six-cylinder seven-bearing car on the U.S. market. Other good value sixes like the Single Six and Twin Ignition Six enabled Nash to ride out the Depression. Despite cutting production to just 14,000 in 1933, its lowest ever, Nash carried on making a profit, quite an achievement in those lean years. The La Fayette name was introduced, but this time as a cheap big car, rather than a true luxury model, and the range was drastically pruned from 32 models to just six. This efficiency was one reason why Nash survived. In 1941, the revived La Fayette was replaced by the all-new Nash 600. This advanced car had unitary construction and was relatively light,

enabling good fuel consumption from its 170.9-cu in (2.8-litre) six-cylinder engine. It could, claimed Nash, cover 600 miles (965km) on each tank of gas, hence the name. Nash's bigger cars, the six- and eight-cylinder Ambassadors, continued alongside the new 600, though car production was ended by war work in 1942.

After the war, the Ambassadors were reintroduced with updated Airflyte styling, complete with wrap-around windshield and semi-enclosed road wheels. But perhaps more significant was the 1950 Rambler, said to be the U.S.A.'s first compact. Around the same time, the Nash-Healey sports car was imported from England, powered by a 219.7-cu in (3.6-litre) Ambassador engine. Another British import was the little Nash Metropolitan, built for Nash by BMC and designed as a miniature version of the Rambler, with a 73.2- or later 90.9-cu in (1.2- and 1.5-litre) engine. Was this the U.S.A.'s first sub-compact?

But Nash was nearing its end. Too small to survive independently, it merged with Hudson in 1954 to form the American Motors Corporation (AMC). Both Rambler and Metropolitan continued, though sales of the bigger Statesman and Ambassador were falling rapidly. In 1957, both the Nash and Hudson names were gradually dropped by AMC, and that was finally that.

ABOVE
1955 Nash Ambassador custom.

ABOVE LEFT
1942 Nash 600 sedan.

LEFT
1926 Nash two-door sedan.

NISSAN/DATSUN (Japan 1912-1983)

Datsun is often regarded in the West as a late arrival, which only began to sell cars in the 1970s. That is true only of Datsun exports to the West, for in reality its roots stretch right back to 1912 and were wholly Japanese. An engineer named Masujiro Hashimoto built a prototype small car in Tokyo, and with financial backing from K. Den, R. Aoyama and A. Takeuchi (DAT), Hashimoto was able to put it into production as the DAT 31 in 1915. This was a simple car powered by a 122-cu in (2-litre) four-cylinder engine, and was followed in 1916 by a larger 140.4-cu in (2.3-litre) version. Almost every part was made in Japan, only the wheels, tyres and magneto being imported.

The DAT company concentrated on trucks after 1926, though for a while it continued to build the Lila light car, whose

narrow track made it the popular choice of Tokyo taxi drivers. DAT was bought by a large industrial concern in 1931, and this proved a turning point, as its new owners wanted to build a mass-produced Japanese car that could be exported.

DAT worked quickly, and in less than a year the little prototype was ready. It was a 30.2-cu in (495-cc) four-cylinder car with a superficial similarity to the Austin Seven, with a top speed of 35mph (56km/h) and a

choice of roadster, tourer or saloon versions. The name was Datson, literally son of DAT. This was soon changed to Datsun, and not simply to allow the company to use the Japanese rising sun as its trademark – in Japanese, 'son' means 'loss'! The company name was changed to Nissan in 1933 but the cars it made were still Datsuns. Production began in 1932 and the 1,000th car was built by mid-1934. There was a substantial boost in engine size

the following year to 44.2-cu in (725-cc).

After World War II the company again concentrated on trucks, but the small cars continued, such as the 52.5-cu in (860-cc) DS of 1949 and restyled Thrift of two years later. The Thrift was then replaced with the Austin-based Bluebird, using a 73.2-cu in (1.2-litre) engine. Through the 1960s and 1970s Datsun production increased rapidly as both home consumption and exports grew. Exports in particular were successful, the company spearheading the new wave of Japanese cars being welcomed by consumers in the U.S.A. and western Europe. Not everyone liked them, but Datsuns were well-made, well-equipped and good value. Although small economy cars predominated, there were big luxury saloons as well, like the President and

FAR LEFT BELOW
1951 Datsun Thrift four-door saloon.

LEFT (top to bottom)
1936 Datsun Type 15.
1937 Datsun Type 16.
1958 Datsun Type 210.

BELOW
1960 Nissan Cedric.

BOTTOM
1972 Datsun 240C saloon.

OPPOSITE
1979 Datsun 260Z.

Cedric, while the 240Z coupé was the world's best-selling sports car for a time. The Datsun Sunny 120Y was a conventional rear-wheel-drive saloon with a 73.2-cu in (1.2-litre) engine, while the smaller Cherry had front-wheel-drive. Up another class, the Violet was a 85.4/97.6-cu in (1.4/1.6-litre) saloon.

In 1983 Nissan dropped the Datsun badge, and all its cars were subsequently known as Nissans. This coincided with a more determined assault on Europe. Nissan bought a controlling interest in Motor Iberica of Spain, which was soon building Nissan Patrol 4x4s. In the following year a brand-new factory was built in Sunderland,

northern England, which began to build the Bluebird, later its replacement the Primera, plus the small Micra, and by 1993 60 per cent of Nissans sold in Europe were built there; moreover, the Sunderland plant was doing wonders for Great Britain's balance of payments. But the company was facing tough times, losing money just when it was

spending out on new models to keep up with arch-rival Toyota. Its Australian factory was closed, though production was increased in Japan, the U.S. plant in Tennessee was extended and Sunderland continued to expand. The new Micra had much to do with this buoyancy. The original Micra was a small three- or five-

TOP
1997 Nissan Primera 2.0 SRi.

ABOVE
1997 Nissan QX.

ABOVE RIGHT
1997 200SX.

RIGHT
Nissan Terrano II 2.7 TDi SR.

OPPOSITE
ABOVE LEFT: Datsun 280Z.

BELOW LEFT: Datsun 240Z.

ABOVE RIGHT: Nissan Micra 1.3 SR.

BELOW RIGHT: Nissan Almera GTi.

door hatchback with a 61- or 73.2-cu in (1- or 1.2-litre) engine. Simple, reliable and easy to drive, it was deservedly popular, and its replacement carried on the same tradition, albeit with a more rounded 1990s shape. Meanwhile, the Almera assumed the mantle of the old Violet, and the 200SX/240SX coupés took over where the old 240Z had left off. The 300ZX had gone up a class, with 300bhp (224kW) from its twin-turbo V6. But Nissan's new performance flagship for the 1990s was the Skyline GT-R. This did not have quite as much power as the ZX (280-bhp/208.8-kW from a 158.7-cu in/2.6-litre twin-turbo straight-six) but boasted viscous-coupled four-wheel-drive and four-wheel steering.

Nissan had long been a high-volume maker of off-road vehicles, with the popular Patrol, and by the end of the 20th

century the range had grown. The Patrol
was a heavyweight beast by now, in Range
Rover territory, so to slot in below it there
was the 164.8-cu in (2.7-litre) Terrano,
developed jointly with Ford, which sold the
vehicle as the Maverick. Latest to join the
range was the X-Trail, one of the new breed
of smaller 'soft-roaders', with only nominal
off-road ability but some of the chunky
looks of their bigger brethren.

ABOVE
The high-tech Nissan Skyline supercar was
updated in 1999.

LEFT
Navarra pick-up truck with crewcab.

FAR LEFT TOP
2000 Almera.

FAR LEFT BELOW
1999 Primera.

ABOVE
2002 X-Trail 2.5 SVE.

ABOVE RIGHT
2003 Primera.

RIGHT
2002 Micra.

LEFT ABOVE
2000 Patrol GR SE+ 3.0 Di.

LEFT
2000 Maxima QX.

LEFT
2003 Nissan Altima.

BELOW LEFT
2003 Sentra.

BELOW
Sentra SE-R.

OPPOSITE
ABOVE LEFT: *350Z.*

ABOVE RIGHT: *Pathfinder.*

BELOW LEFT: *2003 Xterra.*

BELOW RIGHT: *2004 Quest.*

NSU (Germany 1905-1929 and 1958-1977)

To enthusiasts of classic as well as more recent cars, NSU is remembered for its extraordinary Ro80 saloon, an advanced aerodynamic car powered by a Wankel rotary engine. But this Germany company, based at Neckarsulm, already had a long history before the Ro80 was even conceived.

Starting out as a bicycle manufacturer in the early 1880s, NSU later supplied chassis to Daimler and began making motorcycles, for which it became world-famous: during the 1930s, it was one of the largest motorcycle manufacturers in the world. Its first car was a Belgian Pipe built under licence, with its own four-cylinder 6/10 and six-cylinder 15/24 following later. Trucks were produced as well. After World War I NSU's smaller four-cylinder cars were quite successful, but it was unable to

sell them during the Depression, and ceased production of its own cars to concentrate on motorcycles. However, it did sell half of the Neckarsulm factory to Fiat, building Fiats under contract for sale as NSU-Fiats.

Encouraged by the economic revival of the 1930s, NSU commissioned Dr. Ferdinand Porsche to design a cheap 'people's car'. Booming motorcycle sales put an end to that, however, though the prototypes were to influence the layout of the VW Beetle, also designed by Porsche.

NSU did not build another car until 1958, when the air-cooled rear-engined Prinz appeared; this was quite successful and remained in production until the early 1970s. More technically interesting was the Wankel Spyder, a rotary-engined version of the Prinz and in 1964 the world's first rotary-engined production car. It was followed by the more sophisticated twin-rotor Ro80, an advanced mid-sized car of

M12 GTC

NOBLE

impressive smoothness, performance and comfort. Unfortunately, the rotary engine wore out very rapidly, and the car cost NSU a fortune in warranty claims. Although later cars were less troublesome, the reputation of NSU, and indeed the rotary engine, never really recovered. In 1969, the company was taken over by Audi.

NOBLE (Great Britain 2001 to date)

The Noble is a new British supercar, designed by chassis engineer Lee Noble, who went into partnership with businessman Tony Moy to produce it. A mid-engined two-seater in the classic mould, the Noble M12 GTO was powered by a 152.6-cu in (2.5-litre) V6, with twin turbochargers and four overhead camshafts to produce 310bhp (231.1kW). Its road-holding, in particular, came in for praise, the Noble being capable of generating an impressive 1.156g of lateral force. For

2003, an open-top GTC is planned, now with a claimed 340bhp (253.5kW) from an enlarged 183.1-cu in (3-litre) V6. The GTC's claimed weight is just 2,315lb (1050kg).

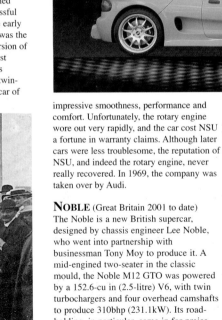

ABOVE
Brochure for the Noble M12 GTC.

LEFT
An NSU in the 1908 Prince Henry Trials.

OLDSMOBILE

(U.S.A. 1896 to date)

One of America's oldest and most prolific makes, Oldsmobile has been in production for over a century. Its early 'curved dash' cars were modest but they worked, and they were followed by a whole string of straightforward, no-nonsense cars. Oldsmobiles were not often to be seen at the cutting edge of technology, though they were also rarely outdated, and gained a

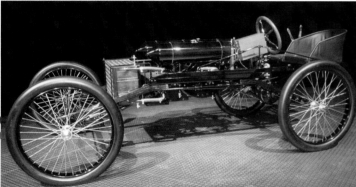

good reputation in the U.S.A. for quality.

Engineering ran in the Olds family. Olds Sr. established a machine shop in Lansing, Michigan, and his son Ransom Eli displayed the same mechanical ability as well as a head for business: in 1892, at the age of 21, he bought his father out and established the Olds Gasoline Engine Works. Ransom Olds was consequently in at the beginning of the new petrol technology, though his first prototype three- and four-wheeled vehicles were all steam-powered. But he soon began experimenting with petrol power, and built his first car in 1897.

TOP
Olds eight-cylinder touring sedan.

ABOVE
1937 Business Coupé Automatic.

LEFT TOP
1903 Oldsmobile curved dash.

LEFT CENTRE
1903 Pirate.

LEFT BELOW
Patrician sedan.

343

Olds also moved to Detroit, which had a larger pool of the skilled labour he would need to become a full-time car manufacturer. The first car offered was too complicated and priced too high to sell, but Olds struck gold with the curved-dash Runabout of 1901. Simple and reliable, this did more than anything else to underline Olds's standing as a serious manufacturer. It was a huge success, and despite a devastating fire at the Detroit factory in 1902, which forced the company to move back to Lansing, 4,000 Runabouts had been sold by 1903. Their fundamental reliability was proved by success in long-distance races like the Tour de France and the U.S.A.'s first 100-mile (160-km) event. Runabouts were even exported to Russia and Europe, and many famous people bought them, including Mark Twain and the Queen of Italy.

The very success of the Runabout enabled Olds to help kickstart an entire industry: an order for 2,000 engines went to Henry Leland (later to head Cadillac) and the Dodge brothers were given an order for a similar number of transmissions.

Olds actually left Oldsmobile in 1905 to start Reo, but by now the company was unstoppable. A new twin-cylinder car launched that year was so successful that the single-cylinder Runabout was dropped; a four-cylinder arrived in 1906, with a six-in 1908, when Oldsmobile became part of General Motors. A side-valve V8 was added to the range in 1914, and by 1919 the company was expanding fast, building 33,000 cars that year. In the 1920s, Oldsmobile kept up to date with such features as four-wheel brakes and chrome plating, with synchromesh transmission, independent front suspension and 'turret-top' all-steel bodies coming along in quick succession. Through the 1930s, Oldsmobile continued to expand, the factory complex of 79 buildings covering 140 acres (56 hectares) by 1935.

In 1937 the automatic safety

ABOVE
1976 Oldsmobile Cutlass.

RIGHT (top to bottom)
1978 Delta 88 Royale sedan.
1988 Cutlass Calais 2.3 Quad 4.
1989 Touring sedan.

ABOVE RIGHT
1995 Oldsmobile LSS.

FAR RIGHT
Oldsmobile Intrigue, launched in 1996.

OPPOSITE
LEFT TOP: 1949 Oldsmobile 88.

LEFT CENTRE: 1940 'Woody' station
wagon.

BOTTOM FAR LEFT: 1952 coupé.

BOTTOM RIGHT: 1961 Cutlass.

ABOVE RIGHT: 1971 sports convertible.

transmission provided a fourth speed and hydraulic gear selection, while 1940 brought Hydra-Matic, the first true two-pedal automatic, an option on all Oldsmobiles in 1944. Oldsmobile was very early with its 'post-war' models. Once peace was restored, Oldsmobile followed industrial trends with sleeker, more aerodynamic body styles, using ever more powerful V8s to replace straight-six power plants. New-Matic air suspension in 1958 was not a success, but Oldsmobile achieved a true technical first with the 1966 Tornado Coupé, a big V8 two-door with front-wheel-drive. Significantly, John Beltz, the engineer who made it work, was also general manager at the time, Oldsmobile being a very engineering-led company.

But Oldsmobile was unable to survive the 1970s unscathed, and production fell sharply after the oil crisis. The company was still producing traditional V8 sedans which drank a lot of fuel, and decided to

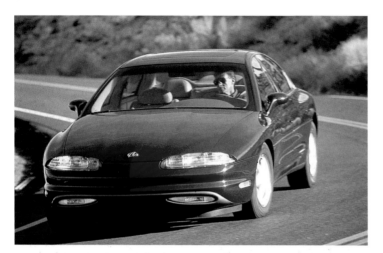

rapidly introduce a range of compacts and smaller cars, while the GM V8 diesels were made available in its 'full-size' cars. The Starfire 2+2 coupé was a typical compact, introduced in 1975, and sharing its bodyshell with the Buick Skyhawk and Chevrolet Monza. By the mid-1980s Oldsmobile was making only front-wheel-drive cars, often with minimal differences from other GM marques.

Despite this, sales continued to plummet, more than halving between 1983 and 1993. But the mid-1990s saw something of a recovery, not least because

of the Aurora, still a luxury V8 saloon but styled along European aerodynamic lines with minimal decoration and barely a piece of chrome to be seen. Despite tough competition from Lexus, Mercedes-Benz, Cadillac and many others, the Aurora had a positive effect on Oldsmobile fortunes, and was followed up with the similar V6 Intrigue. In the late 1990s the Silhouette was launched as Oldsmobile's version of the standard GM people-carrier, with a 207.5-cu in (3.4-litre) engine and four-speed automatic gearbox. The Bravada was another straight piece of badge-engineering, this time with the Oldsmobile badges on the Chevrolet Blazer 4x4. Meanwhile, the ageing Regency and Cutlass were dropped, and a new compact saloon, the 134.25-cu in (2.2-litre) Alero, was introduced.

But these cars will probably be Oldsmobile's last. Late in 2000 General Motors announced that the name would be phased out over the following few years, after more than a century of continuous production.

OPPOSITE
ABOVE LEFT: 1997 Oldsmobile Aurora.

BELOW LEFT: 2003 Bravada.

ABOVE RIGHT: 2003 Silhouette.

CENTRE RIGHT: 2003 Aurora.

LEFT: Alero GL sedan.

ABOVE RIGHT
The Opel Admiral, built 1937-39.

BELOW RIGHT
1924 856-cc Laubfrosch.

OM (Italy 1905-1934)

The Zust brothers were Swiss engineers who began producing experimental cars at the beginning of the 20th century and were soon offering their large Mercedes-inspired machines for sale. By 1906 a separate but related company, Brixia-Zust, had been set up in Brescia to build cheaper cars, among them the 91.2-cu in (1.5-litre) three-cylinder models later used as London taxis. In 1911 the firm was taken over by locomotive builder OM (Officine Meccaniche).

OM continued with the Zust's S305, adding its own designs from 1921. Despite using only side-valve engines, with just a three-speed gearbox on the 1926 straight-eight Grand Prix car, these OMs were quite successful in competition, and the company's first straight-six won the Mille Miglia in 1927. However, OM's commercial vehicle division was more profitable, and when Fiat took over in 1933, car production ceased. A few more OM cars were assembled by the British importer L.C. Rawlence & Co., which had a stockpile of parts to use.

Opel (Germany 1898 to date)

Adam Opel built a flourishing business based on sewing machines, but encouraged by his five sons, he diversified into cycle production in 1886, taking advantage of the late-19th-century cycling boom. When he died in 1895, this was already starting to decline, so his widow Sophie and elder sons Carl and Wilhelm looked around for something else to make.

Motor cars were undeniably a growing market, albeit still a very small one at the time, and the Opels bought the rights to the Lutzmann car, a small 4-hp (2.98-kW) single-cylinder machine. But the Opel-Lutzmann was not a success and the venture

was abandoned after only a few cars had been sold. That might have been the end of it, had not the Opels signed up to become sole agent for Darracq in Germany, Austria and Hungary: part of the deal was that they would build Darracqs under licence. These did better, and by 1902 Opel had launched its own 10/12 115-cu in (1.9-litre) model. Twin-cylinder 'doctor's cars' (in 6/12 or 8/14 form) followed, as well as a large 421.1-cu in (6.9-litre) 35/40. By 1910 Opel was a well-established car manufacturer.

Oddly, the real turning point came after a serious fire at the works in 1911. With the factory devastated, the brothers decided that it would be as good a time as any to

concentrate solely on cars: there would be no more Opel sewing machines. With cars rolling out of the works once more, the range was split between the small twin-cylinder cars (now 5/12 and 6/16) and the flagship 40/100, now with a 622.4-cu in (10.2-litre) engine.

But difficult times hit the company after World War I, not least because its Russelsheim factory was now in French-occupied territory and raw materials were hard to obtain. Moreover, demand for cars had slumped in a Germany that was now impoverished. Opel survived, however, first by making pre-war cars, and from 1924 manufacturing the 4/12 Laubfrosch (tree frog) which was a copy of the Citroen 5CV. This proved to be Opel's saviour, and by the late 1920s it was thriving, an attractive prize for General Motors, which bought 80 per cent of the company in 1929, and the remainder two years later.

Opel now concentrated on smaller cars, such as the unitary-construction 78.05-cu in (1.3-litre) Olympia of 1935, and the 65.54-cu in (1.07-litre) Kadett of two years later, though it also offered the six-cylinder Admiral between 1937 and 1939. After

ABOVE LEFT
'1937-39 Opel Admiral.

FAR LEFT (top to bottom)
1979 Senator CD.
1981 Monza.
1987 Ascona family saloon
1989 Corsa GSi.

ABOVE RIGHT
2002 Agila Njoy.

LEFT (top to bottom)
1994 Tigra.
1995 Calibra
1995 Frontera sport.

OPPOSITE
ABOVE LEFT: 2003 Corsa Eco.
BELOW LEFT 2002 Astra cabriolet turbo.

RIGHT ABOVE: 2002 Frontera.
RIGHT BELOW (from top left clockwise)
2004 Roadster.
2002 Speedster.
2002 Zafira.
2002 Vectra.

making trucks and engines during World
War II, Opel restarted car production in
1947 with the pre-war Olympia, and GM
resumed control the following year – Opel
had been nationalized by the Nazi regime
in 1940.

Genuinely new cars soon followed: the
90.8-cu in (1.49-litre) Rekord in 1953 and a
new 61.02-cu in (1-litre) Kadett in 1962,
which itself was replaced only three years
later. Opel later developed a good reputation
for fine-handling family cars, such as the
mid-sized Ascona and its coupé derivative,
the Manta. These were both given front-
wheel-drive in the 1980s, as was the Kadett
(which later became the Astra) and the new
Corsa. There was also the curvaceous GT
Coupé, which used saloon parts. Into the
1980s, Opel increasingly shared parts and
styling with the British GM subsidiary,
Vauxhall. Opel remained GM's main
European brand, however, with Vauxhall
increasingly restricted to the U.K. market.

By 2002, the range included the small
hatchback Corsa, the Agila (a rebadged
Suzuki Wagon R), the small-medium Astra
(with coupé and cabriolet versions), the

mid-sized Vectra and the executive Omega. The Zafira was Opel's take on the multi-seat people-carrier, while the Frontera 4x4 was by now showing its age. A new model, the five-door long-wheelbased Signum, was imminent, and an interesting sideline at the Paris Motor Show was the diesel-powered

Eco Speedster concept racer, with which Opel hoped to break diesel speed records, which would be second time around: it had done the same with the GT diesel of the 1970s.

PACKARD (U.S.A. 1899-1958)

Alexander Winton, so the story goes, was responsible for the start of Packard cars when he challenged the Packhard brothers, James and William, that they could not improve upon his own car. Suitably fired by the challenge, the brothers formed the New York and Ohio Automobile Co., and in 1899 produced the reliable Model A. In 1901, and after two name changes ending with the Packard Motor Car Co., new finance from a group of Detroit businessmen allowed them to move into a new factory. Oddly, with the company about to begin a new era, this was when the Packhard brothers decided to leave, though James remained as symbolic president until 1909, and of course the name stuck right to the end.

Bigger Packards were soon rolling out of the new factory, first a flat-twin and in

1904 a four-cylinder car, which set speed records at Daytona. Exports began (there were agencies as far-flung as Spain, Hawaii and Latin America by 1908), as did the building of commercial vehicles. The first six-cylinder Packard was launched in 1911, with electric lighting and starting offered from 1913. Shortly after this, ex-lawyer Alvin Macauley took over the presidency, a post he was to hold for over 20 years. Under his leadership, Packard continued to aim upmarket, with cars such as the big Twin Six and Single Eight. The strategy paid off, with over 50,000 cars built in 1928: that made Packard bigger than both Cadillac and Lincoln.

However, the company was about to face its darkest hour. The Depression had a devastating effect on luxury car sales, and in 1934 Packard sold a mere 6,100 cars, barely more than one-tenth that it had

competitors had progressed to V8s. As a defensive measure, the company abandoned the luxury market to Cadillac and began to concentrate on cheaper cars. The final decline began in 1952, when James Nance became president. He tried to move Packard back upmarket, with the Mayfair sports, Caribbean convertible and new limousines. He also sold off the parts section, which was not popular with owners of older Packards. Purchasing Studebaker in 1954 brought a modern overhead-valve V8 to the company, but by the time Nance resigned two years later, Studebaker-Packard was in a poor state, and was bought by aero engine maker Curtiss-Wright. The Packard name remained alive for another couple of years, only on the front of rebadged Studebakers. In 1958 it disappeared for good.

LEFT
1938 32.5-hp straight-eight Packard.

BELOW
1954 Packard Caribbean.

OPPOSITE
TOP RIGHT: *1929 Doctor's Coupé.*

BELOW RIGHT: *1937 limousine.*

BELOW LEFT: *1939 Packard.*

managed six short years earlier. Not surprisingly, it also lost over $7 million that year. But that was the low point, and in 1935 the new lower-priced 120 proved a great success, with advance orders of around 0,000. Then, only two years after, Packard made a profit of $7 million on sales of over 0,000 cars.

Sales were further bolstered by the arrival of the Packard Six, alongside the eight-cylinder 120, though the company continued to offer the traditional Eights and Twelves, with coach-built bodywork and features like electric windows and air conditioning. The 'Senior' Eight lasted until 1948, when production rights were sold to the U.S.S.R., where it was built as the Ziz limousine.

After World War II Packard never gained that 1936 production high. The 'Clipper' style, so fresh when first unveiled in 1941, now looked old-fashioned. It did not help that Packard was clinging to side-valve straight sixes and eights when all its

PAGINI ZONDA (Italy 1999-)

Argentine-born Horacio Pagini was desperate to build his own supercar. He certainly lived in the right place to do so, having moved to Italy and set up as a consultant, working for Ferrari and Lamborghini among others. But the dream to make a car of his own would not go away and in 1999 it was revealed to the world.

The C12 is no clever futuristic high-tech car with advanced features, but remains faithful to a concept that is now over 30 years old, of a low, squat, mid-engined sports car, utterly impractical and blindingly fast. Motive power comes not from a traditional Italian source, but from a 445.5-cu in (7.3-litre) Mercedes V12, modified by AMG to produce 555bhp and

553lb ft of torque, which is fed through a six-speed gearbox to massive 335-section tyres, with all-round independent suspension and disc brakes. An all-out maximum of 220mph (354km/h) is claimed.

It may have a big engine, but the Pagini C12 is not a big car, and weighs just 2756lb (1250kg), according to its maker; consequently, it is not overloaded with convenience features, and piloting a Pagini, with its notchy gearchange and heavy controls, makes it clear that this is a car that puts the raw driving experience first. Don't buy a Pagini if comfort is required – as Horacio Pagini himself might say – get a Fiat instead!

TOP
The curvaceous Panhard 1960 PL17.

ABOVE
1950 Dyna-Panhard 120 cabriolet.

LEFT
Pagini C12.

PANHARD (France 1891-1967)
René Panhard and his partner Emile Levassor were responsible for the standard layout that nearly all cars followed for over 10 years: front-mounted engine, front-wheel steering, rear-wheel drive. The pair had set up to build engines for Gottlieb Daimler in 1886, and were experimenting with their own cars two years later (the first were sold in 1891), while they also diversified into marine engines and commercial vehicles. By 1896, their classic layout (using chain drive) was well established, and the 'Système Panhard' was copied by most manufacturers. Sadly, Levassor died in that year, seriously injured in the Paris-Marseilles race of the previous year.

But the company was reorganized and recapitalized. René Panhard's son, Hippolyte, joined the board (four generations of Panhard would serve the company) and production rose to 336 cars in 1898 and to more than 1,000 by 1902. The company further diversified into aero engines from 1905, but René died in 1908. Despite a decline in sales at the time, Panhard stayed in profit, and had fully recovered by the outbreak of World War I; in 1913 2,100 cars were built, designed by Dufresne and Voisin, while Panhard bought in Knight sleeve-valve engines, as did many other manufacturers at the time.

After the war, during which time Panhard produced an intriguing four-wheel-drive military vehicle with four-wheel steering) the range grew in size and complication. By 1928 no less than eight different engine sizes were available, while the commercial vehicle division built tankers, half-tracks and military vehicles as well as the usual trucks and buses. One interesting sideline was a sleeve-valve diesel engine offered in the 1930s.

Perhaps it was having so many fingers in so many pies that caused Panhard to take his eye off the car business: sales were falling, with the car division operating at only 60 per cent capacity.

Panhard cars did get a boost in 1937 with the launch of the advanced Dynamique. This had a synchromesh gearbox, hydraulic brakes, independent torsion-bar suspension and faired-in wheels and headlamps, plus (until 1939) the unusual feature of a centrally-mounted steering wheel.

After World War II, while Panhard carried on building armoured cars in Paris, a successor to the Dynamique appeared almost immediately, in 1946. In its own way, the little Dyna-Panhard was just as radical, a front-wheel-drive saloon with light alloy bodywork and a flat-twin engine. It sold quite well for a time (over 14,000 were made in 1948) and by 1954 Panhard was offering a supercharged sports version.

But it was too expensive, and after Citroën took a 25 per cent stake in Panhard in 1955, costs were cut by ditching the alloy panels in favour of steel. Ten years later, Citroën assumed complete control, and the last Panhard left the Ivry, Paris factory in 1967.

TOP
Panther J72 with 4.2 Jaguar engine (text overleaf).

ABOVE
The Panther 6 imitated the Tyrrell F1 car.

LEFT
Panther Lima.

PANTHER (Great Britain 1972-1990)
Bob Jankel, founder of Panther Cars, once
said that his company would never have to
close. At the time, Panther was facing a
long waiting list of customers for its replica
1930s-style J72 and De Ville, and looked
set to replicate the success of Morgan, that
other British stalwart. Sadly, it did not
work out like that.

The company's founder was an
engineer who had worked in the fashion
industry for a while, underlining his flair
for both aesthetics and mechanics. These
came together in the Panther J72, a faithful
replica of the 1930s SS100 with a modern
Jaguar engine. At first, Jankel built these in
his spare time, for pleasure, but requests

RIGHT
Panther De Ville convertible.

BELOW
Panther De Ville.

from customers convinced him to go into
full-time production in 1972. Working out
of a small factory in Byfleet, Surrey, near
to the famous Brooklands racing circuit, he
announced a 323.4-cu in (5.3-litre) V12
version of the J72 in 1973, then a replica of
the Bugatti Royale, also powered by a
Jaguar V12. This came first in four-door
saloon, but later in drophead form.
Panther's first volume-market car was the

Lima in 1976, with glassfibre bodywork in
that classic 1930s styling.

But Jankel had ambitions beyond
1930s replicas. As well as the Rio, a
rebodied Triumph Dolomite Sprint, there
was the outrageous six-wheeled Super Six,
shown at the 1977 London Motor Show.
An open two-seater, this aped the Tyrell
Formula 1 car of the time, with two pairs
of front wheels, all of which steered. Power
came from a rear-mounted Cadillac 500.4-
cu in (8.2-litre) turbocharged V8! Alas, the
Super Six was too ambitious and never
reached full production. Moreover, despite
the launch of a turbocharged version of the
Lima, Panther was now on rocky economic
ground. The recession of the late-1970s had
not been kind to makers of specialist cars,
and Panther went into receivership. It was
bought in October 1980 by Jindo Industries
of Korea, which dropped the current range
transferred J72 production to Korea, and
relaunched the Lima in 1982 as the Kallista
with 97.6-cu in (1.6-litre) four and 170.9-
cu in (2.8-litre) V6 Ford engines.

Five years later, 80 per cent of the

company had been sold to another Korean firm, the car maker Ssangyong. Refinanced, Panther was able to develop the Solo and Solo 2, a mid-engined two-seater powered by a turbocharged Ford Cosworth, with four-wheel-drive. This was not a lasting success, however, and Panther simply faded away.

PEERLESS (Great Britain 1975-1962)
Peerless was the short-lived brainchild of Bernie Rodger, who had the idea of building an affordable 2+2 GT for the Britain of the 1950s. Peerless Motors of Slough gave financial backing, and he was off, showing the alloy prototype at the Paris Motor Show in October 1957.

When production began the following year, it was with a multi-section glassfibre body over a spaceframe chassis of square-section tubes. Most of the mechanical components, including the front suspension, came from the Triumph TR3 sports car, though Laycock de Normanville overdrive

was recommended to overcome the low gearing of the standard Triumph transmission.

The Peerless 122-cu in (2-litre) GT was a light and quite good-looking car, but needed a stronger bodyshell that arrived with the Phase II in 1959, which had a one-piece glassfibre shell. However, the company soon ran out of money, and was closed after an attempt to continue production in Ireland fell through. Undaunted, Bernie Rodger restarted production of the renamed Warwick GT late in 1960, but the quality was not what it should have been and this venture too was abandoned in 1962, though not before Rodger had built a re-engined prototype powered by a Buick 213.6-cu in (3.5-litre) V8.

PEGASO (Spain 1951-1958)
Pegaso, the Spanish sports car, was essentially a showpiece to demonstrate the expertise of Empresa Nacional de

Autocamiones (ENSA), a truck maker founded in Barcelona in 1946. It might well have remained just that had ENSA's technical director and chief executive not been Wilfredo Ricart, a talented engineer who had worked for Alfa Romeo and been responsible for Alfa's V16 and flat-12 engines.

Ricart knew the publicity value of racing, and of high-profile sports cars. Coming to ENSA, he also brought with him a troop of ex-Alfa and Lancia engineers. His task was to turn a semi-skilled workforce into skilled vehicle builders, and to him the answer was obvious: showcase ENSA's abilities with an exotic car. This was unveiled at the 1951 Paris Salon and certainly succeeded. Almost every component, other than the Weber

ABOVE
1952 Pegaso Z-102 Spyder.

LEFT
Peerless/Warwick GT from 1961.

RIGHT
1902 Peugeot Type 36 Tonneau.

carburettors and licence-built ZF gearbox, was designed and built by ENSA itself. Powered by a four-camshaft V8 of 152.6 cu in (2.5 litres), later upgraded to 170.9 and 195.3 cu in (2.8 and 3.2 litres), the Pegaso used a De Dion rear axle with integral gearbox. There were up to eight Weber carburettors and dry-sump lubrication, plus an advanced platform chassis.

In practice, this exotic piece of kit proved too heavy for racing, so Ricart brought in Touring of Milan to build some lighter, more elegant bodywork to suit the Pegaso. Less than 100 Z102 Pegasos were built, 42 of them bodied by Touring. They were widely used in Spanish racing, and a few international events, but never with any great success, though a supercharged Pegaso did briefly hold the title of fastest production sports car in the world, recording 151mph (243km/h) in 1953.

Apart from a few restyled Z103s with bigger V8s of up to 286.8 cu in (4.7 litres), the Pegaso never really had the development it deserved, and production ceased after Ricart retired in 1958. ENSA concentrated on trucks from then onward, but the Pegaso had done its job.

PEUGEOT (France 1891 to date)
Most European countries have a single dominant native manufacturer of mass-market cars: in Germany it has long been

Volkswagen, in Italy Fiat and in Britain various incarnations of BMC, British Leyland and Rover. But France has always had two – Renault and Peugeot. A maker of stolid, rather boring cars for many years, Peugeot nevertheless prospered. It expanded by takeover in the 1970s, buying Citroën in 1974 and the European arm of Chrysler four years later. And from the 1980s onwards, after all those years of building sensible cars, it acquired a reputation for family cars with fine driving dynamics.

The Peugeot family had been in the ironmongery business since 1810, branching into bicycles in 1885. Two members went into the car business separately, though they soon joined forces. Armand Peugeot began producing cars in 1891, using V-twin Daimler engines and chain drive, with his own engines following in 1897. Production, and the range of

LEFT TOP
1913 6-hp 'Bébé' Peugeot.

LEFT ABOVE
1920 Type 163 four-cylinder Torpedo.

ABOVE
1913 Grand Prix car.

RIGHT ABOVE
1931 201 saloon.

RIGHT CENTRE
1934 401 D saloon.

RIGHT
1933 301 cabriolet.

models, soon expanded, with the 39.79-cu in (652-cc) single-cylinder Bébé Peugeot arriving in 1902, and a giant 677.4-cu in (11.1-litre) six-cylinder car from 1908. Meanwhile, Robert Peugeot had been making motorcycles before turning to cars in 1906. He worked under the

Lion-Peugeot name (a lion remains the Peugeot trademark to this day) and like Armand built a large variety of cars.

Joining forces in 1910, the two Peugeots came up with a new Bébé, this time a 52.24-cu in (856-cc) car designed by none other than Ettore Bugatti. A tiny two-seater, this led to a long line of mini-Peugeots, and indeed the company's

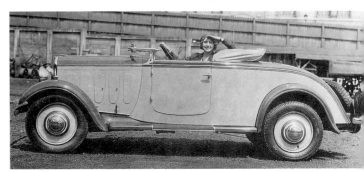

trength has long been in its small cars,
uccess in the executive sector eluding it to
his day. It was replaced in 1921 by the
Quadrilette, another two-seater which
ventually grew to offer five seats. From its
yclecar origins, the Quadrilette evolved
nto a true rival for the successful Renault
CV, produced until 1931.

Through most of the 1920s, Peugeot
roduction gradually grew with no
utstanding successes, though it still
ffered a wide range, from the Quadrilette
o the six-cylinder 12-Six, which was not a
reat success. But the new 201 of 1929 was
ore of a Peugeot milestone. Not only did
begin the well-known three-number
ystem which all Peugeots still use, but it
ffered more interior space than
omparable small cars. It also heralded a
ew generation of Peugeots, based on the
01. So the 301 of 1932 was really a
onger-wheelbased 201, with bigger 8CV
ating and new box-section chassis. The

ABOVE
Peugeot 402B.

ABOVE RIGHT
504 cabriolet.

RIGHT
205 five-door.

401 used a 10CV engine and the 601 a
straight-six 10CV. Once again, the biggest
Peugeot was less successful than its
smaller, cheaper siblings.

Meanwhile, the success of the Citroën
Traction Avant had caused Peugeot to think
again, and in 1935 the new 402 came with
new streamlined styling, new rear
suspension and overhead-valve 11CV
engine (121.5 cu in/1991cc offering
55bhp/41kW). It was soon joined by a mid-
sized 302 and small two-door 202, all with
the same distinctive styling. Peugeots now
enjoyed a family resemblance, and as well

as saloons there were convertibles and coupés, while Parisian dealer Emil Darl'Mart produced sporting Peugeot roadsters from 1937, with tuned engines.

Peugeot's Sochaux factory suffered serious bomb damage during World War II, but was still able to resume car production late in 1945, first with the 202, though it took four years to regain pre-war output levels. In 1948, Peugeot announced its new post-war car, the 203, its first with unitary construction, available in four-door saloon, estate, convertible, or in tuned two-door Darl'Mart form. It was joined by a larger

ABOVE
Pininfarina designed the 406 coupé.

LEFT
The 1997 306 GTi had a six-speed gearbox.

FAR LEFT top to bottom)
1996 106.
The 306 was launched in 1993.
The 406 replaced the 405 in 1995.

403 in 1955; both sold in respectable numbers throughout the 1950s.

The 04 series kicked off in 1960 with the 404, a thoroughly conventional rear-wheel-drive saloon that did well in international rallies. It also introduced a diesel option, which was to be something of a Peugeot speciality (diesel fuel has long been much cheaper than petrol in France). And if the 404 looked very similar to the Austin Cambridge announced a year earlier,

there was a very good reason: both were styled by Pininfarina. The 1965 204 represented a big step forward, being Peugeot's first front-wheel-drive car. As ever, there was a wide range of body styles to choose from: saloon, estate, convertible and short-wheelbased coupé. The 304 of 1969 was an enlarged 204 with more modern styling. By then, the 404 had been replaced by the 504, again with up-to-date styling but very much out of the same

LEFT
806 turbo-diesel.

CENTRE LEFT
2000 406 estate.

BELOW LEFT
2000 406 coupé.

BELOW
2003 307 SW.

and VW Golf. Peugeot had returned to its tradition of offering convertible versions of its mainstream cars, in both the 205 and 306. In 1995, the mid-sized 405 bowed out in favour of the 406, once again leading its class in terms of ride and handling. Later a 134.25-cu in (2.2-litre) direct-injection diesel and 177-cu in (2.9-litre) V6 petrol engine filled its performance gap. There was also a sleek coupé from Pininfarina.

By the late 1990s, no range was complete without a people-carrier, and Peugeot's 806 obliged, being a result of a

LEFT
The 607 was launched in 2000.

BELOW
2003 206 cabriolet.

OPPOSITE
Pierce-Arrow.

mould: a tough, roomy rear-wheel-drive car with petrol or diesel power.

Peugeot made a return bid for the large car market in the 604 of 1975. This used a 164.8-cu in (2.7-litre) V6 petrol engine, designed jointly with Renault and Volvo, plus one of the first turbo-diesel engines (a 128.15-cu in/2.1-litre unit) available in a passenger car. But the 604, with its very conservative styling, was little more successful than previous big Peugeots, especially in export markets. More up Peugeot's street was the little 104 front-wheel-drive hatchback, announced in 1972. Lively and fun to drive, this was the first Peugeot that was a real departure from the previously staid image.

But the car that really broke the mould was the 205 in 1983, with excellent handling and a much sought-after performance variant, the 97.6-cu in (1.6-litre) and later 115.9-cu in (1.9-litre) GTI. If

that was too fast and thirsty, the 109.8-cu in (1.8-litre) turbo-diesel version gave torquey performance at over 50mpg (17.7km/litre). Alongside the 205 were the ageing 305 (which had replaced the 304 in 1978) and the 309 hatchback of 1987, the latter with much the same choice of engines as the 205. The same year, the 405 saloon, now front-wheel-drive, was introduced, underlining the character of modern Peugeots as good drivers' cars. Engine choices ranged from 1.6- to 2-litre 16-valve petrol and turbo or non-turbo diesels. Peugeot persevered in the big sector as well, with the 605 as a scaled-up 405, but yet again, managed to miss the mark.

The 1990s heralded the arrival of the '06' series. The 106 came first, a useful car, its advantages again being the 1.6GTi and an ultra-economical 85.4-cu in (1.4-litre) diesel. Replacing the 205, the 306 advanced half a class to compete with the Ford Escort

joint project with Fiat: there were Lancia and Citroën versions as well, most of them identical. Meanwhile, the 605 was replaced by the 607 (which seemed no closer to gaining big-car stardom for Peugeot) and the 307 replaced the 306 in 2001. Peugeot's advertising slogan is 'The lion goes from strength to strength', which is mostly true.

PIERCE/PIERCE-ARROW

(U.S.A. 1901-1938)
George Pierce made his fortune producing everything from ice-boxes to bird-cages. Quick to spot a market opportunity, he went into bicycles to take advantage of the 1880s cycle boom, and in 1900 turned his attention to cars.

His first prototype was steam-powered, and was discarded in favour of a single-cylinder De Dion engine. Thus powered, the Motorette went into production in 1901.

After a couple of years, Pierce began to use his own engines, while his cars moved rapidly upmarket, with the Arrow in 1903 and $4,000 Great Arrow the following year. Their profile (and sales) were raised by success in long-distance races such as the Glidden Tour; Pierce moved production to a new factory and renamed the company Pierce-Arrow.

Production was still not up to Ford levels, with around 1,000 cars a year being built, but most were pre-sold before they left the factory, and at least two were selected for the U.S. Presidential fleet. George Pierce died in 1910, but he lived to see his final business venture succeed. Underlining the luxury market for Pierce-Arrow cars, the company ran a chauffeur training school, to ensure a supply of safe and competent drivers for its big-engined limousines, the 415-cu in (6.8-litre) 38,

524.8-cu in (8.6-litre) 48 and 823.8-cu in (13.5-litre) 66, with prices up to $8,200.

But it was not only limousines. Pierce-Arrow also started to make trucks in 1910, which saw it through World War I, and provided a solid, profitable base on which the prestigious car line could be based. But after the war, the demand for trucks declined, and Pierce-Arrow found itself in a difficult position. Forced to pay dividends to shareholders, rather than invest in new models, its sales began to fall and the company made a loss of $8 million in 1921. There was one new car in 1924, the 286.8-cu in (4.7-litre) 80, and the firm commissioned Laurence Pomeroy to design an all-aluminium version. But the 80 itself was neglected, and sales again soon dropped off. In 1928, Pierce-Arrow was taken over by Studebaker, which brought in a much-needed new engine for the straight-

eight 133 and 143, while a new V12 followed in 1932. It could not have come at a more inappropriate time, with sales down to a low of less than 2,700, which led to another multi-million dollar loss.

Studebaker collapsed in 1933 and Pierce-Arrow was bought by a group of Buffalo businessmen. Under the new regime, different projects were tried, such as the radically-streamlined Silver Arrow and a new line of trailer-caravans. But the money was running out, and car production ceased altogether in 1938. The V12 engine lived on, however, and was used to power fire engines right up to 1970.

PLYMOUTH (U.S.A. 1928 to date)

Plymouth has always been at the low-cost end of Chrysler, and has spent its 75-year existence battling with Ford and Chevrolet for a slice of the mainstream sales cake. The name was thought up by Chrysler sales manager, Joseph Frazier, suggested by Plymouth Rock, where the Pilgrim Fathers first set foot on American soil.

Of course, as a division of Chrysler, Plymouth used many Chrysler components, but unlike the opposition at Ford and Chevrolet, this included things like all-steel bodies and hydraulic brakes, where its rivals made do with wooden-framed bodies and mechanical brakes. So they were not quite as cheap, but were perceived by many to offer more for the money. As a result, Plymouths sold by the thousands. Even in 1930, with the Depression beginning to bite, Plymouth sold 68,000 cars, quite an achievement for a new marque then only two years old.

Reflecting their market, the early Plymouths stuck with four-cylinder engines, but stole a march on the opposition with rubber mounting, which gave unrivalled smoothness for a four. Plymouth

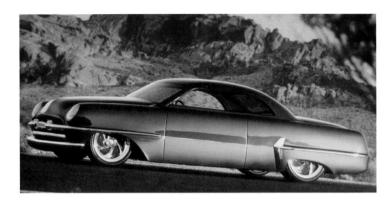

for the new Plymouths, where the fashion was for fastback streamlining. For the first time, Plymouths seemed dull, and sales began to drop away. They recovered in the late 1950s, when stylist Virgil Exner brought Plymouth into the tailfin age, ahead of its rivals, and over 700,000 cars were built in 1955.

But Plymouth seemed unable to regain its steady success of the period before World War II. In the early 1960s, it forecast that American motorists were ready to downsize, and introduced smaller cars as a result. The trend of the time was actually

swept up to third place in the U.S. sales league, beating its own Chrysler parent. It would hold that third place until the early 1950s.

A six-cylinder engine arrived in 1933, which was given a power boost to 82bhp (61.1kW) three years later. The car it powered started at just $495, brand-new, thus consolidating the Plymouth value-for-money philosophy. By 1940, when Walter Chrysler died, Plymouth was churning out half a million cars each year.

This success continued when production resumed in 1945, but Plymouth's fortunes were about to take a turn for the worse. New Chrysler boss K.T. Keller insisted on a sensible three-box style

TOP LEFT
1928 Plymouth.

ABOVE
1955 Plaza.

TOP RIGHT
1954 customized Sniper.

CENTRE RIGHT
Fury convertible.

RIGHT
Barracuda.

FAR RIGHT
Belvedere.

moving in the opposite direction, and Plymouth lost sales, though its compact Valiant was always popular. The late-1960s were happier times, with big cars like the Fury and Belvedere, plus the Mustang-rivalling Barracuda, although in the 1970s Plymouth did seem to hit the doldrums again, and once more this was partly due to cars that looked simply old-fashioned.

There were more radical changes in the 1980s and early 1990s as Plymouth, along with other Chrysler divisions, began to incorporate Mitsubishis as part of its range. The Colt GT hatchback was sold with an 'Imported for Plymouth' sticker, and the front-wheel-drive Acclaim saloon came with a Mitsubishi 183.1-cu in (3-litre) V6. The Laser coupé (in 109.8- and 122-cu in/1.8- and 2-litre turbo forms, with up to 195bhp/145.4kW) was a joint development with Mitsubishi.

However, one new Plymouth in 1996 clearly had nothing to do with Mitsubishi. The Prowler had first been shown three years earlier as a concept car, a 21st-century take on a 1950s hot-rod. The public reaction was so overwhelming that Chrysler

LEFT
2001 Plymouth Prowler.

CENTRE LEFT
2000 Breeze.

BELOW LEFT
2000 Neon.

BELOW
2002 Voyager.

decided to be brave and put it into production. It came with a 213.6-cu in (3.5-litre) V6, which gave good performance, thanks to the car's low weight of 2,830lb (1285kg), the chassis being aluminium, with alloy body panels. But if that was just too much, Plymouth buyers could also choose from practical saloons like the Breeze and Neon, with the Grand Voyager as a luxury people-carrier.

PONTIAC (U.S.A. 1926 to date)

Pontiac was one of the most successful of General Motors' divisions, second only to Chevrolet, and often third in the best-selling league in the U.S.A. In the GM hierarchy, it was a class up from the low-priced Chevrolets, but certainly not in Cadillac territory, and thus more on a par with Oldsmobile and Buick.

It was one of GM's 'made-up' marques, founded in 1926, and named after the town of Pontiac, Michigan, where the cars were built. Like its rival, Plymouth, over at Chrysler, Pontiac met with instant success, and its first car, the Six, was soon outselling its parent's Oakland model: 200,000 Pontiacs were sold in 1929. That slumped to less than 50,000 in 1932, and most of Pontiac's sister marques were dropped altogether.

But Pontiac survived, not least because the energetic GM president Alfred Sloan instituted some serious rationalization, which led to Pontiac sharing many

components with Chevrolet and being sold alongside Buick and Oldsmobile by the same dealers. This might not have worked had stylist Frank Hershey and chief body engineer Roy Milner not conspired to make Pontiacs look different from the corresponding Chevrolets, despite the fact that they often used the same body panels.

All this cut costs considerably, while the new Pontiac Eight of 1933 was a real success, thanks in part to its smooth, powerful straight-eight motor designed by Benjamin Anibal. It was reliable too, and was Pontiac's mainstay until a new V8 took over in 1955. By 1937, Pontiac sales were back up to 200,000, and the recovery was

ABOVE
Pontiac two-door coupé.

TOP LEFT ABOVE
1935 two-door sedan.

TOP LEFT BELOW
1937 four-door convertible.

FAR LEFT TOP
1926 coupé.

FAR LEFT BELOW
1932 model.

ABOVE LEFT
1962 Grand Prix.

OPPOSITE
LEFT (top to bottom):
1964 GTO
1968 GTO
1992 Firebird.

complete. The use of GM's 'turret-top' all-steel bodies, independent front suspension and hydraulic brakes confirmed it, with a six-cylinder engine to back up the successful eight.

After World War II Pontiac enjoyed more prosperity through the 1950s and '60s. It proved sensitive to customer

TOP
1999 Firebird.

ABOVE
2002 Firebird.

demand; having rejected GM's Hydra-Matic auto transmission, it later relented, and was vindicated in 1953 when 84 per cent of its cars were ordered with the two-pedal system. A modern overhead-valve V8 followed in 1955, as did the wrap-around windshield, two-tone paint, tubeless tyres and 12-volt electrics: it was a good year and set new records, in which Pontiac sales soared to over 550,000. Looks had much to

do with this success: Pontiac plugged immediately into the long, wide and low trend, with cars like the Star Chief and Chieftain convertibles.

But as with all the U.S. manufacturers, the 1970s proved a more challenging time due to the oil crisis, tougher emissions and safety legislation, plus the arrival of cheaper imported cars. Pontiac held on to its number three spot in the industry, but

only just, while introducing a new range of compact cars in tune with the times. There was nothing radical about the Pontiacs of the 1970s, however, and the Phoenix, Grand Le Mans and Grand Am were all utterly conventional three-box saloons. The Fiero was a little more exciting as a mid-engined glassfibre sports car, small by American standards. But it was heavy, and the 152.6-

cu in (2.5-litre) four and 158.7-cu in (2.6-litre) V6 engines did not produce the sports car performance to match the looks. More muscular was the Firebird Trans Am, though even this had to be downgraded – the American muscle car was under threat! Fortunately for Pontiac, it had some perennially popular cars like the Grand Prix saloon, that kept the cheques coming in.

OPPOSITE
TOP LEFT: 2003 Grand Am.

TOP RIGHT: 2002 Vibe.

BELOW LEFT: 2002 Sunfire GXP.

BELOW RIGHT: 2003 Atek.

TOP
2003 Montana.

ABOVE
2004 Bonneville.

TOP RIGHT
2004 Grand Prix.

ABOVE RIGHT
2004 GTO.

The company persevered with the Firebird, which was a great image-booster for the Pontiac name, restyling it in 1992 and ensuring it kept the option of a 347.8-cu in (5.7-litre) V8. By now it was the only V8 Pontiac left, and one of the few with rear-wheel-drive. More to the point for mainstream sales was the Sunbird, new in 1994. This was a four-cylinder front-wheel-drive saloon that was relatively economical and, crucially, looked sporty as well, thus maintaining Pontiac's image.

The Grand Am saloon was up a class, with four- or six-cylinder engines, while in 1996 the Grand Prix was restyled. The latter was still a best-seller for Pontiac, with useful performance from a turbocharged 231.9-cu in (3.8-litre) V6. Top of the saloon range was the V6 Bonneville, again with that modern, slightly sporty appearance, and Pontiac's people-carrier was the Trans Sport, V6-powered, with a choice of short or long wheelbases.

PORSCHE (Austria/Germany 1948 to date)

Dr. Ferdinand Porsche was the driving force behind not one major European manufacturer but two, namely Volkswagen, and of course Porsche itself. This engineering genius worked for Austro-Daimler and Steyr before setting up a design consultancy in Stuttgart in 1930. Early projects included two small car projects for Zündapp and NSU: the former was powered by an intriguing five-cylinder radial engine, which not surprisingly turned out to be too expensive.

The breakthrough came when Adolf Hitler commissioned Porsche to design his 'people's car', or Volkswagen, which emerged as a rear-engined beetle-shaped machine with an air-cooled flat-four engine. Production had hardly begun before the war called a halt, and Porsche was arrested by the Americans in 1945 and handed over to the French (he had designed the famous Tiger tank during the war). But the French authorities freed him after two years, when the Italian Cisitalia company paid them a million francs, because they wanted Porsche to design a new Grand Prix car for them!

LEFT
Dr. Porsche pioneered four-wheel-drive.

BELOW LEFT
1964 1600-cc cabriolet.

FAR LEFT TOP
Porsche's 1931 rear-engined car.

FAR LEFT BOTTOM
The 1938 record-breaking Type 64.

OPPOSITE
ABOVE LEFT: *Porsche 356 Speedster.*

ABOVE RIGHT:
1970 Porsche 914 with 2.4-litre 190-bhp engine.

BELOW LEFT: *1987 Porsche 911 turbo.*

BELOW RIGHT: *Porsche 924 Carrera GT with 210-bhp engine.*

Free also to pursue his own work, Porsche almost immediately decided to build sports cars under his own name. These owed much to the pre-war Volkswagen (now back in production), a rear-engined two-seater with a tuned version of the 69-cu in (1131-cc) VW flat-four. Production began in 1948, and moved back to Porsche's original Stuttgart base in 1950, where it grew rapidly: 500 cars were built by early 1951 and 10,000 five years later, helped no doubt by a competition debut at Le Mans. Porsche was to make a habit of winning at the famous French circuit, and had a dozen victories to his credit by 1987.

Ferdinand Porsche died in January 1952, but his son Ferry took over the reins, having been involved with the company as

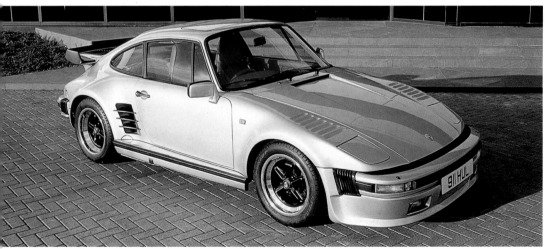

a young man. Under his guidance, the original Porsche 356 acquired bigger engines and more power: a 91.5-cu in (1.5-litre), then a 97.6-cu in (1.6-litre) in 1955 and finally a 130-bhp (96.7-kW) 122-cu in (2-litre) GS, with exports to the U.S.A. under way by the mid-1950s. The 356 was replaced in 1964 by the most famous Porsche of all time, the 911. Designed along the same lines as the 356, with a rear engine and strong family resemblance, the innovation was a new flat-six power unit of 121.5 cu in (1991cc). A four-cylinder 912 came the following year, providing a more direct replacement; but the 911 could only go upmarket, and over the next two decades, that is precisely what it did. The flat-six gradually grew in size to 134.25 cu in (2.2 litres) in 1970, 140.4 cu in (2.3 litres) in 1972, and 164.8 cu in (2.7 litres) in 1973. By 1977 it had been transformed into a 201.4-cu in (3.3-litre) unit with a turbocharger to create one of the fastest-accelerating production cars money could buy. Carrera was the name applied to high-performance variants.

The 911 had by now built up a solid following all over the world, which on its own was not enough to ensure Porsche's survival: by 1975 sales were falling, and an attempt to introduce a 'cheap' Porsche, the VW-engined 914, had not been a success. The company tried again in 1976 with the 924, and this time it worked, reviving

ABOVE
Porsche 968 turbo.

LEFT
Porsche 911 Cabriolet.

FAR LEFT
1997 911 Targa.

OPPOSITE
ABOVE: 1987 944S.

BELOW LEFT: 1999 911 Carrera 4 cabriolet.

BELOW RIGHT: 1999 911 GT3.

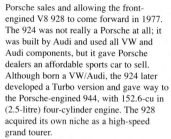

Porsche sales and allowing the front-engined V8 928 to come forward in 1977. The 924 was not really a Porsche at all; it was built by Audi and used all VW and Audi components, but it gave Porsche dealers an affordable sports car to sell. Although born a VW/Audi, the 924 later developed a Turbo version and gave way to the Porsche-engined 944, with 152.6-cu in (2.5-litre) four-cylinder engine. The 928 acquired its own niche as a high-speed grand tourer.

Meanwhile, the 911 was having upgrades of its own, celebrating its 25th anniversary with the Carrera 4, a four-wheel-drive variant with a 250-bhp (186.4-kW) version of that faithful flat-six; however, it was a very different engine to the 1964 original. The Carrera 4 was a 'cheaper' (if that is the right word) variation on the Group B959, an exotic

371

four-wheel-drive twin-turbo car along 911 lines, with 400bhp (298.2kW) and lightweight Kevlar bodywork. Really a competition special, only 250 examples were made.

But once again, Porsche was facing hard times. The 924 had crept upmarket, and the company was again dependent on high-priced sports cars. Fortunately for the workers at Stuttgart, the company had also built up a lucrative consultancy engineering business, selling its considerable skills all over the world. The new generation of Spanish SEATs in the 1980s, for example, used Porsche-designed engines. Meanwhile,

the 944 was replaced by the 968 (now with up to 305bhp/227.4kW). In 1996 Porsche once again produced a cheaper car, this time the Boxster. Not as entry-level as the original 924, this little mid-engined car, with its 2.5-litre water-cooled flat-six, was affordable enough to expand Porsche sales considerably. At the other end of the scale, one of the last air-cooled 911s was the 1993 Turbo, with a 219.7-cu in (3.6-litre) engine and over 400bhp. In 1998, the air-cooled six was finally laid to rest, replaced by a larger version of the Boxster engine.

By 2002, the successful Boxster (now with a 164.8-cu in/2.7-litre six) and 911 (in

turbo or non-turbo form) were making good profits for Porsche, but this still left it vulnerable to the ups and downs of sports car economics. So for 2003 it announced the Cayenne, a luxury 4x4 in the Range Rover mould. Sharing a floorpan with the equivalent VW to reduce costs, the basic non-turbo V8 still cost over £44,000 in the U.K., with the turbocharged version with air suspension coming in at nearly £70,000. It was said to bring a new level of sports car agility to a big off-road machine, though its off-road ability was still an unknown quantity in late 2002.

OPPOSITE
2001 911 turbo.

BELOW
1999 Porsche 911 Carrera coupé.

PROTON (Malaysia 1983 to date)
Proton is one of the youngest
manufacturers currently in production. It
began as a joint venture between the
Malaysian government and Mitsubishi,
with production starting late in 1983, when
the old Mitsubishi Lancer was produced.
As the years have passed, so the Japanese
influence has decreased, but the older
Protons still make use of older Mitsubishi
designs, though they are built in Malaysia.

Exports to Britain began in 1989, with
the angular Mpi available with 79.3- and
91.5-cu in (1.3- and 1.5-litre) engines, with
a 12-valve variant following in 1991.
Hardly cutting-edge, but the Protons soon
proved to be reliable, quite well made, easy
to drive, and very good value. Strangely
enough, however, Proton failed to replicate
its U.K. success on mainland Europe. The
curvy Persona followed the straight-edged
Mpi in 1993, with the executive-class
Perdana arriving in 1996, complete with a
122-cu in (2-litre) 16-valve engine.

In the same year Proton took over
Lotus, using the British company's
expertise to improve the dynamics of its
cars. Despite its best efforts, Proton was
still seen as a bread-and-butter, value-for-
money marque, and it was hoped that some
of the Lotus glamour and mystique would
rub off. But six years after the takeover,
Proton cars were still not seen as drivers'
machines: the Satria was a licence-built
version of the old Mitsubishi Colt, while

the Wira approximated to the Lancer.
Attempts to build upmarket cars, like the
Impian and Coupé, were not taken
seriously; instead, practical values like
reliability and a six-year/100,000-mile
(160,000-km) warranty were the strong
points on which Proton relied.

RAILTON
(Great Britain 1933-1949)
The Railton was Noel Macklin's fourth
car-making venture. In 1919 he worked on
the Eric Campbell, followed by the Silver
Hawk and the longer-lived Invicta. The last
project entailed taking over the old Invicta
factory in Cobham, Surrey, to build cars
designed by Reid Railton, already known
for his land-speed-record machines.

Like a handful of other British makes,
the Railton used a large American engine
rather than a homegrown one, in this case
the Essex Terraplane. This provided the
attractive combination of good
performance and a relatively low price: the

FAR LEFT
1993 Proton Persona.

BELOW LEFT
1997 Proton Compact 1.6 SEi.

BELOW
1937 Railton Carrington.

BOTTOM
1936 Railton two-seater tourer.

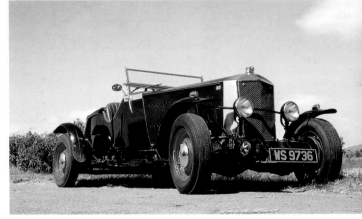

244.1-cu in (4-litre) straight-eight Essex gave the Railton respectable performance, and despite their weight Railtons were quite successful in competition. They also cost around £200 less than an equivalent Alvis or Lagonda.

They also used Hudson engines, notably in smaller 164.8- and 201.4-cu in (2.7- and 3.3-litre) cars, though production was always in the hundreds rather than the thousands. The company was taken over by Hudson Motors Ltd. in 1940 and very few Railtons were built after World War II, the final blow being the difficulty of importing American engines in those austere post-war years. There was a brief revival of the name in 1989, with a Jaguar-based convertible.

RELIANT (Great Britain 1935 to date)
Reliant will forever be associated with those funny little three-wheelers, in themselves a tribute to British eccentricity, but the company also made a long line of sports cars, pioneered the use of mass-produced glassfibre bodies and built the landmark Scimitar GTE high-performance estate.

But a three-wheeler was the company's first product in 1935, when it took over production of Raleigh's three-wheel van. It replaced Raleigh's air-cooled V-twin with the Austin Seven side-valve four-cylinder, and the latter became something of a

LEFT
1984 2.8-litre Reliant Scimitar GTC.

BELOW
Reliant Scimitar with SSI Nissan turbo.

BELOW LEFT
1965 Reliant Regal.

Reliant trademark: it took over production when Austin ceased making the engine in 1938, and it then powered all Reliants until 1962.

The first in-house Reliant design did not appear until 1953, with the glassfibre-bodied Regal three-wheeler. Like all subsequent three-wheelers, this weighed less than 900lb (408kg), which qualified it for lower road tax and allowed it to be

driven on a motorcycle licence. Despite the side-valve engine's mere 17.5bhp (13kW), this resulted in sprightly performance and excellent fuel consumption. In fact, Reliants became famous for the latter, especially after the company's own all-alloy overhead-valve 36.61-cu in (600-cc) unit replaced the old side-valve in 1962. Even when enlarged to 42.72, 45.77 and 51.87 cu in (700, 750 and 850cc), figures of 60-70mpg (21.2/24.8km/litre) were commonplace. The Regal itself was restyled in 1962 to go with the new engine.

Alongside it, Reliant introduced a rakish-looking sports car, the Sabre Six, powered by a Ford six-cylinder engine. This was replaced by the Scimitar coupé in 1966 (now Ford V6-powered) and in 1968 by the hatchback/estate GTE, which uniquely combined near 120-mph (193-km/h) performance, four seats and useful load space. Princess Anne was the most famous customer. The GTE was available right up to 1988, latterly with a convertible GTC version. In the meantime, Reliant also helped set up Anadol cars in Turkey, designing a mid-size Ford-powered saloon to kick off the Turkish motor industry.

Meanwhile, what of the three-wheelers? The Regal was replaced by the more up-to-date Robin in 1973, timed just right to take advantage of the oil crisis, when 70mpg suddenly made a lot of sense. A four-wheel version, the Kitten, was launched two years later, and was also made under licence in India as the Dolphin. The Robin, in turn, gave way to the Rialto in 1982, along with the four-wheel Fox utility. Three years later, the Reliant SS1 heralded a new assault on the budget sports car market. The Michelotti styling was not to everyone's taste, but the car did offer affordable open-top motoring now that MG was defunct. The later Nissan 109.8-cu in

(1.8-litre) turbo gave serious performance.

But by the early 1990s Reliant was in trouble. A reverse takeover by a property company ended in disaster, when the new parent went down in 1994, taking Reliant with it. But after a short-lived takeover by Avonex Industries in the following year, Reliant was back in business, thanks to a consortium of businessmen in 1996. The Rialto went back into production as the restyled Robin, and in 1999 a Robin hatchback was launched. Alas, production of the long-running three-wheeler finally ceased in 2001. Today Reliant Motors imports the Piaggio Ape three-wheeler light commercial and Ligier micro-car, as well as producing spares for the many thousands of Reliant three-wheelers still travelling the roads of Britain.

RENAULT (France 1898 to date)

It was a classic story: Louis Renault built a car to please himself, a little De Dion-engined device with an unusual shaft drive. Friends saw it, liked it and ordered replicas. Thus Louis went into production and a new car manufacturer was born. All this happened before the turn of the 19th century, so Renault was a real pioneer, but his company became the most successful French car maker of all. It was the biggest as early as 1913 and held onto that top slot for over 70 years.

Those early Renaults were distinctive, for the mounting of the radiator close to the dashboard allowed for that classic sloping bonnet that became a Renault trademark. On a more practical note, it also made the radiator less vulnerable in a front-end collision. Bigger Renaults soon followed that De Dion-engined voiturette, with the company's own four-cylinder engine unveiled in 1902, and by 1907 the range was topped by the 482.1-cu in (7.9-litre)

RENAULT TODAY'S MOST OUTSTANDING RANGE

RENAULT 20TD

DIESEL

ABOVE
1937 Renault Celta Quatre.

ABOVE RIGHT
Brochure showing the 1960s range.

RIGHT
Brochure for the Renault 20TD diesel.

OPPOSITE
1912 Renault AX.

A1-C. In the following year, Renault made its first aero engine, an air-cooled V8, and by 1930 was actually the world's largest aero engine maker. It remained a highly diversified company, by that time building trucks, buses, railcars and tanks, as well as locomotive and marine engines.

Renault was now a massive company, the original factory at Billancourt having its own foundries for iron, brass, steel and aluminium. Over 20,000 people worked for the company by 1918, though Renault himself was no longer on good terms with his workforce: a dispute over docking pay for substandard work had seen to that. Meanwhile, Renault continued to offer big cars, such as the 1921 40CV with a 555.3-cu in (9.1-litre) engine, replaced by the straight-eight Reinastella seven years later. But the company also produced small cars such as the Model KJ (1922-29), brought out to rival the successful Citroën 5CV, and later the four-cylinder Quatre series, culminating in the 61-cu in (1-litre) 8CV Juvaquatre. This was a modern small car with unitary construction, and over 27,000 were sold before the beginning of World War II in 1939.

War proved the downfall of Louis. Forced to work under German occupation, he was nonetheless arrested and accused of

FAR LEFT
Brochure for the Renault 5.

CENTRE LEFT
Renault Scenic.

LEFT
Renault Clio Oasis Special Edition.

BELOW FAR LEFT
Renault Alpine GTA V6 turbo.

BELOW LEFT
1997 Mégane coupé.

BOTTOM FAR LEFT
The original MPV, the Espace.

BOTTOM LEFT
1997 Safrane.

collaboration after Paris was liberated. After only a month's imprisonment, during which he suffered brutal treatment, did Louis die. His company was swiftly nationalized, and the rear-engined 45.77-cu in (750-cc) 4CV was launched as Renault's first true post-war car, well over a million being sold by 1961. The bigger, front-engined Frégate was less successful, but Renault produced a whole string of popular cars over the succeeding decades.

The rear-engined Dauphine of 1956 was in the range for many years, and 200,000 were exported to the U.S.A. alone. The open-top Caravelle used an 67.61-cu in (1108-cc) version of the Dauphine's 51.57-cu in (845-cc) overhead-valve engine. The front-wheel-drive Renault 4 (first of the numbered Renaults) was even more successful, designed to offer the comfort and cheapness of a Citroen 2CV, but with more performance from its 845-cc four-cylinder engine. Like the 2CV, it stayed in production into the 1980s. The Renault was a hatchback of sorts, but it took the mid-sized 16 of 1965 to popularize this format for bigger cars. A cross between saloon and estate, it would later become the standard format for European cars. There were still Renault three-box saloons, however, notably the 8, 10 and 12.

TOP LEFT
Renault Laguna saloon.

TOP RIGHT
1998 Clio Sport V6 24V.

ABOVE RIGHT
Mégane Cabriolet Sport 16V.

LEFT
Renault Spider.

ABOVE
2002 Epace.

ABOVE LEFT
2002 Clio Renault Sport V6 255.

LEFT
2002 New-look Mégane.

Renault's most successful car ever, the 5, arrived in 1972 as the first of the hatchback 'superminis'. It used existing Renault engines of 51.6 cu in (845cc) and 58.34 cu in (956cc) in a very roomy but compact three-door (and later five-door) bodyshell. It was also very comfortable for such a small car, and engine options later ranged up to the fire-breathing 160-bhp (119.3-kW) Turbo. So successful was the 5, that when Renault replaced it with a new car in 1985, the family resemblance was strong and deliberate. Some Renaults were less successful, such as the Fuego sports car and big 25, though they were by no means poor sellers.

The 9 saloon and 11 hatchback, plus the upper mid-sized 21 of the early 1990s, were all very conventional, as was the successful 19, but the Espace was

something new. It soon sired a whole new class of car, the 'people-carrier' or MPV (multi-purpose vehicle). Designed and built for Renault by Matra, it offered estate car space with a high roofline and modern looks, plus car-driving dynamics: this was no van conversion. It was a huge success, and the Espace is still in production (though much updated), having inspired a whole raft of similar rivals. The Twingo mini-car was another Renault with character, as was the spartan open-top Spider, though neither was as new a concept as the Espace.

In the mid- to late-1990s, Renault bade farewell to its numbering system. The 5 was replaced by the heavier, more solid Clio, the 19 by the Mégane, 21 by Laguna and 25 by Safrane. The Mégane was one of the best-sellers, growing into a huge range

of hatchbacks, saloons, Cabriolet, Coupé and even an MPV, the Scenic, which was a sort of mini-Espace. Again, most of Renault's rivals followed with their own small MPVs. As if this were not spacious enough, Renault offered the van-based Kangoo from 2001. The avant-garde Avantime arrived in 2002, a futuristic two-door coupé on the Espace floorpan, while the Satis was a new (and radical-looking) attempt to crack the executive market. But Renault's best-sellers were still the Clio and Mégane: small cars remained its forte, just as they had been for Louis.

ABOVE
Renault Kangoo Break'up concept car.

LEFT
2000 Renault Scenic RX4.

REO (U.S.A. 1904-1936)

Reo was the second motor car venture for Ransom E. Olds. He had already founded Oldsmobile, but soon departed after disagreements over the direction in which the company was going. Undaunted, he set up the R.E. Olds Co. in Lansing, Michigan, though the name was soon changed to Reo (after his initials), when Oldsmobile objected to the use of the name.

It must have been satisfying for Olds to see his first 8-hp (5.96-kW) runabout, with its underfloor single-cylinder engine and false hood, not only go smoothly into production, but soon to have the Reo line-up outselling Oldsmobile itself! He insisted on very tight quality control, which nearly led to another falling-out with his colleagues in 1910, but the partnership survived, and the following year Reo introduced a new commercial vehicle, the Speed Wagon.

After World War I, the T-6 car proved successful, while the truck side of the business continued to expand, aided by the takeover of the Duplex Truck Co.'s Lansing factory. Ransom Olds went into semi-retirement in the mid-1920s, and the company brought out the Flying Cloud to replace the T-6, as well as the short-lived Wolverine, a cheaper car. There was also the luxury Royale, though this was badly timed, launched in 1931 in the middle of the

Depression. In fact, Reo never really recovered from these devastating few years. Olds came out of retirement in an attempt to turn the company round, using Graham body dies to produce a car named the Airman, sold by Franklin. But this was not enough, and Reo car production ceased in 1936, though the trucks went on independently for another 20 years.

RILEY
(Great Britain 1899-1969)

One of the British pioneers, Riley lost its independence before World War II, and thereafter was increasingly used as an upmarket badge by BMC until it completely faded from sight in 1969. The Riley family were weavers, but went into the cycle business in the 1890s. The youngest son, Percy, had a talent for engineering, and built a car in 1898, the first production vehicle (quadricycle) following a year later, using a bought-in engine. Motorcycles followed in 1902 and the first true production car in 1906.

By then, Percy had already established the Riley Engine Company, building engines both for the parent company and its rivals. He had also designed a bolt-on wire wheel, and Riley Sr. planned to drop all car production and concentrate on this. But this would never do: Percy and his brothers took over the existing designs in 1913, set up Riley (Coventry) Ltd. and a new era began.

After World War I the company gained a formidable sporting reputation from cars such as the side-valve Redwing. This was reinforced from 1926 by Percy's new twin-camshaft engine in the four-cylinder Nine, followed by a six-cylinder version two years later. There were saloons like the Monaco, but also rakish, open two-seaters, the Brooklands Nine in the late 1920s and the 91.5-cu in (1.5-litre) Imp, all powered by

variations on that twin-cam engine. This sporty veneer rubbed off on the saloons too, such as the fastback Kestrel.

Larger cars were added from the mid-1930s, these including two V8s, but the company may have overreached itself: the receiver was called in and Nuffield (the Morris concern) took over in 1938, swiftly stopping production of the sports cars.

After World War II the new 91.5 cu in (1.5-litre) and 152.6-cu in (2.5-litre) saloons were launched, attractive four-seat, four-door cars that drew on Riley's sporting heritage. But the realities of working as a small cog in a large corporation soon became clear. More rationalization was inevitable, and the Pathfinder, which replaced the 2.5-litre in 1953, made far more use of BMC components, sharing a bodyshell with the equivalent Wolseley. From then on, all Rileys were based on mainstream Austin/Morris cars with a luxury/sporting edge. The One Point Five (1957-65) was a

restyled, bigger-engined Morris Minor and actually a very pleasant, compact sporting saloon. Finally, in the 1960s, Rileys were simply rebadged Austins: the Riley Elf was a Mini, the Kestrel an 1100/1300, and the 4/72 a Cambridge. These all came to an end in 1969.

LEFT
1907 Reo 18-hp tourer.

ABOVE
Riley Sprite.

OPPOSITE
LEFT: 1934 Riley six-cylinder.

ABOVE RIGHT: Riley Imp.

BELOW RIGHT: 1951 2.5-litre roadster.

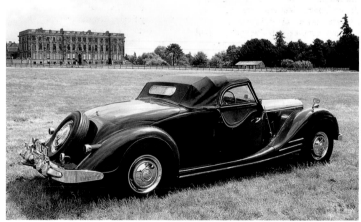

ROLLS-ROYCE

(Great Britain 1906 to date)

The most famous partnership in motoring history was surely that between Henry Royce and the Hon. Charles Rolls. Royce had acquired a Decauville car, and was so dissatisfied with it that he decided to build his own. The resulting 10-hp (7.46-kW) prototype ran like a fine watch, a result of Royce's typically painstaking approach. It also greatly impressed Charles Rolls, so much so that he offered to sell all the cars that Royce could make: thus in 1906 was Rolls-Royce born.

From the start, it was clear that Rolls-Royce would not be making small, still less cheap, cars. The first 40/50 was the sole model, built as a running chassis so that the owner could choose his/her preferred body from proprietary coachbuilders: not until after World War II did Rolls-Royce cars come with standard, factory-built bodies. Demand grew, and production was moved from Manchester to a new plant at Derby; in 1922 a new 'small' Rolls-Royce was announced, more in tune with austere economic times, though of course it was still an expensive luxury car. The Twenty was powered by a new overhead-valve six-cylinder engine of 189.2 cu in (3.1 litres), enlarged to 225.8 cu in (3.7 litres) for the 1929 20/25 and finally to 262.4 cu in (4.3 litres) for the 25/30 in 1936. Rolls-Royce was now a two-model company, and the big 40/50 was replaced in 1925 by the 463.8-cu

RIGHT
1910 Rolls-Royce Roi de Belge Silver Ghost.

OPPOSITE
1929 Rolls-Royce Connaught.

in (7.6-litre) Phantom, a name used on the largest Rolls-Royces for many years. Updated as the Phantom II for 1929, it used a hypoid rear axle to allow lower bodywork, and this was actually the last car designed by Royce himself, for he died in 1933. One romantic story is that the company logo changed colour from red to black soon after, in mourning for its co-founder, but the reality is that Royce had already taken the decision to change it before he died.

Rolls-Royce is always regarded as a quintessentially English car, but exports to the U.S.A. soon became an important part

of its business. So important that in 1919 a factory was set up in Springfield, Massachusetts to build cars specifically for the U.S. market, to get around high import duties. However, it closed in 1931, due to the Depression, but the U.S. influence continued. The Phantom III of 1935 was powered by a V12 engine, to compete with the multi-cylinder cars coming out of Detroit, and independent front suspension, responding to developments at Detroit, again also featured.

Rolls-Royce changed after the war. The conflict had increased the importance of the

aero engine side of the business: the company had made aero engines since 1914, and the famous Merlin had been in great demand during World War II, powering the Spitfire fighter and Lancaster bomber, among a host of other great warplanes. The Derby factory was now devoted to aero engines, while car production was moved to Crewe, where Rolls-Royce had run a wartime factory for the government. But times had changed. Under the guidance of W.A. Robotham, costs were cut by making most cars with standard bodies, rather than coach-built; a new family of engines was

developed for military and commercial as well as car applications, and Bentleys became badge-engineered Rolls-Royces, cutting costs even further. It may seem a heresy to some, but Robotham's rationalization plan, which he had proposed as early as 1940, probably helped Rolls-Royce survive its post-war years, allowing it to carry on profitably after the aero engine business went bankrupt in 1971.

The range now comprised the 'mass-production' Silver Dawn from 1949, the Silver Wraith, mostly with coach-built bodywork, and very small numbers of Phantom IVs. Apart from the Phantom, all used the new inlet-over-exhaust engine in six-cylinder form, first as a 262.4-cu in (4.3-litre) unit, then as 280.7- and 299-cu in (4.6- and 4.9-litre) units for the 1955 Silver Cloud. But the six-cylinder era came to an end in 1959, when an all-new V8 of 378.3 cu in (6.2 litres) was introduced for the Silver Cloud II. Again, the American market was decisive, this time in persuading Rolls-Royce to go the V8 route.

The big Phantom V acquired the new V8 at the same time, and even here standard bodywork (albeit by Mulliner Park Ward rather than Crewe) was the most common option. Mulliner Park Ward was an amalgamation of two coach builders, both of which were owned by Rolls-Royce. The Phantom V became the Phantom VI in 1968, and was actually available in small numbers right up to the late 1980s. The Phantom, of course, had a separate chassis, but the new Silver Cloud of 1965 began a new era of unitary construction for Rolls-Royce. This made bespoke bodywork impossible, but the buyers did not seem to mind, as the new car was Rolls-Royce's most popular ever. It was given an enlarged 411.9-cu in (6.75-litre) version of the V8 in 1971 and better handling with the 1976 Series II. By then it had been joined by the Carmargue coupé, based on the same mechanical parts but with bland two-door coupé styling by Pininfarina.

Bland perhaps, but the new Silver Spirit of 1982, which replaced the Cloud, followed the same rounded-brick lines. This was gradually updated over the years, still powered by the 6.8-litre V8, but now with fuel-injection, plus anti-lock brakes and automatic ride control. There were also several coachbuilt conversions, such as the long-wheelbased Silver Spur produced for Rolls-Royce by Robert Jankel (see Panther), though most were expensive one-offs, due to the nature of unitary construction.

LEFT
1930 Rolls-Royce.

OPPOSITE
ABOVE LEFT: 1989 Rolls-Royce Corniche.

ABOVE RIGHT: Long-wheelbased Rolls-Royce Silver Spur with division.

BELOW LEFT: 1997 Silver Dawn.

BELOW RIGHT
Silver Spur.

But Rolls-Royce was heading for trouble. The market for luxury cars began to suffer in the late 1980s and early 1990s, and Vickers, Rolls-Royce's parent company, began to look around for buyers. In the event, there were two, in the forms of BMW and Volkswagen. BMW had already worked with Rolls-Royce, allowing it access to its V12 engine and sophisticated electronic systems. In 1998, the same year that the Silver Spirit was replaced by the more rounded Silver Seraph, BMW gained control of the company.

A new Seraph-based Corniche convertible was announced in 2000, along with a long-wheelbased Seraph, but more was to happen. It was announced that Crewe, where Rolls-Royces had been built for over half a century, would now be making Bentleys only, and the last Crewe-built Rolls, a Corniche, left the line in August 2002. BMW had decided to build a new factory at Goodwood in Sussex, the plan being to produce an all-new Rolls-Royce early in the following year.

ROVER (Great Britain 1904 to date)
As a badge, Rover is the great survivor. Now the only major British-owned manufacturer, it has outlived countless others, even the doyens of mass-production like Austin and Morris. It has lived through the corporate rationalizations of BMC, British Leyland and Austin-Rover, to emerge (along with MG) as the sole survivor of the many respected names that were once encompassed by that huge umbrella. The reasons are not hard to find. To this day, the brand has kept its strong quality image, supported for decades by the ever-profitable Land Rover 4x4.

Like many European manufacturers, Rover's origins lay in cycle making. It graduated to motorcycles, building its first car in 1904, even though it was a minor player until after World War I, despite a range of single- and twin-cylinder sleeve-

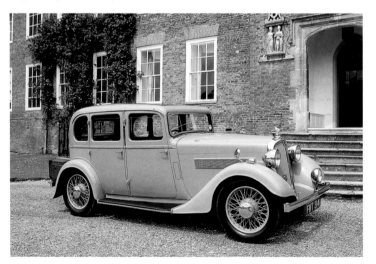

valve engines, not to mention a win in the 1907 Tourist Trophy race. The sleeve-valve cars sold poorly, though a conventional four-cylinder 12-hp (8.95-kW) from 1912 did rather better. Expansion came in the 1920s with a wide range of cars, from an air-cooled flat-twin to the overhead-camshaft 16/50; but it was not until the 1930s, under new general manager Spencer Wilks, that Rover really found its feet and began to achieve profitability.

Wilks introduced an integrated range, with quality a key selling point, and by the beginning of World War II the name was now firmly associated with quality middle-class cars, the sort of thing a bank manager would drive. Reflecting that market, the line-up of saloons and drophead coupés ranged from a 10-hp (7.46-kW) four to a 20-hp (14.91-kW) six. Economy cars and limousines did not feature.

After World War II Rover moved into

ABOVE
1937 Rover 12-hp sports tourer.

TOP LEFT
1922 8-hp with Grose body.

ABOVE LEFT
1904 8-hp model.

LEFT
1937 12-hp saloon.

OPPOSITE
ABOVE LEFT: Rover 95.

ABOVE RIGHT: 1971 Rover 3500.

RIGHT: 1997 Mini Cooper with sports pack.

another factory in Solihull, that it had run for the government during the war. Several British manufacturers (and not only car makers) came out of the war with more modern, spacious factories that had been part of the war effort. At first, the post-war Rovers were mildly revamped pre-war models, but the 1948 P3 sported a new inlet-over-exhaust engine. Even more significant was the Land Rover, launched the same year with that same new engine. Inspired by the U.S. Jeep, it was a simple utility vehicle with selectable four-wheel-drive and twin transmission ranges. It was an instant hit, and in developed form (a choice of wheelbases, diesel or petrol engines and all kinds of body variations) sold in large numbers all over the world for the next 40 years. In 1998, the Land Rover celebrated its half-century, and has undoubtedly been the vital prop that has helped keep Rover and its parent company going, despite the

ups and downs experienced by the cars.

As for these, new styling came with the 1949 P4, a solid, well-made and reliable saloon. The same applied to the bigger P5 of 1959 with a 183.1-cu in (3-litre) six-cylinder engine. Looking at cars like this, it would be easy to dismiss Rover as an ultra-conservative producer of staid, traditional cars. But behind the scenes, buoyed up by Land Rover profits, it was experimenting with gas turbine power: several prototypes were made, of which one competed at Le Mans.

Rover's latent radicalism was also revealed in the P6 2000 of 1963, an avant-garde executive car with overhead-camshaft 122-cu in (2-litre) engine, all-round disc brakes, independent suspension and, as conceived, a gas turbine option. It soon acquired more performance with a 213.6-cu in (3.5-litre) V8, an ex-Buick design to which Rover had acquired the rights. This

engine also found its way into the P5 and was a central part of Rover's range right up to the 1980s. It powered two very significant cars, which once again showed the lateral thinking that lay behind Rover's conservative image. The V8 Range Rover of 1970 was a new concept of luxury off-

roader, comfortable and fast, but highly capable on-road as well. Like the Land Rover, it was a huge success, this time inspiring a whole host of rivals; but the Range Rover remained the true original. Also V8-powered was the Rover SD1 of 1976, a dramatic-looking five-door executive car with impressive dynamics but poor build quality. It was later joined by 140.4- and 158.7-cu in (2.3- and 2.6-litre) six-cylinder versions, and despite its problems, sold in large numbers. Rover even built a mid-engined sports car powered by the same V8 engine, but the promising prototype failed to enter production.

By this time Rover had become part of the troubled British Leyland, the giant

organization that had swallowed up most of the British-owned motor industry by the early 1970s. Saved by nationalization and government funding in 1975, however, BL (and of course Rover) were subjected to constant media exposure and became something of a national joke. Reorganizations abounded in the 1970s when it was realized that the old badges might still have some worth: Rover found

itself slotted into the quality car division with Jaguar and Triumph, while Land Rover was set up as a stand-alone marque. Much later, Land Rover was taken over by Ford.

Oddly enough, as a name, Rover came out of all this rather well. The new regime recognized its appeal, and the others were gradually phased out. But there was not the funding to develop a new range of cars, so the new Rovers for the 1980s owed much

to Honda. The first Rover 200 series of 1984 was little more than a rebadged Honda Ballade, though the big 800 series, which replaced the SD1 in 1986, and mid-sized 600, were closer to real joint ventures. However, the arrangement worked well for Rover, providing it with a range of modern cars, which invariably outsold their Honda counterparts in Europe.

Rover was developing its own engines now, and the 800 came with a choice of a Honda 152.6- and later 164.8-cu in (2.5- and later 2.7-litre) V6 or Rover's new T-series twin-overhead-cam 2-litre unit. The new 200/400 series of the early 1990s used a K-series, an innovative twin-cam 85.4- and 97.6-cu in (1.4- and 1.6-litre) engine. Rover's own V6, the KV6, later appeared,

based on the K-series. Modern diesel engines completed the range.

But Rover was still dogged by business problems. It was sold by the British government to British Aerospace, who in turn sold it to BMW, which didn't last either, and by 2000 Rover was finally independent, the subject of a business consortium and management buyout. It was certainly a great survivor.

ABOVE
2003 Range Rover.

ABOVE LEFT
2003 Freelander.

LEFT
2002 Land Rover Defender.

FAR LEFT
2003 Discovery.

OPPOSITE
LEFT TOP: Rover 600 based on the Honda Accord, but with Rover engine.

LEFT CENTRE: Rover 200 convertible.

LEFT BELOW: 1997 400 series.

CENTRE: 2000 Rover 25.

RIGHT ABOVE: 2000 Rover 45.

RIGHT BELOW: 2000 Rover 75.

SAAB (Sweden 1950 to date)

After World War II many companies in the arms industry began to look around for new products to build, more suitable for peacetime, with Valmet of Finland, for example, turning from cannons to farm tractors. In Sweden, however, aeroplane maker Svenska Aeroplan A.B. (SAAB) decided on cars.

Those first Saabs were clearly influenced by aircraft (the company carried on making planes as well), with rounded aerodynamic bodywork that was said to resemble an aircraft's wing in section. The new car department under Gunner Ljungstrom, who had worked for Standard and Rover in England, came up with a two-door front-drive saloon, powered by a 46.62-cu in (764-cc) two-stroke twin. In 1950, the same year that production began, the Saab 92 won a rally, the first of a long string of such victories over the decades.

A more powerful three-cylinder 45.65-cu in (748-cc) 93 was introduced in 1956 and the 95 estate three years later, then the 51.32-cu in (841-cc) 96, which enabled Erik Carlsson to win the Monte Carlo Rally in both 1962 and 1963. Apart from the mastery of Carlsson, it was a great lesson in the use of superior traction over sheer power. But Saab was one of the last manufacturers to use a smoky two-stroke, so the 95/96 acquired a Ford 91.5-cu in (1.5-litre) V4 engine from 1967, which greatly boosted sales.

The little 95/96 was supplanted by the bigger 99 in 1969: this was originally intended to replace the smaller car, but demand continued and Saab carried on building its original aerodynamic shape for another ten years. The 99 was powered by a slant-four overhead-camshaft engine of 103.7 cu in (1.7 litres), bought from Triumph. It was enlarged to 113.14 cu in (1.85 litres) in 1971 and 122 cu in (2 litres) in the following year, by which time Saab was building the engine itself. It also began building cars with groups of workers, rather than on a moving assembly line, to increase quality and job satisfaction.

The 99 gradually moved upmarket, notably with the 145-bhp (108.1-kW) Turbo

of 1977, one of the first production turbocharged cars, and the following year was supplanted by the long-wheelbased 900, while the 90 was an updated 99. There was a choice of saloon or hatchback bodies. The bigger 9000 was powered by the same 2-litre engine in 130-bhp (96.9-kW) non-turbo or 175-bhp (130.5-kW) turbo form, though it was otherwise completely new.

But Saab's car division, as opposed to its profitable plane- and truck-making arms, was in trouble. With a limited engine range and only one basic model, it was beginning to suffer against bigger rivals. In 1989 General Motors paid $600 million for a 50 per cent stake in Saab. The plan was to make use of Saab's excess capacity to build luxury GM cars, with over 200,000 a year being built by the year 2000. Unfortunately, the plan did not quite work out. Saab's costs were cut by using General Motors components, but in 2002 it still offered only a limited range: the executive 9-3 (still with a family resemblance to the old 99) and bigger 9-5 in saloon and estate forms. It lost money in 2002, and at 130,000, sales were below the break-even point. GM responded by ordering work to start on a smaller 9-2 hatchback and 9-7X luxury off-roader.

ABOVE
1999 Saab 9-3 Viggen convertible.

ABOVE RIGHT
2003 Saab 9-3 estate.

RIGHT
2004 Saab 9-4 convertible.

OPPOSITE
FAR LEFT: Erik Carlsson in his Saab 96
Rally car.

TOP RIGHT: Saab Sonnet.

ABOVE RIGHT: Saab 9000 Aero.

CENTRE RIGHT Saab 900E turbo.

BOTTOM RIGHT: Saab 9-3 Viggen.

SALMSON (France 1921-1957)

Eric Salmson sadly died before the cars that bore his name went into production. His company had been producing aero engines, but on his death, at the end of World War I, it was taken over by M. Heinrich, who diversified into cars in 1921, first GNs under licence, then the Salmson AL. A string of racing wins followed through the 1920s, including the Targa Florio and Brooklands 200-Mile; by 1927 designer Emile Petit had come up with a 67.1-cu in (1.1-litre) straight-eight with twin superchargers that produced an incredible 140bhp (104.4kW).

In the 1930s, the emphasis shifted towards touring cars, rather than sports, and the four-door S4 and other open and closed tourers were available up to and after World War II. At this time, there was also a British Salmson equivalent (see British Salmson). But by the late 1940s they were sadly outdated, and car production actually briefly ceased in 1952. In the following year, the new 2300 GT Coupé wowed the crowds at the Paris Salon, and won the Tulip Rally in 1954. Was this a revival of Salmson's glorious racing past? Alas no, for production ended in 1957 after less than 230 cars had been built.

TOP
1950-53 Salmson Randonnée saloon.

ABOVE
Salmson saloon.

LEFT
Salmson dhc.

OPPOSITE
1934 Salmson 2-seater.

SEAT (Spain)

SEAT is Spain's most successful car manufacturer, although only for a few years did it built cars of its own design. For over 30 years the company built Fiats (as well as Volkswagens) under licence: the 1960 600, for example, was in fact the Fiat 600. But in 1980 Fiat ended the agreement, leaving SEAT to choose between developing its own new car or closing down.

It came up with the all-new Ibiza hatchback and Malaga notchback, powered by 73.2- or 91.5-cu in (1.2- or 1.5-litre) petrol engines, designed for SEAT by Porsche; a 103.7-cu in (1.7-litre) diesel came later. There was also the bargain-basement Marbella, a SEAT development of the Fiat Panda. The new-generation SEATs made a good impression, being competitive with mainstream European cars, and just as well made, though cheaper. This came to the attention of Volkswagen, seeking to expand its capacity in lower-cost areas; it bought 75 per cent of SEAT in 1986, assuming full control in 1990. In the short term, this led to SEAT building all VW Polos, but also ensured a new generation of SEATs using proven VW components. A new Ibiza in 1993 offered the usual range of VW petrol and diesel engines, as did the Cordoba saloon which followed it, together with the bigger Toledo. The Arosa in 1997 was a

RIGHT
2000 SEAT Cordoba S.

FAR RIGHT
2000 Alhambra.

BELOW
2002 Salsa concept car.

BELOW RIGHT
2000 León 20V T Sport

OPPOSITE
ABOVE LEFT: Ibiza 2.0 Cupra Sport.

BELOW LEFT: 1997 100-bhp Toledo SE.

ABOVE RIGHT: 2000 Vario S.

BELOW RIGHT: Arosa 1.4 16V Sport.

small three-door hatchback, the SEAT version of the little VW Lupo.

Despite all of this, SEAT lost money in the early 1990s, and was forced to sell one of its factories; only a massive cash injection from VW kept it afloat. But ten years later, it was still around, selling updated versions of the Arosa, Ibiza, Cordoba, Toledo and Alhambra MPV (the latter almost identical to the VW Sharan/Ford Galaxy) plus the new Golf-based León.

SIMCA (France 1934-1982)

Simca would never have existed had it not been for Fiat. Henri-Theodore Pigozzi was the French importer of Fiats, and saw a business opportunity in producing the Italian cars under licence for the French market. La Société Industrielle de Mécanique et de Carrosserie Automobile – Simca for short – started business in 1934. It was a success, with the Fiat 500 Topolino and 508 being built as the Cinq and Huit respectively. Part of that success was down to Amédée Gordini, who himself had built up a good business tuning and racing Simcas. By 1938, the Nanterre factory on the Seine was building over 20,000 cars per year.

World War II put paid to all this, of course, but full-scale production resumed in 1946, still with the Cinq and Huit, while Gordini simply took off where he had left

off. It was 1951 when Simca produced its first non-Fiat car, the Aronde, which used an existing engine but was otherwise completely new. It was a great success, in export markets as well as in France, and nearly one and a half million were made. Other purely French Simcas followed, notably the Vedette luxury saloon and the little rear-engined 1000, a utility car that sold in large numbers.

Through the 1950s Simca expanded by acquisition. It bought Unic in 1951, and Ford's French operation three years later, the latter bringing much-needed production capacity. Then came the French arm of Swiss truck maker Saurer and finally, in 1959, Talbot. But even as the Talbot purchase was going through, 15 per cent of Simca was already owned by Chrysler, which had been keen to buy a European manufacturing base and would shortly buy into the British Rootes concern as well; by 1963 it had a majority shareholding in Simca. As ever, Simcas of the 1960s were conventional, good-value cars. As well as the little 1000, there were the more modern front-wheel-drive 1100 and 1301/1501 saloons.

In the early 1970s, now wholly owned by Chrysler, the boundary between Simca and Rootes was becoming increasingly blurred, and the cars that both made were being referred to as Chryslers more and more. This lasted only a few years, however: Chrysler itself was now in trouble, and sold all its European interests to Peugeot-Citroën in 1978. The Simca operation was renamed Talbot, but this badge was also dropped after a few years.

SIMPLEX (U.S.A. 1904-1917)

There were four makes of car named Simplex between 1899 and 1920, and the American one began production in 1904. It

was inspired by the contemporary Mercedes, and was actually built by Smith & Mabley, the U.S. Mercedes importer, though designed by Edward Franquist. The company went bankrupt in 1907, but car production carried on after a takeover by textile importer Herman Broesel. A new range was introduced, including a 598-cu in (9.8-litre) 50-hp (37.3-kW), with a wide choice of bodies from Quimby, Demarest, Brewster and Holbrook. Still chain-driven in 1912 (Simplex was said to be the last American car with chain drive) the 50 horsepower was made available with different driving sprockets, according to terrain, and with its large flat radiator betrayed its Mercedes ancestry.

Simplex was sold to Goodrich, Lockhart & Smith in 1913, then the Crane Motor Co. was bought, though the Crane-Simplex Model 5 only lasted a few years, production ending in 1917.

SINGER (Great Britain 1905-1970)

For its last 25 years, Singer was a fairly minor element of the Rootes Group, but not so very long before it had been riding high, the third largest manufacturer in Britain, and employing 8,000 people. Notwithstanding World War II, its fall from grace actually took less than a decade.

George Singer's first cars were licence-built Lea-Francis designs, 8- and 12-hp (5.96- and 8.95-kW) underfloor-engined models. Two-, three- and four-cylinder cars followed before the company suffered both the death of its founder and its collapse into receivership. It was quickly revived, however, and settled down to make small quality cars, such as the Ten, with (unusually) a three-cylinder engine of 82.9 cu in (1.36 litres), later replaced by a 67.1-cu in (1.1-litre) four.

A 122-cu in (2-litre) six followed in 1922, but Singer's core business lay in small cars. In 1926 the Ten was renamed

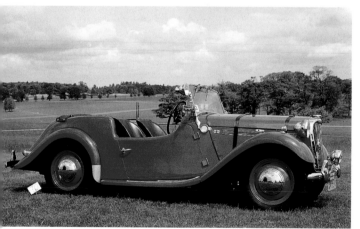

the Senior and was joined by the Junior, with a 51.75-cu in (848-cc) overhead-cam engine. The following year, having bought out both Calcott and Coventry Premier, Singer was able to produce 11,000 cars, and was making most components in-house into the bargain. The Junior was replaced by the Nine in 1932, which was especially popular in sports car form, and was affordable in the same way as the MG Midget. The little 59.32-cu in (972-cc) overhead-cam engine was powerful enough to push the little Nine along as 65mph (105km/h). Meanwhile, an overhead-valve Twelve replaced the old side-valve.

But the company was on the slippery slopes. Profits were slumping so badly that it was forced to close two of its factories, the bigger six-cylinder cars were dropped, and the new Bantam was really a copy of

the Morris Eight. After World War II, the first true post-war Singer was the SM1500 saloon, though this did not appear in large numbers. In 1955, the company was taken over by Rootes (William Rootes, of course, had served his apprenticeship with Singer many years before) and the badge soon became a means of denoting slightly more upmarket Hillmans. The Singer Gazelle was a Minx with better trim, the Vogue a Super Minx and the Chamois the rear-engined Imp. The name was dropped altogether in 1970.

SKODA (Czechoslovakia/Czech Republic 1906 to date)

Vaclav Klement was a bookseller, but in the early 1890s decided to join mechanic Vaclav Laurin to set up a bicycle repair shop. This eventually became Skoda, Czechoslovakia's foremost car manufacturer, and still lives today as the budget brand of the VW group.

Laurin and Klement built a motorcycle, said to be the world's first, in 1888, and their first car in 1905, the twin-cylinder Model A Voiturette.

Bigger four-cylinder cars, the Models D and E, soon followed, along with the B-2 taxi, culminating in the eight-cylinder Type FF, whose 299-cu in (4.9-litre) engine developed 40bhp (29.8kW). The company thrived, building buses and trucks as well as cars, and exporting its products worldwide; it even enjoyed some racing and rallying success. But this happy independence was not to last, and in 1925 Laurin-Klement was taken over by the Czech armaments manufacturer Akciova Spolecnost. From this time forward all their cars would carry the Skoda name.

The company built Hispano-Suizas under licence during the late 1920s, but also offered its own new range from 1928, featuring four-, six- and eight-cylinder engines of 115.9 to 238 cu in (1.9 to 3.9 litres). One landmark among this new generation of Skodas was the Type 420, which used swinging half-axles and a centre tubular chassis, which would be Skoda features for the next 30 years. Facelifted in 1934, this became the Popular, powered by a 55.1- but later 60.72-cu in (903-cc but later 995-cc) engine, whose worldwide sales justified its name. The 73.2-cu in (1.2-litre) Rapid and 177-cu in (2.9-litre) six-cylinder Superb also did well at this time, both receiving larger overhead-valve engines in 1938.

After World War II Skoda concentrated on small cars, with the four-door 1200 launched in 1952, followed by the Octavia and Felicia, all of them powered by a 74.51-cu in (1221-cc) four-cylinder engine. Supplying what was virtually a captive market within Eastern Europe, Skoda expanded into a large new factory in 1964, and during the 1960s concentrated on rear-engined cars, the first of which was the unit-construction 1000MB, powered by a 60.29-cu in (988-cc) 40-bhp (29.8-kW) engine.

Gradually updated with 67.1- and 73.2 cu in (1.1- and 1.2-litre) engines, these were replaced by the Estelle in 1977, still rear-engined, but more obviously a child o the 1970s rather than the 1950s. Low prices ensured a small but steady market i the West, but Skoda also became the butt of bar-room comics, which was somewhat unfair, as the car was better engineered than many of its equally cheap rivals. It also consistently won its class in the RAC Rally for many years. Reflecting this, ther was the Rapid coupé (not as rapid as the name suggests, however), and even a Cabriolet version. There was a radical change in 1988, with the front-engined, front-wheel-drive Favorit. This all-new Skoda boasted an aluminium 79.3-cu in (1.3-litre) engine and up-to-date styling by

RIGHT
1999 Skoda pick-up truck.

BELOW
2000 Skoda Felicia Pacific Limited
Edition.

BELOW RIGHT
Skoda Octavia SLXi 2.0.

OPPOSITE
1958 Skoda 1100cc sports car.

Bertone. Although dogged by a flimsy interior, it still sold well, and like the Favorit proved successful in its rallying class.

A new era dawned for Skoda when it was bought by VW in the early 1990s. One of the first fruits of the new regime was a substantial update of the Favorit into the sleeker Felicia, with better build quality and VW's modern diesel and petrol engines. The logical progression was to launch new Skodas based more closely on VW parts, so this is what the company did. The Octavia, launched in 1996, came with 97.6- and 109.8-cu in (1.6- and 1.8-litre) petrol engines plus a 115.9-cu in (1.9-litre) diesel, and had clear VW overtones in the styling. It was followed by the Superb, using another old name but this time based on a stretched VW Passat with a new front-end. Meanwhile, the Felicia was replaced by the new front-drive Fabia. All this VW influence transformed Skoda's build quality and design, though prices increased to match. It was increasingly looking as though the Skoda would become just another western European badge, with a price to match.

SPYKER (Netherlands 1900-1927)

The Dutch motor industry has never been large; in fact, before World War I Spyker was the only manufacturer. But Jacobus Spijker and his younger brother, Hendrik, were canny enough to rename their cars 'Spyker' to make them more acceptable in export markets. They were rewarded with good sales to Britain, which in fact took the factory's entire output between 1904 and 1906. A typical Spyker of the time was the 152.6-cu in (2.5-litre) four-cylinder tourer, made famous by its appearance in the film *Genevieve*. Spyker also made fearsome-looking 50-hp (37.3-kW) four-wheel-drive racers, but this was in its early days.

But the company's career was blighted by events that had little to do with making cars. Rock-bottom in 1906, it appealed to the British importer to help it out, but he and Hendrik were killed in a storm when travelling to the Netherlands to discuss the matter. A special Spyker was supplied to Charles Godard in 1907 for the 1907 Peking-Paris race. It might even have won, but Godard's unconventional methods of raising sponsorship led to his arrest before the race had finished. The shareholders blamed Jacobus, and sacked him. Bankrupt in 1908, however, the company was soon revived and went on to produce a string of four-cylinder cars up to 1916, and the aircraft-influenced C4 after World War I. There were attempts to sell Mathis cars under the Spyker name, and assemble American trucks, but these schemes did nothing but hasten the end, and Spyker finally ceased to be in 1927.

SQUIRE (Great Britain 1934-1936)

The Squire was an intriguing sports car, advanced for its time, with pre-selector gearbox and hydraulic brakes. Despite this, and the single-minded commitment of its designer, the car actually proved to be too expensive.

Adrian Squire had long dreamed of building his own car, and had worked for Bentley and MG before, at the age of just 24, going into production. He had been encouraged by the announcement of a new engine from British Anzani, a twin-overhead-camshaft unit of 91.3 cu in (1.5 litres) with twin Solex carburettors and provision for a supercharger. It was just what Squire wanted, and by the summer of 1934 he had a running prototype, with the engine giving 105bhp (78.3kW) in supercharged form. There was a great deal of interest in this sleek new sportster, with the choice of short or long wheelbase and open or closed coupé bodywork by Vanden Plas. Alas, when the final price was announced, it seemed far too expensive, and interest fell away. Adrian Squire did have cheaper bodywork supplied by Markham of Reading, but this was not enough to make the Squire affordable. Only a dozen cars were made before the company was liquidated in July 1936, and another three were produced by Val Zethrin, who bought the concern.

BELOW LEFT
1936 Squire Markham-bodied 'Skimpy'.

BELOW 1997 Ssangyong Musso 2.9D SE.

SSANGYONG (South Korea 1954 to date)

Ssangyong is a giant Korean concern and producer of many things, which started building the Korando, a licence-built Jeep, in 1954. It might have remained a commercial vehicle maker for the Asian market, had not involvement with Mercedes-Benz in the 1990s given rise to ambitious plans for expansion.

Ssangyong already had links with the West, having bought British specialist firm Panther. Mercedes bought 5 per cent of Ssangyong in 1992, with the South Koreans contracted to build 50,000 Mercedes-Benz trucks and 80,000 diesel engines in 1995.

Some of the latter were intended to power the Musso, a new luxury 4x4, and a big luxury car would follow. The Musso, styled by a British firm, certainly looked unusual, but sales in the West were helped by a low price and the Mercedes diesel engine. Ssangyong production rocketed from less than 6,000 in 1986 to over 46,000 by 1994.

However, not everything went according to plan. The company was taken over by Daewoo in 1998, which itself was facing bankruptcy only two years later. Ssangyong Motors managed to survive as a separate concern, and for 2003 was producing a range of cars, including the latest Korando, Musso, Chairman saloon, and was about to launch the Rexton 4x4.

STANDARD

(Great Britain 1903-1963)
Standard was the upright English car with the exceptionally modest name. The model names too, spoke of humble aspirations: there were no 'Monte Carlos' or 'Royales' here. Some Standards were named after small seaside resorts, and the Teignmouth and Rhyl perhaps reflected the more realistic aspirations of their owners. Only in the 1930s did Standards show a modicum of glamour, with the slightly more dashing 'Flying' series.

The first Standard was a single-cylinder 6-hp (4.47-kW) in 1903, but sixes were on offer within three years, and the Rhyl was a 9.5-hp (7.08-kW) family car introduced in 1912. After World War I, the dual line of fours and sixes continued, with both overhead-valve and side-valve engines. The company survived the hard times of the late 1920s and early 1930s, due largely to the guidance of Captain John Black, who had previously worked for Hillman. From the mid-1930s, moreover, Standard began to abandon its staid image with the

streamlined Flying Standards, available in 8-, 9-, 10-, 12-, 14- and 20-hp (5.96-, 6.71-, 7.46-, 8.95-, 10.44- and 14.91-kW) sizes. The Eight was actually the first small British car with independent front suspension, while the Twenty could be had with a 164.8-cu in (2.7-litre) V8.

Standard took over the Triumph company in 1945, though ironically the Triumph name was destined to outlive that of Standard by many years. The pre-war Standards were reintroduced after World War II before the all-new Standard Vanguard was ready. It really did live up to its name, with up-to-the-minute styling, unitary construction and an all-new overhead-valve 122-cu in (2-litre) engine. For a while, this was Standard's only model: the British government was encouraging manufacturers to adopt a single-model policy to maximize economies of scale. Only Standard seemed to take any notice, and even it modified the policy in 1953 with the new Standard Eight, followed by the 57.85-cu in (948-cc) Ten. The Vanguard, meanwhile, was later given a six-cylinder engine, and was followed by the 1950s-look Ensign.

The Standard name faded away in 1963, when new models like the Herald and 2000 wore the Triumph badge instead, and were thereby undeniably more dynamic.

ABOVE RIGHT
1930 Standard Avon Special.

RIGHT
1938 Flying Standard.

STANLEY (U.S.A. 1897-1924)

Just for a while, it seemed as if anything were possible. As the 20th century dawned, steam, electricity and gasoline power were all successfully propelling private vehicles. Which was the power source of the future? In the event, gas won, its power and sheer convenience overcoming noise, fumes, unreliability and the need for a gearbox.

That it had won was clear by 1910, but just one major manufacturer of steam cars persisted in the form of the Stanley.

The identical Stanley twins never intended to build cars at all. They were inventors (selling a photographic process to Kodak) as well as violin makers and mathematicians. As is the way of classic stories of budding tycoons, they looked at the primitive models available, thought they could better, and proceeded to do so. There was still no intention to go into production until a Stanley won a race, when the orders flowed in, and the brothers introduced their lightweight steam-driven buggy. Two hundred were made in a former bicycle factory before a publisher named John Brisben Walker bought them out for $250,000. Part of the deal was that they would refrain from making steam cars for a

year. But Walker and his partner soon fell out, leaving the way open for the Stanleys again, now $250,000 richer.

The new Stanleys were better than the old, with twin-cylinder engines bolted to the rear axle and firetube boilers. They looked quite conventional, apart from the lack of a radiator, and the 10-hp (7.46-kW) four-seater was actually made under licence in Gateshead, England. They were fast, too: the wonderfully named Gentleman's Speedy Roadster of 1907 could top 75mph (121km/h), and a streamlined record-breaker managed 150mph (241km/h) before it crashed. Sadly, Freelan Stanley died in a road accident in 1918, while his twin, Francis, semi-retired to run a hotel.

Stanley cars carried on after World War I, but it was increasingly difficult to sell steam in a gas-dominated world. The 735 of 1920 was Stanley's most sophisticated steamer yet, but it had to have a false radiator to make it look like a conventional car. Orders still trickled in, but when Stanley was taken over by the Steam Vehicle Corporation of America in 1924 it was really the end.

LEFT
1908 Stanley Speedy roadster.

OPPOSITE
ABOVE LEFT: 1925 Steyr VIII.

BELOW LEFT
Steyr Porsche-designed Type 30.

ABOVE RIGHT 1935 Studebaker Dictator.

CENTRE RIGHT: 1941 Commander sedan.

CENTRE FAR RIGHT: 1956 Studebaker Golden Hawk.

BELOW RIGHT: 1954 hardtop coupé.

STEYR (Austria 1920-1940 and 1953-1978)

Steyr is another example of 'swords to ploughshares', an armaments manufacturer that had to look for a new product once war had ended. Once the largest producer of arms in Europe, which is saying something, Steyr had a profitable World War I, but was banned from producing weapons thereafter, being on the losing side.

With the brilliant Hans Ledwinka as designer, Steyr unveiled a new conventional car in 1920, though Ledwinka also wished to build a cheap twin-cylinder economy car, which it refused to contemplate. This turned out to be a big mistake. Ledwinka left to join Tatra, where his little twin was a success, and the looming Depression made

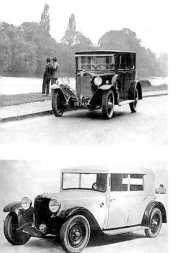

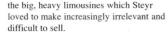

the big, heavy limousines which Steyr loved to make increasingly irrelevant and difficult to sell.

In 1929, another gifted young engineer joined the company: this was Ferdinand Porsche. In the event, Porsche did not stay long, though he carried on working for Steyr on a freelance basis, designing the Type 30 saloon and small Type 50, not unlike the VW Beetle. Now merged with Austro-Daimler-Puch to form Steyr-Daimler-Puch, the company was able to plunge back into arms production with the onset of World War II. This also ensured that its factories were destroyed by the RAF, but it managed to restart production afterwards, first with bicycles, then with scooters and from 1949 assembling Fiats. A line of cars followed, still Fiat-based but with Steyr engines: the last, a 126-based machine, ceased production in 1978, though truck manufacture continued.

STUDEBAKER (U.S.A. 1904-1966)

Studebaker was one of the American independents and, like Nash, Hudson, Packard and Willys-Overland, found it was just too small to survive on its own. But it had not always been so. Back in the 1920s, the company was challenging for third place in the U.S. sales war, so what went wrong?

The Studebaker brothers built wagons and carriages in South Bend, Indiana, and had been in existence since 1852. Electric runabouts (a more popular concept in America than Europe) were produced for a while, and a petrol-powered car in 1904, though Studebaker then sold EMF-built cars. Only from 1912 were all the cars it offered designed and built in-house.

Albert Russel Erskine was a towering figure in Studebaker's history. He became president of the company in 1915 and

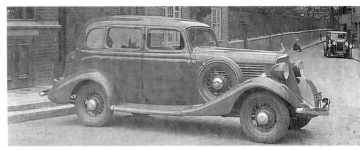

gained a reputation for being ruthless and overbearing. Under his control, however, Studebaker grew rapidly, with its eyes on third place in the sales charts. By the late 1920s it had seven production plants, able to produce 180,000 cars a year between them, and its own 840-acre (340-hectare)

proving ground. It also had the considerable abilities of designer Delmar G. Roos at its disposal, who contributed a straight-eight engine in 1926 and a simple independent front suspension in 1935.

But by then Studebaker's golden summer was already at an end. Erskine, whose strong leadership had achieved wonders during the good times, carried on spending right through the Depression. Studebaker rapidly sank, going into receivership in March 1933 owing $6 million. Erskine committed suicide, but the company fought back. With the sale of Pierce-Arrow stock it was able to restart production, and the new Champion of the late 1930s was a great success, selling over 70,000 in 1939 alone.

The Champion's engine powered a tracked personnel carrier, the Weasel, during World War II, and Studebaker also made trucks and aero engines for military use. When peace was restored, it lost no time getting back into production in 1946 with the Starlight coupé, nicknamed the 'coming or going', due to its 'which end is which?' body shape. The Starliner of 1953 was also well-received. Then there was the attractive, low-slung Hawk; designed by famed stylist Raymond Loewy, this two-door coupé had an Italian look about it, with a touch of Mercedes in the radiator grille.

So Studebaker had good products, but like the other smaller U.S. manufacturers, it found itself in the middle of a price-cutting war between Ford, Chrysler and General

Motors, with which it could not hope to compete; just as Nash and Hudson had joined forces, so did Studebaker and Packard. At Packard's expense, this gave Studebaker another few years of life, and at first the signs looked good. It launched the compact Lark in 1959 (beating the big three to it) and made a respectable profit in that year, though the Studebaker directors had already decided to scale down car production. Instead of trying to beat the big three head-on, it would go for niche markets. The sporting Avanti coupé looked like the car to do this, but in practice only 44,000 were sold in 1963, at a time that 120,000 were needed to break even. By the end of that year, Studebaker had nearly three months-worth of unsold production in stock, and the directors called a halt in

December. Cars and estates did continue at the Ontario plant for another two years, but they too ceased in March 1966, which was the end of Studebaker.

STUTZ (U.S.A. 1911-1935 and 1970-1988)

America's most famous sports car, the Stutz, was small, fast and very well-built. Harry C. Stutz produced the first in 1911, which underlined his multiple abilities by finishing 11th at Indianapolis that year. But that first car consisted mostly of bought-in components: the Bearcat of 1914 was far more of an in-house machine, though even this used a Wisconsin engine. It was the archetypical Stutz, a stripped-down racer for the road, with few concessions to comfort. Its 390.6-cu in (6.4-litre) four-

cylinder engine produced 60bhp (44.7kW) at 1,500rpm, enough to push this relatively lightweight car along at 85mph (137km/h). The Bearcat became a legend in itself, winning many races and breaking long-distance records: one set a new trans-American record at 11 days, 7 hours 30 minutes from San Diego to New York.

Despite this success, Harry Stutz left the company in 1919 (he was to die of

TOP
1930 Stutz Derham Roadster.

ABOVE
1933 Type 29 Club sedan.

LEFT
1919 Stutz Bearcat.

appendicitis in 1930) and it was taken over by steel tycoon Charles Schwab. Stutz began to build its own four- and six-cylinder engines, and in 1925 unveiled the Safety Stutz Vertical Eight. Designed by Hungarian Frederick Moskovics and Belgian Paul Bastien, this boasted over 90bhp (67.1kW) from its overhead-cam straight-eight engine. The 'Safety' element came from hydraulic brakes, wired windscreen glass and the low-slung chassis. The Vertical Eight was a formidable car, and a Black Hawk Speedster version finished second at Le Mans in 1928.

But despite its power and speed, the Stutz was beginning to be overshadowed by the new breed of V12s and V16s from Cadillac, Packard and Lincoln. So in 1931 the company unveiled an all-new Bearcat. Still powered by eight cylinders, but with twin overhead camshafts and four valves per cylinder, this was enough for 155bhp (115.6kW) from the 323.4-cu in (5.3-litre) engine and a guaranteed 100mph (161km/h) top speed. So it was fast, with excellent road-holding and quality, but still too expensive. Sales dwindled, and Stutz stopped building cars in 1935, though light vans were carried on for another three years.

Then in 1970 the name was revived. Businessman James O'Donnell began to produce a new Bearcat, designed by veteran stylist Virgil Exner. It looked like something out of a sci-fi film, a 1960s throwback, but enough people wanted one to keep the new Stutz in business for nearly 20 years. There was an entire range, all powered by General Motors V8 engines: the Bearcat convertible, Blackhawk coupé and later a whole raft of saloons, such as the massive Royale. Production was limited, though, and less than 600 new Stutzs had been built by 1988 when production ceased.

SUBARU (Japan 1958 to date)

In the West, Japanese cars are often seen as well-made, reliable, though boring, with little to differentiate one from the other. If that is true, then Subaru is the honourable exception. With four-wheel-drive and flat-four 'boxer' engines with their distinctive exhaust note, these are Japanese cars for individuals.

Subaru started out merely as a small part of the giant Fuji Heavy Industries, which makes everything from aircraft to industrial machinery. Its first private vehicle was a moped named the Rabbit, in 1956, with the first car appearing a couple of years later. This was a typical Japanese micro-car, with a 21.97-cu in (360-cc) engine. This was followed by the full-sized FE saloon in the mid-1960s, using a flat-four engine, then the updated FF and Leone coupé.

By the late 1970s, Subaru's policy of standard four-wheel-drive across the range, with flat-four engines providing the power, was well established. The 1600 GLF came in both saloon and useful estate guise, and

TOP
1997 Subaru Legacy four-cam 2.5-litre, four-wheel-drive estate.

ABOVE LEFT
1997 Justy GX 1.3.

ABOVE RIGHT
Impreza 2.0GL five-door.

LEFT
1997 Impreza Turbo 2000 five-door.

both found a niche in Britain: there was a pick-up variant too, favoured by farmers. Then Subaru went upmarket with the turbocharged XT coupé in the 1980s, and filled out the bottom of the range with the little Justy hatchback, still in production as one of the few small cars with four-wheel-drive, though Fiat offered a Panda 4x4 in the 1980s, converted by Steyr.

The Justy received a four-cylinder engine in the early 1990s to replace its three-cylinder unit, and 1989 saw the all-new Legacy, an executive saloon with four overhead camshafts for its flat-four engine, and of course four-wheel-drive. The Legacy proved a winner in Group A international rallies, where the four-wheel-drive era was just taking hold, and did much to boost Subaru's image. From 1997, it was available in Outback estate form, with raised suspension.

Meanwhile, the competition mantle was assumed by the Impreza of 1992, based on a shortened Legacy floorpan but with the same power. This won the Rally Championship several times, and became the dream car of boy racers all over the world. The 2002 WRX Sti Impreza produced 305bhp (227.4kW) from its turbocharged flat-four, driven through a six-speed gearbox and, of course, all four wheels. Alongside the sporting Impreza, which also came in cheaper, milder saloon and estate forms, the Forester was a larger estate car, with slightly more off-road bias than the other Subarus.

RIGHT
2003 Subaru Forester.

BELOW
2003 Outback.

RIGHT
2003 Legacy 2.5GT.

OPPOSITE
2003 Impreza WRK sedan.

SUNBEAM (Great Britain 1901-1976)
Sunbeam cars stemmed from the business
interests of John Marston, a former sheet-
metal worker who built up Sunbeamland, a
profitable cycle-making company, in the
late 19th century. He also allowed one of
his former apprentices, Thomas Cureton, to
tinker with prototype cars.

The result was the Sunbeam Mabley of
1901, a curious cross between car and
motorcycle, with four wheels in a diamond
formation, and power coming from a 6-hp
(4.47-kW) Forman engine. The Sunbeam
car business was taken over by T.T.
Pullinger the following year, and by 1907
was working out of 2 acres (0.81 hectares)
of factory space and producing the Angus
Shaw-designed 16/20, which followed
earlier 12-hp (8.95-kW) and 12/16 tourers.

Sunbeams proved successful in
competition, but despite this and expansion
to a 30-acre (12.1-hectare) site by the end
of World War I, the company merged with
Talbot to form STD Motors in 1920. This
allowed Sunbeam to use overhead-cam
Talbot engines in its refined tourers, and
produced the resources to develop racers
and record-breakers; it built Malcolm
Campbell's V12 car, which set a new Land
Speed Record in 1924, at 146mph
(235km/h).

But STD, which included the Talbot
and Darracq marques, itself ran into
financial trouble in the late 1920s: the four-
cylinder Sunbeams were discontinued in
1927, with the sixes and eights following in
1930. At this time Sunbeam was having
more success building trolleybuses than
cars. A new smaller 97.6-cu in (1.6-litre)
Sunbeam was no more successful, and STD
was bought by the Rootes Group in 1935.

From then on, the Sunbeam and Talbot
names were used to sell upmarket and/or
sporting Hillmans. In the early post-war

years there were small Sunbeam-Talbot saloons, though the Alpine sports car (from 1953 and in finned restyled form from 1957) was only ever a Sunbeam. Most potent of these was the Ford V8-powered Tiger. Otherwise, the 1960s saw only the Sunbeam Rapier coupé (a sporting Hillman Minx) and Sunbeam Stiletto (a sporty fastback version of the Hillman Imp). These were all dead by the early 1970s, though the name was revived for the Chrysler Sunbeam hatchback in 1977.

BELOW LEFT
1928 Sunbeam-Talbot.

BELOW
1954 Alpine.

RIGHT
1931 Sunbeam Speed 20.

BELOW RIGHT
1967 1725-cc GT Alpine.

OPPOSITE
1924 four-cylinder 14/40 Sunbeam.

SUZUKI (Japan 1955 to date)

Better known for its motorcycles and scooters, Suzuki has been making cars since 1955, though exports did not really take off until the 1980s. The first car was the tiny Suzulite, designed to benefit from Japanese tax laws, with its little 21.97-cu in (360-cc) engine and cut-price specification. The next Suzuki was also a 360, but the Fronte 360 of 1967 was more of a miniature full-sized car, with front-wheel-drive and a bigger 30.51-cu in (500-cc) version on offer from 1968. The Fronte was actually produced right into the 1980s.

For most Europeans, the first Suzuki they came across was the SC1000 Whizkid in 1977. The rear-engined coupé came with a three-cylinder two-stroke engine for the home market, but a more car-like 59.19-cu in (970-cc) four-stroke for Europe. But more significant for Suzuki exports was the Jimny, a four-wheel-drive mini-Jeep. This was originally powered by a 32.89-cu in (539-cc)

three-cylinder engine, but proved surprisingly capable off-road; engine capacity soon grew to 61 cu in (1 litre), and eventually 97.6 cu in (1.6 litres) in the SJ. It was a great success, and managed to combine useful off-road performance with a

low price and trendy 4x4 looks, thus appealing to both utility and leisure markets.

Successful as the Jimny was, it remained a crude, comfortable and noisy car to drive. The Vitara of 1988 was an altogether more sophisticated proposition:

biased towards pure road use, the 1.6-litre Vitara was aimed squarely at the lifestyle 4x4 market, where cars were never likely to venture off-road. It was a great success, helping to develop a new breed of so-called 'soft-roaders'. Long-wheelbased five-door Vitaras, plus bigger 122- and 152.6-cu in (2- and 2.5-litre) V6 engines in the Grand Vitara, came later. Both the Vitara, and a restyled Jimny, were still available in 2002. Another variation was the short-wheelbased X90, with rounded styling and even more on-road bias.

Alongside its four-wheel-drives, Suzuki also offered a series of unremarkable hatchbacks, such as the small three-door Swift and Alto and Liana compact MPV, while the Wagon R+ is an example of the Japanese predilection for short and tall mini-MPVs.

SWALLOW DORETTI

FAR LEFT
1997 Suzuki Alto.

FAR LEFT BELOW
The Jimny, also known as Tobago in Spain.

TOP LEFT
Suzuki's sports car, the Cappuccino.

LEFT
1997 Vitara Sport soft-top.

OPPOSITE
ABOVE LEFT: 1997 Baleno hatchback.

ABOVE RIGHT
2003 Vitara two-door.

BELOW LEFT
2003 Aerio sedan.

BELOW RIGHT: 2003 Vitara five-door.

(Great Britain 1953-1954)
Swallow, as all Jaguar enthusiasts know, started out as a motorcycle sidecar manufacturer, but was the marque that eventually became the Big Cat. In 1945, the sidecar business was sold off, but by the early 1950s, with the demand for sidecars gradually diminishing, it was clear that Swallow would have to look around for something new to build. It had already built the Swallow Gadabout scooter between 1946 and '51, but the post-war scooter boom had already peaked.

Managing director Eric Sanders had long wanted to build a sports car aimed specifically at the North American market, and this was his chance. Designer Frank Rainbow, who had designed the Gadabout, was given just nine months to come up with the new car, and he did! As for the mechanical parts, they were no problem. Eric Sanders was a personal friend of Standard-Triumph boss Sir John Black, who was happy to supply the drivetrain from Triumph's own TR2 sports car. It must have been a close friendship, for Swallow's planned sports car would surely be a direct competitor for the TR2.

When it was unveiled at the 1954 Motor Show, the new Swallow Doretti was proclaimed to be the most beautiful car in the show. It certainly was, and turned out to be upmarket of the TR2, costing over £200 more. The shapely aluminium body (clothing a tubular frame) was clearly more expensive to build than that of the basic TR2, as was the leather interior, and though heavier than the Triumph, it could still manage 100mph (161km/h). Alas, the car was in production for a mere 10 months, during which time 280 were built. Why was it so short-lived? Had Triumph called 'foul'? Did no one want to buy the beautiful Swallow? Neither was the case.

Ironically, it was Jaguar which objected: evidently it saw the Doretti as dangerous competition, and threatened to stop buying components from the TI Group (Swallow's parent company) unless production ceased forthwith. It did.

SWIFT (Great Britain 1900-1931)
Swift cars were never particularly advanced, or as fast as their name implies, but were simple, well-made cars with a good reputation. Swift the company built sewing machines and bicycles before unveiling its first car, a single-cylinder voiturette, in 1900. This was powered by an MMC engine and featured an unusual transmission with a twin-pinion and double-geared crown-wheel. This lasted only a few years before a more conventional transmission was adopted.

The company produced its own engines (singles, twins, threes and fours) from 1904 and by 1912 the range included a 7-hp (5.22-kW) cyclecar and 10-hp (7.46-kW) light car, with twin-cylinder 59.32-cu in (972-cc) and four-cylinder 67.13-cu in (1100-cc) engines respectively. After World War I these were joined by a

122-cu in (2-litre) 12-hp (8.95-kW) with four-speed gearbox, and from 1926 the new 14/40 used an enlarged 1.2-litre engine based on that of the 10-hp.

Other small cars followed, such as a new four-speed 10-hp and the 8-hp (5.96-kW) Kadett, but Swift was too small to compete effectively with the giants of the industry, and production ceased in 1931.

TALBOT (Great Britain/France 1903-

1959 and 1979-1986)
Talbot was originally set up to import French Clément cars into England in 1903, but it soon began making cars itself, the 1906 231.9-cu in (3.8-litre) 20-hp (14.91-kW) being considered the first truly British Talbot.

The company combined with Sunbeam and Darracq to form STD Motors in 1920, which made use of the Talbot name, selling Darracqs in France as Talbots and as Talbot-Darracqs in England. By now, Swiss designer Georges Roesch was a key figure at Talbot: he had joined the company in 1916, produced the 10/23 model in 1923 and was put in charge of the division two years later. In the late 1920s the 115.9-cu in (1.9-litre) 14/45 was another Roesch design and was actually Talbot's only offering for a couple of years.

It was soon followed by the 140.4-cu in (2.3-litre) Type 75 and 90, 183.1-cu in (3-litre) 95 and 105 and 207.5-cu in (3.4-litre) 110. These were highly successful in competition, and Talbots finished third at Le Mans three times, won the Alpine Rally in 1932 and 1934 and finished the Alpine Rally Trials without penalty on three occasions. This was to be Talbot's golden era, however, as STD collapsed in 1935, and both Talbot and Sunbeam were bought up by the Rootes Group.

Both badges were then increasingly used to denote upmarket Hillmans and, seeing the way things were going, Georges Roesch left the company in 1938, the year in which Rootes merged them to become

ABOVE LEFT
1911 Swift single-cylinder 7-hp two-seater.

LEFT
1925 Swift 'Q'-Type tourer.

he Sunbeam-Talbot marque, the Talbot half being dropped in 1954. But that was not the end of the story. The French arm of Talbot had continued to produce small numbers of cars throughout the 1930s, supported by Anthony Lago, who kept the name alive in France until 1959 with his exotic Talbot-Lago line, culminating in the BMW V8-powered America Coupé of that final year.

The name was also revived in 1979 by Peugeot-Citroën. The Rootes Group and Simca in France had been taken over by Chrysler in the 1960s, by now facing problems of its own. The U.S. giant sold its European interests to PSA in 1978, which swiftly renamed all British-made Chryslers and French Simcas Talbots. This included the Sunbeam three-door (a Lotus-powered version of which won the World Rally Championship in 1981) and Horizon five-door hatchbacks, and a new executive saloon, the Tagora. But by 1986 all of these had gone, and with them the Talbot name.

TATRA (Czechoslovakia/Czech Republic 1923-1999)

Tatra's main business has always been trucks and railway rolling stock, but it also built cars, and only stopped doing so very recently. The company is inextricably linked with the name of Hans Ledwinka, an engineer of genius who was never afraid to introduce new ideas. But as well as being unconventional, his cars worked, and worked very well indeed.

Carpenters Ignac Sustala and Adolf Raska started making horse-drawn carts, later branched into railway wagons and in 1897 into cars. The Nesseldorf car used a

LEFT
Talbot 105 tourer.

BELOW LEFT
1959 Talbot-Lago America Coupé.

RIGHT
1923 Tatra TII.

BELOW
1963 Tatra T2-603.

Benz engine, and by the turn of the century a truck was added.

Hans Ledwinka took charge of the car side of the business in 1906, and was soon offering the 183.1-cu in (3-litre) S Type, an innovative car which later added four-wheel braking and an overhead-cam engine, and all of this before the war. After the war, and now part of the new state of Czechoslovakia, the company renamed itself Tatra, while Ledwinka designed a new small car, the Tatra 11 in 1923. Rugged and simple, it was a huge success, and not the

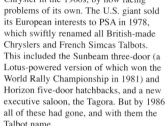

least in competition.

But Tatra is better remembered for its streamlined cars, and the first hint of these arrived in 1934 with the Ledwinka-designed Type 77. This was the world's first enclosed streamlined production car, and a range was soon available with a choice of engines: the 77A, 87 and 97. But another war forced Tatra to concentrate on trucks instead of cars, and the firm was nationalized in the late 1940s.

At first, just a trickle of pre-war models was built, but 1948 saw the all-new Tatraplan, a 122-cu in (2-litre) rear-engined car with streamlined styling similar to that of the original Type 77. It was only four years in production, however, when the Czechoslovak communist regime dictated that production was destined for top officials only. Tatra returned to making trucks until 1955, when it unveiled the big T603. Rounded, rear-engined and very streamlined, this was out of the same mould as the Type 77 and Tatraplan, but now with a big air-cooled V8 engine. It was produced

right through to 1973, when it was replaced by the 613, similar under the skin, but now with decidedly ordinary 1970s styling by Vignale. It was fast though, with 166bhp (123.8kW) and a claimed 120mph (193km/h); there were several variants such as a four-door cabriolet, prototype coupé and ambulance conversion.

The 613 was in turn replaced by the T700, now with smoother styling but still with an air-cooled V8 sitting in the tail. This was short-lived, as times were changing, and after the transformation of Eastern Europe in the early 1990s, Tatra went back into private ownership. Realizing the need for new products, it produced a prototype of the MTX, a mid-engined sports car with a 220-bhp (164-kW) V8. This came to nothing, however, and T700 production finally ended in 1999. Since then, Tatra has concentrated on making trucks.

TOYOTA (Japan 1936 to date)
Early in the 21st century, Toyota remains one of the largest, if not the largest, car manufacturers in the world. This being the case, it highlights the difference between car enthusiasts and the main mass of car buyers. Enthusiasts may carp that many Toyotas are soulless and boring, devoid of an ounce of character. The bulk of the population, however, counter that they are reliable, well-equipped and good value for money.

As a car manufacturer, Toyota has been around for over 60 years. Sakichi Toyoda ran a successful business making weaving looms in pre-war Japan, later selling the patents to a British company. With the money, his son Kiichiro set up a car division: he had already studied production methods in the U.S.A. and England, so the AA car (using a Chevrolet chassis but Toyota engine) made a trouble-free appearance. Within two years, Toyota (changed from Toyoda because it was easier to pronounce) was making 2,000 cars, trucks and buses a month: in 1941 over

FAR LEFT
Tatra T603.

LEFT
1944 Toyota B model.

BELOW LEFT
1955 Toyota RSD Crown Deluxe.

BOTTOM LEFT
1981 Toyota Starlet 1200 GL.

BOTTOM
1983 Corolla 1.3 GL.

OPPOSITE
LEFT TOP: *1984 MR2 sports car.*

LEFT CENTRE: *1990 Celica.*

LEFT BOTTOM: *1997 Rav-4.*

LEFT BOTTOM CENTRE; *Short-wheelbased Landcruiser.*

RIGHT TOP LEFT; *1997 Carina E.*

RIGHT TOP RIGHT: *Corolla four-door.*

RIGHT CENTRE: *Toyota Hilux.*

RIGHT BELOW: *Paseo 2+2 coupé for the US market.*

BOTTOM RIGHT: *Previa MPV.*

exports began to rocket skywards. In 1955, the company was building just 700 cars a month; a few years later, the figure was more like 50,000. Between 1961 and 1971 car exports rose more than a hundred-fold.

Central to this massive growth were simple, affordable cars like the 1000 UP10 of 1961, Toyota's first mass-market car, which later became the Starlet, the 61-cu in (1-litre) Corona of 1959, and the first

40,000 trucks were produced.

After World War II, car production began again slowly with the little Toyopet and small four-wheel-drive vehicles, but founder Kiichiro Toyoda was soon forced to resign after a series of losses and long strikes. The new management had also studied U.S. production methods, and this soon began to bear fruit. In fact, the late 1950s and 1960s would be a time of very rapid growth for Toyota, particularly as

Corolla, launched in 1966. There were big cars too, such as the American-influenced Crown. All of these were rear-wheel-drive; the company came to front-wheel-drive fairly late, with the 85.4-cu in (1.4-litre) Tercel and Corsa in 1978. Meanwhile, long-running lines like the Corolla were also updated to the front-wheel-drive format.

Toyota diversified into new markets with the mid-engined MR2 sports car in 1984. This was technically interesting and highly competent, with the added attraction of a relatively low price and the now almost legendary Toyota reliability. Of course, there had long been Celica coupés from Toyota, based on equivalent saloon mechanics, and these continued. Only from 1989 did the Celica become more of a dedicated sports coupé, though still with four seats, later including the four-wheel-drive GT-Four. The Supra, launched in 1986, was Toyota's sporting flagship, with a 183.1-cu in (3-litre) 24-valve twin-cam straight-six engine.

But on a worldwide basis Toyota is probably better known for its four-wheel-

drives than its sports cars. The big Land Cruiser was the world's best-selling 4x4 in 1985, and there was a whole range of short- and long-wheelbased variants, backed up later by the smaller RAV-4, a road-biased 4x4 to rival the Suzuki Vitara. Toyota also produced a four-wheel-drive version of the Tercel Estate, though no one was pretending that this was a genuine off-roader.

Toyota's very wide range remained one

of its strengths as the 20th century came to a close. As well as the specialist sports cars, coupés and 4x4s, the solid, sensible Toyota saloons and hatchbacks kept on selling by the thousand. The Corolla, the executive Camry and mid-sized Carina (now built in Britain for the European market) all had a strong presence in the 1990s. By 2002, the Carina had given way to the Avensis (now also available in Verso MPV form), but it was still possible to buy a Corolla (as hatchback or Verso) and a Camry.

The smallest Toyota on sale in Britain is the round-faced Yaris, while the Prius is a petrol/electric hybrid. The MR2 has been transformed into a back-to-basics open roadster, while the Celica remains a comfortable closed coupé. And to rival the Renault Espace, Toyota offers the large, boxy Previa. Most of these are practical, sensible cars, bought by practical people who can do without 'character' in their cars.

TRIUMPH (Great Britain 1923-1984)
Triumph of Coventry built its first car in

TOP
2003 Avalon XLS.

ABOVE LEFT
2003 Camry XLE.

FAR LEFT
2003 4Runner.

LEFT
2003 Solara coupé.

OPPOSITE
ABOVE LEFT: 2003 Celica GT.

BELOW LEFT: 2003 Corolla.

ABOVE RIGHT: 2003 Landcruiser.

BELOW RIGHT: MR2 Spyder.

1923, though it had been making motorcycles since 1902 and bicycles for 15 years before that. In fact, the Triumph motorcycle range was highly respected, and remained more important than the cars until the 1930s. It was not really until after World War II that the Triumph name reached the height of its popularity, with popular, best-selling sports cars such as the Spitfire and TR series.

The early Triumph cars were not very startling, though in 1925 one was the first British car to be equipped with hydraulic brakes. They were conventional small- and medium-sized saloons, perhaps slightly upmarket when compared with an Austin or Morris, as typified by the Super Seven of 1928. Things began to get interesting in the 1930s, when the abortive Dolomite, a supercharged straight-eight and direct copy of the Alfa Romeo 8C appeared. But the cars that did reach production included handsome roadsters and coupés, such as the Gloria and its faster tuned sister, the Vitesse. The Dolomite reached production with a mid-sized range that replaced both of these in the late 1930s.

By 1939 Triumph was bankrupt, overstretched by a range that was too complex and, with the end of World War II in sight, the company was sold to Standard. This might have been the end of the Triumph badge, as it had been for so many other famous names following a takeover. But Standard recognized the value of the name, and applied it to the Standard-engined Mayflower saloon and 1800 Roadster, culminating in the 1952 Triumph TR2. The latter was a huge success,

BELOW
1936 Triumph Monte Carlo tourer.

OPPOSITE
1954 Triumph TR2.

offering 100-mph (161-km/h) performance at a low price. It was so successful that the Standard name was dropped altogether in the late 1950s, when all saloons and sports cars were badged as Triumphs. The TR series would stretch right up to the 1980s, when the TR2 and the updated TR3 became the Michelotti-designed TR4, six-cylinder TR5 and fuel-injected TR6. The 1976 TR7 had a less happy time: unlike the others, it was at first sold only as a fixed-head coupé, designed for the U.S. market when it seemed as if open-top cars would be outlawed altogether. An open TR7 did follow eventually, along with the 213.6-cu in (3.5-litre) V8-powered TR8. Another long-running Triumph sports car was the little Spitfire, unveiled in the early 1960s with an 70-cu in (1.14-litre) engine, and later growing with 79.3- and 91.5-cu in (1.3- and 1.5-litre) units.

But there was also a range of Triumph-badged saloons. The 1959 Herald was the first Triumph styled by Michelotti, and later came in six-cylinder Vitesse guise. The six-cylinder 2000 (later 2500) was Triumph's executive car, which would be an early user of fuel injection. The front-wheel-drive 1300 was transformed into the memorable Dolomite rear-wheel-drive sports saloon, notably the 16-valve 122-cu in (2-litre) Dolomite Sprint. The Stag was a stand-alone model, a 2+2 sports tourer, with its 183.1-cu in (3-litre) V8 developed from two Dolomite engines spliced together. Its unreliability led to its nickname, the 'Snag'

By the early 1980s all of these were either dead or about to be dropped. It was

not quite the end of the Triumph name, however, which was used to sell a rebadged Honda Ballade, built by British Leyland at Cowley. Sold from 1981 to 1984 it heralded the beginning of BL's co-operation with Honda, and the end of Triumph.

TROJAN (Great Britain 1922-1936)
The Trojan was a brave attempt to build a

ABOVE
Triumph TR5.

ABOVE FAR LEFT
Brochure for the Spitfire 1500.

ABOVE LEFT
Triumph TR3.

LEFT
1992 Triumph Stag Mk I.

OPPOSITE
LEFT: 1926 Trojan shooting brake.

ABOVE RIGHT: 1962 TVR Grantura.

BELOW RIGHT: 1979 TVR Ford V6-engined convertible.

cheap, basic car that many people could afford. However, the omens were not good: even when launched the basic design was a dozen years old. Production began in 1922, but the first Trojan stemmed from a 1910 design by Leslie Hounsfield.

It was financed by Leyland Motors, which wanted to diversify into car production, alongside its main business of commercial vehicles. That first Trojan was a 10-hp (7.46-kW) car, powered by a four-cylinder engine of 93.31 cu in (1.5 litres). There were many variations on the theme in its 14-year production run, such as the final LW and RE (introduced 1930 and '31 respectively), both powered by a 90.8-cu (1.48-litre) unit.

TVR (Great Britain 1949 to date)
Blackpool-based TVR derived its name

from that of its founder, Trevor Wilkinson. An apprentice mechanic at the age of 14, he set up Trevcar Motors after World War II and within a couple of years joined up with Jack Pickard to form TVR Engineering. At first, the pair concentrated on one-off specials, but began building series production cars in 1953, already with that familiar dumpy TVR look.

The cars gradually grew in size, first with Austin A40 and Ford side-valve mechanics, later with 97.6-cu in (1.6-litre) Ford and 152.6-cu in (2.5-litre) six-cylinder Triumph engines. Available in factory-built or kit form, the latter enabling the purchaser to take advantage of a U.K. tax loophole, TVRs became an established part of the British specialist car industry. Scariest of them all was the Griffith V8:

423

U.S. dealer Jack Griffiths imported TVRs and fitted Ford V8 engines, selling them as Griffiths. Some were also sold by TVR itself under the name Tuscan.

In the meantime there was a series of collapses and takeovers, with several different owners attempting to pull TVR round through the 1960s. A measure of stability was provided by Martin Lilley, who bought the firm in 1968 and remained in charge until 1981. Under his rule, TVR survived by developing the original sports car with Ford 183.1-cu in (3-litre) V6 power, the Tamar hatchback version and a convertible. It was also an early proponent of turbocharging, which gave the lightweight TVR extraordinary performance.

A new era began for TVR in 1981, when chemical engineer Peter Wheeler took over. He remains in charge to this day, replacing the old-shape TVRs with the new wedge-shaped Tasmin in 1982. At first powered by Ford's latest 170.9-cu in (2.8-litre) fuel-injected V6, in both coupé and convertible forms, this later adopted the venerable Rover V8 in tuned 238- and 256.3-cu in (3.9- and 4.2-litre) as well as the standard 213.6-cu in (3.5-litre) forms. The traditional TVR body shape returned in 1989 with the Tuscan S roadster.

Twenty years on from the Wheeler takeover, TVR was thriving, very different from the days when it was producing cars in kit form, offering a range of high-priced sports cars with straight-six or V8 engines. All, from the Chimaera (still with that Rover V8) to the Tamora, Cerbera (powered by TVR's own 274.6-cu in/4.5-litre V8) and Tuscan, offered unsophisticated sports car appeal.

VAUXHALL (Great Britain 1903 to date)
In 2003 Vauxhall celebrated its centenary,

ABOVE
1973 TVR Vixen.

LEFT
1982 TVR Tasmin.

OPPOSITE
ABOVE LEFT: TVR Cerbera.

BELOW LEFT: TVR Chimaera.

BELOW RIGHT: Old Vauxhall.

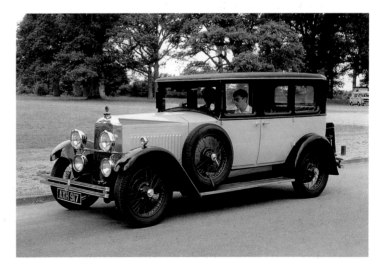

making it one of the longest-lived British marques of all, although for most of that time it has been under American ownership, since General Motors bought the company back in 1926.

Vauxhall's roots were in the Vauxhall Iron Works, which began to make marine engines in 1857, and produced its first car in 1903, with an improved 6-hp (4.47-kW) model appearing the following year. The next year Vauxhall moved to a new factory in Luton, and it has been there ever since. But in these days of global production, Vauxhalls are just as likely to be made in Japan, Germany or Spain as in Luton, though by the early 21st century the brand was effectively used for the British market only.

Although Vauxhall is now associated with mainstream bread-and-butter cars, its early years were sprinkled with more exotic offerings. Most famous of all was the 30/98 Prince Henry, a sporting 274.6-cu in (4.5-litre) car that was produced from 1913 right through to 1928. It was updated during that time, ending its days with an overhead-valve engine and hydraulic brakes, and capable of over 80mph (129km/h). Vauxhalls were successful in competition too, notably with the 4.5-litre 130-bhp (96.9-kW) Grand Prix.

The smaller 140.4-cu in (2.3-litre) 14/40 was more mundane, offering a four-speed gearbox from 1925 and Wilson pre-selector two years later. But by this time the company was facing financial problems, but a saviour appeared in the form of General Motors; Ford already had a strong manufacturing presence in Britain, and its arch-rival had little choice but to follow suit. The GM influence soon manifested itself in the Vauxhall 20/60, while 1930 saw

OPPOSITE
ABOVE LEFT: Vauxhall six-cylinder tourer.

ABOVE RIGHT: Vauxhall F-type Victor.

BELOW LEFT: 1959 E-type Wyvern.

BELOW RIGHT: 1959 Vauxhall Velox.

RIGHT
Vauxhall Viva HB.

BELOW LEFT
Vauxhall Nova SR.

BELOW RIGHT

the 122-cu in (2-litre) six-cylinder Cadet that was the first British car with a synchromesh gearbox, but was soon replaced by the 12- and 14-hp (8.95- and 10.4-kW) Light Sixes.

No one could accuse Vauxhall of lagging behind the times. The new 10 of 1937 featured unitary construction, torsion-bar front suspension and a lively overhead-valve 73.41-cu in (1.2-litre) engine. It filled out the bottom of the range nicely, beneath the bigger sixes, and all Vauxhalls had hydraulic brakes by 1939. The first new post-war Vauxhalls in 1948 (the pre-war 10, 12 and 14 were offered at first) were the 88-cu in (1.4-litre) four-cylinder Wyvern and 140.4-cu in (2.3-litre) six Velox. Both were restyled in 1952 with more power (40 and 65bhp/29.8 and 48.5kW respectively), thanks to shorter-stroke engines. They were replaced in 1957 by the four-cylinder Victor and six-cylinder Velox and Cresta, all with American-influenced styling. Both lines would be updated regularly through the 1960s and early 1970s, with a sporting VX4/90 derivative of the Victor available from

1963 and a 201.4-cu in (3.3-litre) six-cylinder engine for the Velox.

But the big news came in 1963, when Vauxhall finally returned to the small car market with the Viva. As the name suggested, this Ford Anglia rival had a lively nature, due largely to its 64.5-cu in (1.06-litre) 44-bhp (32.8-kW) unit. The

Viva became Vauxhall's big seller, updated as the HB in 1966 with curvier styling and a wider range, including engines up to 97.6 cu in (1.6 litres) and a 2-litre in the flamboyant Viva GT. The HC came four years later, with a bigger body, and still the choice of two- or four-door saloon and estate, plus the Firenza coupé. Engines now ranged from 1.3 to 2.3 litres. The Chevette in 1975 hinted at a closer relationship with GM's German subsidiary, Opel, as it was a restyled version of the Opel Kadett. First as a hatchback, later as a saloon and estate, the Chevette was on sale for eight years.

RIGHT
1997 Vauxhall Tigra.

BELOW RIGHT
Frontera SWB.

BELOW
1997 Corsa.

BOTTOM LEFT
Omega estate.

BOTTOM RIGHT
The Monterey, a rebadged Isuzu Trooper.

Similarly, the Cavalier of 1975 was a modified Opel Ascona.

Vauxhall's front-wheel-drive era began in 1980 with the boxy little Astra, a wide range of hatchbacks and estates from 1.1 litres eventually up to 2 litres. It also offered a diesel option for the first time. A new front-wheel-drive Cavalier followed in 1981 (again with petrol or diesel options) and the small Nova in 1983. The old Velox had long since gone by now, and in the executive class Vauxhall was offering Opels rebadged as the 109.8-cu in (1.8-litre) Carlton, 152.6-cu in (2.5-litre) Viceroy and 170.9-cu in (2.8-litre) Royale. The last was replaced by the 2.5- and 3-litre Senator, another Opel import, while the new Carlton arrived in 1987, later with V6 petrol and four-cylinder turbo-diesel engines. The Carlton, incidentally, was briefly offered as the 170-mph (274-km/h) Lotus Carlton in the early 1990s, and claimed to be the fastest four-door saloon in the world; but a high price, and press criticism of such outrageous performance, kept sales low. The Carlton in all its forms was later replaced by the Omega.

Meanwhile, a friendly, more rounded styling theme was on its way, notably in 1984 with the new Astra and its Belmont saloon version, and in 1993 with the Corsa, which replaced the Nova. The Cavalier had a serious update, and gained the Calibra coupé, later available with Vauxhall's new 2.5-litre V6 and four-wheel-drive. If that was too much, the Tigra was a small mid-engined coupé based on Corsa parts. Vauxhall was lacking in four-wheel-drives until the Frontera was launched during the 1990s in both short- and long-wheelbased forms. It was really an Isuzu, however, assembled by Vauxhall in the U.K., while the bigger Monterey was no more than a

rebadged Isuzu Trooper, imported directly from Japan. Neither made great inroads against established rivals like Land Rover and Nissan.

For the 21st century, there was a new Vectra (the original had replaced the Cavalier in the mid-1990s), the Zafira compact MPV and the Signum, claimed to be a cross between an MPV, estate and coupé.

VOISIN (France 1919-1939)

RIGHT
Vauxhall Astra.

BELOW RIGHT
Signum.

BELOW
Vectra.

Voisin cars reflected the idiosyncracies of   their designer, Gabriel Voisin, who was better known for his aircraft but built cars sporadically for 20 years. Voisin was more interested in experimentation and development than in churning out cars simply for commercial profit. He considered building the Artaud & Dulfresne steam car, going on to develop Knight double-sleeve-valve engines and researching an easier system for changing gear, trying both the Sensaud de Lavaud and Cotal set-ups.

Belgian Imperia cars were built under licence at the Voisin factory in the early 1930s, but more interesting were some of the prototypes that Gabriel himself came up with. There was a front-wheel-drive V8, and an in-line 12, the latter so long that two of the cylinders poked into the cockpit. Experiments like this were expensive for no return, so it is hardly surprising that Voisin was taken over in 1937 and a conventional Graham-engined car put into production. Gabriel was horrified that such an ordinary

car should bear his name, and reassumed control, going on to built a variety of electric vehicles, and also Gnome-Rhône aero engines under licence. No Voisin cars were made after World War II.

VOLKSWAGEN (West Germany/Germany 1936 to date)

The world's most popular car, for it overtook the Ford Model T in terms of numbers in 1972, the Volkswagen Beetle was the result of both Adolf Hitler and Ferdinand Porsche's ambition to build a 'people's car'. However, the similarities between the two men ended there. It was an extraordinary story: production flickered back into life in a bombed-out factory in

BELOW
Voisin.

BELOW RIGHT
1967 Volkswagen Beetle.

1945; within ten years the Beetle was a huge success; by 1970, its maker was losing its pre-eminence, overly-dependent on the now outdated rear-engined concept; but it fought back with an all-new range of front-wheel-drive cars to re-establish its place as a major European manufacturer.

It was May 1934 when Hitler invited Porsche to submit designs for a 'Volkswagen'. Porsche should have been delighted: as a designer, he had been striving to complete such a project for years. The snag was that Hitler wanted the car ready for production in double-quick time, and at a price of no more than 1,000 Deutschmarks, less than half the price of the cheapest car then available. Despite these hurdles, and the hostility of existing German manufacturers, Porsche set to work, and by late 1936 the first prototype of this little beetle-backed car, with its air-cooled flat-four engine mounted in the tail, was being tested. A vast new factory was

hurriedly built with a town to house its workers, while the first KdF-wagen (as Hitler called it) rolled off the production line in April 1939. A special advance-purchase plan was announced, so that any German worker would be able to afford the new car, and 350,000 accounts were quickly opened. But the outbreak of World War II put a stop to all this after only 210 cars had been built, and the new factory was turned over to war work.

In 1945 the factory emerged from World War II in a badly damaged condition and under British control. Several car manufacturers were offered the VW design as war reparations, but they all rejected it. But Major Ivan Hirst, in charge of the Wolfsburg factory, set the production lines running again. He handed control back to the Germans three years later, and when production was booming.

Through the 1950s, production and exports increased year on year (there had

TOP LEFT
Polo five-door hatchback.

TOP CENTRE
Sharan.

TOP RIGHT
Vento.

CENTRE LEFT
The Mk III Passat, launched in 1997.

ABOVE
Golf Gti.

LEFT
Mk 3 Golf cabriolet.

been nothing quite like this since the original Model T): the five-millionth Beetle was built in 1961 and from then on more than a million were built every year. With this huge success, it took VW some time to come up with variations on the Beetle theme (though the Transporter van was available from 1950, and the Karmann cabriolet from 1949). The bigger 1500 saloon, with a 91.11-cu in (1.49-litre) flat-four, appeared in 1961 and was soon followed by a Variant Estate, TL fastback and unitary-constructed 411.

But VW was in danger of becoming complacent. The Beetle had made it the biggest car maker in Europe, but it eventually lost that slot to Fiat in 1969, and was overtaken by Opel in Germany two years later. The first attempt to diversify, the front-wheel-drive K70 of 1971 was not a success. But VW had better luck with the new Passat in 1973. Based on the Audi 80, it had a water-cooled engine and front-wheel-drive (K70 apart, the first VW so-equipped) and sold well. But the company was still on the verge of going under, and was only saved by the all-new Golf and Scirocco the following year. The Golf was

engines for the Scirocco and Golf Gti, plus a four-wheel-drive Golf Syncro. The Scirocco was replaced by the Corrado coupé in 1990, which was available with a supercharged 136-bhp (101.4-kW) power unit. The Golf was updated into Mk II and then more rounded Mk III forms, while a new Polo appeared in 1994. VW could not afford to ignore the growing MPV market, and a joint venture with Ford provided one in the form of the VW Sharan, otherwise Ford Galaxy or even SEAT Alhambra, as by now the Spanish maker was part of the VW empire, and all of its cars were VW-derived. A new Passat followed in 1996, with the top petrol engine an unusual V5, while VW was also pioneering the use of electronically controlled injection diesel engines. The turbocharged TDI range was available across the range, and combined good performance with excellent economy. With the Polo moved upmarket, the smaller, cheaper Lupo was brought in as the entry-level model, though these days a VW would never be the cheapest car on the market.

The new Beetle was aimed at a very

different buyer. Unashamedly nostalgic, it sought to evoke a family resemblance to the original, while making a 21st-century statement. It looked cute, but cost more than the Golf on which it was based. No one cares what Hitler would have thought of that, but it is more than likely that Ferdinand Porsche would not have approved either.

VOLVO (Sweden 1927 to date)
The idea behind the Volvo was simple: it would be a substantial car able to withstand

TOP LEFT
2003 Jetta.

TOP RIGHT
2003 Passat Estate.

LEFT
2003 Golf Gti.

BELOW
2003 Beetle.

OPPOSITE
2003 Beetle cabriolet.

simply the Passat 'writ small', a front-wheel-drive hatchback in the modern mould, while the Scirocco was an attractive coupé based on the same parts.

From this point on, there was no stopping VW. The little Polo hatchback arrived in the following year, giving VW a full range of modern front-wheel-drive cars; meanwhile, the Beetle remained in production until 1979 in Germany, though in Mexico it simply carried on. There were notchback versions of the Polo and Golf as

the Derby and Jetta in the late 1970s, but more memorable for most was the Golf Gti. With a 97.6-cu in (1.6-litre) fuel-injected engine of 110bhp (82kW), this was the first of the hot hatchbacks and VW had founded a new class. At the top of the range, the Santana four-door saloon was a rebadged Audi.

Not everything was so rosy, however. By the mid-1980s VW was facing tough times again, and was losing money, though it underlined the sporting image with 16-valve

the rigours of the Scandinavian climate, and Assar Gabrielsson and Gustav Larson were able to fulfil this plan. Both men had worked for SKF bearings, and it was their former employer which funded the first production run of 1,000 cars in 1927.

That first model, the OV4, lasted for two years before being replaced by the bigger 183.1-cu in (3-litre) six-cylinder PV650 in 1929, which was later fitted with 195.3- and 219.7-cu in (3.2- and 3.6-litre) engines. One interesting variation was the PV36, a streamlined car similar to the Chrysler Airflow. The PV53 took over in 1938 and was produced right through World War II as a result of Sweden's neutrality, though very few were made in 1942. By this time, Volvo was also building taxis and small trucks.

Volvo's car for peacetime was the

PV444, a solid rear-wheel-drive saloon like its predecessors, but now with independent front suspension and coil springs at the rear. It was a success, and was even exported to the U.S.A.: for the first time, Volvo cars were outselling Volvo trucks, and half a million PV444s (including the 544 saloon and 210 estate) were made before the car was replaced in 1965. Alongside the PV, from 1961, came a real departure, the P1800 sports car, with styling by Ghia and Frua. It was a good-looking car, and achieved fame in the TV series *The Saint*, driven by Roger Moore. An estate variant, the P1800ES, was produced up to 1973.

Meanwhile, Gabrielsson and Larson had departed, but they had already initiated the next-generation Volvo, the P120 series. Named the Amazon for the home market, this was another good seller, and was also built in Canada and Belgium, while the new

ABOVE
Volvo B18.

ABOVE LEFT
The debutante Volvo, the OV4 of 1927.

BELOW LEFT
The U.S.-influenced PV36 Carioca of the 1930s.

OPPOSITE
ABOVE: 1960s P1800 coupé.

BELOW: 1967 Volvo 121.

140 was announced in 1966, followed by the six-cylinder 164. The 140 became 240 in 1974, then 244 saloon and 245 estate, now with a diesel option. Volvo had also collaborated with Peugeot and Renault to develop a new 164.8-cu in (2.7-litre) V6 engine, and this was used to power the 260 saloon from 1974.

All of these had the Volvo family resemblance; but the 760, launched in 1982, was an angular, wedge-shaped car which no one could claim was any more beautiful than the brick-like 240. The 760 was the new flagship, but Volvo was also offering a range of smaller cars by now, thanks to its tie-in with Daf. It had bought 75 per cent of the Dutch concern, and consequently the Daf 66 became the Volvo 343, with a range of engine and transmission options. It was later replaced by the 440 in the 1980s, and its coupé spin-off, the 480.

For much of this time, Volvo had been concentrating on building its image as a producer of solid, sensible and, above all, safe, cars. The 850 saloon of 1992 changed all that. Not only was it front-wheel-drive (a

LEFT TOP
1997 Volvo S70 saloon.

LEFT CENTRE
Volvo old-style 960 saloon.

LEFT
V90 estate.

TOP
1997 V40 saloon.

ABOVE
Volvo S40 saloon.

departure for a big Volvo) but it offered fiery performance from its five-cylinder petrol or diesel engines, some of which were turbocharged. An 850 T5 Estate was actually entered in the British Touring Championship, and did not disgrace itself. This sporting image, along with Sweden's entry to the European Union, allowed Volvo to transform its losses of the early 1990s into profits, and sales increased healthily.

More change came in the late 1990s, when the sharp-edged 440 was replaced by the rounded S40, a joint venture with Mitsubishi. There was a V40 estate as well, though by 2002 both were starting to look dated, and a replacement was planned for two years hence. Meanwhile, the S70/V70 had replaced the 850 in 1996, and by the end of the century were offered as the updated S60, V70 estate, C70 coupé and four-wheel-drive V70 XC. If none of those was big enough, Volvo also took a stab at the luxury car market with the S80 saloon. Now part of the Ford empire, Volvo should have the stability for long-term survival.

WESTFIELD (Great Britain 1982 to date)

LEFT
2003 Volvo C70 convertible.

CENTRE LEFT
2003 S40 saloon.

CENTRE RIGHT
2003 S80 saloon.

BOTTOM LEFT
2003 S60 saloon.

BOTTOM RIGHT
2003 V40.

In 1982 Chris Smith began to build Lotus

RIGHT
2003 Volvo XC90

OPPOSITE
2003 XC70.

Eleven replicas in a factory north of Birmingham. Two years later, he did the same with the Seven, which again was a fairly faithful copy of the original, apart from its all-glassfibre bodywork. In its ultimate form, this came with a 213.6-cu in (3.5-litre) Rover V8 engine, as the Seight. It was later treated to a tuned 238-cu in (3.9-litre) version of the same unit to provide 285bhp (212.5kW) in the tiny flyweight Seight.

It was of course blindingly fast, able to spin the rear wheels in fifth gear, if the roads were wet. If they were dry, it would accelerate from 50-70mph (80-113km/h) in just 2.5 seconds. A Ford limited slip differential helped to keep things in check, but its excessive power and ultra-fast steering made it a car for experienced drivers only. More accessible fun was provided by the Westfield TD, using a tuned Ford 109.8-cu in (1.8-litre) turbo-diesel engine. With lots of mid-range torque, this made the lightweight Westfield

fast enough to be fun, and of course it was a little less thirsty than that big V8.

In 2002, Westfield was still offering its Seven replica with various engine options, all either factory-built or in a do-it-yourself kit. As well as the basic 1800, the Seight was still there, as were the motorcycle-engined Megablade and Megabusa, the latter with a Suzuki Hayabusa 79.21-cu in (1.3-litre) unit providing 172bhp (128.2kW). If that was not race-orientated enough, Westfield announced the XTR-2 in

BELOW
Westfield Seight.

2002, also Hayabusa-engined, but designed as a track day machine that was also (just) legal on roads.

WHITE (U.S.A. 1900-1918)
White was one of the few manufacturers to succeed in making the transition from

steam to petrol car building. Rollin H. White worked for his father's firm, which produced a number of products from roller skates to sewing machines. It added steam cars in 1901, after Rollin had built a successful prototype with a single-cylinder engine mounted on the floor.

It was very popular, selling 200 in its first year, and in 1903 a two-cylinder version was added. White steamers soon settled down to a front-mounted engine, armoured wooden chassis and a condenser where the conventional radiator would have been. A two-speed rear axle was standard from 1905, and by 1906 1,500 steamers were being made each year. White steamers were not cheap, but they were well-made and reliable. Some were fast, too: an underslung chassis special, rejoicing in the name of 'Whistling Billy', was timed at 74.04mph (119.15km/h).

But Rollin White could see the way things were going: despite their advantages,

steam cars were too expensive and far less convenient than the rapidly improving petrol alternative. So the company turned to making petrol cars in 1911, having bought the Waltham Manufacturing Company as a short cut (Waltham had been making cars since 1901.) Three years later, Rollin left White to set up on his own, but back at

White, car sales were slowly declining. By 1918 series production was halted, and cars were made to special order only, leaving the company to concentrate on commercial vehicles.

WILLYS (U.S.A. 1907-1963)
Willys is best known for the U.S. military Jeep, which for many years was the

LEFT
1906 White Steamer.

BELOW
'Town car' on White 158 chassis.

FAR LEFT ABOVE
1911 petrol-engined car.

FAR LEFT BELOW
2.4-litre Rollin-bodied White.

company's sole product, but it had been building cars 30 years earlier. John North Willys bought the Standard Wheel Company in 1907, and within a couple of years had transformed its product line from single- and twin-cylinder runabouts to full-sized cars with four- and six-cylinder engines. In 1909, the Overland name was added, and 'Willys' dropped the year after.

Extraordinary as it may seem now, Overland was the best-selling car in the U.S.A. in 1914, six years after the Model T appeared, and second only to Ford the following year. Sleeve-valve-engined cars were added to the range after 1914 (badged Willys-Knight) and a V8 in 1917, though between 1919 and 1925 only side-valve fours were produced.

Sixes were reintroduced, and sales continued to climb, but they peaked in 1929 and Overland was almost wiped out by the Depression. The four-cylinder cars were dropped in 1931, and the Willys-Knight the year after. The company actually went into receivership in 1933, but managed to carry on producing the cheap Model 77 (sold under the Willys name), which kept it afloat while it pulled out of receivership after three years.

Fortunately, Overland was about to produce its saviour, the Jeep. Production began in 1941, and although Ford made the Jeep too, Overland retained sole rights; after World War II, therefore, the company was well set-up with a proven, unique vehicle in high demand. Civilian versions

followed and the production lines hummed: no Overland cars were built until the Aero saloons of 1952. But none of this prevented Overland from being taken over by Kaiser in 1953, and from 1957 Willys-Overland production was back to Jeeps only. The name was changed in 1963 to Kaiser-Jeep.

WINTON (U.S.A. 1897-1924)
Winton was the best-selling petrol car in the U.S.A. at the turn of the 19th century.

LEFT
1949 Willys Jeep.

BELOW
2001 Willys concept vehicle.

BELOW LEFT
1940 Willys Jeep.

Alexander Winton, a Scot, had made bicycles before experimenting with cars in 1897. He began to sell them the following year, little two-seat single-cylinder buggies typical of the time.

Expanding fast, Winton moved into a new factory in 1902 and added a twin-cylinder car. He also tried his hand at racing, with 518.7-cu in (8.5-litre) four-cylinder and twin-engined 244.1-cu in (4-litre) cars, the 'Winton Bullets'. Driven by Percy Owen and Winton himself in the 1903 Gordon Bennett Cup, neither car finished, though they both later had successes in sprint racing. Four-cylinder production cars were sold from 1904, and in 1908 Winton decided to concentrate entirely on luxury limousines with six-cylinder engines. Some 1,200 of these were sold in 1909.

Winton evidently had a change of heart, for he was producing cheaper cars again by 1915, and these formed the backbone of the Winton range until 1920. But by then, cars had become a relative sideline. Since 1912, Winton had been producing marine diesel and stationary engines, and in the early 1920s his shareholders decided that this was a more promising line of business. Winton car production ceased in 1924.

LEFT
One of the first Wintons – a model from 1899.

BELOW
The 1903 Winton Bullet racing car.

WOLSELEY (Great Britain 1896-1975)
Wolseley was one of Britain's earliest car manufacturers, and it survived (albeit as a badge on other cars) right up to the late 20th century. Like Standard and Singer, it came to represent quality motoring for the British middle classes, with the odd sporting model appearing here and there.

The first was built by none other than Herbert Austin, then the company's general manager, who would go on to form his own motoring dynasty. It was a simple three-wheeler powered by a 2-hp (1.49-kW) single-cylinder engine. A four-wheeled car followed in 1899 with 3.5-hp (2.61-kW), and in 1901 it was joined by a 97.6-cu in (1.6-litre) 10-hp (7.46-kW), plus a four-cylinder five-speed racer, the latter available only to special order. Wolseley's reputation was anything but sporting, but its flat-four-engined Wolseley Beetles were very successful in 1904-05 events.

The biggest Wolseley yet, the 201.4-cu in (3.3-litre) Wolseley-Siddeley (co-named after its designer J.D. Siddeley) appeared in 1906, and by 1910 the company was offering a wide range of cars, including two big sixes by 1914, the 24/30 and 30/40. In fact, Wolseleys would gradually become more sophisticated, with overhead-cam engines built after World War I. During the 1920s, the range consisted of the 7, the 10, later replaced by the 11/22, and the 15, later replaced by the 16/35 types.

But the company was also bankrupt, and was soon swallowed up by the rapidly growing Nuffield empire in 1927. Rationalization ensued, but Wolseley was not reduced to badge-engineering just yet. A Morris Isis-derived 21/60 appeared in 1929, with six-cylinder engine and hydraulic brakes, while 1930 saw the advent of the 79.3-cu in (1.3-litre) Hornet. The latter, with its smooth, powerful little six-cylinder overhead-cam engine, was a cut above other small cars. There was an open two-seater sports as well as the

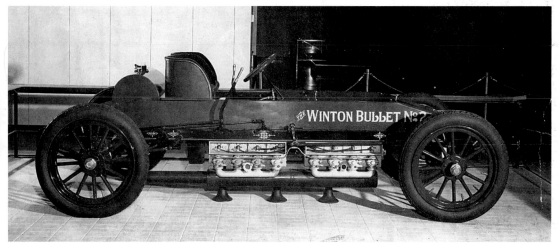

standard saloon.

The range developed through the 1930s, both in breadth (there was an eight-cylinder version of the 21/60) and technical sophistication (synchromesh and pre-selector gearboxes). It was around this time that the famous illuminated Wolseley badge was adopted, which the cars would retain to the end. The six-cylinder Hornet engine was enlarged to 85.4 and then 97.6 cu in (1.4 then 1.6 litres). After World War II the Eight, Ten and Twenty-five were offered at first, with two new cars launched in 1949 as the four-cylinder 4/60 and six-cylinder 6/80, both with overhead-cam engines. In 1953 the 4/44 showed signs of more obvious rationalization, sharing its unitary-constructed body and 76.3-cu in (1.25-litre) engine with the MG ZA Magnette. This trend continued with the later 6/90 (very similar to the Riley Pathfinder) and 1500 (Riley 1.5), both based on the Morris Minor floorpan. Now part of the BMC, Wolseley offered its own variation on the Farina-styled, mid-sized saloon from 1959. As well as the Wolseley, there were Morris, Austin, MG and Riley versions of this same car, with only minor

differences between them, but solemnly treated by BMC as separate models.

The same was true of the big 6/99 and 6/110, while the Hornet name was revived with a Wolseley-badged Mini, which did at least have a larger boot than the front-wheel-drive car from which it derived. In fact, on paper, Wolseley was offering a complete range, including the front-wheel-drive 1100 from 1965 (1300 from 1967), big 18/85 and six-cylinder 2200. The new wedge-shaped 1800/2200 with Hydragas suspension appeared early in 1975. It was to be the last Wolseley model, however, since it was renamed Princess by British Leyland in October of the same year. So ended Wolseley's career as a car badge.

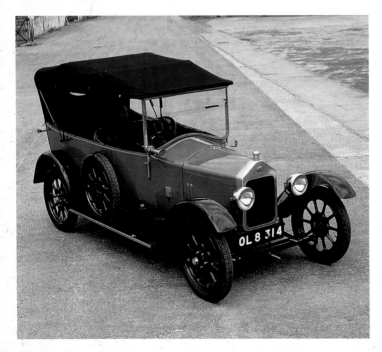

ABOVE
Wolseley Hornet.

LEFT
Wolseley 10-hp tourer.

OPPOSITE
1924 14-hp Wolseley.

INDEX

INDEX

ACKNOWLEDGEMENTS Andrew Morland: Pages 3, 4, 5, 6, 9, 10 top and bottom, 11, 12 all, 13 all, 14 below left, 16, 18 all, 19 all, 20, 21 top right, bottom right, top and centre left, 22 top, 23 right, 24 all, 26, 27 top and bottom right, 30 all, 31 all, 32, 33, 34 top, 38 bottom, 42, 43 both, 44, 45, 46 both, 47 all, 48, 49 both, 50 both, 51 bottom left, top left and centre left, 52 bottom right, 53 all, 54 all, 60 both, 61 both, 62 all, 66 bottom, 67, 68 top, 69 all, 70 left, centre top and bottom, 71 top and bottom left, 72 bottom right and left, 74 all, 75 all, 76 all 77, 90 all, 94 all, 95 all, 96 bottom, 97, 99 top, 100 all, 111 top right and left, 112 both, 113 all, 114 centre right and bottom right, 115 all, 116 bottom, 117 bottom left and centre, 120, 121 top left, 122 all, 123, 126, 127 all, 128 both, 130 both, 132, 133 all, 138, 149 top and bottom left, 142 all, 143 all, 144 all, 145 both, 146 all, 147 both, 149 both, 150 both, 151 all, 155, 156 bottom, 157 both, 159, 167 top left and right, 168 left, 172, 173 all, 179 top left, 180, 181 top left and bottom, 182 all, 184 all 185, 200, 202 top, 203, 205 all, 206 left and top right, 216 top and bottom right, 217 both, 219, 221 right, 222, 223, 224 all, 225 both, 226, 227, 230 bottom right and left, 231 bottom, 232 all, 234, 235 all, 236 bottom, 237 left, 238 bottom left, 240, 241 all, 242, 243 both, 244 all, 245, 246, 247, 248 both, 249, 251 top and bottom right. 252, 253 both, 267 bottom right and left, 286, 269 both, 270 all, 271, 272 both, 273, 274, 275, 276 top, 278, 279 both, 280 all, 281, 283 all, 291, 292 both, 293, 294, 295 both, 301, 310 both, 311 all, 312 all, 313, 314 both, 313, 316 top right, 319 bottom right, 324 all, 325, 326 both, 327, 328, 330 left, 332 right, 333 right, 335, 336 top left, bottom left, 342 top, 350 all, 351 top, 352 bottom left, 353 top right and bottom left, 354 both, 357 all, 359 right, 360 bottom, 361, 388 top and bottom right, 369 all, 370 bottom right, 371 top, 374 top and bottom right, 375 top and bottom right, 376, 377 all, 376 top left, top centre, top right and centre left 380 all, 381 all, 382 top, 383 all, 384, 385, 386, 387 top left, 388 bottom left and top right, 389 top right and left, 392 top right, 394 bottom left and bottom right, 395, 396 all, 397 all, 398 both, 399 top and bottom left, 400, 403 both, 404, 406 bottom left, 410, 411 all, 415 all, 416 top left, 420, 421, 422 all, 423 all, 424 both, 425 all, 426 all, 427 all, 429 left, 430 both, 435 bottom, 440, 444 both, 445.

Asia Motors: Page 29 all. Aston Martin: Pages 34 bottom left and right, 35 both, 36, 37 top left. Audi: Pages 40 all, 41 all. Bentley: Pages 55 all, 56 all, 57. BMW: Pages 63 all, 64 all 65, 66 top. Chrysler Motors: pages 2, 105 top and bottom right, 106 all, 107 all, 108 all, 109 all, 136 centre and below right, 137 all, 230 top, 231 top, 233 all, 362 top right, centre right, bottom left and right, 362 all. Citroën: Pages 114 left and top right. Daewoo: pages 119 all. Edward Herridge: Page 351 bottom. Fiat: Pages 152, 153 all. Ford: Pages 154 all, 156 top, 158 all, 160 all, 161 all, 162 all 163, 164, 165 all, 167 bottom left, 169 all, 170 all, 171 all, 174 all, 175 all, 176 all, 177 all, 178 both, 262 all, 263 all, 264, 265 all, 304 top and bottom right, 305 all, 306 all, 307 all, 308 all, 309 all. General Motors: Pages 78 all, 79 top and bottom left, 80 all, 81 all, 82 all, 83 all, 84 all, 85 all, 86 all, 87 all, 88 all, 89 all, 93 both, 96 top left 98 all, 99 bottom left, bottom left and centre left, 101, 191 top right, bottom right, bottom, centre and middle left, 192 all 193 all, 343 top and centre left, 344 centre and bottom left, 345 top and bottom right, 346 all, 348 top right, 349 all, 365 all 366 all, 367 all, 428 all, 429 top and bottom right. Honda: Pages 194 bottom left, 195 bottom, 197 top right, centre and below, 198 all, 199 all. Hyundai: Pages 7, 210 all, 211 all 213, 214. Jaguar Cars: Pages 228, 229. Lada: Page 239 all. Lancia: Pages 256 all, 257 all. Lexus: Pages 259 all, 260 all. Mazda: Pages 286 all, 287 all, 288 all, 289. Mercedes-Benz: Pages 296 all, 297 all, 298 all, 299 all, 300, 302, 303. Mitsubishi: Pages 320 all, 321all, 322, 323. Nissan: Pages 336 top and bottom right, 337 all, 338 all, 339 all, 340 all, 341 all. Peugeot: Pages 358 all, 359 top left, centre and bottom left, 360 top. Porsche: Pages 370 left and top, 371 bottom left and right, 372, 373. Proton: Page 374 top and bottom left. Renault: Pages378 bottom left, bottom right, centre right, 379 all. Rolls-Royce: Pages 387 right, bottom left and right. Rover: Pages 316 bottom and top, 317, 389 bottom, 390 all, 391 all. SAAB: Pages 393 all. Skoda: Page 401 all. Ssangyong Page 402 right. Subaru: Pages 407 all, 408 all, 409. Suzuki: Pages 412 all, 413 all. Toyota: Pages 417 bottom left, centre and right, below and above centre right, top centre and left, 418 all, 419 all. Volkswagen: Pages 431 all, 432 all, 433. Volvo: Pages 436 all, 437 all, 438, 439. Kaiser-Jeep: Page 442.

Neill Bruce/Nick Baldwin: Pages 10 bottom left, 14 both right, 15 all, 17 all, 22 bottom left and right, 23 left top and bottom, 25 all, 37 top right, middle right and bottom right, 38 top, 39 all, 51 top right, centre right and bottom right, 52 top left and right, 58 all, 59 all, 68 top and bottom left, 70 bottom right, 71 bottom and top right, 72 top right and left, 73 all, 79 top right, centre and bottom right, 91 all, 92 all, 96 bottom right, 102 all, 103 all, 104, 105 top and bottom left, 110 all, 111 bottom left and right, 116 top, 117 right, 118 both, 120 bottom and centre left, 121 bottom and top right, 124 all, 125 all, 129 all, 131 all, 134 all, 135 both, 136 top and bottom left, top right, 139 bottom right, 140 all, 141 all, 148 all, 166 all, 168 top right, centre and bottom right, 179 top and bottom right, 181 top right, 183 all, 186 all, 187 all, 188 all, 189 all, 190 all, 191 top left, 194 top and right, 195 top left and right, 196 all, 197 top left, centre left, bottom left, 201 all, 202 bottom left, bottom centre and bottom right, 204 all, 206 middle right and bottom right, 208 all, 209 all, 215 all, 216 bottom left, 218 all, 220 both, 221 top and bottom left, 236 top, 237 right, 228 top and bottom left, 250 both, 251 top and bottom left, 258 all, 261 all, 266 all, 267 top, 278 bottom left and right, 277 all, 282 all, 284 both, 285 all, 290 all, 304 bottom left, 328 both, 319 top, above left, centre left, bottom left and centre right, 329 both, 330 top left, centre right and bottom right, 331 all, 332 left top and bottom, 333 top and bottom left, 334 all, 336, 342 bottom, 343 bottom left, top and bottom right, 344 top left, bottom centre, top right, 345 top left, bottom centre left, above left and centre right, 347 both, 348 top left, bottom left, bottom and top centre, 352 top and bottom right, 353 bottom right, 355 all, 356 all, 362 top and bottom left, 365 all, 368 top and bottom left, 375 bottom left, 382, 388 top and centre left, 392 bottom. 394 top right, 399 top right centre right and bottom right, 405 all, 406 top and bottom right, 414 both, 416 top and centre right, bottom left and right, 417 top and centre left, 434 top and bottom left, 435 top, top all, 443 both.